Distributed – Book Masters
30 Amberwood Parkway
Ashland Ohio: 44805
(877) 312-3520 INT'l (419) – 281-5100

Also Distributed by New Leaf Distributing:
401 Thornton Rd, Lithia Springs, GA 30122
(770) 948-7845

Cover art by Jill Mattson

The Lost Waves of Time

www.JillsWingsOfLight.com – Art Galleries

Disclaimer

Please know that this book is not intended to serve as medical advice or make any recommendations or prescriptions for medical treatment. The book is written for educational and informational purposes only. Any action taken based on what is presented here is solely, the reader's responsibility.

Thank you. *Jill Mattson*

The Lost Waves of Time

Overture

A Sprite approached me; her energy was bright, radiating with peace and grace. She had the body of a pixie; an engaging smile, combined with an instant aura of optimism. Her voice was enthusiastic but I quickly realized that this vital being who had just introduced herself as a writer and musician was much more than she seemed to the naked human eye.

She was sharing information that she may have learned but it was obvious that the knowledge she held was from lifetimes of layered wisdom. As I got to know her, I think I now realize that the insights and talent she possesses were uniquely supported by the music and art that seems to effortlessly spring forth from her at every turn. I think her violin must have whispered to her in some ancient language that only innate musicians understand; we have at work some primordial stream of consciousness that provides information well beyond what is known to us common folks.

And so it is with *The Lost Waves of Time*. This book is filled with secret knowledge unassumingly shared by someone who thinks we common mortals need to know these ancient secrets. She's convinced we just forgot those musical math lessons from eons past. In our busy world, I don't think it occurred to most of us that we should even look for the information that she has put to paper from the very depths of her every cell. She represents the wisdom from our past and makes it vibrant using today's nomenclature; not an easy task.

The Lost Waves of Time will take you back to the beginning and ahead to the potential that we have forgotten. Prepare for a ride through history in a way that will move you to your very core. You will recognize information from a deep inner place that you likely didn't know even existed within you.

I cried more than once with a deep appreciation and recognition of what we somehow left behind. An incredibly important part of our heritage will propel us into an enlightened reality and it is patiently waiting for us to accept that math–based frequency combinations, that we call music, holds the keys to understanding the depths of our potential and to see beyond what we have been allowed to claim as our own. Jill Mattson puts it all together from her heart and soul. This book is sure to become a classic in many fields of study: music, math, healing, human potential, frequency, ancient knowledge, sound, light, architecture…and more.

Sharry Edwards, Founder, BioAcoustics

www.JillsWingsOfLight.com – Art Galleries

Chapter 1

Sound Energy

Energy.
Energy is life.
Energy is information.
Energy is matter made quick.
Energy enables all.
Without Energy... we have nothingness.

The energy of gravitational attraction drives the formation of stars in deep space. The energy of our sun powers all life on Earth (deep ocean volcanic vents aside). The power of our winds and storms have their roots in the nuclear fusion reactions constantly going on in our sun (nuclear energy) – transmitting energy to the Earth in the form of photons (sunlight – electromagnetic energy). The relentless ocean tides are due to the gravitational attraction of our moon (gravitational energy). Bio–chemical energy allows new life to begin – as an egg is fertilized and cells begin to divide, multiply and specialize. Electro–chemical energy powers our brains, thoughts and memories. On a finer level, *subtle* energy flows through our bodies, minds and souls – representing and nourishing our consciousness, our "self," our qualities and inspirations.

This book is about Sound energy – an often overlooked and vastly underrated form of energy. Sound energy has a multitude of capabilities, as it consists of a large spectrum of vibrational frequencies that can be adapted for an incredible variety of applications. The energy is selective and powerful for focused uses. We are all familiar with many common types of sound energy: ultrasounds and sonograms in the medical field, sonar for naval and aquatic purposes, sonic booms, car horns and high pitched dog whistles... there are many, many more examples encountered in everyday life.

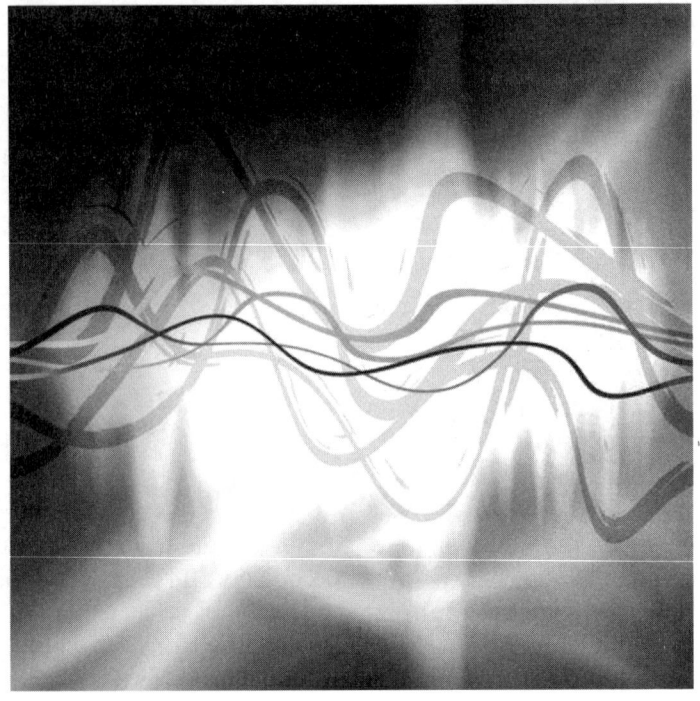

Sound Energy: Tremendously Varied & Complex

Subtle, influential energy – disguised as music – has affected mankind for many thousands of years. In ancient times, music was considered critical for survival. It was used for diverse applications: strengthening warriors, striking enemies, inducing rain, building psychic skills, enhancing crop growth, creating trances, curing physical, emotional and mental health issues and even more. Music was a powerful "vibratory wand" wielding magical–like energies. Thousands of years later, music's mystique has faded; it is considered only as a form of entertainment, a tragic loss to mankind.

Some sounds (frequencies of specific energy) interact with our minds fostering a certain type of brain wave state and hence a specific state of awareness or consciousness. Other sounds, *help our bodies heal themselves* – in the face of almost any illness or malady (including cancer, emphysema, flu, muscular and skeleton injuries and much more). Sound energy can enhance our consciousness by interacting with our subtle energies and associated systems, such as the chakras and meridians. Sounds can heal emotional and physiological problems. Often, sound can replace or simulate physical items – such as vitamins or other nutrients; even pathogens or beneficial microbes can be neutralized or simulated by sound. I created *The Healing Flower Symphonies* incorporating the sound vibrational counterparts of the Flower Essences. I believe that listening to the Flower Symphonies supplies the same benefits as ingesting the traditional flower essences. Other special sounds can enhance intelligence.

Modern man applies sound in a variety of useful ways; we can greatly expand on this – to the good of all – by returning to our ancient forefathers.

Sound: A Window on the World

Ancient peoples understood many things by connecting them to music. Sound was a "window on the world". Music was a way of viewing reality – just like science or religion. Music was a paradigm to understand the universe. The mechanics of music explained everything for the ancients, just as science does for many people today. Pythagoras explained the universe with mathematical equations derived from simple vibrations of a lyre string.

Music was often a prerequisite for all higher learning – as it explained the Heavens and Earth (again music bridges science and the spiritual). Ancient leaders believed that minuscule sound vibrations impacted all facets of life. In fact, sound was intimately related to math, science, religion, philosophy and many other studies.

Music was viewed as a lens for viewing the universe and sound was used in ways that we would not even dream of today. These cultures deliberately used special music for practical and spiritual purposes. It was used to control areas ranging from the environment and health, to the population's values and attitudes.

An entirely new way of thinking is required to accept these ancient ideas. We can easily miss their reasoning. Fatal errors of understanding occur when we interpret ancient music based on today's norms, namely music's prime value is to entertain us; *not so for the Ancients.*

Worldwide religions[1] describe sound as the source of creation.[2] Indeed, the *Bible* says, "In the beginning was the Word, and the Word was with God, and the Word was God."[3] Creation was related to the vibrational energy of words. It is no wonder that sound and music were sacred in the ancient world. Sound was God's tool.

Music can display intricate, coherent information when you translate it mathematically. Think how much information the combined output of a large symphony orchestra playing a classical masterpiece contains. Music's hidden mathematical patterns, not listening preferences, were of supreme importance to ancient leaders. Ancient music mimicked naturally occurring numerical patterns or laws, such as those found in a star's movements across the heavens. Music emulated nature, reflecting its perfection. When man vibrated in sync with Heaven and Earth, he was in harmony with God and all cosmic forces.

Ancient man used numbers to understand God's creation. Numbers were not considered to be only symbolic, but infused with sacred essence. God surrounded us with mathematical revelations, hidden in nature. Recall that Pythagoras said, "All is number." As numbers and music were interchangeable, ancient people believed that music was another means of expressing God's sacred language.

---

[1] Hindus, Egyptians, Mayans, Hopi, Buddhism, Christianity and others
[2] Hindu tradition states in the <u>Vedas</u>, "In the beginning was Brahman with whom was the Word. And the Word is Brahman." Thot, an Egyptian God, was believed to have created the world with His voice. According to Mayan tradition, in the *Popul Vuh* (the book on creation), humans are given life by the power of the Word. In the Hopi Indian tradition, "Spider Woman" sings songs of creation to produce animated life. The *Satapatha Brahmana* reads, "In the beginning was God with power through speech. God said, 'May I be many...may I be propagated through subtle speech, he united himself with that speech and became pregnant.'" In Chinese Buddhism, the Divine Voice calls forth the illusive form of the universe.
[3] <u>Bible, John</u> 1:1

12

Music and Subtle Energy

Subtle energy is sometimes viewed as a universal life force – present within all things, even inanimate objects. Subtle energy connects things. Subtle energy has infinitesimally small vibrations that are currently undetectable; not identified within the electromagnetic spectrum. It has been called qi, chi, orgone, prana and kundelini energy. Yet others link this fine energy to the energy of thought, intention and intuition. Some disciplines refer to this fine energy as an aura, a field or universal life force.

Some modern scientists scoff at the concept of subtle energy, however, consider that after 400 years of modern scientific study we still do not understand how the force of gravity works. Further, in the past 15 years, modern physics has discovered that the universe consists mainly of *dark energy* and *dark matter* – neither of which we can directly detect! Ancient mystics knew of subtle energy since the dawn of our existence.

Ancient people believed that the properties of subtle energy explained psychic occurrences. They described subtle energy acting more like waves than fixed particles (similar to modern physics theory for how things like electrons work). For example, during the psychic phenomenon of remote viewing or past life regression, a person animates one body, while viewing events at another time or location. The ancient Buddhists exposed people to specific colors to activate healing energy within their bodies. The ancient Greeks listened to sorrowful music to vibrate and release negative emotions. In a classic example of sound resonance, a plucked "A" string on one violin makes a nearby violin's A string vibrate. The energy of the A note transfers to the other violin. Analogously, subtle energy readily transfers between things.

In the physical world we perceive fixed, permanent things. We perceive a table to be separate from its surroundings. Yet if we observe the infinitesimally small atomic energies within it, we see that the table is largely empty space occupied with small forces of constantly moving energy. Ancient people described subtle energy as infinitesimally tiny, moving streams of energy. This clearly displays their vibrational understanding of reality.

We are holistic vibratory beings constantly interacting with many types of energy. The energies of our mind, body, and spirit and the environment surrounding us are deeply connected and interrelated; each aspect impacts the others. Every cell in our body emits and absorbs frequencies.[4]

Our internal vibrations resemble music; all music that we listen to intermingles with our internal vibrations. The effects of a single song may be too small to notice, but the cumulative effects – after extensive listening – can be significant.

Our ancestors were well aware that subtle energy, influenced by music, could be used to shape our world. By focusing on small subtle energies they discovered amazing capabilities of sound and music. For example, ancients used rhythmic patterns to encourage specific types of thoughts and attitudes. They prized tuning practices, to curtail negative emotions. The selection of instruments colored people's attitudes. A diet of flutes provided a different impact than one of ringing horns and booming drums. We know these things instinctually.

Biology of Music

The phonetics of language changed throughout time. New languages developed, others merged or became extinct. Various combinations of sound came and went. The unique sound patterns of languages influenced civilizations, just as music did. Were the sounds of extinct languages different than those of languages today? Did each language have unique strengths and influences?

Early man did not possess all of the physical hardware that we use to speak with today. Spoken language changed as man evolved. For example, Neanderthals had less sophisticated organs for speech. The larynx, tongue, teeth, jaw and lips evolved to better enable us (homo sapiens) to form complex sounds. All evidence indicates that homo sapiens developed the most capable and advanced organ systems for speech – of all hominids.

---

[4] Thaut, Michael. Rhythm, Music and the Brain, Scientific Foundations and Clinical Applications, Routledge: NY, 2005, Pg. 205.

Language and musical sounds have much in common. American author and scientist, Michael Thaut, noted that music and language follow similar rules; they both have a grammatical structure. Similar to a verbal language, music is a complex, rule based sensory system.[5]

Russian scientists, Grazyna Fosa and Franz Bludorf, challenged what was previously considered "junk" DNA, by conventional theory. They propose this (heretofore unassigned) "junk" DNA is used for information storage and communication. The Russians also found that the building blocks of DNA follow regular grammatical rules, just like our languages. Author Brendan Murphy made a remarkable claim regarding this research: "Human language seems to have emerged from the grammatical and syntactical structures in our very own DNA, the massive junk portion."[6]

Scientist, Michael Thaut, concluded that music is related to the biology of the human nervous system and served *evolutionary* purposes. "Music must be viewed as a biological fact, not just as a cultural phenomenon."[7]

Emerging scientific experiments are showing that the biology of living organisms is musically hardwired in a multitude of surprising ways. Recent findings by a multidisciplinary, MIT research team demonstrates the phenomenon. The large research team, including engineers, biomedical experts, mathematicians and *musical composers*, undertook a project to formulate synthetic silk. They identified the underlying bio–materials responsible for the unique light weight, subtleness and extraordinary strength of spider silk.

After synthesizing a number of "artificial silks", the MIT team analyzed their results by using a surprising analytical tool, music! Greatly simplifying the details... the various components of the silk's biochemical formulation (the proteins, their relationships, and underlying structures) were translated into musical

[5] Thaut, Michael. *Op. Cit.,* Pg. 31.
[6] Murphy, Brendan. "Junk DNA: Doorway to Transformation," *Nexus Magazine*, Aug. – Sept. 2012, Pgs. 42–45.
[7] Thaut, Michael. *Op. Cit.,* Pg. 57.

compositions. The end result: the strong silk proteins that would not form usable threads produced music that was harsh and displeasing. The proteins that formed usable silk fibers played as soft, fluid, pleasing music. The fact that the above process (based on the silk proteins) resulted in anything even remotely resembling music is remarkable; the fact that pleasing music was produced from "good" silk and harsh music resulted from "bad" silk is near miraculous.

One of the researchers, Markus Buehler of MIT said, "There might be an underlying structural expression in music that tells us more about the proteins that make up our bodies. After all, our organs – including the brain – are made from these building blocks, and humans' expression of music may inadvertently include more information than we are aware of." Music may soon tell us much more about our biology and reveal new insight into our humanity. Expanding on this, the processes that produced our biology, DNA and building–block proteins may be encoded in a universal song.

In a separate, but strikingly similar experiment, French physicist Joel Sternheimer developed a system for converting the amino acid sequences in plant protein into music. Sternheimer found that the compositions based on these amino acid sequences produced aesthetically pleasing music. In fact, when the "song" made from a plant's amino acids was played back to the plant, its growth rate increased markedly and its resistance to drought and disease also improved. Just as with the proteins in the spider silk, music composed from the biological building–blocks in plants was consonant, musical, logical and positive in feelings.

There is extensive evidence – that has been growing for years – that demonstrates our inborn affinity for music. Infants seem to have innate musical preferences; at as early as two months, babies will turn towards consonant or pleasing tones and away from dissonant sounds. Modern medical images of the brain show pleasure centers light up while listening to an orchestra play beautiful symphonies. These are the same pleasure centers that respond to sex, eating chocolate and taking cocaine. What is it about music that seems to be imprinted in our cells?

Sound and music – could these be far more than we have thought them to be? Musical compositions are grand "stories" employing numerous instruments, notes, pitches, rhythms, octaves and so on; classical symphonies are layers upon layers of intricate sound frequencies, an astoundingly rich matrix that can produce holistic effects vastly beyond the sum of the parts. Music could be the universal language of nature – and deeper – mirror the grand plan that makes us what we are.

Like a person plucking notes on a lyre, music "plays" and cements certain brainwaves and emotional states in its listeners. In a diverse sampling, the writings of Lao–tzu, Plato, St. Augustine and Dante describe music as a force that can mold admirable human behavior. A civilization is the sum of its individual people – the totality of their characteristic thoughts, emotions and actions. Since music influences thoughts, emotions and ensuing actions, it is far more important than providing entertainment. The distinctive musical practices of a culture create unique subtle energies that correlate to and reinforce the key characteristics displayed in that civilization.

Ancient music was closely linked to math and numbers. Ancient people routinely translated musical notes, rhythms and intervals to a corresponding set of numbers; music and numbers were different symbols for the same information. Music was converted to numbers by gematria, (a system of assigning numerical values to words, phrases or music). Music was correlated to the energy of other things (plants, colors, animals etc.) with identical numerical values.

Beyond the translation of musical fundamentals to numbers, the music of a culture usually had a *"signature"* number. This number was used in many important ways to compose the fundamental musical system. Notes, intervals and rhythms reflected this signature number. The signature number was used over and over again in the dominant music of a culture; the music became connected to that number and its associated energy. The importance of the signature number in the music of ancient civilizations can hardly be overemphasized!

An example of music possessing a signature number can be found in the Chinese musical system. The ancient Chinese typically included five notes that were a fifth apart in their musical scale. Each note correlated to one of the five elements, one of the five directions (including center) or one of the five colors. Their signature number was – no surprise – five.

When one examines the signature musical number of cultures throughout the ages, the signature numbers appear to unfold in reverse numerical order (9, 7, 6, 5, 4, 3, 2, 1). The earliest number (9) was found in Lemuria (based on legend) followed by Atlantis (with 7), then Sumeria (6) and later China (5), Greece (4) and so on, up until modern times.

In ancient times a number was equated with certain energy and associated with certain virtues, such as strength, courage or the divine. Numbers served important roles beyond mere counting.

Various cultures were historically known for certain qualities. For example, the Greeks developed great beauty in their art; the Romans showed tremendous military power and the Egyptians were respected for their knowledge. Perhaps each great culture developed its own "collective unconscious," and the key knowledge was stored in this energy pool of a collective consciousness. This book suggests that the signature number of a culture's music was associated with its dominant characteristics.

Often in antiquity when a mature culture was established – and its supporting music was in place – leaders established strict parameters for maintaining and preserving the music. When the music never changed, the associated subtle energy became permanent. The mature civilization showed little change; the net effect was a very stable culture. Stability was desirable in countries that enjoyed power and wealth. For this reason, the Egyptians insured that their art and music remained constant, without innovation, for 3,000+ years. Music helped stabilize the country, keeping its people united and dedicated... to the many dynasties and their grand monument building obsession.

Were the ancient leaders correct in believing that constant subtle energy from art and music provided stability in their country? Do fields of sound and subtle energy guide human thoughts and emotions? This book will strive to answer these questions.

Sages of ancient times believed that when the music of a civilization changed, the demise of the regime would follow. Did the music, and the associated constant subtle energy grid, fall before the civilization? Or rather, after societies reformed or morphed, was the music vulnerable to new influences? History shows that many factors contributed to the demise of a civilization. This is not being debated, but the role that music played has not been heretofore acknowledged. In all of the examples examined by the author, the legacy or foundational music of an epoch faded away and new musical norms arose prior to the demise of the status quo. This finding is consistent with the earlier idea that a constant musical style and its associated subtle energy produces cultural stability.

To summarize: sages of all important ancient cultures well understood the role of music in supporting and maintaining subtle energy for a variety of important purposes. As cultures advanced and flourished, a sophisticated musical system along with other techniques helped the ancient leaders stay in power and control their people. This book describes many of these techniques. Some practices were common knowledge and others were "secrets," closely guarded by leaders. Most of these obscure secrets are elusive, but many are about to be revealed!

How I came to Write this Book

Writing a book is an extraordinarily personal experience. This is the fourth book that I have written for publication and I am still amazed, how writing passionately fills me with deep emotions. Innately, I understand the importance of bringing back these ancient traditions; revealing the ancient secrets and sharing the information with modern readers is immensely satisfying.

Looking back, I now understand that the two major influences on my life – that continue to direct and drive me in my quest – are my love of music and deep personal spirituality. As I eventually learned, combining these two passions was the right path for my life, actually the only possible path.

I seemed to know naturally, that what I sought, had roots in ancient cultures and lore. Being a musician, my excitement grew every time I read a technique about using music to increase intelligence, health, energy or one's relationship with God. Hence, I undertook a journey to read and immerse myself in everything available, regarding antiquity's uses and beliefs, regarding sound energy and music.

I read hundreds of volumes, particularly about secret societies such as: the Tibetan monks, Christian monks, Druids, ancient Egyptian priests, ancient Chinese sages, accounts of numerous mystery schools and many more. As the years rolled by, I devoured and recorded every scrap of information that I could find. No source was too obscure.

I always perceived ancient history through the eyes of a musician. Scholars have yet to scrutinize history using a musical lens. This approach will yield new insights; music was sacred and interconnected to many systems of thought throughout the ages. Perhaps the time is ripe for this to occur.

Ancient leaders did not divulge their mysteries and musical secrets, so extracting this information was anything but easy. It was often like finding a needle in a hay stack. The ancient "mystery" schools that had the information I sought, had very few written documents. Their students were selected based on moral fiber as well as psychic abilities. Students were divided according to their degree of moral and psychic advancement into categories of initiates, disciples, adepts and masters. Secrets of sound were *verbally* passed to "tested" masters only… for safe keeping. Almost nothing was written down.

So how could I unearth these secrets? Most mystery schools divulged a few teasers, but never the entire story. Each group may have only recorded an occasional musical secret, but when dozens were studied, the information added up. Over more than twenty years, I accumulated a wealth of information on musical practices for targeted benefits – from dozens of mystical sources – written over thousands of years from all corners of the globe. These secrets are only part of the unique story told in *The Lost Waves of Time.*

After I collected information from ancient mystery schools, around the world, I decided to broaden my search. Some references suggested that Mayan stories refer to a time as far back as 50,000 BC. In stark contrast, the oldest written history begins about 3000 to 4000 BC. Much of the information that I wanted was from time periods with no recorded history.

Emerging archeological finds are changing the way we view ancient peoples. Early writings in extinct languages present translation difficulties, but we are beginning to decipher them. In Central America, newly found Mayan inscriptions have been translated, giving us fresh historical information about the ancient civilizations of Atlas (Atlantis) and Lemuria. The old writings relate applications of music so startlingly creative that music resembles the "magic" in a faerie tale.

Prehistoric artwork on cave walls and other durable materials are preserved in original form, but understanding ancient music remains elusive. Drums, skins and soft materials used to construct most musical instruments have typically perished by now. We do have some clues from archeology including: bone artifacts used as flutes and other musical instruments, special harmonic resonance points marked in caves and paintings of musical instruments and rituals.

Ancient art left valuable clues, reflecting musical practices in prehistoric cultures. For example, 30,000 year old cave art displays rituals of people who appear to be in a trance, with a shaman drummer. Many are cloaked in animal skins. Perhaps this "altered state of consciousness" allowed them to locate animals, producing a successful hunt.

Often, throughout history, artistic developments paralleled changes in music. We can glean insight into musical practices by observing art. In an example, the ancient Egyptians created a highly stylized art that remained unchanged for 3,000 years. Their music was just as static. No creativity was tolerated. Permanence and constancy were highly valued. Leaders enjoyed their power, wanting nothing to change. A subtle energy shift produced by innovative art and music was believed to change people's thoughts and emotions – risky indeed.

I have an advantage when reading ancient history, as I possess many psychic and spiritual gifts. These skills enable me to recognize psychic manipulations in ancient history. I was able to understand the significance of practices that affect subtle energy and that helped me grasp how ancient people used music's subtle energy.

Many people shy away from channeled[8] information, questioning its validity. Ideas revealed in this way are often incredible, but yet make sense. They include innovative ideas of how music and vibrations can be used for our benefits. These ideas are so revolutionary that they greatly expand most people's imaginations. Just reading them (whether or not you believe them) opens up your mind. I recommend considering these ideas, no matter what your beliefs are regarding channeling. For those who are skeptical of channeled information, a footnote identifies when this type of information was used.

My psychic abilities gave me insight into how ancient musicians were inspired to create their music. This experience made me wonder about, not only how I received music, but to question, was there an overarching pattern of music that was transmitted to composers over the ages?

I once had a vivid personal experience that gave me insight into how composers may have been influenced, allowing them to create music that subconsciously incorporated a special musical pattern that would benefit mankind.
Years ago, while attending a symphony concert I experienced a sensation that could only be a spiritual being penetrating my body. Actually, I was sitting down, but it seemed like someone came

---

[8] Channeling occurs when a spirit takes control of a person's body and voice to relay a message.

22

inside me from the back of my seat. It created a light pressure all through my body. Using all my might, I grabbed on to my seat to prevent "him" from wildly conducting the orchestra from my body.

I heard thoughts that were clearly not my own. I was aware of and felt the emotions of another being. This being felt masculine, so I shall refer to it as "he," but that is all the further that I can identify him. He was extremely agitated, desiring to conduct the orchestra. He wanted to stand up (in the audience) and conduct the orchestra using my body. Summoning all my strength, I held on to my seat to prevent him from yanking me to my feet and conducting the orchestra.

His intensity was remarkable and it intermingled with the music. Inside my head, he shouted when a musician lost precision or intonation. Towards the end of the piece he got angry, annoyed that the musical score (Hayden) was incorrect. He argued that someone had changed the last few notes of *his* music. When the song was over, he was gone. No goodbyes. He had no bedside manner. I was left trembling, sweating and holding on to my seat with all my might.

Several days later, I was home alone, and I again felt this same being's presence. I recognized him as he entered into my body from the back. He raised my arms to conduct an orchestra that I could *not* see. This time I let him use my body… and the music began. Internally, I heard an incredible orchestra and the music was divine! As he conducted the invisible orchestra, music filled my being, yet I heard nothing with my outer ears. A mouse in the corner would have enjoyed watching me "conduct" the dining room table, but this musical experience was more real to me than any other that I had ever experienced.

When the symphony was over he was gone, but I was left with the musical score in my head. Quickly, I ran to the piano, recreated the music and jotted down the melody. I didn't remember each part and ornamentation exactly so I improvised to the best of my ability. Hence, I added my own touch to the music that I recorded.

This original symphony can be heard on my CD, *Deep Wave Beauty* and is entitled *Symphony of the Stars.*[9]

Other musicians have reported receiving music, as I did. There are many written testimonies from classical composers, admitting that they just "heard" the music that they composed. Often, in antiquity, it was believed that such inspiration was bestowed for mankind's benefit. Author David Tame has credited music with forming the characteristic qualities of a civilization. "In the hands of the illumined, music was a tool of beauty and power which could lead the way for an entire race to a golden age of peace and prosperity."[10]

Summary

Many sources including: musical history, legends and folklore, ancient spiritual music, archeological finds, science, art history, psychic practices and channeled information have been used in this book. The information from hundreds of sources resembled a jigsaw puzzle. After I organized this massive data, a powerful overarching theme emerged, revealing an ancient hidden treasure – sound.

The modern interpretation does not appreciate the true importance of music. Lacking the ancient perspective, we cannot ascertain that tiny sound vibrations impact all things. Only a privileged few possessed this ancient knowledge. This information was used with intent to control people. The general population had no possibility of understanding these methods – until now.

The universal power of music is a new concept to the Western world. Unaware of the potential impact of vibrational energy, we are helpless to manage its influences. We must take control of sound energies that subtly drive us. With diligent research and education we can understand and control our sonic intake. This book is a step in that direction: to understand the role that music and sound play in shaping collective thinking, emotions and physicality.

---

[9] Sample the music at www.jillswingsoflight.com and at www.jillshealingmusic.com.
[10] "A greater force is that of the Illumined Mind, a Mind no longer of higher Thought, but of spiritual light." http://www.kheper.net/topics/Aurobindo/Illumined_Mind.htm

After reading *The Lost Waves of Time* you will never consider sound as mere entertainment again. At the very least, you will wisely consider about what you listen to. Better yet, you will open yourself to new possibilities and growth through readily available vibrational frequencies.

www.JillsWingsofLight.com – Art Galleries

25

Chapter 2

Involution and Evolution

Before we can enter the magical worlds of ancient civilizations and understand how they used music as a powerful force in shaping their lives, we must prepare. The concepts that follow may not be new to experienced readers, however, they are critical to understand the rest of the book. So bear with me; I will try to make this chapter as brief a detour from our main trip as possible.

The topics addressed in this chapter concern *involution* and *evolution* of spirit and matter. That is, how did the spiritual aspect of human beings enter the physical world and what will be the ultimate fate of us all? Also, we need to talk further about subtle energy and how it is the conduit between the material and the spiritual realms.

Recall that music can interact with subtle energy (present in all things) to profoundly impact people. As you have already seen, ancient sages were well schooled in the interconnected relationship of music and subtle energy. Intentional (and accidental) changes in music throughout the ages caused corresponding changes in the prevailing subtle energy fields available to civilizations. Often the ancient leaders desired to maintain the status quo of music and subtle energy – preserving the ruling elites and value systems of their cultures.

To further illustrate the subtle energy concept: the universe is full of subtle energy – analogous to photons filling empty space throughout the entire universe. Subtle energy travels on its endless voyage through space – back and forth across the universe – forever... like an endless river, reminiscent of the spectrum of electromagnetic energy. At any one point in time, human beings are open to only parts of the subtle energy continuum; we can only absorb so much of this universal force. As we change, the portholes within us receive different "frequencies" of subtle energy – OR put differently – as the prevailing subtle energy field around us changes, our receptiveness changes; we are now "open" to different subtle energy forces and our resulting selves change in very fundamental ways. For example, we no longer believe that human sacrifice is acceptable; we stop enslaving other people; we "discover" a Jesus or a Buddha. Because we have been "tuned" by subtle energy, all of our values, beliefs and even emotions have changed. Each of us has a "lock" that only the appropriate subtle energy "key" can open. Higher functioning mortals – such as Tibetan monks – can access more of the universe's subtle energy – so can mystics and other "talented" people. This explains many mysteries that have puzzled us for eons... connections with subtle energy open up the spiritual world; divine information and energy that we associate with God and the highest powers are available to those skilled in connecting with and manipulating the subtle energy surrounding us.

www.JillsWingsofLight.com – Art Galleries

This book paints a picture of HOW music/sound healing works; that is, music interacts with the subtle energy, which can reach our spiritual and nonphysical selves. Music additionally has the ability to reach human beings on a direct experiential level – clearly we enjoy listening to music – it affects our moods and emotions; we relax with music; some say we learn better with music; certain binaural beats can facilitate whole brain functioning etc. This connection reveals key components of our theory regarding how music/sound healing actually work; music directly affects our physical selves (in the traditional listening ways) *and* our non–physical selves through the subtle energy connection. This breakthrough observation changes the way we understand our world!

My *secret finding* – that you will discover throughout this book – is that music has played a pivotal role in each major culture, affecting the subtle energy that we get "tuned to." This dramatically shaped the spiritual and physical drivers of each era.

After years of research I detected that the dominant, overarching musical patterns changed over the ages and such changes correlated to shifts in major emotional and value characteristics of the culture. I want to explain this idea only once, so it is done here – to lay a foundation for the reader to grasp the significance of the changing subtle energy (from music) in each culture.

Involution of Spirit

Our modern understanding of how the physical form adapts – Darwin's Evolution – is well established and supported by a voluminous body of research and data. In contrast, the scientific community has largely "passed" on offering any explanations for the spiritual aspects of reality. Specifically, the understanding of our divine selves – our souls and our mystical aspects – has been left to fringe scholars (leaving organized religions out of this discussion – who universally rely on faith for accepting such mysteries). One explanation for the nature of our souls is based on subtle energy. However, our modern insight into subtle energy is very limited. Even the objective confirmation of subtle energy is sketchy, with only a few studies validating its existence. Yet, one of the lost triumphs of ancient cultures was an understanding of the workings of subtle energy and its ability to influence matter as well as the nonphysical realms.

A keystone concept presented by this book is the theory of the nature of subtle energy. The energy of the physical world is fundamentally different from subtle energy. The evolution of physical matter and the transformation of subtle energy through time are based on vastly different, distinctive processes.

Widely accepted scientific theories cover the physical aspects of the universe and the emergence of biological life; though important, these areas are not in the scope of this book. The critical concepts that are addressed here concern the ***involution*** and ***evolution*** of spirit. Specifically, we have interconnected processes responsible for human consciousness and destiny:
1. The ***Evolution*** of physical matter (Darwin's evolution)
2. The ***Involution*** of spirit (the nonmaterial) into matter
3. The ***Evolution*** of spirit (the nonmaterial) out of matter

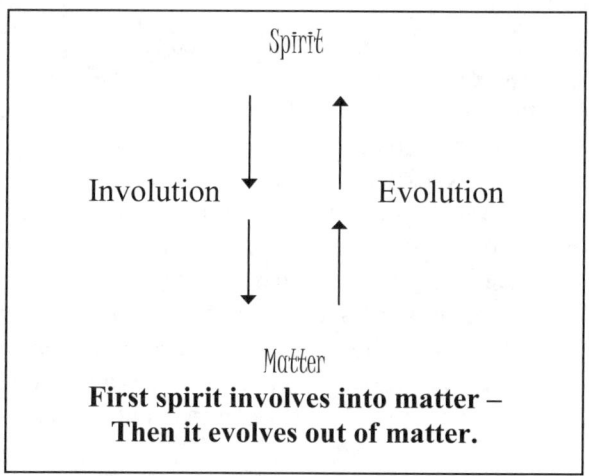

**First spirit involves into matter –
Then it evolves out of matter.**

The Cycle of Involution & Evolution of Spirit

Involution of spirit into matter is the process of subtle energy moving into, animating and elevating matter. Ancient beliefs held that energy is comprised of information and consciousness. Subtle energy can occupy many forms, including a human body. Spirit inhabiting matter in an orderly fashion is described in many sacred traditions. The intricate transformation begins as small units of subtle energy connect to matter. These energy units group together, forming increasingly complex structures. Slowly, over time the energy (involved spirit) becomes increasingly complex, identifying with matter to a greater extent.

The ancients described the stages that subtle energy took before it inhabited a human body. Spirit first merged into matter as a simple energy configuration that associated with an elementary compound or basic physical organism. For example, a rock is far less complex than a living being; its subtle energy is also much simpler. Gradually, over eons, living organisms evolved and the spirit that occupied them advanced in complexity as well. Inevitably, with time, Darwin's evolution of physical organisms progressed; life advanced in complexity and diversity. Spirit followed suit as it matured "inside" these more sophisticated life forms. The involution of spirit into matter grows and corresponds to increasing advancement in the physical organism's complexity.

As evolution continued, plants emerged and the energy of conscious spirit occupied these forms too. Gradually, more complex subtle energy units *involved* into the animal kingdom. Finally, upon completion of these stages, the ultimate organized unit of subtle energy, a soul, is ready to inhabit a human body. The advancement of spiritual involution (for humans) is accompanied by the progression of physical evolution that accommodates increasingly complex subtle energies, such as feelings, thoughts, awareness and free will. This idea can be found in many traditions around the world. For example, many years ago the Persian poet, Rumi, said, "I died as a mineral and became a plant. I died as a plant and rose to an animal. I died as animal and was as Man."[11]

It is yet to be revealed, but my feeling is that each individual type of higher being (human beings, alien beings on other planets and so forth) have their own destinies and fates. We humans may not aspire to the heights that other species reach – just as the animal species on earth do not reach the same levels that humans do. Key takeaways: subtle energy is the vehicle used for spirit's involution into matter and thus the bridge to access the nonmaterial world.

---

[11] Rumi. *Mathnawi*, III, 3901.

The involution – evolution cycle drives the beginning and ultimate fate of human beings. And our spiritual nature is coupled to matter for important purposes.

Timing of Major Events on Earth[12]

Event	Approximate Years Ago
Earth's age is well established	4.6 billion years
The simplest cells (prokaryotes)	3.6 billion years
Cyanobacteria photosynthesis	3.4 billion years
Complex cells (eukaryotes)	2 billion years
Multicellular life	1 billion years
Simple animals	600 million years
Fish and amphibians	500 million years
Land plants	475 million years
Mammals	200 million years
Primates	60 million years
Great apes	20 million years
The genus Homo	2.5 million years
Anatomically modern humans	200,000 years.

To implement decision making required for survival, a human being needs complex physical systems; these interpret wave information from the five senses. The body evolves (Darwin's evolution) physically to acquire the capabilities for higher intellectual thought, understanding and decision making. Simple souls occupied the earliest primitive men; more sophisticated souls involved into the more advanced men that emerged later. The combined processes of Darwin's physical evolution and the

---

[12] http://en.wikipedia.org/wiki/History_of_the_Earth

involution of spirit resulted in modern man who came to dominate the planet. When the dateline shown above is reviewed, it is amazing how quickly modern humans came to rule their world. This could only happen with the infusion of the divine or more advanced spirit.

Darwinian evolution does not consider the impact of subtle energy, but ancient shamans did. Shaman masters believed that everything housed consciousness. Every object (a rock, a pool of water etc.) or energy (sunlight, sound and so on) that we come into contact with, has some tiny effect on us. Ultimately, everything has minuscule, vibrational qualities; the movements are just too infinitesimal for us to observe. By selectively using the subtle energy of certain objects, a shaman positively affected the health and success of his clan. Since the earliest days of humankind, certain objects, such as crystals and precious stones, created positive healing effects. For example, certain rocks can calm or give energy. This is due to the rock's subtle energy. Shamans believed that this subtle energy had consciousness. Archeology and oral legends consistently show shamans making extensive use of special plants, musical instruments and chants.

www.JillsWingsOfLight.com – Art Galleries

Early Beings

The earliest souls inhabited a transparent, ghost–like or faerie–like body. The first *involved spirit* played with matter, while still being aware of and connected to group consciousness. Early beings were connected to the One through subtle energy. Their awareness or connectivity was also present through telepathy, clairvoyance and clairaudience. Gradually involution of spirit into matter progressed and the bodies became completely grounded and physical.

The early Atlanteans used their right brain hemispheres predominantly, which connected them to higher energy sources. Using the right brain resulted in perceptions that they were all connected: nature, the night sky, and all living things. Use of their left brain, with logical, sequential and comparative abilities, enabled them to experience themselves as separate. In addition, they became stressed when they strived for material things. This caused their thoughts and feelings to become separate. Eventually their independent feelings made them perceive that they were apart from nature, enabling them to contaminate and harm it.

The Law of Conservation of Energy from physics states that energy can change form, but can neither be created nor destroyed.[13] The soul is an eternal energetic entity, with neither birth nor death. Early sexless ethereal beings inhabited a body for a very long time, but their long lifetimes proved problematic. These beings formed habits; they got stuck in their ways and stopped growing during very long lives. Persistent legends suggest that birth and death "developed" to give people fresh starts, dropping older habits, through reincarnations. Ancient stories portray a "veil" that prevented man from remembering the (often hurtful) past. In each returning life one could begin afresh and open up to new ideas. Death and the "veil" helped man identify as a physical person, rather than a spiritual being.

With multiple lives, a soul has opportunities to experience and hone the results of his thoughts, emotions and actions. He "reaps what he sows." Recall that the record of man's thoughts and actions are retained in his subconscious – an eternal energy unit. This self–created energy attracts like–energy, providing unlimited chances to overcome obstacles and develop positive emotional and mental states. The energies a man creates outlast his physical body.

---

[13] The law of conservation of energy, states that the total amount of energy in an isolated system remains constant and conserved over time. For an isolated system, this law means that energy can change its location within the system, and that it can change form within the system, for instance chemical energy can become kinetic energy, but that energy can be neither created nor destroyed. http://en.wikipedia.org/wiki/Conservationof energy

Group Consciousness versus Individuality

In this book we shall refer to God, as "All That Is" or the "One". All That Is naturally includes consciousness and awareness of all energies. There are many subsets included within the One. Each major species of living organism, has a *group soul*, a collective energy pool, also called the *collective subconscious* (or unconscious). The most important and prevalent thoughts and feelings of the species dominate this energy pool. Each individual's energy contributes to the group's energy and can slightly alter it. A powerful soul – with greater connections to All That Is – can overcome the lesser group consciousness of lower living beings.

It is hard to go against the flow – to be the black sheep. We esteem inventors, pioneers and scientists who discover and introduce new ideas; it is a hard thing to introduce new ideas and we honor those few that do. The energy of prevailing attitudes and ideas is powerful, but individuals are *not aware* of this influence. Mainstream thought (as reflected in the energy of the group soul) influences us in many ways. Recall how difficult it is to think and act differently than your peers. Courage and perseverance, in the presence of a group of like–minded people, are required to stand out from the crowd. We progress by a few people coming up with better ideas – fighting against mainstream resistance – gaining acceptance and then spreading; the new ideas become mainstream. One hundredth monkey Avatars, such as Jesus and Buddha, come along to demonstrate a way to greater involution. Their energy is strong enough to overcome group consciousness as they gain followers.

The plant and animal kingdoms are strongly connected to their respective species' collective energies (group souls). The energy animating lower forms of life, such as an ant, shows surprising awareness and connectivity. To illustrate, when a queen ant is separated from her colony, building and maintenance of the hive continue according to plan; but if she is killed, the other ants do not know what to do. In the *Secret Life of Plants,* studies showed that plants responded to the wellbeing of their owners, even when the owner traveled across the country. Animals are aware of approaching bad weather. During the recent tsunami at Sri Lanka, the smaller animals fled in advance of the tidal waves. This demonstrates connectivity to and awareness of events in nature. Finally, what we call *instinct* is the undeniable connection of animals to their collective soul.

Author Jon Young, an expert on bird language, observed that animals receive communication from other species. Young describes a "sound canopy" in the woods, where various species pass their alarm through rippling sounds. For example, birds and squirrels, high up, detect the abrupt movements of a spooked deer. They sound their concerns to the entire forest community. With this warning, animals can estimate where a predator is and how fast it is moving – by the direction of these flowing sounds. The bird alarms even differentiate whether the predator is in the air or on the ground.[14]

Young suggested that humans were once tied into this network. Our sensory equipment is still designed for this interspecies awareness – it is just deeply buried. We can still read the moods of other people, but our primordial communication has become dormant. We are disconnected from the wider network of living things. Some sensitive people still retain this ability. We can regain these abilities if we try. Such insights are useful for many things such as: weather warnings, hunting, building relationships, nature photography, sensing danger signs and more.

In the beginning of the involution process, the human soul was keenly aware of its group energy. In contrast, today's humans have lost connectivity to this type of information; each person perceives himself as less connected – more independent.

There are many examples of how earlier ethereal beings lost awareness of group consciousness. As man's body developed keener eyesight, he simultaneously lost clairvoyance. Since man could not see subtle energy connectivity, he lost faith in this force. As time passed, he felt isolated and trusted only his senses; information obtained from psychic means was ignored.

---

[14] Young, Jon. <u>What the Robin Knows</u>, birdlanguage.org. *The Press – Republican News*, Plattsburgh, NY, Vol.119, No 329. Article by Elizabeth Lee.

Eventually, souls became increasingly individualized and autonomous.

The trend from group to individual consciousness is clearly seen in history. In older civilizations, autocratic rulers made all the decisions, while individuals labored and followed orders. Russian DNA scientists, Gosar and Bludorf, recognized that in earlier times humans operated like pack animals and were strongly connected to the group consciousness. In order to develop individuality, humans had to decouple from group consciousness.[15]

Today, we perceive ourselves primarily as individuals; we are distinct from our leaders and conduct ourselves with autonomy. With greater involution, people deemphasize the expectations of family, neighbors and other peer groups. They make choices freely based on personal preferences and independence grows. Free will becomes dominant as people make their own choices. There has been a noticeable change in individuality in just the past 60 years; compare the 1950s to the 2010s!

As the soul became more invested in matter, its source of information gradually transferred from telepathic, intuitive and group energy to the physical senses, especially sight and hearing. The new entity's perspective gradually shifted from that of an eternal, all–knowing soul to that of a time–limited man, who mainly operated based on sensory information.

People no longer identify with the soul and the nonmaterial, but with the world of physicality. Today, most people do not seek information from psychic sources, they doubt the validity of the spiritual. Many who practice this ancient art, do so poorly, further adding to the lowly regard of anything nonphysical. Ancient psychic energy connections are now largely dormant.

People can effectively target selective information. For example, a student can amplify the voice of the teacher or the hot gossip from the next student. What we pay attention to, dominates our

---

[15] Gosar, Grazyna and Bludorf, Franz. "Russian Discoveries," (*Vernetzte Intelligenz,"*) *ISBN 3930243237.* http://www.luisprada.com/Protected.russian_dna_discoveries.htm

awareness. We see this same trend in Darwinian evolution. If a species focuses on developing a new ability for self–defense from an enemy, the physicality slowly evolves to meet the need; if the adaption is not made, extinction may occur. As man focused on the physical world, he developed greater abilities to understand and manipulate physicality. The soul learned to direct life with only the input of the five senses, perceiving the world physically. Reflect on the adage, "Seeing is believing." Man has become completely grounded in the physical world.

The most advanced involution of spirit into matter is linked with the greatest perceived separation from God. Logically one might link the greatest involution with a person's greatest negativity, but this judgment does not automatically hold. People can make selfish or altruistic choices while perceiving themselves as individuals. However, with great involution, the person makes his own positive or negative choice – not the choice of the group. I would argue that the potential of making ethical personal choices – and the accompanying growth and grace – is one of the reasons for the involution–evolution cycle altogether.

In conclusion, most early beings were highly psychic, deeply and frequently accessing the collective consciousness. With the passage of time, psychic practices faded; people used special techniques (meditation, shaman journeys, spiritual practice…) to access subtle energy information.[16] In modern times portholes to this special information closed and man stands on his own – fully functioning and alone in physicality.

Duality

As involution progresses, the soul not only experiences increasing individuality, but also duality. Duality reflects opposite poles of energy, like positive and negative, night and day or *yin* and *yang*.

---

[16] The Old Testament described extraordinary hearing. "Oh, wondrous ear! It is the Lord that gives the hearing ear." Proverbs, XX.12, Bullinger, E.W. Number in Scripture: Its Supernatural Design and Spiritual Significance. "He wakenth the ear to hear."[16] Isaiah 1.4, *Ibid*, "It is the Lord that openeth the ear." Isaiah1.5, *Ibid*, "The natural ear does not hear spiritual sounds; it cannot discern them."[16] Isaiah IXiv.4 and 1 Corinthians ii, 9, *Ibid*, Today most people don't know what clairaudience is, let alone value or trust it.

Incarnate souls make many choices. Some prefer positive energies, while others experiment with negative alternatives. Recall that a soul is a small packet of energy of the One. With free will the soul becomes the sum of its energetic creations stemming from all thoughts, feelings and actions. For example, those who largely create negative energies eventually become comprised of them. Over time, these energies accumulate, become habits and influence the personal characteristics, creating a great diversity among souls.

Intense duality enhances the perception of separation. Author and scientist, Dean Hamer notes that people who experience being "at one" with others and the environment, are less self–centered than those that perceive themselves as separate.[17] People who do not sense strong connections to others feel less responsible for the world and its inhabitants. They also tend to exploit nature rather than protect it. Likewise, as man became an isolated individual, he polluted the Earth and acted primarily with self–interest.

Various species exhibit different degrees of duality awareness. The dog has a limited perspective of duality. Dogs are simpler and live in the moment, without planning for the future. The dog is conscious of good and bad times, night and day, but does not judge like humans do. The dog experiences less polarity.

The dog shows strength of character. To illustrate this point, note that the animal maintains joyful energy around a sick or depressed person – showing the dog's stability and emotional strength. Many dogs exhibit unconditional love to their masters, which is an uncommon trait in humans. Animals gain strength from their group consciousness. The human soul, fully involved in matter, draws on *its own* positive energy, not that of the group. The infinite goodness is **increased** with a generous soul acting freely, responsibly and producing positive energy and actions.

The dog enjoys greater connectivity to nature than humans do. A wolf does not survive for long on its own. Wild coyotes and wolves survive in a "pack," relying on information from their

[17] Hamer, Dean. The God Gene; How Faith in Hardwired in Our Genes, Doubleday: NY, 2004, Pg. 18.

group collective consciousness. Instinct clearly comes from the group consciousness.

Evolution of Spirit

Initially, the vibrations of higher subtle energy were "slowed down," that is, lowered in frequency, so that this higher energy could inhabit and associate with matter. At the end of the cycle, the vibrations of the subtle energy speed up again, quickening and preparing to exit matter. After reaching the apex of involution and perceiving himself being fully immersed in duality, a soul *evolves* back to unity or "All That Is." This is the process ancient people called enlightenment and we are calling evolution of spirit.

Each soul returns to the Earth many times in different bodies, personalities and circumstances in order to learn and grow while inhabiting a material form. Karma returns the energy that man creates, giving him endless opportunities to respond in a "higher energy" fashion. As a soul "masters" himself, he discards negative emotional habits, and obtains positive emotions, like forgiveness, compassion and happiness. The sensations of loving, forgiving and helping are lighter, "higher," energetic feelings than revenge, hatred and treachery. Man raises his overall energy, enabling him to return to the divine group consciousness again.

At the pinnacle of complete enlightenment, polarities and conflicts disappear. Man rises above duality. The soul no longer incarnates; Nirvana is attained.[18] In Buddhism, Nirvana refers to the state of eliminating desire and delusion with the accompanying freedom from samsara – the repeating cycle of birth, life and death.[19]

Since man is operating as an individual, each person reaches enlightenment or returns to "All That Is," on his own schedule. Some individuals have evolved back to spirit well ahead of the rest of humanity. A few are well known, such as Jesus, Buddha and Muhammad.

---

[18] http://en.wikipedia.org/wiki/Nirvana
[19] http://en.wikipedia.org/wiki/Saṃsāra

www.JillsWingsOfLight.com – Art Galleries

As the soul evolves, it gains greater conscious connectivity to group energies, at first only with his species or group collective energy and then with other, higher energies as well. An individual abiding in positive energy, elevates the collective unconscious energy – uplifting – to a small extent, the world around him. He now enjoys intuition, telepathy and other psychic abilities, while retaining what he learned in the physical realm.

Historical Impact of Involution

Ancient people frequently relied on subtle and psychic information in their daily lives. They instinctively believed in spiritual realms and they perceived reality differently than modern man. Modern man relies on sensory information, and the logic of science and technology for his understanding of the world. Depending entirely upon material and sensory qualities makes it nearly impossible for people to understand cultures that lived thousands of years ago. Magic and the mysterious were very real to ancient cultures. A revealing example from ancient Central America illustrates this point. Tournaments were a big part of celebrations of holy events or special occasions. In the tournaments, fierce competitions were held – all participants striving vigorously to win. The "winner" was then often sacrificed, earning a high spiritual honor in the afterlife.[20] In contrast, modern values would consider this murder. Who would want to be killed for any reason?

Believing strongly in an afterlife changes one's view of death. One who is certain that death of the body is not the end of his existence, is far less intimidated by death. Ancient people viewed the "dropping of the physical body" like changing clothes – no big deal – because the soul can always occupy another body, perhaps in a better experience. In contrast, if one doubts what happens when he dies, death is formidable, uncompromising and forever.

Ancient people were near unanimous in their belief of an afterlife. In contrast, today, non–belief is widespread, and with it comes the associated fear of death; consequently people are "all in," and "living for today."

www.JillsWingsOflight.com – Art Galleries

The earliest phases of involution – where a soul inhabited a faerie– like body of insubstantial material – obviously did not leave any traces for later discovery. However, early stages of involution are described in ancient tales – as archeological finds emerge – we see

---

[20] http://www.aztec–history.com/aztec–ball–game.html,
http://www.criscenzo.com/jaguarsun/ballgame.html,
http://en.wikipedia.org/wiki/Mesoamerican_ballgame

this process documented in history. Recall that people make decisions based on the information that they use to perceive reality. We will document an example of one historical Earth–wide trend (below) and then see how ancient people made choices based on subtle energy information (contrasted with today's physical sensory approach).

Human sacrifices are sometimes thought to be the stuff of legend and movies. Archeology clearly shows that human sacrifice was a worldwide practice in early cultures. Numerous examples of human sacrifice are found in burial remains, including:

- The city of Ur in Mesopotamia (the City of Abraham according to the *Bible*) – there exist remains from 60 human sacrifices accompanying Queen Puabie in 2650–2500 BC.
- Sumeria in the epic of Gilgamesh – when a man dies, his wife, family and court members willing submit to death to accompany him.
- Lindow Moss near Manchester, England – the Druids ceremoniously sacrificed young people in bogs.
- Chinese Emperor Qin Shihaungdi in 250 BC – all concubines with no children were sacrificed to accompany the emperor in the afterlife.
- Ancient Peru with the Moches and Mayans (100 AD to 800 AD) – human sacrifices accompanied sacred rituals.
- Oseberg Mound near Oslo, Scandinavia – the Viking queen is buried with her maidens, animals and supplies for the other world.
- During early times in various parts of the globe, children were buried in the foundation of ordinary homes, perhaps sacrifices to insure good fortune for those who dwelled in the structure.

Many sources tell us, those sacrificed believed that their souls benefitted from their selfless acts. Families of sacrificed individuals were often elevated in community position. One could choose to be sacrificed as a gift to his family. We can observe remnants of this behavior today. Devotees of radical Islam strap bombs to their bodies to blow up an enemy (and themselves). They believe that their eternal souls will benefit. Ancient people regularly accessed spiritual dimensions, contacted ancestors and "obtained" information from the spiritual realm. Such practices made sacrifice more palatable.

With partial involution on the soul, a more physical man lost direct access to the pool of subtle energy information; he utilized trances and mystical practices to access this subtle information. Early cave drawings found in France[21] and Spain[22] display drawings 15,000 – 16,000 years old. The cave art depicts shamans contacting the spirit world on behalf of the tribe. The shaman, often dressed as an animal, which helped him become one with its spirit. By tapping into the animal's spiritual energy he determined the physical location of the herds, aiding the hunt and/or asking its permission to sacrifice it.

Shamanism was widely practiced in: Africa, the South Pacific, the Americas, China, Australia, Europe and the Middle East. The practice of contacting the spirit world was well documented in far reaching cases: Atlantean stories, Neanderthal cave drawings and surviving practices of primitive people living in isolated locations in modern times. Drumming, playing music, whirling, chanting, dancing, sweat lodges and psychoactive plants helped shamans reach this shadowy place. All tribe members did not directly receive psychic information, but they still relied heavily upon it.

As man's perspective shifted to the preeminence of the physical world – the human life became valued enough to be spared from sacrifice. Animals took the place of men on the sacrificial alter. The remains of the Hebrew Temple in Jerusalem, referred to in the *New Testament*, can be seen today. At the time of Jesus, during Passover, seven priests slaughtered animals around the clock with the overpowering smell of burnt flesh and the animal carnage cloaking Jerusalem. That is a very large number of live animals killed. Animal sacrifice was an integral part of the Jew's world. Several thousand years later the same acts are viewed as horrific, disgusting and inhumane. People have developed compassion for animals, and live sacrifice is no longer required to atone for sins.

---

[21] French caves of Trois Freres/Lascaux
[22] Caves in northern Spain: Altamira

Around 210 BC, a transitioning practice is seen in ancient China with the reign of Emperor Qin Shihaungdi. Although his burial included human sacrifices, it also boasted an army of thousands of life–sized statues; each statue was sculpted realistically out of clay, representing soldiers, horses and chariots. Earlier, the Egyptian pharaohs' tombs included symbolic statues and artwork. Symbolism was gradually replacing live sacrifices. Progress was uneven around the world but all places eventually reached similar values.

After the life of Jesus, many religions used symbolism to replace live animal sacrifices for purification and forgiveness. Some examples are communion (Catholic Church) and *pooja*[23] (Hinduism). These symbolic sacrifices helped the faithful to achieve nearness to God; self–improvement and repentance aided in this realization. In Hinduism, flowers are given to the guru. The flower is plucked instead of the animal sacrifice.

Jesus was believed to be the "sacrificial Lamb" that enabled Christians to accept that their sins were forgiven. In this way, Jesus is a bridge to a time when people can forgive themselves – no sacrifice required. Religious beliefs and traditions dictated how people should behave. People were obedient to prescribed rules, but as people's souls involved further, they actively created their own guidelines. As people make choices, they learn and grow. As each individual assumes increasing responsibility, he becomes stronger and more independent.

Jesus predicted mankind's next step in spiritual development. He said, "Anyone believing in Me shall do the same miracles I have done and even greater ones."[24] To perform these same miracles people will need greater connectivity to higher consciousness. Jesus is referring to a time when more and more souls make the

---

[23] The following are some *pooja* offerings to a Hindu deity: the deity is invited to a ceremony from the heart; the deity is offered a seat; the deity's feet are symbolically washed; water is offered for washing; flowers are offered before the image, or garlands draped around its neck; incense is burned before the image; foods such as cooked rice, fruit, clarified butter, sugar and betel leaf are offered; the worshipper and family bow or prostrate themselves before the image to offer homage.

[24] Bible: John 14:12

leap in spiritually *evolving* back to God (advancing enlightenment).

Across the globe we find historic records documenting man's activities to gain God's favor; chronologically we have:
* Human Sacrifices... giving way to ↓
  * Animal Sacrifices... giving way to ↓
    * Gifts/Flower Sacrifices... giving way to ↓
      * Baptism/Symbolic Rituals... giving way to ↓
        * No Sacrifice, Ceremony or Deity

In modern times there are clear and strong trends to highly value life and respect the individual. The 19th century saw the practice of slavery greatly reduced. The differences in class structure were pronounced at the beginning of the 20th century but largely torn apart by the end of the century. During the 1900s most women gained the right to vote and by early in the 21st century we see great inroads made in treating women, minorities and gays better (although not fully as equals and not everywhere). These trends must be part of the evolution of the soul. Kindness, love and empathy are at the root of the involution and evolution cycle. This reminds me of escaping samsara in Buddhist teachings...

In recent times societies have steadily raised standards for personal responsibility and integrity. President John Kennedy's adulterous relationships with women were hushed up during his presidency. Thirty years later President Bill Clinton did not enjoy the same laxness. The moral standard clearly moved higher. Racial bigotry is greatly reduced around most of the world, ethics in business and politics are generally improved (of course there are still offenses). Over time, people demanded higher standards from their leaders and these expectations then trickled down to the general population.

When a significant percentage of souls reach a certain level of enlightenment, this behavior becomes the norm in the collective unconscious. The energy of each individual adds to that of the group energy, whether or not the individual is consciously aware. If enough individuals' energies change, then the group energy will follow suit. This has a lasting impact.

Decision making behavior was affected by the degree of awareness of group energies. Early humanity was tightly connected to its group consciousness and acted with uniformity. Tribes and ancient people lived and died with their group. An individual's identity and survival was inseparably linked to the strength of his group. Nowadays neighbors often do not know each other, let alone associate together. Long ago, decisions were made to enhance the group's strength, not to honor individual preferences. Today, the rights of individuals are not sacrificed for the group.

Changes occurred as man lost awareness of the group energy:
- Tribalism for survival was replaced by modern individualism.
- Acceptance of slavery is abandoned for the belief that every man should be free and autonomous.
- Kings and queens, and autocratic rulers give way to elected leaders – democratically selected by the population.
- Feminine or masculine dominated civilizations are replaced by a male – female balance. Both genders enjoy similar opportunities in modern societies.

Why Spirit Involves into Matter

The research of sacred music throughout the ages reveals that mystics lamented the loss of ancient wisdom and musical/spiritual traditions as civilizations fell. What was not often appreciated were the gains from mankind's growth in physicality. Surely there is a purpose for a spirit involving into matter. What was learned? What is the purpose for the adventure of a soul in matter? Why bother?

In duality, man has opportunities to experience forgiveness, mercy, generosity and so on. Many emotions are not available in a unified consciousness. For example, if "All is One," how can you generously give to another? Everyone has everything. Virtues are nonexistent in the group energy of The One. For example, how can you show mercy or self–sacrifice when everything is perfect?

During the journey through duality, the soul develops its uniqueness. People express their singularities in writing, music, art, architecture, service and more. Small businesses abound. Utilizing the Internet, musicians, artists and writers are blowing past publishers and promoters, with everyone getting a chance. Scientists are advancing world knowledge, quickly publishing results, blogging and making videos on their own. With greater availability of material merchandise, people express their individuality to a greater extent. Information and free communication is the new currency. Each person may develop unique skills and abilities that he can offer to the world as his gifts. Everyone can be his own master, choosing his desired life path with less pressure from society and family.

After spirit involves into – and later evolves out of matter, it retains mastery of thoughts and emotions that were learned during this cycle – this creates habitual virtues. The soul learns to care for others. The spirit becomes independent and able to do good on his own. As the spirit attains higher energies (through positive emotions and virtues) the soul's energies rise and connect to the higher subtle energies.

There are always growth opportunities for souls, and they can progress beyond being loving to enable unconditional love – loving all people no matter what they do. Unconditional love is outside the boundaries of duality, but within the enlightened consciousness. Here there are no mistakes that cannot be forgiven. In fact, there is nothing to forgive.

As we spiritually evolve, we do not revert back to earlier herd–like consciousness. We know how to make our own independent choices and be responsible for them. Yet, we can consciously access subtle, group information. The Internet serves as a symbol of collective unconsciousness that is accessible by individuals. Yet, no one loses his individuality when he uses the Internet. The soul again experiences the interconnectedness of life, but "oneness" does not obliterate its identity. It is both; it is the One and the All.

Spiritual evolution continues, but not necessarily in the physical realm. After Earthly spiritual evolution is complete, there are bigger gifts in a soul's "toy box" to create with. Perhaps your next adventure will be that of an ascended master, helping mankind from the spiritual realm or another adventure within our broad universe. At the completion of the involution – spiritual evolution cycle, there are vast opportunities for more growth cycles to participate in.

This is what this book is about – our spiritual roots, growth and ultimate destinies. It teaches the power of music, the ability of music to connect with and "tune" the subtle energy realm. Going forward we will see the characteristic aspects of ancient cultures and their use of music in defining their core values – maintaining them and pushing them forward. If we understand the connection between triumphs of a great civilization and their music, we can use music purposely for our goals. We can recreate the grid that allowed for the greatness of epochs past.

An avatar comes (Jesus & Buddha) and lifts people up inch by inch. They teach us how to rise above challenges associated in a musical energy matrix. Buddha taught about freedom from materiality and matters of the heart. Jesus gave an example of grace, understanding and wisdom. Quan Yen showed us compassion, mercy and forgiveness.

Subtle energy is still subtle, as strong as a house of cards. When the music changes drastically, liken it to a subtle energy tsunami – the structures of the past are destroyed and the new epic will rise. A new playground is created. Each civilization provides the playground for new lessons.

We are like a toggle lock. During each civilization we learn mastery of its characteristic energy – each skill lines up different types of energy like the toggles in a lock. When we master all lessons, the toggles all line up – we are unlocked and free from constraints.

Chapter 3

Lemuria and Atlantis: The Story & Music

The title of this book: *The Lost Waves of Time,* has its roots in numerous myths and legends – none more controversial or mysterious or wonderful than the legends of Atlantis and Lemuria... These two long lost lands were Eden to early master races that lived tens of thousands of years before the full emergence of our direct ancestors – homo sapiens. Of course, both island continents met with separate cataclysmic demises – perhaps due to massive floods, Earthquakes or polar shifts. Or, perhaps, the inhabitants sunk their own island homes after their work was accomplished.

Folklore originating from all over the globe makes reference to the Motherland of Mu (Lemuria). Mu or Lemuria clearly is older in origin than Atlantis; it is possible that there was a period of time that the two mysterious lands were simultaneously occupied. It is widely accepted that Lemuria was situated in the Indian or Pacific Ocean basin. The beings that were the Lemurians may never have been fully involved into matter. Many sources cite ethereal Lemurians who may have been more spirit than matter. To be fair, there is not enough evidence that allows us to definitively categorize the Lemurians. They did live on this planet for many years, starting at least 100,000 years ago – perhaps even far earlier. Their music and their relationship to the Atlanteans – as well as their heritage to us – will be addressed later in this chapter.

The evidence for the existence of Atlantis is voluminous – truly remarkable in its scope and depth. Some background on Atlantis will be provided for the uninitiated reader, however, our focus will be on addressing this legendary race's music and wondrous application of sound.

Atlantis – The Story and People

Atlantis is probably the most enduring grand mystery of all time... an enigma that was famously recorded by Plato around 360 BC (and it was an ancient tale at that time). Atlantis has captured the interest and imagination of countless generations; over 2,000 books have been written on this most famous "Lost Continent." Some suggest that the longevity of the "myth" and mankind's fascination with Atlantis is due to the memory of Atlantis written into our collective subconscious.

Plato's account of Atlantis is based on a trip that Solon, a respected Greek lawyer, took to Egypt around 580 BC. While traveling in Egypt, Solon learned of Atlantis from priests who received knowledge passed down from very old reliable sources. They told of a land beyond the Pillars of Hercules (Strait of Gibraltar) that was lost to the Atlantic Ocean 6,000 years before (this account gives a final demise date for Atlantis of approximately ~ 6600 BC – 8,700 years ago; sources usually date the disappearance of Atlantis beginning 30,000 to 40,000 years ago and finishing up 8,000 to 11,000 years ago; the destruction occurred in phases).

Edgar Cayce, famous for revealing alternative health information while in a trance state, has provided us with prolific and carefully documented, channeled sessions, about Atlantis and its people. During trances, Cayce learned of people who had lived previous lives in Atlantis. He provided startling detail on this ancient land and its destruction. Amazingly, many of Cayce's channeled revelations were later confirmed with scientific discoveries – after his death! Ancient sources referring to Atlantis are incredibly numerous and pervasive. Information on Atlantis is also found in Central American cave writings. The ancient Tibetans refer to Lemuria as *Ra Mu*.[25] In the Yucatan, monuments are dedicated as

---

[25] Andrews, Shirley. Lemuria and Atlantis: Studying the Past to Survive the Future, Llewellyn Publications: Minnesota, 2006, Pg. 1.

a memorial to those lost in Mu's flood.[26] Stories of a devastating flood are part of old oral legends of the Lancandon Indians in Mexico. The Cherokee history begins with beings from the Pleiades star system, who migrated to America prior to the sinking of Atlantis.[27] The book, *Popul Vuh*, from Central America described a visit by three princes "in the East on the shores of the sea whence their fathers had come."[28] The Toltecs of Mexico trace their heritage to Atlan (Atlantis). Montezuma (Aztec) told the Spaniards that his people came from the East, where their homeland of Azlan sank into the seas. The Dakota Indians insist their ancestors lived in a city now underwater. Similar stories are found in stories from: the Iroquois, Sioux, Delaware and Mandlan tribes.[29]

Geological finds support the existence of "lost" continents in the Atlantic and Pacific oceans. For example, nearly identical flora and fauna exist on lands widely separated by oceans. Fossil remains of the camel are found in India, Africa, Kansas and South America. Many similar fossil remains, of closely related species, are found around the globe. How did they cross the ocean barriers? The banana tree, native to Africa and Asia, with no small seeds, got to the Americas. The mid–Atlantic ridge has some of the highest peaks (submerged) of any mountains on Earth – are these remnants of the original Atlantis island continent?

Traces of mysterious language links abound; the old language of Basque from early Western Europe resembles the aboriginal languages of America. One third of the Mayan language is *pure Greek*. The first 13 hieroglyphs of the Mayan "alphabet" resemble the Egyptian Hieroglyphs. Many Hebrew words resemble the Chiapenecs' language of Central America.

In 1920, the British–born James Churchward published *The Lost Continent of Mu*, after 50 years of research and explorations throughout Asia and the South Asian Sea. Churchward described the Naacal, the people of the lost continent of Mu (Lemuria).

---

[26] Andrews, Shirley. *Ibid,* Pg. 30.
[27] Andrews, Shirley. *Ibid,* Pg. 57.
[28] Scott–Elliot. <u>The Story of Atlantis and the Lost Lemuria</u>, The Theosophical Publishing House: London, 1925 with editions up to 1968. Pg. 13.
[29] Andrews, Shirley. *Op. cit.,* Pg. 58.

Churchward claimed that he gained this knowledge after befriending an Indian priest, who taught him to read the ancient (dead) Naacal language. The priest revealed several ancient tablets, written by the Naacals. Churchward found that the writings of the early Naacal tablets were in the same language as geologist William Niven discovered on artifacts in Mexico.[30] How did these language influences cross the oceans? Did land once connect the east with the west?

The Guatemalan sacred text, *Popul Vuh,* claims that all people originally spoke the same language; this link was lost as groups moved away from their homelands. When the Spaniards first came to America they were surprised that natives had religious customs similar to their own, such as the worship of crosses, baptismal practices, fasting, confession, marriage, virgin mothers and communion. Ancient stories all over the planet tell of an archaic flood.

Numerous underwater archeological ruins of ancient cities have been discovered. One of the most notable is near Cuba on the Bahaman Plateau. Massive stone tiers that look like streets and walls have been found underwater, with carbon dating to 12,000 BC. The shapes are tetragonal and polygonal and precisely interlock. One formation appears to be the base of pyramid, 55 by 43 meters.[31]

Book after book presents extremely specific evidence of Atlantis. Numerous stories – from widely diverse cultures around the globe – refer to Atlantis. We find skeletal remains of homo sapiens (anatomically modern man) dating 150,000 to 200,000 years back.[32] We also know that cataclysmic events changed the surface of the Earth many times over. It is not hard to believe that the civilization of Atlantis existed at one time... only to disappear with hardly a trace.

Legends tell of a fantastically advanced Atlantis – with sophisticated technology AND spiritual and psychic capabilities

---

[30] Andrews, Shirley. *Op. Cit.,* Atlantis: Insights from a Lost Civilization, Pgs. 17–18.
[31] Muck, Otto. The Secrets of Atlantis, Times Books: NY, 1976. Pg. 34.
[32] Tattersall, Ian. The World from Beginnings to 4000 BC, Oxford University Press: NY, 2008, Pg. 67.

unlike we have ever known. At the same time, numerous species of hominids as well as homo sapiens were walking the planet – using stone tools and wearing animal hides. How can we reconcile these mysteries?

www.JillsWingsOfLight.com – Art Galleries

An Atlantis Theory

Science tells us that there have been numerous – surprisingly many – possible ancestors of modern homo sapiens (modern man). Often, several of these races of "early men" were present at the same time, co–inhabiting the same geographical regions. Why where there so many of these early hominid species and why did only one emerge – and emerge so quickly – to become modern man? Enter Atlantis theory... with the idea that some form of *"Divine Designer"* was watching developments on Earth and waiting for the right moment to arrive – when one species of early man was ready – or when the overall environment – or the planet or cosmos was right. Perhaps then the Divine Designers intervened and elevated the "chosen" race of early primitive man to the status of *modern man* – where the preceding species was animal only.

According to some schools of thought, Atlantis was where the early "chosen" human ancestors were taken by the Divine

Designers. Perhaps in this isolated, pristine land – the spark of divinity – the soul, or the everlasting spirit – was added to the animal form and what we know as true human man was born! These Divine Designers could have been truly divine – say the Angels of a traditional God; myths tell of Atlantis being home to Poseidon and his descendants. Even *Bible* stories echo this idea, as some versions of *Genesis* describe Giants who found Earth women pleasing and mated with them. If you are rooted in a more physical or scientific explanation, these super beings could have been advanced extraterrestrial aliens who had visited the early Earth for many millennia – watching and waiting until the time was ripe... This "creation" event dates at approximately 100,000 years ago, as closely as it can be traced.

Perhaps guardians watched over the small population of early "true men" for thousands of years in the isolated, paradise–like Atlantis. There, the Divine Designers educated them, nurtured them to grow and explore. The ability to use agriculture to enable permanent settlements started in Atlantis, as did advanced language and artistic skills. Early true men multiplied across Atlantis; then, starting about 50,000 years ago small vanguard parties of the true men began to move out into the wider Earth where they initiated small outpost settlements. These ancient vanguards – our earliest true fathers – went out in many different directions. Europe, Africa, Asia, and the Middle East were the first destinations for establishing proto–civilizations. (This theory, if true, could explain many enduring mysteries that have long baffled scientists and archeologists.)

As the years went by, more parties departed Atlantis – to supplement and extend the populating of our planet. The new settling parties went in varied directions – venturing into North and South America including Mexico and Central America. Others entered remote islands in the Pacific including Australia; some groups went to the same areas as previous settlers, to insure that a healthy population was developing.

Early true humans from Atlantis began to interbreed with suitable animal–like primitive men. The results of their offspring were mixed – some of the offspring thrived and the divine spark burned bright in them. Others retained a baser nature and lead to inferior species or died out altogether. The Designers saw that their efforts were succeeding.

Earlier we posed this question: why did modern humans emerge so quickly, after numerous hominid species existed for millions of years with little progress? Homo sapiens man, was chosen for his biological features; these allowed souls to develop emotional, mental and physical control. After emergence of this physical body, Middle Earth's purpose was concluded and the other human–like species faded away. This time period, called Middle Earth in stories, featured many human species existing at the same time. Perhaps these stories awaken our subconscious recognition and emerge repeatedly in works such as Tolkien and others.

It has been convincingly argued that some Atlanteans departed their doomed continent and spread around the globe, joining established populations of early men. These Atlantean refuges began the Shaman or Wiseman traditions in the primitive peoples that they "seeded." Often these transplanted Atlanteans and their direct heirs, passed on remarkable powers and skills to the primitives. This can explain many of the early wonders of primitive and early cultures – such as the monument building accomplishments and reported psychic abilities.

When the preeminence of modern man was certain, forces were put in motion that would eventually destroy all traces of Atlantis. The first destruction is traced to approximately 45,000 years ago when Atlantis was divided into five major islands. At 28,000 years ago the Earth's magnetic poles shifted and an Ice Age began. Complete destruction of Atlantis occurred approximately 9 to 10 thousand years ago.

From a spiritual point of view, a physical body can be likened to a container, skin or vehicle for a soul to use. Just as a variety of people can drive the same car, a Lemurian, Atlanean, dwarf, ogre or higher celestial soul can incarnate in the vehicle of man. The gamut of souls could incarnate into the human body. Not only is Earth a melting pot for different ethnic races, but for a wide variety of souls. The hermetic saying, "So as above, so below" reflects the mixing of spirits and races. If one believes in reincarnation then it follows that the souls of these earlier races can be reborn into today's human bodies.

Everything that was proposed earlier in this chapter, as an explanation for the rise and fall of Atlantis, can easily be considered as also true for Lemuria. It is probably unknowable today, but it seems logical that Lemuria and Atlantis fit together in the overall master plan for Earth and mankind. The main differences being that Lemuria came earlier than Atlantis (and was situated in the Pacific); we have far less evidence surviving for the Mother continent of Mu.

Lemuria

One of the primary goals in this book is to examine the music (and its associated subtle energy) from ancient periods. An extensive study of Lemurian music would be hard to comprehend without describing these people and their lives. They used music for purposes that we would not understand, because their lives were vastly different than ours. This book describes early cultures' uses of subtle energy and psychic practices in their daily lives. With this context, it is easier to understand how music, with its subtle energy effects, was utilized.

Channeled sources[33] described early Lemurian souls that were not at all human (homo sapiens). These ethereal beings entered the physical realm and began to interface with matter. The Lemurians belonged to strong soul groups, which interconnected the energy of all their thoughts and feelings. In a similar way God has been referred to as: All That Is, The One, the totality of all group souls, the ultimate repository of vibratory information.

According to many channeled stories, these early beings lived in the astral (or fourth) dimension and placed little value in the physical world. Existing outside of birth and death, they were close to God or All That Is.

---

[33] Many sources have been combined, including: Steiner, Rudolf. Reading the Pictures of the Apocalypse, Anthroposophic Press: USA, 1909 and 1991.

The Lemurians associated strongly with their souls and not so much with a physical body. They interpreted subtle information rather than sensory information. It is claimed that the early Lemurians did not experience sensory input from eyes or ears.[34]

Gradually, the Lemurians deepened their association with matter, exploring a new world, a physical one. As this occurred, vision, hearing and other sensory intake systems developed.

H. Spencer Lewis, a Rosicrucian, described the Lemurians as more psychic than physical. "The Lemurians were about seventy–five percent a psychic race, so far as development was concerned and twenty–five percent a physical race."[35] The Lemurians communicated telepathically and conveyed images mentally. They spent considerable time in altered states of consciousness or meditation, and had little time for material affairs.

These early beings were not fully incarnate into matter as we are. They were more faerie–like or spirit–beings. Tales describe some Lemurians as mermaids. There are also many tales of giants, mixed species, like the centaur (a combination of a man and horse) and the Minotaur (man and bull). In a later example, the legends suggested the oracles at Delphi, Greece were water nymphs, spiritual beings inhabiting water bodies.

Some Lemurians were described as twelve to fifteen feet tall.[36] The idea of giants seems farfetched, but there are artifacts suggesting otherwise.[37] A skeleton of a nine foot tall man was dug

---

[34] Steiner, Rudolf. Reading the Pictures of the Apocalypse, Anthroposophic Press: USA, 1909 and 1991, Pg. 55.
[35] Lewis, Spencer, H. Lemuria and its People – extracted from *Mystic Triangle 1926: A Modern Magazine of Rosician Philophy*, Kessinger Publishing, Pg. 62.
[36] Scott–Elliot. *Op. Cit.,* Pg. 88.
[37] Some newspaper articles about discoveries of "giant" skeletal remains in the USA in the late 1800s and early 1900s: New York Times (NYT) 2/11/1902 (skeleton with 4' arm); NYT, 5/4/1908 (200 skeletons in cave in Mexico about 8 feet tall); NYT, 3/5/1894, (found 11' skeleton in Ohio); NYT, 7/14/1916 (68 skeletons in PA about 7' tall); NYT, 11/21/1856 (skeleton found 11'); NYT, 8/10/1880 (2 skeletons found 12' tall in York, PA); NYT, 2/91/1890 (skeletons burial ground with extreme height in Mays Landing NJ); NYT, 12/25/1868 (Skull found 31 inches in circumference, 11' tall, Sank Rapids, MI); NYT 9/8/1871 (Skeletons about 8' with 1 inch thick skulls and flat tops, 8' tall, VA); NYT, 5/4/1912 (giant skeletons with skulls that recede straight back directly over eyes, nose above cheek bones and jaws long and pointed. Madison, WI).
http://www.sydhav.no/giants/newspapers.htm

up in the Pacific Islands, near the suspected location of Lemuria. In 1885, in Mississippi, a ten foot–nine inch skeleton was unearthed. A giant skeleton was also found in California.[38] Photographs exist of an archeological find of a crown, made for a man with a head twice as large as the priest, who discovered it.[39] Also, the Greek legend of the Titans boasts of their giant stature.

Many skeletons and fossil records reflect the existence of numerous human–like species. Archeological artifacts of some early skulls reveal that the average brain size (cranial capacity) for some humanoid species was larger than the modern human brain by up to 200 cubic centimeters. The contents of the brain could have been arranged differently due to the different size and shape of the skull. Some skulls were lower, broader and elongated in contrast to the higher doming of a modern skull.[40] Perhaps such variations reflect that different areas of the brain were more developed than in modern humans.

Hominid Species approximate Time Spans of presence on Earth

Species	Approximate Time Span
Homo erectus	2 million years ago to 200,000 years ago
Homo Heidelbergensis	600,000 years ago to 250,000 years ago
Homo Neanderthalensis	200,000 to 25,000 years ago
Homo Floresiensis	800,000 to 40,000 years ago
Homo Sapiens	200,000 to present

The Lemurian and Atlantean time periods overlapped somewhat according to channeled sources. The Lemurian civilization was an

[38] Andrews, Shirley. Lemuria and Atlantis: Studying the Past to Survive the Future, Pg. 12.
[39] Andrews, Shirley. Ibid, Pg. 72. (See the photograph!)
[40] en.wikipedia.org/wiki/Neanderthal Wikipedia™

older culture than Atlantis, and experienced its demise much earlier. Channeled stories describe "beings" visiting between the continents and "inter–racial" children. At this time the fossil records show numerous species of hominids with different facial characteristics, varying heights and different arrangements of the brain cavity. Stories from this time describe a variety of races, with skin color ranging from red, black, blue, yellow and white. Many types of men walked the Earth in these days, namely: anatomically primitive men (of several unique strains), modern man (homo sapiens) and the near–divine Atlanteans and their cousins. Popular stories parallel this scenario. Perhaps the Lemurians can be likened to the Elves.

Helena Blavatsky (1831–1891), a Theosophist, described the early spiritual development of humanity. In the First Age, humans were pure spirit. They were sexless beings in the second state.[41] In the Third Age the giant Lemurians used spiritual impulses to develop awareness of the physical world and sexual reproduction.

www.JillsWingsofLight.com – Art Galleries

In a similar vein, *Genesis* (6:1–6:4) refers to the "sons of God," or in other Biblical translations references are made to "the giants."[42]

---

[41] Other sources indicating that these early beings were sexless at first: Steiner, Bailey, list, Willugut, Randall–Stevens, Cayce, and Tom.
[42] Giants were also referred to in Numbers 28–31, Deuteronomy 1:28, with David and Goliath.

Perhaps these "giants" or the "sons of God" are from an older civilization, such as the Lemurians.[43] These giants found favor with the Earth women who bore their children. Atlantean mythology has similar stories with advanced beings mating with Earth women. Other sources also report that some Atlanteans were giants.[44] The story that the Greek's Poseidon (a god) mated with Earth women is in a related tradition. Similar stories exist in Sumerian texts;[45] the gods from Sumer are referred to as "visitors from heaven" in Mesopotamian tablets. The extraterrestrials seemed powerful and came from above, which classified the extraterrestrials as gods.[46]

Blavatski mentioned a race, cited in the *Popol Vuh,*[47] whose sight was unlimited and they knew all things at once.[48] These early beings were not fully materialized and exhibited an intuitive, clairvoyant state of consciousness. Perhaps these were the advanced beings mentioned frequently in ancient texts.

The Musical Number

Today, associating energy with a number sounds ludicrous to some; that is the case because we have lost our awareness of subtle energy. Our ancestors demonstrated mastery in this area. The idea that "numbers are subtle energy" prevailed for many thousands of years. This way of thinking was consistent with their overall deep connection to the spiritual world.

In antiquity, a number was equated with a characteristic energy. Numbers were found throughout nature and the heavens above. Whether a number was observed in a star configuration, a plant or the math behind music – people believed the number carried a unique quality. The actual number per se was not as important as

---

[43] The composite frequency of an object changes with its dimensions, according to Barbara Hero. See her chart: *Unified Theory of Color and Sound as Related to the Physical Body, The Chakras and Human Dimensions*: Hero, Barbara. The Glass Bead and Knot Theory of Relationships, Strawberry Hill Farms: ME, 1992 –1996. Pg. 45.
[44] Bellamy, Saurat, Steiner, Heindel, Oahspe, Scott–Elliot and Heindel
[45] Andrews, Shirley. Atlantis, Insights from a Lost Civilization, *Op. Cit.,* Pg. 32.
[46] Andrews, Shirley. *Ibid*, Pg. 32.
[47] *Popol Vuh* is a mytho–historical narrative from Guatemala. The title translates "Book of the People."
[48] Godwin, Joscelyn. Atlantis and the Cycles of Time: Prophecies, Traditions and Occult Revelations, Inner traditions: VT, 2011, Pg. 67.

its energy. Remnants of this art still exist today. It is called Numerology.

John Mitchell and Christine Rhone, in *Twelve Tribe Nations and the Science of Enchanting the Landscape,* convincingly described that ancient civilizations adopted numeric signatures and rules that enabled people to live in "enchantment." Numbers were used for this end, not only in music, but also in calendars, weights, measurements, land allocation and monumental architecture.[49]

Numbers were also *expressed* with music. When counting cycles per second of sound waves, calculating rhythmic beats and measuring the timing of musical phrases we are "doing math" with music. When a number was used to create sound (such as a number of cycles per second or pitch), the feeling of that sound was correlated with the number. In this way, numbers and music were closely linked.

Sources indicate that the music the Lemurians played was far different than ours today. Lemurian music had intervals in which the smallest distance between adjacent tones was equivalent to **nine** of our notes[50] – this represented huge jumps from note–to–note. Due to clairaudient abilities and their "quick" natures, the Lemurians had no problem listening to music with such vast intervals or frequency ranges. We would only be able to hear a handful of Lemurian notes before the frequencies were out of our hearing range. To make a crude comparison the Lemurians could hear tones higher than a dog whistle – or well beyond the hearing range of dolphins and whales!

According to Steiner, the Lemurian music connected the listener with divine energy. (Remember higher frequencies are higher energy and faster vibrations.)

Nine is the recurring number used in Lemurian music; it is the most humanitarian of all numbers. Nine symbolizes completion, fulfillment, gestation and self–awareness. A numerologist often

[49] Heath, Richard. Matrix of Creation: Sacred Geometry in the Realm of the Planets, Inner Traditions: VT. 2002, Pg. 49.
[50] Godwin, Joscelyn. Cosmic Music: Musical Keys to the Interpretation of Reality, Inner Traditions: VT, 1989, Pgs. 183–185.

applies the Pythagorean skein or gematria[51] to the letters of a person's name. When the number nine is obtained from one's name, it is associated with social consciousness; the person is described as idealistic, visionary, tolerant, imaginative, creative, compassionate, romantic, selfless and generous. [52, 53]

An interesting correlation – to the musical number – exists in crop circles, which have patterns that can be grouped by numbers. Crop circles, called circles of the gods in South Africa, can be as large as football fields, yet the delicate plants are usually bent and not harmed.

Author, Shirley Andrews, suggested that extraterrestrials are responsible for most crop circles and they impact our subconscious minds with these symbols and numbers. Investigators have measured energy emanating from the vicinity of the circles.[54] MIT and Princeton trained physicist, Dr. Claude Swanson, echoed this discovery, finding that crop circles give off energy based on their patterns, which can create sacred feelings and perceptions.[55]

Freddy Silva, crop circle expert, relayed his thoughts on the significance of crop circles: Since the late 19th Century, these mysterious geometric symbols have materialized in 29 countries, near sacred sites. Both the crop circles and the sacred sites are believed to be on subtle energy grid lines, which act like subtle energy veins for the Earth. Both the sacred sites and nearby crop circles create uplifting energy that travels on these ancient grids. Silva believes this uplifting energy explains why some people experience spontaneous healing near genuine crop circles?[56]

---

[51]Gematria is a system of assigning numerical value to a word or phrase, in the belief that words or phrases with identical numerical values bear some relation to each other. http://en.wikipedia.org/wiki/Gematria

[52] http://www.spiritual–numerology.com/numerology–number–meaning/numerology–meaning–of–number–9.html

[53] Weaknesses linked to the number nine: aloof, withdrawn, distracted, possessive, moody, timid and uncertain, unsatisfied with results and careless about finances.

[54] Andres, Shirley. Lemuria and Atlantis: Studying the Past to Survive the Future, Pg. 105.

[55] Coast to Coast am radio, George Noory interview with Dr. Claude Swanson, May 10, 2010.

[56] http://www.greatmystery.org/GMEmail/humanevolution.html

Silva believes that the shapes of crop circles subtly influence our world. It should be noted that the subtle energy of each crop circle varies with the shapes within the circle. The crop circles can be characterized by counting the *number* of times a design element is present. Likewise, some ancient sages would link the number in the crop circle with a musical system built around the same number.

The Number Nine in Crop Circles[57]

The Music and Sounds of Lemuria

Lemurian verbal communication was composed of singsong–like utterances that expressed pleasure, joy, pain and other sensations. These sounds resembled words[58] but were strongly musical. Most Lemurian communication – particularly in the beginning – would have been telepathic.

Language is a special attribute of humans. In apes and human babies the *larynx* (AKA the voice box) is located in the top part of the throat. The larynx is an organ that holds the vocal chords, responsible for manipulating pitch and volume of the voice. Until the larynx drops, some sounds commonly used in speech, cannot be produced. If the skull base is flat, then the pharynx – an organ in the back of our mouths – has limited ability to modify sounds. As the human baby grows, the skull base curves and the larynx drops, allowing a greater range of vocalizations. On the basis of

---

[57] Used with permission from Peter Sorensen.
http://cropcircleconnector.com/Sorensen/circles/1999/main.html
[58] Steiner, Rudolf. Cosmic Memory, Prehistory of Earth and Man, Harper & Row: San Francisco 1959. Pg. 72.

the curvature of skulls in the fossil record, *potential* for speech existed 600,000 years ago. Yet the pharynx and oral cavities were not balanced as they are now; the vocal apparatus we have now was not like theirs.[59]

Ancient words often contained the energetic force of what the word represented. One way ancient priests figured out the sound energy of an object was to place sand on a drum head and create a sound underneath the drum for up to 15 to 30 minutes. The priests experimented with the same sound at a variety of pitches. The sand would sometimes vibrate and create shapes when the pitch was right, often making recognizable shapes, like a dragonfly. When this happened, the sound became the word (or part of the word) associated with the image that it produced. Words were analogous to vibrational energy and were used for healing. For example, Atlanteans sang their impressions of being healthy.

Excavators, Augustus Le Plongeon and his wife, encountered some Mayans at Chichen Itza (now Yucatan Peninsula) who were isolated from the rest of humanity until about 100 years ago. It is believed that their language was one of the oldest on the Earth. The Le Plongeons listened to a chant, a song of the tribe's ancestors. The sounds changed in pitch, intensity and amount of vibrato depending on the meaning to be portrayed. The Le Plongeons were able to understand the singsong story – before it was translated to them. By listening to the chanted sounds they correctly interpreted a story about the frantic actions and terror of a hunter as a jaguar attacked and killed him.[60] The communication was achieved with pitches and vibrato – not symbolic words. Likewise, the Lemurians used sounds to express feelings and experiences, but did not use words symbolically like in today's languages.

Dr. Rudolf Steiner, born in Australia in 1861, was a brilliant Theosophist[61] and master of occult sciences. He founded a

---

[59] Tattersall, Ian. *Op. Cit.,* Pg. 72.
[60] http://en.wikipedia.org/wiki/Chichen_Itza. Steiner, Rudolf. <u>Cosmic Memory, Prehistory of Earth and Man</u>, Harper & Row: San Francisco 1959. Pg. 51.
[61] Theosophy is a doctrine of religious philosophy and mysticism. Theosophy holds that all religions are attempts by the "Spiritual Hierarchy" to help humanity evolve to greater perfection. Each religion therefore has a portion of the truth. The founding members,

spiritual movement, Anthroposophy, featuring an esoteric philosophy that was developed from transcendentalism and linked to Theosophy. In this system of thought, musical vibrational patterns were linked to the energy of a higher source – God. As sound matrices transferred energy to physical levels, we experienced increasing independence from God.

Steiner taught that the Lemurians listened to *descending* tonal passages that facilitated their spirits involving into matter. Author and spiritualist, R. J. Stewart described subtle benefits from ascending and descending tones. Descending scales carry inner power outwards, while ascending scales send consciousness inwards.[62] Descending chants enable spirit to occupy matter, while ascending tones help spirit to leave matter. (This is an important concept that we will revisit later.)

Steiner described ancient Lemurian music as if it floated, like the sounds of wind chimes, with no beginnings or endings. This music has also been referred to as the "music of the spheres."

The Lemurian rhythms copied nature's patterns found in animal sounds and rhythms created by cycles, such as the sound of ocean waves. Nature's rhythms help energy flow into the chakras and up the spine (in the enlightenment process). Today, remnants of these rhythms are used in the Hindu musical system.[63]

Nature sounds were believed to have different influences. For example, bird song produced a different energetic effect than the cricket's chirp. Words also incorporated nature's original divine energy. Words were also used to advance plant growth and tame wild animals.[64]

Helena Petrovna Blavatsky (1831–1891), Henry Steel Olcott (1832–1907) and William Quan Judge (1851–1896) established the Theosophical Society in New York City in 1875. http://en.wikipedia.org/wiki/Theosophy

[62] Stewart, R. J. The Spiritual Dimension of Music: Altering Consciousness for Inner Development, Destiny Books: VT, 1990, Pg. 101.

[63] Prophet, Elizabeth. Science of Rhythm for the Mastery of the Sacred Energies of Life: Uses and Misuses of the Word in the Music of the East and West, The Summit Light House: CA, 1978, cassette tapes.

[64] Steiner, Rudolf. Cosmic Memory, Prehistory of Earth and Man, *Op. Cit.,* Pg. 51.

Jane Roberts[65] channeled an entity called Seth. Seth (through Roberts) described additional Lemurian uses of sound, "The Lemurians had telepathic gifts, and ways of manipulating and understanding sound far beyond anything we can conceive. They used sound to create brilliant images before the inner eye and also as their main source of physical energy."[66]

Due to their telepathy, there was little reason for Lemurians and early Atlanteans to communicate by the spoken word. Sound was mainly used like a vibrational tool, to quicken or slow down matter. They used sound to levitate heavy objects, for healing and other targeted purposes. Sound was effective in moving and altering dense physical matter.

Author Bruce Cathie wrote about an eye witness account – of a Dr. Jarl – who witnessed the Tibetan monks using musical instruments and their voices to move huge boulders. The positioning of the singers and musicians was crucial for the "anti-gravity effects" to work.[67] Numerous sources suggest that the Atlanteans also used directional sounds as a means of applying mechanical power.[68] Details of this account can be found in the chapter on Egypt.

According to ancient wisdom, the power of sound increased with large numbers of participants singing. Each individual accessed energy that originated from the heavens. The Lemurians believed that two singers together created more energy than each singing separately – as if their combined voices increased energy exponentially. Singers drew on heavenly energy – continuously singing in large choirs to make their countries potent. Perhaps Jesus also suggested that there is power in numbers, "For where *two or three* gather in my name, there am I with them."[69]

Kryon, a channeled entity who said that he was a being from Lemuria, gives an interesting account on the music of Lemuria. In

---

[65] 1929–1984
[66] Roberts, Jane. The Education of Oversoul 7, Pocketbooks: NY 1976, Pgs. 104–107.
[67] Cathie, Bruce, *Acoustic Levitation of Stones: Monastery Construction, Tibetan Style*. See Appendix B.
[68] Theosophists, Brown, Neate, D. Leslie, Seth, Tom
[69] Matthew 18:19–21

Lemuria he conducted a choir of 800 people chosen for their vocal abilities. Four hundred singers on a side, faced one another singing back and forth to a partner. Many cultures had similar practices for large musical ensembles throughout the ages. The group's energies were believed more powerful than the sum of their individual components. A moment of silence is also a remnant of this practice. When people create group–thoughts in the prescribed moment, their energy becomes powerful.

The locations of musicians were carefully mapped for musical performances. Think of each singer as a point and the sound coming out of his mouth as a vector of energy, like water shooting from a water pistol. The ancients arranged where musicians stood, directing sound energy to produce etheric geometries for desirable effects.

Life in Atlantis

The last phase of the Atlantean culture endured over 50,000 years; there were significant and lengthy earlier phases, according to channeled sources. Life was different in the beginning and changed significantly as the continent endured. The Atlanteans started out more involved into physicality than the earlier Lemurian race; they were spiritual and harmonious beings that gradually mixed their energies with matter. The early Atlanteans were not like today's human species.

They were highly capable of manipulating malleable and subtle energies. For example, the power to produce rain at will was common, as water is pliable.

The early Atlanteans did not see objects with clear and sharp edges, but as hazy objects surrounded by auras or soft lights. The early Atlanteans possessed clairvoyance and clairaudience. To them, the astral world was enormous and rich, while the physical world appeared diminished and small. Music that we hear only with our external ears is described as a shadowy reflection of the "inner music" that they enjoyed.

The people of Atlantis communicated telepathically.[70] (Comprehensive speech as we know it emerged relatively late in human evolution, roughly corresponding with the emergence of homo sapiens.[71]) This may seem fanciful, but today even humble ants receive long distance, nonverbal communication from the queen of their colony.

Telepathy was widely used to communicate with beings other than humans, such as plants and animals. The Atlanteans believed in *nature spirits* – the intelligent consciousness of energy in all living things. The ancient Hindu religion calls this consciousness, divas.[72] Sound is used by some Hindus as a bridge to other dimensions, such as the divas.

In the later days of Atlantis, people were involved into matter to a far greater extent. Their physical bodies were perfected to better interpret vibrations in the physical world, such as sight and hearing. In the later years, when telepathic skills lessened, thought transference was taught in the temples in attempt to retain these skills. The students practiced specific techniques – they relaxed while breathing deeply to low pitched, rhythmic sounds. This enhanced the mental state required to produce telepathy.[73] In any society in which everyone can read minds, secrets were uncommon. With transparency, people's behavior was impeccable.

Edgar Cayce reported many details about the Atlanteans. Prominent was their great mind power; they could use their minds to strictly control their bodies. Many of the priests could levitate; others were "magicians." Religion, science and magic were considered almost the same thing. Their schools of magic served the role of both church and school. This land did not have stark contrasts between rich and poor. No one lived in want. Items most valued were not material, but psychic skills and abilities. Their country relied on seven famed oracles – who foretold the future by accessing subtle energies from future times.

---

[70] Andrews, Shirley. Atlantis: Insights from a Lost Civilization, *Op. Cit.*, Pgs. 68, 80.
[71] Perrault, C. and S. Mathew. "Dating the origin of language using Phonemic Diversity." *PLoS ONE* 7(4): e35289. Doi:10.1371/journal.pone.0035289. 2012.
[72] Andrews, Shirley. *Op. Cit.* Pg. 138.
[73] Andrews, Shirley. *Op. Cit.*, Pg. 74.

Atlantis had rich soil and enjoyed a temperate climate (as you would expect for a large island in the Atlantic). Their diet included fish and fowl, but no red meat, although there are stories that they drank fresh blood.[74] Lions were kept as pets; felines enhanced psychic work and protected against the "lower astral" energies.

Atlantean houses were built with the help of sonic gongs; huge stone blocks were raised without machinery or human effort. Power from the sun was harnessed for energy. Stories of these abilities are found all over the world. We will go into more detail about using sound for moving large objects in the chapter on Egypt.

The Atlanteans developed amazing skills unimaginable today. In one account, they used hypnotism and magnetic therapy to raise the consciousness of criminals, to rehabilitate their thinking, so that they would never commit a crime again.[75]

The sound of one's name was believed to resonate with the gifts that the soul wished to create while in the physical body. Care was taken to say someone's name with love. If a child heard his name in a judgmental, demeaning way, the child was expected to experience difficulties in expressing his potential.[76]

Even when they were young, these highly evolved beings often chose to pass over once they accomplished what they had incarnated for.[77] The process of dying was perceived as simply separating from the physical body. When a person died, the body was "disintegrated by the occultist priests with the use of certain cosmic forces."[78]

The Mayans have a legend about a practice of willful death. When a medicine man or shaman got too old to perform his duties, a young person, who was trained to replace him, would sit with the

---

[74] Scott–Elliot. *Op. Cit.,* Pg. 51.

[75] Andrews, Shirley. Atlantis: Insights from a Lost Civilization, *Op. Cit.,* Pgs. 80, 90, 92.

[76] Cooper, Diana. Discover Atlantis: A Guide to Reclaiming the Wisdom of the Ancients, Findhorn Press: Scotland, UK, 2005. Pg. 172. (channeled information)

[77] Andrews, Shirley. *Ibid,* Pg. 86.

[78] Helio–Arcanophus, Atlantis Past and To Come, (London: The Atlanteans, 1959), Pgs. 8–9. Godwin, Joscelyn. *Op. Cit.,* Pg. 194.

aged shaman and a crystal skull. During a ceremony, they would both put their hands on the skull; in this way the knowledge and wisdom of the older person would pass to the younger. When the ceremony was completed the older person passed. The Mayans credit the Atlanteans as their ancestors. Mayans believed the people from Atlantis created the crystal skulls, which according to some reports, several have now been found.[79]

In Atlantis seeds were given an energetic boost with music. Loud drum beats and passionate dancing were believed to inject energy into the Earth. The soil's energy was activated with vibration for best results. Additional instruction was received telepathically from the growing plants to produce optimal results. Examples include: plant root vegetables during a full moon for best growth; tomatoes prefer to live alone and a quartz stone in the middle of gardens amplifies plant growth.[80]

"Boji" stones were composed of dense sand, in which the outside felt like iron particles. Many perfectly round balls were smooth, while others had protrusions. The smooth ones were considered feminine and the others masculine. Both varieties were arranged in gardens to benefit crops.[81]

In *The Secret Life of Plants,* a study showed that ultrasonic frequencies stimulated plants' enzyme activities and respiration rates. Plants that were exposed to frequencies for insect control grew faster than those not exposed. However, the frequencies that stimulated one plant often inhibited the next. In conclusion, exposure to frequencies greatly impacted the growth of plants and seeds.[82]

The Kairos Institute of Sound Healing in New Mexico tested if sound vibrations enhanced crop growth. They played tuning forks and hand chimes over seedlings. The forks were tuned to the frequency made by Mars and Venus moving in their orbits and

[79] Morton, Chris and Thoman, Ceri Louise. The Mystery of the Crystal Skulls, Bear & Co.: Santa Fe, N.M., 1963, Pg. 26.
[80] Andrews, Shirley. Atlantis: Insights from a Lost Civilization, *Op. Cit.,* Pg. 139.
[81] Cooper, Diane. *Op. Cit.,* Pg. 47. (channeled information)
[82] Tompkins, Peter and Bird, Christopher. Secret Life of Plants, Allen Lane, 1974 Article by Sherwood, Ed. http://www.cropcircleanswers.com.

other special frequencies found in space.[83] Their findings showed that sound vibrations improved seed germination, quantity and quality of produce, longevity of production, pollination, and plant size.[84]

The Atlanteans used a healing technique that specified treatments depending on brain hemisphere dominance. Dr. Richard Gerber reported that ancient civilizations, such as the Atlanteans, altered their medicine depending on a patient's primary brain usage. Today, Sharry Edwards, who developed the science of BioAcoustics, does the same thing. One of her discoveries is that each brain hemisphere uses opposing methods to determine frequencies.

Rosenzweig, a scientist with studies published in *Scientific American*, conducted experiments to validate that each brain hemisphere is hardwired with its own sound processing center.[85] This has significant implications. For example, medicine and food have their own unique frequencies. A medicinal or chemical compound is in essence a frequency, a vibrational energy. Since the right and left hemispheres of our brains process frequencies differently, which brain hemisphere is being used makes a critical difference in which frequency (or medicine) is most effective. Perhaps this explains why some antibiotics work on one person, but not another. The Atlantean civilization altered the type of medicine used on people depending upon their brain dominance.[86]

Author and teacher Diana Cooper presented a channeled explanation for the many stone circles that we see around our planet. She reported that the heavy stones were transported by telekinesis (dematerializing something and rematerializing it elsewhere), together with sound and crystal power. The stones were often concave, so that the circle created great acoustics for chanting. The circle location usually included an underground

---

[83] They also used planetary gongs tuned to the "three cycles of the Earth: the four seasons, the Earth spinning on her axis, and the Earth going through its processional cycle."
[84] Leeds, Joshua. The Power of Sound: How to be Healthy and Productive using Music and Sound, Healing Arts Press: VT, 2001, 2010, Pgs. 207–209.
[85] Rosenzweig, 1961. The Science of Audio Based Beat Brainwave Entrainment, http://web–us.com/thescience.htm
[86] Gerber, Richard, MD. Vibrational Medicine, third edition, Bear and Co.: VT, 2001, Pg. 330.

stream crossing. The people's chanting and prayers blessed and purified the water that the people drank. The stone circles were built on ley lines (subtle, magnetic energy currents of the Earth). The circles were also aligned to special star systems. For example, when the stones matched the star positions of Orion, they connected with the wisdom of the Orion Masters. Perhaps they aligned the stones to the Pleiades star grouping, to receive healing energy from the Pleiades. In another example, the stones may align to Sirius to receive energy to create spiritual technology, originating from that star.[87]

In the ceremonies, people entered the circle by walking on the ley lines, to receive uplifting energy. They chanted as they walked in clockwise circles that got smaller and smaller. This was done to amplify the energy of the participants, as well as the power of the circle stones, the earth and water. Eventually, the location and stone accumulated healing powers; people brought their sick to these stone circles. In their ceremonies, the priests gave thanks and led people in further chanting. At the conclusion of the session, chanters walked in circles that gradually got larger in a counter clockwise direction to close the ceremony. The creation of labyrinths evolved from this practice. Walking a labyrinth strengthens one's right brain, meditative abilities.[88]

Sound temples were often located in circular buildings; the height of the building was half of the length. The windows were made of quartz crystals. This created a reflection pattern that was excellent for sound waves. Sound was used for healing, regeneration of limbs and detoxification. To regenerate a limb, a person was placed within a crystal chamber. Chanters sounded the resonant frequency of each tissue to be regrown. Within their minds they held the image of the regrown limb. In this same way, they provided a rejuvenating treatment to counteract the impact of aging.[89]

I have had numerous "visions," in which I woke up in what I believe to be Atlantis. On one occasion, I perceived I was in a

---

[87] Cooper, Diana. *Op. Cit.,* Pg. 66. (channeled information)
[88] Cooper, Diana. *Ibid*, Pg. 67. (channeled information)
[89] Cooper, Diana. *Ibid,* Pg. 85. (channeled information)

building, formed with several wings; there were no straight lines in the design of the building. The building segments were circular and connected. The windows were made of quartz crystal. There was a crystal skull in the center of the building. It glowed with red dots of light, and I believed the crystal skull was the generator or power source for the building.

A person missing an arm stood in the center of one of the circular rooms. Six of us (and at other times five) surrounded this person in a circle, equidistant apart. We were wearing hooded, midnight blue robes, similar to that of medieval monks. We used our voices, aiming our voice streams to the section of the arm that we were trying to regrow. Our voice energy-streams created the shape of a five or six pointed star (depending on the number of people in the circle). We had crystals and colored lights behind us that also amplified this energy.

In another vision, I believed that I had twelve strands of DNA. I understood DNA to be like radio antennae. The longer an antennae, the better the reception. Likewise the more strands of DNA one had, the greater his connectivity to other energy sources. People with "developed DNA" were more psychic and possessed other useful skills. I believed that DNA was resonant with love. Love could be compared to white light, which can be broken down into the component colors of the rainbow. Love was made up of many qualities. For example, two aspects of love were compassion and wisdom. As people lost their telepathic and clairvoyant abilities, they hid their mental and emotional energies – if they expected condemnation. When they denied their emotions, this energy hung around them like little balls of dark energy. As it accumulated, their DNA recoiled, losing strands of connectivity.

Theosophy sums up changes that the people of Atlantis experienced towards the end of this civilization: Their spiritual world gradually diminished as the Atlantean society came into its ultimate prominence. The soul became more attached to its physical environment. People relied on information from their senses; the use of intuition and subtle energy information faded. As spirits increased their identification with matter, the Lemurians and Atlanteans utilized sound as spoken words to communicate in place of mental means.

Theosophist, Helena Blavatsky, wrote that modern humans developed on the continent of Atlantis, and that this developmental age is not over. The final accomplishments will be the reawakening of psychic gifts. Blavatsky hinted that the psychic gifts that mankind will develop may be intuition and telepathy.[90]

The Musical Number of Atlantis

The Atlantean scale used notes that were closer together than the Lemurians – but still much further apart than we know today. The smallest distance between neighboring notes was equivalent to **seven** of our notes. According to Steiner, the music of the Atlanteans connected them to their own Divine Spirits; this was a somewhat lower spiritual level than the Lemurians.[91] The Atlantean man was also more involved into matter than his predecessor, the Lemurian. The music of Atlantis used patterns of seven, while the Lemurian style incorporated patterns of nine. Steiner maintains that different vibrational patterns in music correlate to varied attributes in consciousness, creating different experiences for listeners.

The Atlanteans, like the Lemurians, deeply believed that numbers carried subtle energy. By using a number – seven in the case of the Atlanteans – in the design and composition of the music, certain energy configurations were created that link to emotional, mental and physical states. Using a repeating number pattern (seven in Atlantis) in the music, locks in and strengthens a specific influence of music. The listener in ancient Atlantis received a great many doses, eventually shaping his brain waves, emotions and even physicality.

Seven is a uniquely spiritual number. There are seven colors of the rainbow, seven notes in a diatonic scale, seven major chakras and numerous flowers with seven petals. People refer to seventh heaven, seven years of bad luck and seven deadly sins. Seven can

---

[90] http://www.katinkahesselink.net/blavatsky/articles/v12/y1890_053.htm
[91] Godwin, Joscelyn. Cosmic Music: Musical Keys to the Interpretation of Reality, Inner Traditions: VT, 1989, Pgs. 177–179.

symbolize reflection, preparedness, independence, discipline and inner work.

 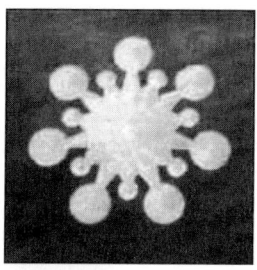

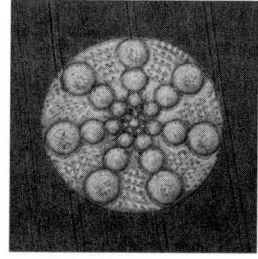

The Number Seven in Crop Circles[92]

The number seven, the featured energy in Atlantean music, is the most spiritual of all numbers. Numerology reveals that people with this number in their name[93] are analytical, intellectual, focused, scientific, inventive, contemplative, meditative, spiritual and enigmatic. They seek truth and accumulate knowledge and wisdom. They prefer working alone as they need space and privacy. They enjoy solitude, but also display their knowledge in public. They think abstractly, are self–oriented, are perfectionists and possess mental acuity.[94, 95]

---

[92] Used with permission – Peter Sorensen.
http://cropcircleconnector.com/Sorensen/circles/1999/main.html
[93] The number in your name is found by applying the Pythagorean skein and gematria. Gematria is a system of assigning numerical value to a word or phrase, in the belief that words or phrases with identical numerical values bear some relation to each other, or bear some relation to the number itself as it may apply to a person's age, the calendar year.
http://en.wikipedia.org/wiki/Gematria
[94] http://www.spiritual–numerology.com/numerology–number–meaning/numerology–meaning–of–number–7.html
[95] Negative characteristics of people associated with nine: egocentric, arrogant, self-pitying, sentimental, discontent, fickle, cold or mentally unstable.

75

Sounds and Music of Atlantis

Atlanteans enjoyed musical instruments made from reeds and animal bones. Before an animal died, they would ask permission to use its bones for the instrument; they respected the animal in this way. Bones of different lengths could be wrapped together and used like pan pipes. They would hit the pipes with something covered in a soft material to create beautiful notes. They also made music with the sounds of hanging crystals. Stringed instruments, such as the harp, were widely enjoyed.[96]

People liked to chant together. They isolated a specific emotion that they wished to experience, such as peace or playfulness. Their music would create this wonderful feeling, allowing everyone to experience this vibration of peace internally. Likewise, they created art. It was displayed so that people experienced a playful feeling when viewing the artworks; in another room the art would radiate a feeling such as peace. They would desire a beautiful feeling and then create art and music to experience it.[97]

Being clairvoyant, the people saw that certain sound patterns lit up their auras, making them feel uplifted. They listened to these sounds often. Today, Kirlian photography allows us to see one's aura. Certain sound patterns – such as solfeggio frequencies, tones associated with the Fibonacci pattern of numbers and sounds calculated from the planet's orbits – all create light in one's aura.

Every cell creates a frequency, as it seemingly breathes. When all sounds were perfectly in tune, the person's "song" is glorious. Through life's difficulties, many notes are suppressed or out of tune. By listening to, or singing, the missing tones, the Atlanteans reestablished their perfect sounds, health and "divine blue prints."

These ancient people applied sounds to tune patients to their natural harmonic states. This was particularly helpful with depression and other mental issues. Rhythms restored normal, calm and internal balance.[98]

---

[96] Cooper, Diana. *Op. Cit.,* Pg. 42. (channeled information)
[97] Cooper, Diane. *Ibid*, Pg. 42. (channeled information)
[98] Andrews, Shirley. Lemuria and Atlantis, *Op. Cit.,* Pg. 80.

The Atlanteans believed that everyone had a composite frequency. Author Ted Andrews described how the ability to know and work with their fundamental frequency benefitted them, "The Atlanteans developed the ability to transmute physical conditions – to alter the physical vibrations – through fundamental tones. Many believe that the misuse of this knowledge contributed to the collapse of the civilization."[99]

Intuitive channeler, Margaret Brown,[100] described the Atlantean command of sound: "They had a mastery of sound that we cannot imagine. They had instruments not played by the hand, but by electric mechanism. The Atlanteans had different vocal chords from ours, which enabled them to produce more efficacious vibrations."[101]

Cyril Scott reflected on Atlantean musical practices, "It was the priests who by degrees improved the primitive types of song and transformed it into a species of chanted spell. These spells were committed to memory and handed down generation to generation.... They increased religious fervor, with the result that men swayed with their bodies, to dance and clap their hands.... The priests discovered the potency of 'mantrams' or spells. They realized that if certain notes were reiterated, definite results could be obtained and powers brought into action. They used this particular form of magic – for magic it was – for noble and constructive ends during the earlier periods of the Atlantean history."[102]

Edgar Cayce related channeled stories describing healing chants in Atlantis. People intoned sounds such as *Arrr, Urrr,* and *Ouuu,* while using crystals and symbols to obtain purity, raise their vibrations to a higher level and absorb more light for healing.[103]

---

[99] Andrew, Ted. Sacred Sounds: Magic & Healing through Words & Music, Llewellyn Publications, Minn., 2008, Pg. 26.
[100] 1867–1925?
[101] Gareth Knight. Pythones: the Life and Work of Margaret Lumley Brown, Thoth Publications: Loughborough, U.K., 2006, Pgs. 220–221.
[102] Scott, Cyril. Music: Its Secret Influences throughout the Ages, Samuel Weiser: London, 1958, Pg. 152. Reprinted in 2013 by Inner Traditions.com
[103] Andrews,Shirley. Lemuria and Atlantis, Op. Cit., Pg. 114.

Music was a central component of the Atlantean society. Part of training for the priesthood included learning to play musical instruments, such as flutes and harps. The Muses taught students chants for healing and ceremonial purposes.

Women could go to a "Temple Beautiful" to learn to be good mothers. Music was used when they were ready to prepare their bodies and minds for procreation.[104]

Like the Lemurians, the Atlanteans enjoyed a descending musical scale. This descending pattern of sounds lowered frequencies linked to their minds, bodies and spirits. This resulted in a greater association with physical energies.

Stones and crystals were thought to have consciousness and absorb energy. Healing ceremonies were conducted near circles of large rocks, while people chanted. The musical energy hovered around the rocks, infusing them with harmony. The priests added tantalizing, hypnotic music for tranquilizing effects. Gauss meters, which measure static magnetic field strength, have recorded elevated energy around ancient stone circles. Further tests suggested that the stones acted as amplifiers.[105] In a manner reminiscent of plants responding to music, the rocks' subtle energy was altered with music. This musical harmony combined with the energy from the Earth at sacred spots to induce healing. These healing energies were then easily accessible to the entire community.

Atlanteans associated metals with the celestial bodies – associating certain metals to energy from the planets and sun. Gold and an unknown metal, orichalcum, were associated with the sun. Copper was associated with Venus and tin with Jupiter.[106] Likewise, Tibetan masters insist that the sounds made from different metals produce specific effects. They prescribe singing bowls of different metals for specialized purposes.

---

[104] Andrews,Shirley. *Ibid,* Pg. 45.
[105] Michell, The New View over Atlantis, Pg. 208, as quoted in Andrews, Shirley. Atlantis: Insights from a Lost Civilization, Llewellyn Worldwide: MN, 1997, Pgs. 97and 85.
[106] Andrews, Shirley. Atlantis: Insights from a Lost Civilization, *Op. Cit.,* Pg. 120.

Exactly why Atlantis was destroyed we may never know... many who have closely studied the available information believe that the Atlantis masters destroyed all trace of their homeland – when their work was done. Some others blame black magicians and their "black" music for the destruction of Atlantis. After the fall of Atlantis, information regarding subtle and spiritual energy, including information about powerful sound frequencies and their application, was hidden by priests and leaders who possessed this knowledge. The vibratory and musical secrets were buried deeply; it was feared unscrupulous people could use this information to control and destroy others. Only those who proved themselves to be virtuous were allowed to carry the torch, keeping the information alive though oral transmissions.

Civilization Dates

Age	Approximate Peak Years
Lemuria and Atlantis	100,000* to 6600 BC
Sumer	5000* to 2004 BC
China	2850 to 206 BC
Egypt	3200 to 664 BC
India	3102 to 483 BC
Greece	200BC to 600 AD
Middle Ages	479 AD to 1,400 AD
Renaissance	1400 to 1900 AD
Modern	1900 AD to present

*Dates uncertain

Chapter Four

Prehistoric Music
Circa 50,000 to 4,000 BC

As we leave the misty legends of Atlantis and Lemuria – where almost everything we have learned comes indirectly through stories and myths, or channeled sources – we next visit the earliest physical records of music. Our sources are now more conventional: archeology and fossil remains.

This chapter deals with artifacts and findings of early proto–human and true human musical traditions. Archeology has well documented the dynamic presence of music in homo sapiens and Neanderthals as early as 40,000 – 50,000 years ago. In related studies, modern day musicologists have traveled to pockets of primitive cultures that remain untouched by modern civilization. The adventurers describe the tribe's musical traditions, which reveal strikingly similar patterns in widely separated places on Earth; these modern discoveries are consistent with the emerging vision of the Stone Age civilizations.

The focus of this chapter is "Prehistoric Music", that is, music from civilizations and people before the advent of writing. This era, which spans many tens of thousands of years, bridges the "lost" civilizations (Lemuria and Atlantis) with the historic societies which follow this chapter starting roughly about 8 to 9,000 years ago. (The emergence of writing varied widely from civilization to civilization; our definition of "prehistoric" is more of a convenient convention for this book than a hard fast one.)

Neanderthals and pockets of early homo sapiens existed simultaneously up until approximately 25,000 years ago. For eons, a number of human–like species walked the earth at the same time. New archeological finds continually add to the diversity of skeletal remains of various hominid species. Musical artifacts date to as early as 50,000 years ago. It is interesting that the use of music *did not* belong exclusively to homo sapiens – our species!

Approximate Date Ranges of Hominid Species

Years Ago (YA)	~3 - 4 Million YA	~2 Million YA	~.5 - 1 MYA	~.4 - 0 MYA
Pre-human Primates	1.5 – 4 MYA			
Homo – Habilis		1.4 – 2.4 MYA		
Homo – Erectus		200,000 – 2 MYA		
Homo Heidelbergensis			250,000 – 600,000 YA	
Homo Neanderthalensis				25,000 – 200,000 YA
Homo Floresiensis			40,000 – 800,000 YA	
Homo – Sapiens				Today - 200,000 YA

The existence and importance of music to Stone Age peoples is revealing and significant. After years of investigation, the picture is becoming clear – *music was a fundamental and crucial part of prehistoric life*. Ancient peoples accepted the spiritual and magical as a matter of fact. Music and its deep role in prehistoric societies was also a given. Medicine men and shamans used music in many forms: drumming, singing, and chanting – a versatile tool in their mystical arsenals.

Musicologist Carl Engel suggested that drums and rattles were among the first instruments in prehistoric groups around the world. Later wind instruments without finger holes were made; they were typically crafted from reeds or wood. Animal horns, with a mouthpiece cut out, were the forerunners of brass instruments.[107] Percussion sounds were produced by striking two objects together. Strings were made from animal guts and sinews; when attached to a length of wood, this produced the earliest string instruments.

Over thirty flutes carved from long bones have been found, dating from about 10,000 to 50,000 years ago. Several flutes have been dated to 45,000 to 50,000 years old.[108] A 50,000 year old Neanderthal flute produced five tones in odd intervals. The pitches could be altered with finger maneuvers over the openings. The end result sounded like a modern flute with a narrow pitch range.[109]

Many flutes were made of hollow bird, reindeer or bear bones. The flutes have three to seven holes, and are played like penny whistles, unlike our flutes today. Given their length, they produced tones in the piccolo range. Reindeer phalanges (small foot bones) were used as shrill whistles. At cave sites in the Pyrenees Mountains, flutes made from vulture bones were found, dating back 30,000 years. They were capable of making complex sounds.[110]

From the same time period some bird bone tubes with no holes have been found. These bone instruments make blasts similar to a trumpet. The sounds were thought to lure in beasts of prey.

A number of small bone and ivory objects, pierced with a hole, have been unearthed; they make a loud humming noise when whirled around on a string. In another example, a large animal's rib cage was used to create sounds similar to a xylophone.

Dating from 20,000 BC, mammoth bones were discovered that are thought to be musical instruments: a hip bone xylophone, skull and shoulder blade drums and jaw bone rattles. These instruments

---

[107] Engel, Carl. The Most Ancient Nations: Assyrians, Egyptians and Hebrews with Special Reference to Recent Discoveries in Western Asia and in Egypt, Murray: London, 1864, Pg. 10.
[108] McBurney, 1967; Marshack, 1987. Bahn, Paul and Vertut, Jean. Images of the Ice Age, Facts of File: NY, 1988. Pg. 68.
[109] http://whyfiles.org/114music/4.html, Neanderthal Jam.
[110] Tattersall, Ian. The World from Beginnings to 4,000 BCE Oxford University Press: NY, 2008. Pg.98.

were successfully played by Soviet archeologists; they even cut a record![111]

We can only speculate how many musical instruments were made from perishable materials, such as wood, fibers, feathers and hides. Sadly, old wooden instruments, reed pipes and stretched skin drums have perished by now.

The human voice was definitely the first instrument of primitive music. All music started with singing. The first "instruments" modified and enhanced the voice, such as a conch shell placed in front of the mouth. The cavity of the shell acts as a resonator for the voice. In Northern Siberia, "the shaman uses his drum for modifying his voice, placing the drum directly in front of his mouth, turning the drum at an oblique angle."[112]

Calcite formations in caves make tonal sounds when struck – as with beating a drum. The entire cave can be likened to an instrument, with a resonating chamber. Stalactites are often present in large "rooms" within caves that could hold an audience. Mario Ruspoli, a photographer of ancient caves, described the opening of a cave as the "orifice leading into the womb of mother Earth."[113]

Some caves had painted dots and lines on walls and floors. These markings, smeared in isolated points in the inner recesses of caves, have puzzled historians. Initially researchers assumed that the colored symbols were trail–markers... until they discovered that the markings denoted resonance points for sound. Using sophisticated equipment, researchers were able to reproduce frequencies similar to those made by bone flutes. Red spots marked points where harmonic resonance was produced from the flute sounds.

---

[111] Bibikov, 1975. Bahn, Paul and Vertut, Jean. Images of the Ice Age, Facts of File: NY, 1988. Pg. 69.
[112] Sachs, Curt. The Rise of Music in the Ancient World, East and West, Dover Publications: Mineola, NY, 1943, Pg. 23.
[113] Redmond, Layne. When the Drummers were Women: A Spiritual History of Rhythm, Three Rivers Press: NY, 1997, Pg. 36.

www.JillsWingsofLight.com – Art Galleries

Musical archeological finds include many clues, suggesting that ancient people filled their world with sound – just as we do with our iPods, movie sound tracks and car stereos. Iegor Reznikoff, an anthropologist from the University Paris Quest, visited caves in southern France, containing cave paintings 25,000 years old. He found that the location of drawings often corresponded with the areas of greatest auditory resonance.[114] Steven Waller, a biochemist and archeologist from California, studied hundreds of rock art sites found around the world, and confirmed that ancient people created art that was connected to acoustics.[115]

Some historians believe that ancient temples were constructed with acoustical engineering in mind. For example, when the priests at Temple Chavin De Huantar, in Peru, sounded their conch shells 2,500 years ago, the sound bounced off smooth stones creating the illusion that the sound came from every direction. Archeologist–acoustical engineer, Miriam Kolar, discovered that the ducts at this temple amplified the sounds of the conch shells, due to the frequencies and acoustical design of the structure; other sounds were dampened.

Stanford University archeologists reported that ancient builders used ducts, shafts and galleries to channel sound. For example, in El Castillo Mexico, if you clap your hands at the base of the

---

[114] Starr, Douglass. "Echoes from the Distant Past: Ancient Acoustical engineers designed subterranean soundscapes as stirring as any special effects." *Discover Magazine*, Nov 2012, Pg. 28.
[115] Starr, Douglass. *Ibid*, Pg. 28.

pyramid a series of chirps are heard. They sound like the cry of the quetzal, a bird the Mayans greatly respected.[116]

Sound and architecture may have been used to create a mystic experience. These efforts may have been rooted in their attempts to reach the divine.[117]

Musical Archeology

Discovery	Approximate Years Ago
Neanderthal Flute	50,000
Hollow Bone "Trumpets"	30,000
Caves with special Acoustics	25,000
Xylophones and Rattles from Bones	20,000
Hypogeum Temple – Acoustic Resonance	6,000

Primitive Rhythmic Beats

The dominant feature of much primitive music is its lively and accentuated rhythmic beats. Rhythms are a natural part of life. In the womb, the sound of the mother's heartbeat is louder than you would expect because sound travels better through the embryonic sac's fluid than in air. Air is not the best conductor of sound; the body is much better. Instinctively, mothers hold babies near their heart where they hear the familiar sounds of the womb – the reassuring heartbeat.

Ancient people naturally mimicked the natural rhythms of nature. Without using an artificial device, like a clock, people adjusted to the rhythms of the sun, stars, seasons and weather patterns. Nature's cycles were rhythms, wave–like movements that they

---

[116] Starr, Douglass. *Op. Cit.,* Pg. 28.
[117] Starr, Douglass. *Op. Cit.,* Pg. 28.

mimicked. Primitive people were in tune with nature's rhythms, making it easier to balance their own energies.

www.JillsWingsofLight.com – Art Galleries

Rhythms are currently used in physical therapy for gait disorders, present with Parkinson's disease and stroke patients, to help patients regain and coordinate their movements. Primitive people used drum beat patterns to heal members of their tribe. Today, witchcraft and ritual music from tribes of Kenya and Tanzania feature healing rhythms.[118] David Fanshawe received a grant to document a near extinct musical practice found in East Africa. According to Fanshawe, "Music takes on the power of medicine, and medicine becomes associated with the healing sounds of the drums, interwoven with beautiful threads of melody." Writer Jeff Strong added that this practice of using rhythms to heal is ancient. Strong said, "Auditory rhythm has a long history of use for affecting neurological function, with the earliest uses being documented tens of thousands of years ago."[119]

Every culture weaves rhythms into different facets of daily life. It is fascinating how so many aspects of ancient cultures are unique, while the same therapeutic techniques – such as drumming – are common, even in isolated parts of the globe.

---

[118] Fanshawe, David, *Kenya & Tanzania Withchcraft and Ritual Music*, a musical CD made by WEA Manufacturing, a Time Warner Co., 1973.
[119] Strong, Jeff. "A Look at Rhythmic Entrainment Invention by its Creator," *SI Focus Magazine*, winter: 2008.

Excavators at Catal Huyuk (Turkey) showed that this ancient town sported a population of ~6000 in 4500 BC. The people of Catal Huyuk worshipped goddesses and were an agricultural society. German scholar, Doris Stockmann, believed that sacred dance rituals enhanced the dancer's senses, making it a vivid experience.[120] The drums were a driving force in Catal Huyuk's ritual ceremonies.

Author, Layne Redmond, suggests that rhythms conveyed divine energy. "The drum was the means our ancestors used to summon the goddess and also the instrument through which she spoke. The drumming priestess was the intermediary between the divine and human realms. Aligning herself with sacred rhythms, she acted as summoner and transformer, invoking divine energy and transmitting it to the community."[121]

Redmond continued, "Invoking the elemental powers of the deities, the voice of the drum called forth the cyclical rebirth of nature. Its vibrational force woke the sleeping life within the Earth. Drummers played over freshly sown seeds to quicken their ripening, and later over the burgeoning vegetables to protect and enhance their growth."[122] The drum also drove away evil spirits and disease; it created sacred space. According to Marija Ginbutas, expert on ancient goddess practices, the priestesses enjoyed "an intimate language between the drum and the goddess."[123]

Shamans listened to drumming to supposedly travel to "invisible worlds," beyond ordinary reality to retrieve information. The shaman sought information about spirituality, health, work and relationships. To lend credence to this idea, research has revealed that deep shamanic states of consciousness can be accessed by listening to drumming at about 4 to 4.5 beats per second.[124] "The drums have to be monotonous and maintain a consistent beat between 240 to 290 beats per minute. At this beat, the brain is

[120] Hart, Mickey. Drumming at the Edge of Magic: A Journey into the Spirit of Percussion, Harper Collins: New York, 1990, Pg. 72.
[121] Redmond, Layne. *Op. Cit.,* Pg. 21.
[122] Redmond, Layne. *Op. Cit.,* Pg. 21.
[123] Hart, Mickey. *Op. Cit.,* Pg. 73. Marija Ginbutas, Language of the Goddess.
[124] http://www.sunflower–health.com/popups/journeying.htm

stimulated to synthesize natural beta–endorphins."[125] The brain creates theta brain waves and a dreamlike awareness (like just before waking or sleeping) by listening for at least 13–15 minutes. The dream images contained information that shamans valued and perceived was from beyond ordinary reality.

Author Robert Moss' research confirmed the idea that shamans can reach other planes of reality: "Some physiologists believe that shamanic drumming may harmonize neural activity inside the brain with the frequency of the beat…. The pace of the drum beat corresponds to brain–wave frequencies in the theta wave lengths (four to eight hertz) associated wave lengths with transitional states to and from sleep and its dreamlike imagery…. Our brain waves get in step with the beat, carrying us into the patterns of the theta state and the corresponding flow of images."[126]

Melinda Maxfield, Ph. D., matched drumming patterns with brain waves, as measured by cortical EEG. The drums used by indigenous cultures in rituals created specific neural–physiological effects.

Maxfield observed images or sensations produced by "shaman–like" drumming. Temporary changes in brain wave activity were observed that facilitated imagery, even when the experience was separated from ritual, ceremony and intent.

Drumming elicits strong subjective experiences and images with common themes. Maxfield cataloged common reactions to shamanic drumming:

- Loss of time continuum
- Movement sensations, including pressure on or expansion of various parts of the body
- Body image distortion
- "Energy waves"
- Sensations of flying, spiraling, dancing, running, feelings of being energized, relaxed, sharp and clear, hot, cold

---

[125] *Howard G. Charing,* http://www.shamanicjourney.com/article/6051/shamanic–journey–drumming

[126] Moss, Robert. Conscious Dreaming: a Spiritual Path for Everyday Life, Crown Trade Paperbacks: New York, 1996. Pg. 148.

- Feeling physical/mental or emotional discomfort – emotions, ranging from exaltation to rage
- Vivid images of natives, animals, people and landscapes
- Remarkable altered states of consciousness
- Out–of body experiences (OBE's) and visitations.[127]

Shamans engaged in chants, dances and prayers, using their will and strength for many things, such as drawing energy from the clouds, to cool the air and create heavy water droplets producing rain. Clouds and water are more malleable than solid matter, making this task within reach.[128] In a simple experiment, observe your finger and imagine, with intense focus, that it is hot. Do this for about five minutes. Your finger will begin to feel warmer. The focused thought and intention subtly affect the temperature. Numerous chanters in rituals, such as rain dances, increase the sonic impact.[129]

Primitive music was composed of simple melodies with little to no harmony. These early peoples' brains were not over stimulated from many pitches or harmonies in their music. This freed up their attention to focus on complicated rhythm patterns. Primitive music included complex, repetitive rhythm patterns. Tribal witch doctors beat rhythmic patterns that morphed into a frenzied climax, while their melodies spanned a narrow pitch range.

Many primitive societies used physical movement to accompany their songs. When the movements were large, such as a jump or leap, musical intervals were also large. When the movements reflected small motions, the intervals were also small. Music and dance were choreographed to create similar energy.

When a woman in a certain African tribe knows she is pregnant, she goes out into the wilderness with a few friends. Together they

---

[127] Maxfield, Melinda, PhD. "Effects of Rhythmic Drumming on EEG and Subjective Experience" (Ph.D. diss., Institute of Transpersonal Psychology, Menlo Park, Calif., 1990).
[128] Almost all the air is moist; it contains water in the form of vapor (a gas that can't be seen). Water condenses in the clouds as it gets cooler. It forms water droplets that merge with other droplets, getting heavier. After the droplets grow, they become too heavy to say floating in the cloud and it rains.
[129] Andrews, Shirley. Atlantis: Insights from a Lost Civilization, Llewellyn Worldwide: MN, 1997, Pg. 176.

pray and meditate until they hear the song of the unborn child. They recognize that every soul has its own vibration that expresses its unique flavor and purpose. Once the women attune to the song, they sing it out loud. Then they return to the tribe and teach it to everyone else.

When children are born into the village, the community gathers and sings their song, one unique melody for each unique child. Later, when children begin their education, the village gathers and again chants each child's song. They sing when the child passes into the adulthood initiation, and again at the time of marriage. Finally, when the soul is about to pass from this world, the family and friends gather at the bedside, as they did at birth, and they "sing" the person to the next life.

In the African tribe there is one other occasion upon which the villagers sing to the child: If at any time during a person's life, he or she commits a crime or aberrant social act, that individual is called to stand in the center of a circle formed by all members of the tribe; once again the villagers chant the person's song. The tribe recognizes that the proper correction for antisocial behavior is not punishment, but love and the affirmation of identity.

Musical historian, Curt Sachs, suggests that rhythm and dance parallel characteristics of men versus women. Men strive for a release, moving forward and upward, while women keep low to the ground; their movement draws energy inward. These differences are reflected in both tones and rhythmic patterns. In the Eskimo boat songs, women sing the same melodies as men but change the rhythm to create a three beat pattern, avoiding the masculine stride of one hard beat followed by one soft (a two beat pattern).[130] Author and healing drummer, Richard Flatischler, taught that dual and triple rhythms are rooted in our psyches. A triple pattern leads to inner stillness, while the double pattern creates extraversion and activity.[131]

---

[130] Sachs, Curt. *Op. Cit.,* Pg. 40.
[131] Flatischler, Reinhard. The Forgotten Power of Rhythm, Liferhythm Publisher, 1992, Pg. 242.

Societies and their leaders have long understood that music can help control peoples' states of mind; peaceful music calms people, but certain other music can encourage aggression and war. Musicologist Daniel Levitin suggests that, "Native Americans sang and danced in preparation for launching an attack, as did other prehistoric aggressors. The emotional and neural–chemical excitement that resulted from the preparatory singing gave them the mettle and stamina to carry out their attacks."[132]

At first glance, these ideas of receiving special energy from listening to music appear farfetched, but reflect on the absence of music. With approaching war, music stops and silence reigns, heavy with the feeling of upcoming devastation. Osama Bin Laden outlawed all music for his followers. It makes common sense that it is difficult to direct young people to be suicide bombers, while exposing them to any type of uplifting music. They are easier to control and influence with the absence of music.

Drumming helped warriors achieve victory. "There are kettle drums from ancient India from the ancient holy text the *Mahabharata* that measure five feet in diameter and weigh approximately 450 pounds. You needed an elephant to lug them around. 'There arose a tumultuous uproar caused by the blare of the trumpets and the thundering of drums, the blowing of the conch shells,' said the *Mahabharata*. 'The very sky was rent by the beating of drums.'"[133] This music energized warriors and terrified enemies.

Primitive societies lived or died as a group. If a neighboring tribe overpowered them, the entire group was harmed. Primitive cultures created group karma and lived in accordance with group energy. People in primitive groups did not express individuality. The music of primitive societies reflects this. Primitive music is the song of the tribe; it represented all of their energies.

Dr. James Powel, former director of the American Bureau of Ethnology, stated that importance of rhythm parallels the "hunter

---

[132] Levitin, Daniel. The World in Six Songs: How the Musical Brain Created Human Nature, Penguin Group: NY, 2009, Pg. 47.
[133] Hart, Mickey. *Op. Cit.,* Pg. 78.

stage" in man's evolution. As man evolved to the "shepherd state," he developed melody.

Music historian, Curt Sachs,[134] researched music worldwide, including that of isolated and primitive groups. He discovered common trends. The earliest primitive melodies have two notes, usually three or four notes apart. A two tone melody is well established before a third tone appears at the end of a phrase. This trend has been amazingly persistent.

Musicologist, Carl Engle, discovered that the most primitive songs used only a few notes, rarely extending beyond the interval of a fifth.[135] Only after the group had clearly advanced, the music then included the interval of the octave.

Babies babble in the same language, a universal song. When children begin to speak, they do so in characteristic intervals. Across the globe, children of ages 18 months to 2.5 years spontaneously sing musical phrases with the intervals of a second, minor third and a major third. (These intervals are in the children's song, "This Old Man.") In their second and third years the child advances and uses intervals of fourths (as heard in "Old McDonald") and fifths. Beginning at the age of three, the particular culture's musical style becomes the dominant musical influence. Once again, small intervals are associated with early development.

American conductor and composer Leonard Bernstein[136] suggests that early singing in children includes repetitive, descending minor thirds that are often accompanied by another descending step to the interval of a fourth. Musical patterns in children's songs seem to be hardwired. The musical development of primitive groups also appears to be hardwired.

---

[134] Sachs, Curt. *Op. Cit.*
[135] Engel, Carl. The Most Ancient Nations: Assyrians, Egyptians and Hebrews with Special Reference to Recent Discoveries in Western Asia and in Egypt, Murray: London, 1864, Pg. 21.
[136] In 1973 at Bernstein's lectures in Harvard. Tame, David. The Secret Power of Music: The Transformation of Self and Society Through Musical Energy, Destiny Books: VT, 1984, Pg. 230.

Decline of Primitive People

Micky Hart, drummer for the Grateful Dead, researched the early roots of drumming and its role alongside sacred worship. "During the Great Hunt, we found the sacred in the wandering rhythms of the herd (the way of animal powers). With the rise of agriculture the sacred shifted to the seeded Earth and its cycles of vegetative growth and decay. Now, with the so–called dawn of civilization, the sacred manifested itself in the rhythms of the stars and planetary gods – the male sky gods. The new temple towns were bigger than Catal Huyuk... Towns of Ur, Kish and Uruk, in what is known as the Sumerian civilization. In terms of the sacred, Sumer lies at the cultural crossroads between the declining mother goddess of the Neolithic, and the rise of the male sky gods, who responded to their predecessor by converting her most sacred symbols – the snake, the bull, the naked female body – into their most feared ones."[137] Female–ruled civilizations declined many thousands of years ago, although the healing rhythmic patterns influenced subsequent cultures.

Music created the energetic skeleton that helped shape a society's values and framework. This idea echoes from culture to culture. Author David Tame reflected that this belief is found in ancient, technologically advanced civilizations from Mesopotamia to India and Greece.[138] It is unclear whether some of the ideas were passed among cultures or if each culture discovered these concepts anew.

The ancients believed that when a culture's music fell, the civilization's demise would follow. Ancient civilizations firmly believed that listening to the "wrong" music produced disastrous effects. Author Corinne Heline described the fate of the city of Ur, the city of Abraham, "Esotericists understood that it was by the magic of music that a cloud of evil and terror, which enveloped the city, was being transmuted. The city's vibratory rhythms correspondingly were raised. This important function of music will someday be rediscovered and used."[139] The author strongly believes that similar musical fates occurred to the prehistoric peoples, but evidence is very difficult to find.

---

[137] Hart, Mickey. *Op. Cit.,* Pgs. 74–5.
[138] Tame, David. *Op. Cit.,* Pg. 17.
[139] Tame, David. *Op. Cit.,* Pg. 280.

The Sophistication of Some Ancient Civilizations

Stories of Atlantis suggest that it was extraordinarily advanced, at an early time period. It is hard to imagine the stories about Atlantis with their strange technology – at a time when we envision only cave men. This section presents archeological evidence of ancient, sophisticated practices and technology, although they were very different than modern ways.[140]

Neanderthals and other ancient people[141] demonstrated precise knowledge of geographic measurements.[142] All over the globe, ancient people incorporated the latitude and longitude positions into their temple's orientation and dimensions. Also, the location

---

[140] Graham Hancock in <u>Fingerprints of the Gods</u> and <u>Heaven's Mirror</u> presented evidence of prehistoric, highly developed, worldwide cultures.

[141] The Neanderthal is an extinct member of the *Homo* genus, classified as a subspecies of modern humans or a separate human species. The first proto–Neanderthal traits appeared in Europe as early as 350,000 – 600,000 years ago. These characteristics disappeared 50,000 to 30,000 years ago. http://en.wikipedia.org/wiki/Neanderthal

[142] Godwin, Joscelyn. <u>Atlantis and the Cycles of Time: Prophecies, Traditions and Occult Revelations,</u> Inner traditions: VT, 2011, Pg. 27.

of sacred sites globally forms a precise grid that cannot be a mere coincidence.[143]

Astronomical numbers were used to calculate distances, such as the distance to the equator and locations of meridians. For example, stars rotate around the North and South Celestial Poles directly above the geographic North and South Poles. The Earth's axis of rotation intersects the Celestial Poles. The number of degrees the celestial pole is above the horizon is equal to the latitude of the observer.[144] With this type of information the ancients located buildings so that structures on Earth mirrored the locations of planets or "heaven." In this way, their building strategies replicated "Heaven on Earth."

Ancient people were fascinated with the movements of the stars. They made advanced astrological predictions. Locations of sacred buildings oftentimes mimicked the shape of a constellation, creating a little celestial energy on Earth. Pyramids and temples were built so that important star light would enter openings and illuminate sacred spots during the equinoxes.

Extremely early populations moved mammoth stones. Prehistoric people created megalithic monuments in Europe, Egypt, Mexico, Peru, Bolivia, India, Cambodia and the Pacific Islands. An archeological site in Gobekli Tepe, Turkey, dating back 12,000 years (thousands of years before Stone Henge and the Great Pyramid) features a large building complex. Circular stone monuments with 19 foot pillars, each weighing 15 tons, reflect their advanced building capacities. The pillars and carvings are elegant and refined, but no tools to cut stone have been found.[145]

Puma Punku is one of four structures of Tiwanaku in South America. The age of the megalithic ruins is controversial since it has been looted and compromised. There are claims that it is up to 15,000 years old. Massive stones used in the construction bear no chisel marks and were finely cut to precisely interlock, reflecting extremely sophisticated engineering and geometry. The city also

---

[143] Hancock, Graham. Fingerprints of the Gods and Heaven's Mirror.
[144] http://www.astronomynotes.com/nakedeye/s4.htm
[145] History, HD.com, "Unexplained Structures," http://www.cpakonline.com/content/

had a functioning irrigation system, waterproof sewage lines and hydraulic mechanisms. Metal inserts were used in building structures. Metal was poured into stone indentations, which means the builders had portable smelters that operated at very high temperatures.[146]

In Bosnia, a series of temples has been discovered under heavy vegetation. One of them, the Sun pyramid stands over 722 feet high – one third taller than the Great Pyramid of Giza in Egypt. Radiocarbon dating shows the pyramid to be at least 24,800 years old. Material analysis reveals that the structure is made from man–made concrete.

Bosnian Pyramid

Moving on to Egypt, the Sphinx's erosion is mainly due to rainfall before the area became a desert – dating the Sphinx to at least 7,000 to 9,000 years ago. The rise of the great ancient Egyptian civilization that we are familiar with was predated by an equally sophisticated one (at least in some ways) in earlier times.

An underground temple was found at Malta, called Hal Saflieni Hypogeum, dated about 4000 BC.[147] This three level underground temple required 2,000 tons of stone removal for its creation. At certain spots there is powerful acoustic resonance, amplifying a male baritone voice at 110 hertz, "one hundred times". *Popular Archeology* reported, "Low voices within the Hypogeum's walls

---

[146] http://listverse.com/2013/04/12/10–mysteries–that–hint–at–forgotten–advanced–civilizations/ 10 Mysteries That Hint At Forgotten Advanced Civilizations, Hestie Barnard Gerber, April 12, 2013
[147] D. Trump and D. Cilia. Malta: Prehistory and Temples, Midsea Books, 2004.

create eerie, reverberating echoes; a sound made from words spoken in certain places can be clearly heard throughout its three levels. Now, scientists are suggesting that certain sound frequencies – created when sound is emitted within its walls – are actually altering human brain functions of those within earshot."[148]

A study by Ian Cook in *Time and Mind Magazine*[149] reported information about the impact of 110 hertz vibrations, which were used in this ancient structure: "In a pilot project, 30 healthy adults listened to tones at 90, 100, 110, 120, and 130 Hz while brain activity was monitored with electroencephalography (EEG). Activity in the left temporal region was significantly lower at 110 Hz than at other frequencies. Additionally, the pattern of asymmetric activity over the prefrontal cortex shifted from one of higher activity on the left at most frequencies to right sided dominance at 110 Hz."[150] The 110 hertz frequency fires up the section of the brain responsible for mood and emotional processing.

"These findings are compatible with relative deactivation of language centers and a shift in prefrontal activity that may be related to emotional processing. These intriguing pilot findings suggest that the acoustic properties of ancient structures may have influenced human brain function, and chanting might have been used to enhance right brain activities."[151]

Stonehenge may also have been designed with acoustics in mind. A team of researchers from the University of Salford in the UK spent four years studying its acoustic properties – attempting to crack the mystery of why it was built. The researchers theorized that Stonehenge transformed ordinary music into robust sound that Neolithic man would respond to. Since the site is in disrepair, the team travelled to Maryhill in the U.S.A. where a full–sized concrete reconstruction of Stonehenge was built in 1929, as a memorial to the soldiers of WW I. They created a video

---

[148] *Popular Archaeology*, March 5, 2012.
http://www.Earthfiles.com/news.php?ID=1974&category=Science
[149] March 2008 issue
[150] ttp://www.Earthfiles.com/news.php?ID=1974&category=Science
[151] ttp://www.Earthfiles.com/news.php?ID=1974&category=Science

demonstrating the sound amplification that was created at this site. The link is in the footnotes.[152]

South of Paris, scientists found a 7,000 year old skeleton that had underwent surgery. Tests showed that a successful amputation was performed. Impressively, the patient was even anesthetized and the wound was not infected – suggesting that the surgery was conducted in relatively antiseptic conditions.[153]

Near Crete in 4000 BC, the Minoans used paved streets, functioning sewers, water piping and drainage systems, advanced air management systems (similar to air conditioning), hot and cold running water, water flow for toilets and even earthquake resistant walls.[154]

The *antikythera* device was retrieved from the bottom of the sea in a Roman shipwreck near Crete. This device, dating back to 80 AD, was found in 1900 and took decades to understand. It computes the synodic lunar cycles by subtracting the effects of the sun's movements from the effects of sidereal lunar movements by calculating the movements of the stars and planets. It is an analog mechanical computer, a sophisticated navigational tool. An electric battery was unearthed in Baghdad, dating back 1,800 years before Voltas invented it in 1798.

Prehistoric/ancient people were far more sophisticated than we would suppose. They were certainly not barbaric cave men. The evidence, though meager, clearly demonstrates that these people understood and utilized music in all important aspects of their lives and throughout official ceremonies and functions. Music was held in high esteem. This reverence was closely passed on to the Historic Civilizations, which we will cover next.

As we clearly see, there were pockets of surprisingly advanced civilizations coexisting with primitive hunter–gathers. We also know that the continents on the Earth have drastically changed in

[152] http://www.dailymail.co.uk/sciencetech/article–2131519/Was–Stonehenge–designed–sound–Researchers–recreate–ancient–site–sounded–like–Neolithic–man.html#ixzz2IcxlLe00
[153] http://www.auxmaillesGodefroy.com/The_Scroll
[154] History, HD.com, "Unexplained Structures," http://www.cpakonline.com/content/

size and shape over the eons. It is not such a stretch to believe that Atlantis existed, and was an advanced civilization.

www.JillsWingsofLight.com – Art Galleries

Advanced Ancient Civilizations

Discovery	Approximate Years Ago
Bosnia's Pyramids	25,000
Puma Punku, Tiwanaku S America	15,000
Gobekli Tepe, Turkey	12,000
Skeleton showing surgery & anesthesia	7,000
Hypogeum, Malta	4,000

Chapter Five

The First Civilizations: Sumer and its Music
~5,000 to 2,000 BC

In this chapter – for the first time, we enter a new age – we leave the mythic days of Atlantis and Lemuria, legends that are not accepted by all; we also move on from the meager records enduring from the Stone Age and Prehistoric Civilizations to arrive at the earliest true "historic" civilizations.[155]

Sumer, probably better than any other land, truly deserves to be called the cradle of civilization. This region – between the modern rivers, the Euphrates on the west and the Tigris on the east – is the location of modern Iraq. Many thousands of years after the arrival of its earliest settlers, the Romans renamed the region: Mesopotamia. Eventually, eons later, it became known as

---

[155] Strict use of the terms "prehistoric" and "historic" relies on the existence of written records – for a civilization to be considered historic and the absence of written records for a prehistoric civilization. We are taking a more casual use of the terms here where a "historic" civilization may not possess writing at the earliest times of its existence, but developed writing along the course of a significant record of progress along with important accomplishments such as monument building, technological advances, advanced societal structures, cities, farming with irrigation, art, music and so forth. In this vein, our Sumerians did not develop writing on their clay tablets until circa 3000 BC; however we consider the Sumer of 5,000 BC a historic civilization. The case is similar with the Egyptians; they discovered that papyrus, when properly processed, could make convenient sheets to lay down writing on with a brush and ink; the pliable papyrus was far superior to hard clay. We do not consider the earliest forms of representational art – such as cave paintings – equivalent to the systematic use of the writing systems in Sumer and Egypt. Further, the peoples who first expressed themselves with cave drawings lacked the other important characteristic on an advanced "historic" civilization as described above. Bauer, Susan. History of the Ancient World from the Earliest Accounts to the Fall of Rome, W.W. Norton, NY, NY, 2007, Pg. 5.

Babylon, home to the infamous Tower and hanging gardens that were numbered among the Seven Wonders of the ancient world.[156]

The name of the first Sumerian king has come down to us through the long annals of time; history, first kept through an oral tradition then later written on clay tablets, names Alulim, as the first king of Sumer, circa 2100 BC. As with similar Egyptian and Chinese lists – the Sumerian king list is clearly from a much older tradition.

Modern scholars stress that the people of these long ago cultures all had one thing in common: they all believed strongly in the supernatural. In fact, they believed in magic and the supernatural as integral parts of their reality. This strong mystical aspect, made them more open to and sensitive of, the supernatural in their lives.

According to the Sumerian king list: Alulim was recorded as having reigned for 28,000 years; his son, Alalgar, reigned 36,000 years. We truly neither know how long ago, nor for how long, Alulim ruled, but it was many thousands of years ago indeed. Alulim ruled the walled city of Eridu, in the south of what became known as Mesopotamia.

Strictly speaking, historians use the term "Sumerians" for the people who occupied the Mesopotamian plain from 3200 BC forward. We are interested in the total culture that arose in this region – much of it far earlier. For that reason, we are interested in the peoples that predated the historians' Sumerians, and eventually became melted into later day Sumer. Modern day archeology tells us that the region that became Sumer, was inhabited long before 4500 BC. The people who lived in the Mesopotamian region before 5000 BC are referred to as of Samarra, Hassuna and Halaf. For our purposes we will refer to all forerunners and later inhabitants as Sumerians.[157]

The Sumerian king list documents eight kings before the Great Flood. (The Sumerians have a Great Flood story as do numerous ancient civilizations around the globe. It appears that the Biblical

---

[156] Heline, Corinne. Healing and Regeneration through Music, The New Age Bible and Philosophy Center: Santa Barbara, CA, 1943, Pg. 38.
[157] Bauer, Susan. Ibid, Pg. 5.

101

story of the flood in *Genesis* is a different account than the Sumerian one – but based on the same **real** event.) Scholars of Sumer refer to kings before the Flood as "mythical" and kings afterwards as "quasi–historical". We interpret the differences as being the result of the fact that the earliest kings reigned far in the past allowing deep legends to work into the accounts; the more recent kings – still long ago – had their stories less varnished with the passing of time. With the arrival of formal writing, the histories became relatively stable.

It has been established that Sumerians, circa 5000 to 4000 BC, were successful farmers; their population grew and the culture became more sophisticated. It was this growing wealth and complexity of life that created the need for a king – to help organize the society and its dealings. By this reckoning historians place the arrival of Alulim – first king of Eridu – in this approximate time frame. This is the very edge of history – the birth of the first true historic civilization.

In 3200 BC, the evidence suggests that country dwellers moved into walled cities.[158] Around 3800 BC each town had its own gods and leaders, but this changed in 2700 BC. As the epic of Gilgamesh relates, he conquers neighboring towns, making himself the first ruler of all Sumer.

There are many reasons why it was advantageous to be in power and control a vast area. Valuable trade routes and resources for building, weapons and other items were secure with a vast kingdom. Rulers killed conquered peoples, took them as slaves or made them pay tribute to support the elite's grand lifestyle.

Having a victorious king and army was vital to a group's survival. The ancient ideas of morality were not in accordance with today's standards. Rather than embracing the idea of good versus evil, the concept of power being prized versus weakness (resulting in death and decimation of your city) was prevalent. People lived and died with their group. The group's survival was far more important than an individual's rights.

---

[158] Bauer, Susan. *Op. Cit.*, Pg. 18.

The tradition of passing kingship down to heirs, based on blood relations, began in Sumer. With the creation of a royal family we see – for the first time – the rise of an aristocratic class. In these times, a dozen walled cities in Mesopotamia came to compete for power. These cities were independent, ruled by a local prince.

The city of Kish, in the north valley, was in a strategic position, and eventually the King of Kish became the most powerful leader in Sumer. The other cities did retain their independence; they were not conquered by Kish. Sumer was not an empire so much, but a collection of independent cities that traded with each other and interacted widely and freely. Kish was first among equals.

Ancient Sumer displays the earliest and most extensive archeological remains and written records for a true civilization. From 4800 – 4500 BC, the development of extensive canal networks in major settlements were built in Sumer.[159] Five millennia old architecture used vaults and arches. These inventions took a long time to surface in other areas of the world.[160] It is most remarkable that the Sumerians were using this technology so long ago.

At Ur, a great Sumerian city, a spectacular treasure trove was found that rivals King Tut's tomb. Royal family members were buried with elaborate gold jewelry, including a queen's headdress made of gold leaves and studded with lapis lazuli. Other objects dating to about 3000 BC included a gold and lapis lyre, *one of the first known historical musical instruments*.[161] The skills to make such objects must have developed prior to this time.

Approximately between 3800 BC – 3000 BC, the first Sumerian writing on clay tablets glorified the deeds of great men and warriors, and also kept track of livestock, grain and important possessions – that were numerous enough to need writing down. Sumerian scribes wrote of their long past.

---

[159] http://en.wikipedia.org/wiki/Ubaid_period
[160] http://www.thenagain.info/webchron/MiddleEast/Sumer.html
[161] http://www.csmonitor.com/World/Middle–East/2013/0327/Ancient–Iraq–yields–fresh–finds–for–returning–archaeologists

The old history of Sumer, written on these clay tablets, begins with fantastic legends and the story of creation. Sumerian mythology described their first king, Alulim of Eridu, who descended from heaven and reigned for 28,000 years.[162] A third century Babylonian priest, Berosus, also describes Sumer's origins: "Sumer's religion and magic were one and had half fish and half men, who came out of the Red Sea under the guidance of Eu, the water god and patron of learning. They established the first metropolis, the city of Eridu."[163] An old Sumerian poem describes this strange species as coming from the land of Shinar (place of light/Sumer) and as "wearing no garments and eating herbs."[164] Stories describe that other early kings live up to 30,000 years.[165]

Many consider these legends as fanciful; other historians attribute the early stories to advanced beings from other planets that ruled on Earth. The complexity of their architecture, mathematics and building skills brings up questions of where did this information come from? There is no evidence that this information gradually developed among humans. This "step jump" in technology in ancient Sumer brings the role of Atlantis to mind... Sumer historian, Zecharia Sitchin, maintains that the gods of the Sumerians were alien beings from another planet, who used humans as slaves.[166]

Laurence Gardner, a Sumerian historian, reflected on the Sumerian's mathematical achievements, "To this day, everyone concerned is baffled by the sudden, extraordinary emergence of the Sumerians, seemingly from nowhere. But there is no doubt that upon their advent in southern Mesopotamia, they were already highly advanced, to a level far beyond that recorded or sustained in any place from where logically they could have emanated. Nowhere on Earth was there a culture like that of the Sumerians, who appeared soon after 4000 BC."[167]

---

[162] Bauer, Susan. The History of the Ancient World: From the Earliest Accounts to the Fall of the Rome, Norton: NY, 2007, Pg. 3.
[163] Heline, Corinne. Op. Cit., Pgs. 38–39.
[164] Heline, Corinne. Op. Cit., Pgs. 38–39.
[165] Bauer, Susan. Op. Cit., Pg. 3.
[166] http://www.lightbridgemusic.com/sumer.htm
[167] http://SumernGods.blogspot.com/

In a similar vein, historian Carl Engel believed that Sumerian music came from an earlier time period than contained in their records; their music was too sophisticated to have been developed in just one culture. He believed they received their music – in an advanced state – from nations unknown to us.[168]

Ernest McClain, musicologist and historian on Sumer, described the Sumerian's mathematical sophistication. The earliest writings in 3500 BC were not words, but numbers drawn on clay tablets. They used tables of reciprocals, multiplications, squares, square roots, cubes, cube roots, exponential functions, coefficients for practical computation and calculations of the areas of rectangles, circles and other shapes. Numbers, up to 60, were shown with their reciprocals. The Sumerians' sophisticated math is extraordinary, especially in view of how early in history this was.

When counting and the number 60 was reached, the Sumerians began counting all over again.[169] In contrast, today we use base ten math. Our measures – of 60 seconds in a minute and 60 minutes in an hour – are borrowed from the ancient Sumerians. They also divided the year, which they measured to be 360 days, into twelve months. They were the first to divide a circle into 360 degrees.[170]

The ancient Sumerians closely studied the laws of mathematics; they were particularly interested in proportions and ratios. Some numbers were considered sacred. The Sumerians worshiped gods, symbolized as fractions. Simple fractions of 60 were deified (1/6, 1/5, 1/4, 1/3, 1/2, 2/3 and 5/6).[171] Each one of these numbers symbolized a god. It is an abstract concept to worship numbers (or what the numbers represent) and it is remarkable that these people were using fractions in 3500 BC.

Early towns built spectacular temples to their gods. The gods were their power source. Their temples, called ziggurats, were

---

[168] Engel, Carl. The Most Ancient Nations: Assyrians, Egyptians and Hebrews with Special Reference to Recent Discoveries in Western Asia and in Egypt, Murray: London, 1864, Pg. 27.
[169] Waerden, B. L. Science Awakening: Egyptian, Babylonian and Greek Mathematics, Wiley & Sons: NY, 1963, Pg. 39.
[170] Channam, Talal, Ph.D. The Mystery of Numbers: Revealed through Their Digital Root, Create Space: South Carolina, 2011, Pg. 10.
[171] http://SumernGods.blogspot.com/

considered actual homes for the gods. Sumerians believed they had a duty to feed and shelter their gods.

The precursors of the ziggurat were raised platforms – built to be closer to heaven. Later, temples were erected on the platforms. Ziggurat designs ranged from simple bases upon which a temple sat, to marvels of mathematics and construction which spanned several terraced stories and were topped with a temple. The ziggurat steps led to the heavens and the actual god or goddess. Modern chemical testing suggested that the temples were painted dark indigo, matching the color of the sky.

Great Ziggurat of Ur
Near Nasiriyah, Iraq[172]

The grand temple changed the emotional dynamics of the people and the warrior class; a powerful god and temple created feelings of invincible strength. One early Sumerian temple, called the *Etemenanki*, means "temple of the foundation of Heaven and Earth." Even the temple name exudes strength. The date of its original construction is unknown, with suggested dates ranging from the ninth century BC and earlier, with textual evidence suggesting it existed in the second millennium BC.[173]

From 2700 BC on, there are many documented wars, invasions and exchanges of power and territory. In 2334 the Akkadians

[172] http://en.wikipedia.org/wiki/File:Ziggurat_of_ur.jpg
[173] George, Andrew. "The Tower of Babel: Archaeology, History and Cuneiform Texts," *Archiv fuer Orientforschung*, 51, (2005/2006). Pgs. 75–95.

conquered Gilgamesh's territory. Glutian hordes attacked Sumer from 2278 to 2154 BC. They were driven out of Sumer, but in 2004 BC the Elamites conquered, killed, destroyed palaces and leveled Sumerian towns.[174] This marked the end of the Sumerian civilization.

Sumerian Music

The discovery of numerous musical instruments in royal burial sites, along with illustrations of musicians, showed the importance of music in Sumer. Music was an integral part of their community. Sumerians enjoyed songs for work, social events, religious ceremonies and celebrations for important victories. Music in Sumer went hand in hand with daily activities. Music was a tool for all purposes: peace, battle, crop growth... to contacting the divine.

The Sumerians preferred string instruments, such as: the *asor*, harp and lyre, which produced soft and sentimental music.[175] Some instruments played the pentatonic scale, which includes remarkably melodious intervals. In contrast, the Egyptians used many harsh percussion instruments and the Hebrews liked loud trumpets.

The three instruments primarily used in the temples were the drum, flute and the harp. The *balag* or god–drum would "assuage tears," calm and uplift people. The priestess used the drum to summon the gods in the outer court of the Temples. The flute was heard in the inner court and the harp within the "sacred" place. The seven note flute, the *imine*, was used for hymns of penitence and adoration. It "connected" one to the seven planets known at that time. The temple harp, called an *algar*, had eleven to fifteen strings. A hymn to the goddess Ishtar[176] in 2100 BC reveals: "I will speak to thee with the *algar*, whose voice is sweet." Sacred harps were lavish, adorned with gold, lapis lazuli and precious

---

[174] Bauer, Susan. *Op. Cit.,* First third of book.
[175] Engel, Carl. *Op. Cit.,* Pg. 107.
[176] Ishtar was the East Semitic Akkadian, Assyrian and Babylonian goddess of fertility, love, war, and sex.

stones. Snki, the God of Music, described the harp: "It glittered like the stars by day; it was holy by night; it poured forth song."[177]

Sacred songs were chanted in the temples. Cantillation: singing words with tones and accents, was common; temple singers recited phrases and the audience sang back. Music was accompanied by drones and choirs using pleasant chords, perhaps of fourths and fifths. Ancient religious texts created patterns of accents (rhythmic patterns) with words. These were sung, adhering to prescribed rhythms. Notations were developed for rhythm and accent. Singing the scriptures was a custom adopted by many cultures. For example, the Hebrew *Talmud* scorned people who read their scriptures without singing them.

A Sumerian hymn containing the oldest form of musical writing was discovered in Asshur, depicting majestic music and words with cuneiform writings on clay tablets. According to Dr. Curt Sachs, the symbols represented melodic riffs.[178] Sumerian music radiated dignity, power and mastery.

Temples were the earliest form of universities. Stephen Langdon, in *Babylonian Liturgies*, suggested that each large temple had its own musical school[179] that related music to astrology. The priests taught people how to play instruments. In the third millennium BC, the records from the great Temple of Ningirsu in Lagasj, recorded the employment of a choir director and a singing teacher.

Music was a powerful and practical tool. Sumerian hymns were credited with bestowing beneficial energies, such as aiding people in distress and protecting against demons. For example, the hymn, "Ahuna Vairya," in the *Avestas* (an ancient Zoroastrian scripture), creates the energy of victory[180] and encourages the truth.[181, 182] The hymn, Vendidad, heals and protects the body – the energy increasing with each recitation.

---

[177] Heline, Corinne. *Op. Cit.,* Pg. 42.
[178] Heline, Corinne. *Ibid,* Pg. 40.
[179] Langdon, Stephen. *Babylonian Liturgies*, Paris, 1913, Pgs. xii, xix.
[180] "The most victorious" – Yasht 11.13, *Avestas*
[181] "Veracious word" – Yasna 8.1, *Avestas*
[182] "The sacred gift" – Yasna 27.7, *Avestas*

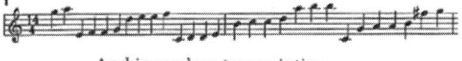

MS 5105

Old Babylonian cuneiform musical notation. Babylonia, 2000-1700 BC

And in modern transcription

A cuneiform tablet displays the notation of ancient Sumerian music. It has been roughly translated to modern musical notation.[183]

The spiritual energy of highly evolved musicians was believed to combine with their music. Before playing an instrument, the musician washed and purified his hands.[184] The music was sacred, therefore the purity of the musician mattered. Purity was further heightened by mental and emotional mastery. These qualities, in turn, enhanced the music and the listener.

---

[183] http://lauravaleri.com/2012/12/07/sumerian–music–the–real–deal
[184] http://en.wikipedia.org/wiki/Sumern_music

The Greek scholar Philo stated that the Mesopotamians sought "world–wide harmony and unison through the musical tones". Sitchin agreed that the Assyrio–Babylonian civilizations, who lived in Sumer, used music as a force for global peace. The Sumerian's soft and beautiful instruments provided a calming and uplifting influence. To illustrate, consider how incompatible war is with soft soothing music. This was important in avoiding war in this period.

Historian Carl Engel's research concluded that Sumerians used elemental harmony.[185] Leon Crickmore suspected that the ancient Mesopotamians used base 60 arithmetic – from their standard tables of reciprocals – to create their musical scales. The resulting scales would have notes created from ratios of whole numbers rather than notes created by the interval of a fifth.[186, 187]

McClain believed that the Sumerian base 60 mathematical system incorporated the main patterns of harmonic theory that later appeared in India, Egypt and Greece. Zecharia Sitchin, a historian on Sumer, agreed with this idea, "Sumerian music had the same scale that is characteristic of contemporary Western music and of Greek music of the first millennium BC.... Until now it was thought that Western music originated in Greece; now it has been established that our music – as so much else of Western civilization – originated in Mesopotamia."[188]

It is widely suspected that invaders that occupied the land once called Sumer learned about music from the indigenous people. This thread of passed knowledge can be seen even today in Arabian music. Remnants from ancient Persia (now Iran) reveal a surprisingly advanced and complex musical system. When the Arabs conquered Persia in 641 AD their captives demonstrated a more sophisticated civilization and music than their conquerors. Musicologist Carl Engel remarked, "There can be no doubt that

[185] Engel, Carl. *Op. Cit.,* Pg. 116.
[186] Crickmore, Leon. "New Light on the Babylonian Tonal System," Pg. 11. *Babylonian Music* edited by Richard Dumbrill & Irving Finkel, Proceedings of the International Conference of Near Eastern Archaeomusicology, 2008.
[187] http://en.m.wikipedia.org/wiki/Portal:Ancient_Near_East
[188] http://SumernGods.blogspot.com/

the musical system exhibited by the earliest Arab writers was based on an older system of the Persians. Their octave is divided into seventeen 1/3 tones."[189] The ancient Persian's instruments were precisely constructed to accurately use tiny intervals. Who were these early people with such sophistication in their music?

A Babylonian script on a clay plaque recounts a creation story, written in verse, perhaps the words of a song. Worldwide legends reflect that the misuse of sound contributed to the sinking of Atlantis. Afterwards, secrets of sound–based power were hidden to prevent unscrupulous people from misusing them, again. This powerful information was only given verbally to participants in elite groups, called mystery schools. Students (classified as initiates, disciples, adepts or masters) were given information, only after they had proven themselves worthy. The Babylonian story/song appears incomplete. The text of these verses ends with the words, "Secret – the initiated may show this to the initiated." The final secrets of creation were not available to the general population, only to those few who were admitted to the mystery schools. This reflects that many ancient secrets were passed along verbally only.

Musical Definitions

Pitch – relates to frequencies that can be measured in cycles per second (CPS).

Interval – is the difference (or interval) between two pitches (or CPS). An interval may be adjacent pitches in a melody or simultaneously sounding tones, found in a chord.

Octave – is an interval between two frequencies, having a ratio of 2 to 1.

Harmonic (also called overtone or partial) – is a component frequency that is an integer multiple of the fundamental frequency, i.e. if the fundamental frequency is f, the harmonics have frequencies $2f$, $3f$, $4f$...

Harmonic Series – pitches within the harmonic series may be calculated by dividing an instrument's string as follows: 1 + 1/2 + 1/3 + 1/4 + 1/5 + 1/6 + 1/7 + 1/8...to 1/16.

---

[189] Engel, Carl. *Op. Cit.,* Pg. 163.

Zoroastrianism

Mystic legends point to the special music of the Zoroastrians creating strong influences on ancient people in the land now called Iran. Due to close geographic proximity, there may have been exchanges of musical ideas with Sumer.

The Zoroastrism religion was inspired by the ancient Iranian prophet, named Zoroaster or Zarathustra, meaning living star. The date of his lifetime is greatly disputed. Prior to the 17th century, classical writers such as Plutarch the Greek historian, proposed dates earlier than 6000 BC.[190, 191] Other Greek sources reported that the original Zoroaster was born into the priestly Athrawan tribe around 7100 BC – in what is now Iran and Afghanistan.[192] In 7200 BC Kai Vishtaspa became ruler of Persia and reportedly ruled for 120 years. Zarathustra was a contemporary of King Vishtaspa. On the basis of astronomical observations at the time, many Greeks placed Zoroaster's time around 7052 BC. None of these dates are confirmed by historians or archeologists. Today, Zoroastrian religious leaders suggest that Zoroaster lived about 3000 BC. Historians date the original Zoroaster's life between 1750 and 1200 BC on the basis of his writing style. Part of the confusion regarding the time period of Zoroaster resulted from the custom of selecting new Zoroasters – to replace the former one – who had passed away. Likewise, in the history of Tibetan religion, Dalai Lama after Dalai Lama was named (fourteen so far). Since many share the same name it is difficult to isolate information about a specific person thousands of years ago.

Zoroastrianism is one of the world's oldest living faiths. Earlier religions worshipped Mother Earth or a group of gods. Followers were born into their religion, but Zoroastrianism is *not* exclusive to only one race. Zoroastrianism is the first documented religion to have been divinely *revealed.* In a similar manner, Jesus revealed truths about God and the "way" to live; Islam was revealed through Mohammad; Buddhism came about by the teaching of Buddha. In Zoroastrianism, religion was a set of beliefs, rituals

---

[190] Nigosian, Solomon. "*The Zoroastrian faith: tradition and modern research*," McGill–Queen's University Press, 1993, Pg. 15.
[191] *Ammianus Marcellinus*, xxiii.6.32, 4th century AD
[192] As a reference point, the end of the ice age was approximately 9844 BC.

and activities to become pure and worthy. Ethics were of primary importance.

Zoroastrianism had many defining ideas, such as free will, and good versus evil. Early Zoroastrians were pacifists, monotheistic and equally supported both genders. They emphasized meditating to harmonize with the original pristine state of nature. Neighboring groups did not believe in the equality of women, peace being more valuable than war and monotheism.[193]

Each person was believed to have a divine spark – that needed to be developed. Fire is a visible symbol of this inner light, physically representing the illuminated, divine spark and truth. Ancient Zoroastrians revered fire so much that they recognized five different types of fire with names for each: 1.) Useful fire for keeping homes warm and cooking 2.) Energy in plants that makes them grow 3.) Lightning 4.) Energy that keeps our bodies warm and functioning 5.) Holy fire burning in the presence of the creator.

In ancient Iran, fire temples had many functions using the various aspects of this element. Folk tales described miracles that took place at "sacred" eternal fires.

The original Zoroastrian fire supposedly came from God, and the Zoroastrians kept the fire – without ever letting it go out. Separate fire temples with sacred/eternal fires were built for priests, warriors and farmers. When enemies took over the country, the Zoroastrians saved the ashes of the perpetual fire to provide a link in a new fire in another location, thus keeping their fire "eternally".

Archeologists found a site, Takht–i Sulaiman in Iran, with a lake – well above sea level – that was fed by thermal springs. The area around this lake was the site of the Zoroastrian "sacred fire" for kings and warriors. Long ago the warmth naturally spouted due to thermal springs. This natural phenomenon also occurs at Mount Olympus today.

---

[193] Bauer, Susan. *Op. Cit.,* Pg. 127. Moses left Ur, an Akkadian city devoted to the worship of the moon goddess, approximately around 2166 BC.

In the Zoroastrian religion, water and fire are used in rituals to "purify" members' souls. Spiritual insight and wisdom are gained through the energy of fire and water. Both are still considered life–sustaining and are in fire temples today. Likewise in Christianity, water is used for the baptismal rites; Fonts provide holy water for blessing Christians as they enter and leave a church. Ashes, created with fire, are placed on a believer's forehead on Ash Wednesday.

Zoroastrians usually pray in the presence of some form of fire or light. Similarly, spiritual masters of many traditions recommend meditating in the light – not the dark.

The Moguls and warriors of Islam persecuted the Zoroastrians. After the death of the *mobeds* (priests), many Zoroastrian customs were lost. Today, in India, there is a small community of Zoroastrians, the Parsees. This is the principal remaining Zoroastrian stronghold.

Zoroastrian Music

The conquerors of the Zoroastrians destroyed much of their history, sacred texts and musical practices. The deeper understandings of their music have been lost. A significant portion of the Zoroastrian's religious book, *The Avestas*, was destroyed. The lost portions are referenced and quoted in the later works. Most liturgies survived.

Zoroastrians believe that four spiritual powers surround God – music being one of them. Current religious thoughts can be traced to Zoroastrian ideas. For example, the Sufis are set apart from other Muslim traditions for their admiration of music. The Sufis communicate with God through music.

Zoroastrian music accompanied religious and traditional rites. Zoroastrian fire temples possessed one or two bells that chimed at certain times during ceremonies, providing awakening sounds.

Zoroastrians enjoyed choral and solo performances prior to the arrival of Islam in Persia. These songs are no longer performed, although they still endure. The words are from either *The Avesta* or *The Gathas*, which translate to "songs" (both attributed to Zoroaster). The religious text, *The Avesta*, was chanted with characteristic rhythmic patterns. Zoroastrian music boasted of a natural rhythmic cadence similar to the inflections in speech.

Zoroastrian ideas influenced the development of philosophy. Among the classic Greek philosophers, Heraclitus incorporated Zoroaster's thinking. Zoroaster perceived the human condition as the mental struggle between truth and lies. One's word is sacred and not to be broken, however difficult the circumstances. When one lies (or breaks a promise) he creates two energies. His words (the lies) are energies, but his mind/subconscious knows the contrasting truth. These combined energies create internal dissonance that feels like "guilt." This dissonance is like a small dose of "subtle–energy–poison," afflicting the liar. In contrast, speaking the truth creates internal harmony. Over and above speaking the truth, one must think and act in an honest way.

There are many reasons why the sound of a word (not its meaning) is impactful. Ancient people carefully noted the vibratory impact of a word and how it affected them. The energy of the word and its meaning were connected. The sound of ancient languages formed stronger energetic associations with the meaning of the word than languages do today. This design made ancient words potent. For a prayer, they carefully selected words for their uplifting energy. Similarly, the song of a nightingale brings joy, with no one understanding a word.

The Zoroastrians believed that the act of chanting *The Avesta Manthras* uplifted their souls more so than the meaning of the prayers. Prayers are recited in many original languages for this reason.[194]

Zoroastrian music accompanied many critical events in life. An individual sang to help himself through difficult passages. There was music to lament, eat a meal, praise God and accompany all rituals in the temples. Temple music bounced between a soloist and the choir.

---

[194] Levitin, Daniel. The World in Six Songs: How the Musical Brain Created Human Nature, Penguin Group: NY, 2009, Pg. 173.

Author Michael Hayes stated that ancient music was an interactive part of people's lives, and this practice improved their genetics. "The musical symmetry dictated the evolution of the human gene pool. It was not only identified by ancient peoples, but it was actively employed in their daily lives as a complete way of being."[195]

Among his many accomplishments, Zoroaster was a famed mathematician who predicted rare star configurations in the sky, without the aid of telescopes. Zoroaster employed "musical astrology". Zoroastrian music changed every day of the year to balance the movement of the celestial stars.[196] Zoroastrians perceived that the stars were divine living beings. Believing that the planets were embodied by great beings (many suggest the spirit named Gai "ensouls" Earth), their relationship to the planets was most important; each planet influenced them. Harmonizing to subtle star energy was a revered spiritual tradition.

The Earth, sun and moon were believed to affect our astral bodies (feelings), while the planets affected our etheric bodies (health energy). The signs of the zodiac affected our physical bodies.[197] These ideas are among the earliest references to astrology.

Curt Sachs wrote that the ancient desire to hear the "harmony of the spheres" developed from civilizations' fixations on the stars. Sachs believed that this sacred information was given to the Babylonians[198] (who occupied territory now Iraq) and from there passed to the Jews, Greeks and Egyptians.[199] The heart of the Music of the Spheres was that one planet was to another planet, as a certain pitch was to another pitch. Musical relationships were linked to astronomical relationships; very profound on deep reflection. Sounds were produced by the planets' movements –

---

[195] Hayes, Michael. The Hermetic Code in DNA: The Sacred Principles in the Ordering of the Universe, Inner Traditions: VT, 2004, Pg. 22.
[196] More information will be given later in this book on how this was done. There is an entire chapter on methods to do this in an upcoming book of Jill Mattson's.
[197] Steiner, Rudolf. Reading the Pictures of the Apocalypse, Anthroposphic Press, NY. Lectures from 1909, 1993, Pg. 44.
[198] In October 539 BC, the Persian king Cyrus took Babylon, the ancient capital of an oriental empire covering modern Iraq, Syria, Lebanon and Israel.
[199] Sachs, Curt. The Rise of Music in the Ancient World, East and West, Dover Publications: Mineola, NY, 1943, Pg. 111.

creating actual tones below our hearing range. These unheard vibrations can also be thought of as astrological influences.

The Sufi whirling dervishes are reminiscent of Zoroastrian dancers. The Sufis wear tall felt hats, looking like truncated cones, and broad skirts that stand out as they whirl. Their hats are said to be tilted at the same angle as the Earth's axis. This musical and sacred rite displays twirling dancers with drum and reed–flute accompaniment. The dancers whirl, tracing the Fibonacci spiral symbol, found so abundantly in nature. They also mimic the movements of the planets, as seen slowly moving in the night sky. Energy is created by dancing in spiral figures, giving the dancer and the audience harmony with all things in nature – from the smallest cells to the immense stars.

The human body is a replica of the cosmos and nature's cycles. Our blood flows around the body and people revolve through the stages of life. These cycles are natural and unconscious. The whirling dervish intentionally represents the shared cycle of life.

The ancient tambourine music of Kermanshah, in Iran, is similar to some Zoroastrian music. Remnants of this ancient music are heard today from Kurds who live in the nearby mountains. The Kurds create hypnotic and trance–inducing–music with frame drums and other percussion instruments, such as their *shirmshals.*

The beating drums sounded like thunder and were used to create conditions to produce rain. Shamans in the Kalari Desert, Iran, used whirling music, chanting, intense concentration and breath control to achieve a state, in which they accessed information from the spirit world.

The Musical Number Six

Mystic legends connect the original Zoroaster's music to the energy of the "Planetary Logos," (a highly evolved being thought to have assisted in creation and guidance of the solar system). Rudolf Steiner described the original Zoroastrian music as providing a spiritual experience;[200] it produced a lower type of

---

[200] Godwin, Joscelyn. Cosmic Music: Musical Keys to the Interpretation of Reality, Inner Traditions: VT, 1989, Pgs. 180–182.

energy than the Atlanteans enjoyed, but had greater spiritual energy than music emits today.

According to Steiner, Zoroastrian music incorporated the number six in its compositions. Numbers were used in music to represent both pitches and rhythms, and were used in constructing musical instruments.

Numbers were naturally used in many other arenas. Mathematics was used by ancient people, who closely recorded what they saw in the night sky. The phases of the moon and movements of celestial bodies were counted and mapped. The farmer marked the seasons. Herbs were identified by the number of plant leaves and their dominant patterns.

People noted how a numeric pattern subtly felt. For example, the energy of a five pointed star fish felt similar to subtle feelings emitted from plants with five petals. The predominate number–design created a defining feeling. Music that was created with patterns of five would also have this same feeling.
Arithmetic was considered necessary in the shop, but it was vulgar. The "true" study of numbers freed people from the physical world and introduced abstract principals and archetypes. The study of numbers was the root of all other studies and was referred to as the primary reflection of reality.[201]

The Zoroastrian's music incorporated the signature numeric pattern of six, which correlated to things with "six energy," such as snowflakes and crystals formed with six sides. A hexagon shape is found in the middle of a carrot and on the top of a pepper. Each cell of a honeycomb has six sides. Insects have six legs. There are six lines in each hexagram in the Chinese sacred book, *I Ching*. During an orbit, Mercury traces a six pointed star in the skies.

Mercury's yearly movements between two successive conjunctions[1] and its repetition of evening and morning stars,

---

[201] Plato follower, Thomas Taylor in <u>Theoretic Arithmetic</u>, Michell, John. <u>The Dimensions of Paradise: Sacred Geometry, Ancient Science, and the Heavenly Order on Earth</u>, Inner Traditions: VT, 2008, Pg. 49.

traces a perfect six pointed Star of David. The Star of David has a feeling of "six–ness", as there are six points on the circle.

www.JillsWingsOfLight.com – Art Galleries

119

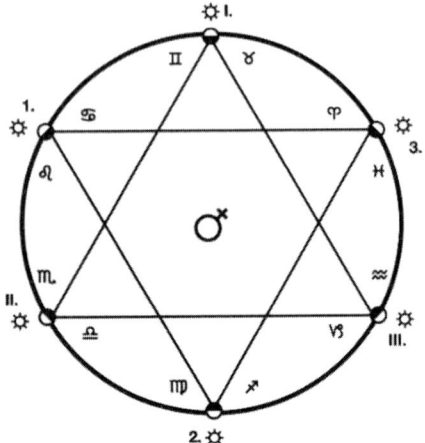

Mercury's Movements

♉	Taurus. _____		♍	Virgo. _____
♈	Aries. _____		♎	Libra. _____
♓	Pieces. _____		♏	Scorpio. _____
♒	Aquarius. _____		♌	Leo. _____
♑	Capricorn. _____		♋	Cancer. _____
♐	Sagittarius. _____		♊	Gemini. _____
◑	Conjunctions. _____		☼	Sun. _____
♂	Mars. _____			

Movement and Rhythms of the Stars; Schultz, Joachim (translated by John Meeks); Edinburgh, Floris Books (Anthroposophic Press); 1986. The information came from Chapters 15 and 17.

"Six–energy" is described in numerology. Six is the most loving of the numbers. The energy of six is similar to the qualities of exuberance, mercy, justice, love, divine power, wisdom, perfection and majesty. Numerology suggests that people with the energy of six have compassion, responsibility, unselfishness, harmony, balance, generosity, kindness, humility, charisma and charm. They are committed, protective, nurturing, domestic, community conscious and family oriented. [202, 203]

The Number Six in Crop Circles [204]

A fascinating aspect of an interval of a sixth is that the golden ratio (1.618033…) numerically lies in between intervals of a minor (8/5 = 1.6) and a major sixth (5/3 = 1.666.) When two waves combine and create the golden ratio, the final wave has the lowest amplitude of possible vibrations. In contrast, the major sixth is the greatest point of amplification and resonance.[205] Areas of the lowest amplitude (golden ratio and nearby minor sixth) and the greatest resonance (major sixth) are nested next to each other. Creating a musical system based on sixes, shapes and sculpts subtle energy in powerful ways.[206]

---

[202] http://www.spiritual–numerology.com/numerology–number–meaning/numerology–meaning–of–number–6.html

[203] Each number radiates a positive and negative expression of energy. The challenging energies associated with the number six are being too emotional, overly sentimental, susceptible to flattery, imbalanced between helping and interfering, self–righteous, stubborn, egotistical and dominating.

[204] Used with permission by Peter Sorensen
ttp://cropcircleconnector.com/Sorensen/circles/1999/main.html

[205] Merrick, Richard. Interference: A Grand Scientific Musical Theory, Merrick: Houston, 2009, Pg. 136.

[206] Richard Merrick discussed phi in relation to a tritone (Aug. 4th/dim 5th) and the location of phi in a 7–step diatonic scale: "The center of resonance (harmonic center) of a resonating tone is the ninth partial in the natural harmonic series. For the tonic C in a C major scale, this is the supertonic D, called the ninth. It forms naturally as part of the harmonic series

In Summary: Music of Sumer and Zoroaster

As we glimpse at our first real historical civilization, we observe the powerful and complex role that music assumed. Music was interwoven into every aspect of life, both divine and practical. Music was used for healing and power. People sang at important events and transitions in their lives. They sang to create energetic support – to get through difficulties.

Recall that the musician was to possess purity and honor, even cleansing himself before a performance. Musical instruments of gold and precious gems demonstrated that music was not taken lightly. It was certainly more than mere entertainment. The first universities taught music and manipulation of subtle energies.

Music was mathematical and correlated to the gods – their source of power. A god was the energy associated with a fraction, and fractions were used to create musical intervals. A song would then

---

(for fundamental C in the example) and acts as an axis or pivot around which all of the other harmonics balance (or orbit). So, recognizing the ninth as the harmonic axis in an octave, the inverse harmonic center is a tritone away or G# in our example. Thus, {D, G#} act as a harmonic axis of symmetry in the harmonic series and diatonic scale of C. Measuring phi upward and downward from G# we land in the gaps between {B, C} and {E, F} which are symmetrically balanced around the harmonic center D. The tense diatonic tritone (and only tritone in the diatonic C major scale) is then {B, F} which we anticipate and recognize resolving to the tonic major third {C, E}. This is where the relationship of phi to the tritone comes in. The two phi–damping locations in a diatonic scale over an octave are measured from G# or the inverse harmonic center of C. The tritone function (driving force in music harmony and human music perception) then oscillates across these two phi–damping locations from {B, F} {C, E} {B, F} {C, E} ... Our perception of musical harmony is based on recognizing this oscillation across the phi–damping locations relative to the harmonic axis {D, G}.
My definition of resonance: the major sixth is the most resonant because the wave partials in the harmonic series naturally combine in such a way that it is the interval in an octave least damped or deadened by phi. Another way of saying it is energy sharing is least bound or constrained at a major sixth. The first major sixth interval in the harmonic series occurs between the third and fifth partials (or {G, E} for fundamental C), thus 5:3 = 1.666. The least resonant interval in a 12–step octave is the inverse harmonic center, which is G# for fundamental C and harmonic center D (see pg. 124 in Interference). This is because G# is the furthest away from the harmonic center D. But within the 7–step diatonic scale over an octave, the least resonant intervals correspond to perfect fourths from the harmonic center or {D, G} and {A, D}. They are equivalent to perfect fifths from the tonic major third as {C, G} and {A, E}. In traditional music harmony, perfect fifths and fourths are considered the most stable, most calm and most resolved intervals, thus confirming them as the least perceptually resonant intervals in a diatonic scale. Notice that {G, A} balance symmetrically around inverse harmonic center G#."

122

be a pantheon or chorus of the gods. The Zoroastrians believed that music was an attribute or quality of a god. No wonder these people, who believed in supernatural powers, cherished music, which was divine magic. Music was a tool to call, commune and please the divine. It created sacred space. It mimicked elements of nature, which was the signature of God. Contrast these ideas to current society.

Sumerian documents display complex math, which is at the roots of their music. Their advanced music was present at the dawn of the first civilization, when the only historical records we have sound like faery tales. Without more extensive records, we do not know the complete role that music played to maintain or contribute to Sumerian accomplishments or demise. We do know it was cherished and was equated with the heavens and the divine.

www.JillsWingsOfLight.com – Art Galleries

Chapter Six

Ancient Chinese Music
2850 to 206 BC

Records enduring from the reign of Emperor Shun (~2600 – 2500 BC) give a rare glimpse of the unique role music was afforded by the ancient Chinese – considered critical to their world's stability and security:

> "Each 5th year, in the second month, Emperor Shun journeyed to check upon his kingdom and ensure that everything was in order in the vast land. Yet he did not do so by auditing the account books of the different regions. Neither, by observing the state of life of the populace or by receiving petitions from them. Nor by interviewing the regional officials in authority. No, by none of these methods. In ancient China there was considered to be a much more revealing, accurate and scientific method of checking on the state of the nation. According to the Chinese text, *Shu King*, the emperor Shun went through the different territories and… tested the exact pitches of their notes of music.[207]

> … "But most important of all, he believed he should listen to, and to check, the five notes of the ancient Chinese scale. He had eight kinds of musical instruments brought back to him and played by musicians. Then he listened to the local folk songs and also to the tunes that were sung in the court

---

[207] Tame, David. The Secret Power of Music: The Transformation of Self and Society Through Musical Energy, Destiny Books: VT, 1984, Pg. 15.

itself, checking that all music had perfect correspondence with the five notes.[208]

"If Emperor Shun, on his travels about the kingdom had discovered that the instruments of the different territories were all differently tuned from each other, then he would have considered it a foregone conclusion that the territories themselves would begin to (if they did not already) differ with each other. They might even lose their unity and begin to squabble among themselves unless the tuning was not corrected at once and made uniform from one place to another. And if the music that he heard in the villages had begun to become vulgar and immoral, then the Emperor would have expected immorality itself to sweep the nation unless something was done to correct the music.[209]

"According to the philosophy of the ancient Chinese, music was the basis of everything. Civilizations were shaped and molded according to the kind of music performed within them. Was a civilization's music wistful or romantic? Then the people themselves would be romantic. Was it strong and military? Then the neighbor's better beware. Furthermore, a civilization remained stable and unchanged as long as its music remained unchanged. But to change the style of music which people listened to would inevitably lead to a change in the very way of life itself."[210]

According to author Curt Sachs, when the emperor evaluated his country, he listened to the six pitches, the five notes of the scale and the eight kinds of musical instruments; he tested the court modes and ballads of the villages to insure that they corresponded to the five tones.[211]

Music embodied a village's moral qualities. Music contributed to the vitality and strength of a nation when it maintained purity of sound. To monitor this, the ancient Chinese maintained a

---

[208] Tame, David. *Ibid*, Pg. 15.
[209] Tame, David. *Ibid*, Pg. 16.
[210] Tame, David. *Ibid*, Pg. 15.
[211] Sachs, Curt. <u>The Rise of Music in the Ancient World, East and West</u>, Dover Publications: Mineola, NY, 1943, Pg. 112.

Department of Measurements. One of its functions was to insure that all provinces tuned instruments in a harmonious way with each other. By controlling the instrumental designs and/or frets of instruments, they insured that musical notes were the same frequency and harmonious with each other.[212] The physical lengths of instruments and range of scales were also carefully correlated to special numbers found in Heaven and Earth.

Roots of Chinese Civilization

To provide a better context of the beginnings and early days of Chinese culture we will digress to the roots of this civilization. The earliest permanent settlements trace to wanderers who began to settle the great plain between the Yellow and the Yangtze rivers by 5000 BC. Settlers raised rice in the wet ground near the rivers. Archeological records show that the earliest significant villages developed near the Yellow River.

www.JillsWingsOfLight.com – Art Galleries

---

[212] The ancient Chinese measured intervals by their wave length, not their pitch. Science does this with the formula: $F = V / W$. V = the speed of sound through air (1,130 feet per second), F = frequency (in cycles per second) and W = wavelength (in feet). One can measure a pitch by wavelength, which determines pitch. A good example of this can be seen by observing organ pipes. Each different pipe length creates a different pitch. The lengths of instrument were regulated in ancient China to maintain their vibratory control.

Important Events – Prehistoric & Ancient China

Historical Events	Approximate Dates
Flutes constructed from crane bones	~7000 BC
Domestication of dogs & chickens	~6000 BC
Settlements of Yellow & Yangtze River Areas	~5000 BC
Oldest utilization of Silk	3630 BC
Fu Xi (First King)	2850 BC
Shennong (The Farmer King)	Dates assigned vary
Huangdi (The Yellow King)	2696 BC
Yao (First Sage King)	Dates assigned vary
Shun (Second Sage King)	2598 BC
Yu (Third Sage King)	Dates assigned vary
Yu's off spring establishes Xia Dynasty	2205 – 1766 BC
Confucius	551 – 479 BC

Stories of ancient China, set down several thousand years afterwards, tell of the first king who discovered the essential order of all things – his name was Fu Xi. Such accounts are idealized, but contain basic truths.

Sima Qian (historian) tells us that Fu Xi began his rule about 2850 BC. Notably, Fu Xi created the eight Trigrams, a series of straight and broken lines used for record keeping, divination and interpreting a deeper understanding of events. The trigrams were modeled after the markings on a turtle shell. He meditated on these geometries and used them to communicate with "higher beings." He is revered for connecting patterns of nature to the body, mind and soul.

Fu Xi is followed by the second Great King: Shennong, the Farmer King. Succeeding the Farmer King is perhaps the greatest of these times – Huangdi, the Yellow Emperor. Huangdi, the last of the three great kings, was followed by Yao – the first of the Three Sage Kings.

Emperor Shun was the second of the Chinese Sage Kings. His reign began about 2600 BC as he was named the successor to Emperor Yao. Yao named Shun as his successor – bypassing his son who was not up to the job. He chose a poor peasant with great virtue and wisdom as his successor. Yao established that wisdom, not birth, was the standard for a king. Everything that we know from this period was passed down, for many centuries, by oral histories – and much later put down in writing. According to legend, Shun was a simple farmer who had a difficult life. After years of living a selfless existence, Shun was elevated to share the responsibilities of ruling the great empire at the age of 30. As we have glimpsed, Shun was an impeccable Emperor; he had remarkable leadership abilities and administrative skills. He was also noble of character, generous and just. According to records, Shun served as Emperor for 47 years and like Yao before him, went outside his family to name Yu as his successor. Yao and Shun – the first two Sage Kings – were considered the ideal leaders of Ancient China. To this day, no greater compliment can be paid to a ruler than to compare him to Yao and Shun.

Shun began the tradition of touring the country every fifth year to inspect the health of the empire and its people. He used the health and purity of Chinese music as a gauge of the civilization's wellbeing. It is noteworthy that Shun passed this musical tradition down to future generations of Chinese Emperors.

Shun skipped over his son and selected Yu as his heir – the Third and last Sage King. The Si–clan, descendants of Yu, established the first Chinese Dynasty, the Xia, which endured for hundreds of years. [213] (Circa 2200 – 1700 BC). Yu the Great continued the strong, early tradition which valued music highly. Yu decreed that there would always be five court instruments present at the entrance to this throne room: a gong, drum, stone instrument, bell and rattle. Visitors were to strike a tone on one of the instruments. The use of the instruments instantly communicated information regarding the visitor and his purposes to the King. Bad omens could also be detected in the subtle feelings accompanying notes of the instrument used by a troubled visitor. The music also set the vibratory matrix for the session with the Emperor and helped facilitate productive outcomes.

After Yu, the throne in the Xia Dynasty and future Chinese dynasties, ceased to be passed on by merit and succession became based on hereditary.

The Xia Dynasty fell about 1700 BC followed by Tang's Shang Dynasty (ca 1700 – 1050 BC). Dynasties continued, but split into various states or kingdoms. For over a thousand years this patchwork group of states held uneasy peace interrupted by wars, often changing the boarders of kingdoms. Enormous wastelands in the northern and western parts of the country were inhabited by nomadic societies. Although the nomads were poor, they were superior in military strength. In the southern and eastern parts of the country fertile river areas supported agriculture, which led to great communities. These two groups exchanged goods, but conflicts often appeared. The farming areas were constantly attacked by the northern barbarians. Internal power struggles also challenged the dynasties over the years.

After the birth of Buddha in India (563 BC), Kong Fuzi (Confucius – 551 BC to 479 BC) was a respected poor individual who became a great reformer of a fractured and warring China. Confucius loved antiquity and brought back many of their ancient customs. He performed rituals in the courts of the Zhao and Lu kings featuring hundreds of songs that he knew by heart. These

---

[213] http://heim.ifi.uio.no/~huut/xia.html

songs were of ancient origins, reviving the art of establishing harmony and balance with music. Confucius believed that orderly performance of duties developed virtues and tranquility. Putting aside gruesome wars, Confucius offered a way to control their society and develop virtues, which included the strategic use of music. According to the philosophy of the ancient Chinese, music was the basis of everything. Civilizations were molded according to their music.

The final powerful Chinese dynasty, the Chi'ing Dynasty of 1644 –1912 AD, was ended after the old musical ways were silenced as the Republic of China took power.

Creation of Chinese Music

According to some sources, the Chinese attribute the invention of their music to supernatural beings;[214] their sing–song language is often linked to the ancient Lemurians.[215]

The *I Ching* (*Book of Changes*) is one of the oldest classic Chinese texts. Long held traditions teach that the *I Ching* had its beginnings with Fu Xi around 2850 BC and his trigrams. In the *I Ching,* Fu Xi claimed credit for the Chinese musical system, according to documents written around 645 BC.

In 2697 BC the Yellow Emperor established the original *kung* as the cosmic note. The *kung* – or first note of the scale – was believed to be the original note of creation. In a universal theme, many religions credit sound with the creation.[216] There are various

---

[214] Elson, Louis. Curiosities of Music; A Collection of Facts Not Generally Known, Regarding Music of Ancient and Savage Nations, O'Ditson Co. 1908 and 2009. Pg. 64.

[215] Scott–Elliot. The Story of Atlantis and the Lost Lemuria, The Theosophical Publishing House: London, 1925 with editions up to 1968. Pg. 95.

[216] "The Beginning of the World" stories from many religions give sound or the spoken word a vital role in the creation of the universe: "In the beginning was the Word, and the Word was with God, and the Word was God." John 1:1 (A spoken word is a sound.) Hindu tradition states in the *Vedas*, "In the beginning was Brahman with whom was the Word. And the Word is Brahman." Thot, an Egyptian God, was believed to have created the world with his voice. The ancient hieroglyph for the word mouth is in the shape of a seed.[216] According to Mayan tradition, in the *Popul Vuh,*[216] humans are given life by the power of the Word. In the Hopi Indian tradition, "Spider Woman" sings songs of creation to produce animated life. The *Satapatha Brahmana* reads, "In the beginning was God with power through speech. God said, 'May I be many... may I be propagated through subtle speech,'

130

translations for the word *kung: haung, zhong, haung chung, gong,* yellow bell, the fundamental tone and the cosmic tone. They all describe the same note.

Today, science confirms that sounds can affect brainwaves and human emotions. Since frequencies influence people, the precise pitch of notes was considered critical. Music must be closely controlled due to its potential to impact thoughts and emotions. Measures to control music included: precisely setting musical scales, tuning notes to set frequencies (for example, today the musical note A is set at 440 hertz), restrictions allowing the use of only certain notes, and dictating when instruments can be played, were some methods employed in ancient China to maintain close control of the music. Early on, this subtle influence was perceived to be so powerful that its stability was policed. "It was due to their music's tremendous power that for ages the Chinese kept their music under state supervision to guard against any stealthy introduction of tones contrary to their rigid ordinance."[217]

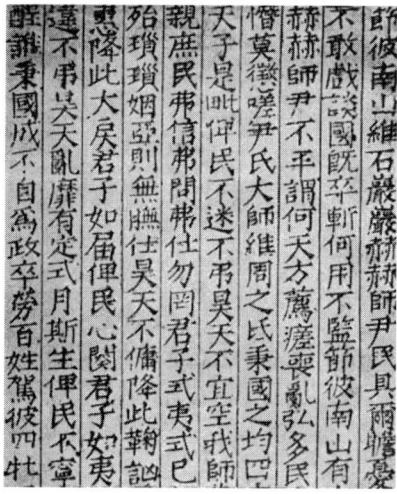

The *I Ching* [218]

he united himself with that speech and became pregnant." In Chinese Buddhism, the Divine Voice calls forth the form of the universe.

[217] Heline, Corinne. Healing and Regeneration through Music, The New Age Bible and Philosophy Center: Santa Barbara, CA, 1943, Pg. 44.

[218] Image from Wikipedia

For the Chinese, music was not primarily for entertainment, but was considered *far more* important. Its stability was safe guarded to protect national interests. Modern leaders categorize military and economic problems as the issues of utmost importance. Confucius believed that the purity and quality of music were more significant; improper music led to problems that could ultimately threaten the civilization.

Confucius taught that good government was not possible without good music. Good is always stronger than evil in our world. Evil is disharmonious and cannot exist in a strong field of harmony. The stronger vibration overcomes the lesser. Music can create strong harmonic vibrations, which can overcome negativity. In an example, Liu Kun was defending Chin Yang against the Tartars. One midnight during the siege he played Tartar music on a Tarter pipe, making the attackers emotional and homesick. The great horde went home. In this example, music was used to change the emotions of the enemy. Courage and determination in the warrior, were replaced with the desire for the comforts of home – when the familiar music was played.

Confucius believed that the power of music altered the attributes of a population. "Would'st thou know if a people be well governed, if its manners are good or bad?" asked Confucius. "Examine the music that it produces!"[219]

The book *Yao Chi* states, "In the ancestral temples rulers and ministers, high and low, listen to the music and all is harmony. Within the gates of the family, fathers and sons, brothers and cousins, *listen together and all is harmony and affection.* In this way fathers and sons, and rulers and subjects, were united in harmony and then people of myriad states were associated in love. Such was the method of the ancient kings when they framed their music."[220] The ancient Chinese closed the generation gap by enjoying the same music. A consistent musical diet unified and strengthened the cohesiveness of the people.

---

[219] Mulcahy, Pat. Esoteric Harmonics: Tuning to the Occult Scale of Sound, AstroQab Publications: Australia, 2009, Pg. 67.
[220] Mulcahy, Pat. *Ibid,* Pg. 67.

A written account from 227 BC described the impact of listening to a sound outside of prescribed parameters. "Gao Jianli played the *zhu* (a musical instrument) and Jing Ke sang along in *Bianzhi* pitch (a note outside of the approved pentatonic scale; it was similar to the seventh note of today's scale). All who were present wept."[221] Over 2,000 years ago someone sang a rogue pitch, causing the listeners to cry.

In contrast, today, a huge variety of musical styles exist and they change significantly and quickly. In the midst of constant vibratory change, it is difficult to keep a president in the USA past four years. Ancient Chinese sages would credit the fleeting musical styles with our rapid national changes and fleeting values.

History shows that similar to the ancient Chinese, most important civilizations that revered and preserved their music endured for long periods of time. Musicologist David Tame reflected on the security of a country listening to stable, sublime music, "A civilization which mirrored the above (musical stability) would never pass away, for every institution and object within it provided a medium for the containments of life–enforcing, invigorating cosmic forces."[222]

Although the emperor closely monitored the empire's music to prevent unwanted change, defects in the music inevitably arose. China was comprised of thousands of distant villages and vast territories; maintaining musical purity was not always effective. Many small villages, that were great distances from the Emperor, enjoyed local theater and folk music. This music (deemed vulgar by the aristocracy) creatively stretched outside the fixed musical parameters.

Control of Chinese Music

In the Chinese musical scale, each note was linked to a government authority or certain group of people. Each group was responsible for maintaining harmony for their tone. This was another means of insuring that the civilization was continually

---

[221] Ho Lu–Ting and Han Kuo–Huang. "On Chinese Scales and National Modes," University of Texas Press: *Asian Music*, Vol. 14, No. 1 (1982), Pgs. 132 –154.
[222] Tame, David. *Op. Cit.*, Pg. 56.

energized and harmonized with appropriate music. Musical historian, Danielou, reported that: "The dukes and ministers heard the *lu* (the musical note) of each month in the court's assemblies (and harmonized with this tone), to move heaven and accord themselves to the Earth's influx."[223]

Responsibility for Harmonious Notes

Note of the Scale	*Kung* 1st *note in a scale*	**Shang** 2nd *note*	**Chiao** 3rd *note*	**Chi** 4th *note*	**Yu** 5th *note*
Responsibility of ...	Emperor or prince	Ministers	Loyal subjects	Affairs of State or public works	Produce or Material things
Season		Autumn	Spring	Summer	Winter

Responsible Parties for Harmonious Pitches[224]

Brain waves and emotions are vibratory, just as musical tones are. Some believe that all vibratory waves in close proximity combine; hence – ultimately – the energy of sound interacts with the energy of thoughts and emotions. The ancient Chinese meditated while listening to a single tone. Listeners superimposed the feeling of harmony on the sound. In this way, they controlled emotional, mental and physical energies associated with a frequency.

The Emperor bore the responsibility to harmonize his primary tone. The other tones were derived from this *all important* note. The welfare of the empire depended on the *kung*'s pitch being exact. It was the emperor's job to adjust the frequency of creation

[223] Guenon, Rene. *Orient et Occident*, Pg. 70. Fu Xi's date is about 3468 BC according to a chronology based on the exact description of the condition of the sky at the time. Danielou, Alain. Music and the Power of Sound: The Influence of Tuning and Interval on Consciousness, Inner Traditions: VT, 1943, Pg. 30.
[224] From Grove's *Dictionary of Music and Musicians* (1954 edition)

– as he sensed the need. If the tone felt discordant to him, then he changed its pitch. When a tone felt compromised, devastation was expected. For example, the Chinese were certain that the prior emperor would not have died unless his tone was out of harmony.[225]

An ancient text warned: "If the *kung* is disturbed, then there is disorganization; the prince is arrogant." If the *kung* was out of tune, then the celestial realm had changed; disorder in society would follow. This vital frequency changed overtime as everything in the universe changes. As cosmic influences moved on slowly, consequently the *kung* did too. If the *kung* frequency changed, then the harmony of Heaven and Earth followed suit. Being in tune with Heaven and Earth was literally the purpose of life.

Numerous sources suggested that the *kung* was close to our musical note of F; as we have seen, it changed over the eons. D'Olivet matched the *kung* to 708.76 cycles per second, an F natural.[226] The final Chinese dynasty placed the *kung* pitch at D or 601.5 cycles per second.[227] The ancient Chinese would have believed that this *kung* was incorrectly tuned or this would <u>not</u> have been the last dynasty.

In the second century BC, Doug Zhongzu described the ongoing energy exchanges between Heaven and Earth: "The vital spirits of humankind, tuned to the tone of Heaven and Earth, expressing the tremors of Heaven and Earth, just as several *cithars* (musical instruments) tuned on gong (*kung*), all vibrate when the gong sounds. Harmony between Heaven, Earth and humankind does not come from a physical union; it comes from tuning to the same note.... In the universe nothing happens by chance, there is no spontaneity: all is influence and harmony, accord answering accord."[228]

---

[225] Sachs, Curt. *Op. Cit.*, Pg. 112.

[226] According to Father Amiot, D'Olivet, Pg. 73. Danileou, Alain. <u>Music and the Power of Sound: The Influence of Tuning and Interval on Consciousness</u>, Inner Traditions: VT, 1943. Pg. 42.

[227] According to musicologist Van Aalst in 1884. Tame, David. *Op. Cit.*, Pg. 58.

[228] Danielou, Alain. <u>Music and the Power of Sound: The Influence of Tuning and Interval on Consciousness</u>, Inner Traditions: VT, 1943, Pg. 2. Quoted by Preau in 1932 from the second century BC.

Disciples of Confucius were taught to gauge harmony within sounds. In an example, a pupil visited a distant village to determine what state the community was in. At sunrise, the student walked to the village center, sat, closed his eyes and listened until after sunset. The apprentice soaked in sounds of the village. He listened to the sounds of children laughing and playing, mothers speaking, merchants shouting, people arguing, the movement of materials, the sound of equipment being used in foundries, the sound of the wind and the background sounds. Like a doctor taking the pulse on the wrist of a patient, the pupil diagnosed the energetic pulse of the village and knew if famine was close, if rebellion was brewing. He could determine if chaos or harmony would prevail within weeks or months.

Danielou credited the Chinese with musically balancing energy to create harmony in the world.[229] The Chinese did not have the passionate desire for union (with God) that haunted the Indians. They strove to maintain order and harmony on Earth by harmonizing all things with appropriate sounds. "Music can express the accord of Heaven and Earth... and produces harmony between men and spirits."[230]

Listening to One Tone

The Chinese understood that sound energies combine. To illustrate this idea, Confucius recited a verse and then struck a percussive instrument to "receive the tone and transmit it to the following word."[231] The instrument's sound vibrations literally combine with the sound waves of the word and subtly fill the air until the next word is spoken. The silence after notes creates a variety of subtle feelings. Ancient listeners noticed and appreciated these fine details.

Today, who would listen to just one tone and marvel at its beauty? How boring. Yet when playing one tone, the Chinese made endless subtle variations that we would not appreciate. In the duration of *mere seconds,* the Chinese prescribed a multitude of volume and speed variations in vibrato. (Vibrato is created by

[229] Danielou, Alain. *Op. Cit.*, Pg. 123.
[230] Zu Xiaosun, quoted by Courant and Danielou, Alain. *Op. Cit.*, Pg. 30.
[231] Sachs, Curt. *Op. Cit.*, Pg. 108.

fluctuating a tone up and down a tiny bit.) Ancient Chinese music dictated fast vibrato – then slower, slower still and then none… all this in a second or two. The ancients documented 26 variations in the rate, volume and pitch of a vibrato. Today we employ one. We are conscious of only one.

The Chinese created subtle differences within a single tone in many ways. The same pitch can be created on different strings. The timber sounds different on each string due to its thickness and the material the string is made of. They dictated which string a note was to be played on, controlling subtle tonal color. They also prescribed lightly or firmly placing your finger on the strings, creating an airy or solid feeling. Finally, which finger was used to pluck a string created another subtle variation of strumming sounds.

Ancient people perceived subtleness within a tone that today we would never notice. The listener and musician were "in the zone" to notice such minute detail. By focusing on extremely fine effects, they refined and mastered their perception of subtle energy, which was most useful in many contexts.

The Musical Number

In Chinese music each note (a *lu*) and its neighboring note create the interval of a *fifth*. An open string and a note, *five* notes away, create an interval called a perfect *fifth*, a 3/2 ratio. (The upper note makes three vibrations in the same amount of time that the lower note makes two.) Notes in the Chinese scales were created by using the ratio of 3/2 between notes.

The ancient Chinese music had a predominant numeric pattern, based on the number **five.** This is consistent with their high regard of the number five: They identified five elements, five "seasons" of the year, five major colors, five planets and five directions on their maps (including center). The main Chinese scale was composed of *five* notes corresponding to these things. Another, more intricate scale, used twelve notes generated by the frequency of sequential musical *fifths*.

Patterns of fives are found many places in nature. A host of plant leaves create a pentagram–type shape. Countless flowers have five petals. Humans have five fingers and toes; we have five senses. There are five seeds in a dissected apple. A sand dollar has the same pattern. The presence of five in nature is pervasive.

Rudolf Steiner taught that listening to music created by *"fives"* stimulates the imagination.[232] In numerology, the energy of five – the most flexible of numbers – correlates to creativity, conflict, challenge, desire, obstacles, bridges and adaption, being upbeat, inspirational and a good communicator. People with the energy of five are dynamic, persuasive, inspirational, friendly, upbeat, adaptable, versatile, curious, courageous, bright and quick–witted.
[233, 234]

---

[232] Godwin, Joscelyn. Cosmic Music: Musical Keys to the Interpretation of Reality, Inner Traditions: VT, 1989, Pgs. 183–185.

[233] http://www.spiritual–numerology.com/numerology–number–meaning/numerology–meaning–of–number–5.html

[234] Difficulties associated with the energy of five are committing to just one relationship and difficulties finishing projects, impatience, restless, easily distracted, impulsive, lack of discipline and overindulgence in sensual pleasures.

The Number Five in Crop Circles[235]

Musical Scales

A scale is a "set" of notes that increase in pitch (frequency).
When you reach the end of the scale you arrive (musically) at the
next octave – which is now the original note in the scale raised up
by a factor of two. Today we only use one scale in music, but that
was not true in ancient times. In antiquity people never heard
music in the common scale of today. There can be thousands of
different possible notes in some octaves, yet scales usually select
only a handful – typically five to eight – of notes and exclusively
use them in songs. In a similar way, you may color an amazing
picture using only the few colored crayons available in a particular
box. Different pallets have different colors and numbers of colors
to select from. Music can be thought of as a numbering system –
where you count the cycles–per–second of a note (frequency). In

---

[235] Used with permission – thanks to Peter Sorensen
http://cropcircleconnector.com/Sorensen/circles/1999/main.html

antiquity, scales were made from number patterns that correlated to pitches. Ancient scales generally used two methods to select pitches.

A. The Up and Down Principle

The up and down principle, started with selecting a tone, in the easy speaking range. The second tone in the scale was perhaps set five notes higher, that is, an interval of five notes. The third note was created by raising the pitch up five more notes and then down four notes. This "up five–down four" interval pattern was repeated to create more notes to fill out the scale. Intuitively, one would question – rather than go up five notes and then down four – why not just go up one note? Ancient sages created scales to form number patterns, so the mathematics showing their signature number was important to them. There were several variations of the up–and–down principle, but the basic idea remained the same. The distance between whole notes created by a pattern of up–five–notes–then–down–four, creates a ratio of 9/8. A scale with a ratio of 9/8 between tones later became known as Pentatonic Tuning.

B. The Divisive Method

For string, woodwind or brass instruments – a different method was often used to create notes. The first note is created by plucking a string on an instrument. Shortening this string (or length of a string instrument) to one–half, one–third and one–fourth of its original length, created new tones that were used in the scale. When combined with the initial string length/tone, intervals of an octave, a fifth and a fourth were created. Musicians logically continued this process and divided the string into a 1/5 ratio (producing a major third), a 1/6 ratio (producing a minor third) and so on. This process is called the *divisive* principle.

Scales created by both systems shared the same notes for the octave, fourth and the fifth intervals. Other scale notes were different. For example, with the divisive method, the third scale note was deeper in pitch than the third note of the up–and–down scale. Further, the distance between the divisive semitones was different than the distance between semitones made by the up–and–down system.

The five note Chinese scale (F, G, A, C, D) was often used in pentatonic modes[236] and songs. The key of F was the most common scale, as the key of C is today.[237] Half–tones and the notes E and B were rarely used.[238] (Both E and B create a half note if added to the scale.) Pentatonic music[239] lacked dissonant intervals between pitches so any notes may be played in any order or combination without clashing. This is the reason Chinese music is so harmonious.

In another method of scale creation, the first note was the *kung*. The Chinese musicians moved up five notes (or a musical fifth) to get the next note. This process was repeated 12 times to form a twelve note scale. The higher notes were above human singing capabilities. These high pitched notes, were lowered by octaves, into the appropriate range for singing ease. This created a 12 note scale which the Chinese related to the 12 months of the year and also to the 12 zodiac signs in astrology. Each note, or *lu*, harmonized the energy that occurred during one of the 12 months and 12 constellations.

The Chinese felt that the energy of the number five was critical for the country's stability. Many songs/modes allowed only five notes, corresponding to the five elements that described all possible energies. They would use the number five over and over again to establish this energy and stability. In another scale, the Chinese started with a note and counted up five possible notes – to get the next note, which they selected for the scale. In a similar process, as described in the paragraph above, they went up 5 notes to select a scale note, but instead of doing this 12 times as above, they did it 60 times. Their reasoning was that there are 12 half notes in some scales and they wanted to incorporate the number five in the musical system, $12 \times 5 = 60$. All 60 tones were transposed down

---

[236] There are no minor seconds, major sevenths or any tri–tones in a pentatonic scale. http://en.wikipedia.org/wiki/Pentatonic_scale.

[237] Engel, Carl. The Most Ancient Nations: Assyrians, Egyptians and Hebrews with Special Reference to Recent Discoveries in Western Asia and in Egypt, Murray: London, 1864, Pg. 143.

[238] Engel, Carl. *Op. Cit.*, Pg. 125.

[239] A pentatonic scale is a musical scale with five notes per octave, in contrast to a heptatonic (seven note) scale, such as the major scale and minor scale. Pentatonic scales are very common and are found all over the world. Pentatonic scales, without semitones, and lacked dissonant intervals; there are neither any semitones nor any tri–tones.

into singing range; this required highly discriminating hearing on the part of the musician, to play such tiny pitch differences. In comparison, we currently use 12 notes (7 whole notes and 5 half notes), not 60, in the span of our octave.

Think of other uses of these same numbers: the length of a day, division of a year into 12 months, the relationships between the hour – the minute and seconds. Perhaps this is the origin of 12 months in a year, 12 hours of daylight and 12 hours of night in a day (at equinox), 60 minutes in an hour and 60 seconds in a minute.

Pentatonic guitar chords fit together like pieces of a puzzle.

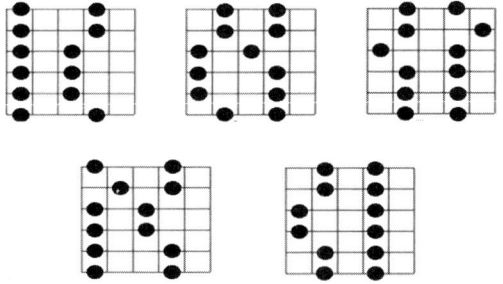

The chord patterns of a pentatonic scale for the guitar contain an intriguing pattern. Each graph above represents a musical instrument's frets and strings. The dots represent finger positions or notes that have been dampened. This finger pattern creates pentatonic chords.

If you were to create shapes from each pentatonic chord by coloring in between the dots, then the shapes could be interlocking puzzle pieces. The second chord's shape could be moved to the left to fit into the first chord's shape. The third chord's shape could slide perfectly into the second chord's shape and so on.

The Chinese deeply felt the energy of each day and experimented listening to all possible notes – to select ones that balanced and harmonized their feelings. They discovered that balancing notes were also subtly louder (without the musician making a louder note), confirming their selection. These daily frequencies were prescribed to be used by musicians on the corresponding day.

As we have seen in the Sumer chapter, ancient mathematical skills were surprisingly sophisticated thousands of years before Christ. The Chinese wrestled with minute mathematical discrepancies when taking music up many octaves. To create an octave, one doubles the cycles per second of a note, and a note that is an octave higher is produced. Both notes sound the same, except that one is higher or lower. For example, one might play a high or low musical note C and both sound like the same note. This process worked going up a handful of octaves, but as one went up about 12 octaves the rule no longer worked. To make the new octave note sound like the ones below it, one had to double the cycles per second of sound and then add a cycle or a fraction of a cycle to make the note harmonious. This was disturbing to ancient sages. Recall that the Sumerians worshiped gods as whole number ratios, not complex fractions. Ancient sages wanted their math to include whole numbers and be consistent. Today, this extra wavelength is called the Pythagorean comma. Long before Pythagoras was born, the Chinese calculated the frequency of the comma and then tried unsuccessfully to balance this messy math.[240] Pythagoras also correctly observed and defined the comma, but was equally disturbed that it reflected minute fractions rather than whole numbers.

Sound vibrations – above or below our hearing range – were believed to express in other forms. The ancient Chinese believed energy transferred through octaves, even when the vibration went up so high or low that it left the range of sound and entered the spectrum of light, taste, smell or other unseen vibrations.[241] A quote from *Theosophy* magazine stated, "The priests of ancient nations understood the secret power of music not only upon the human spirit, but as well upon the health of the body. They understood, perhaps the vibrations constituting the notes of the musical scale are strictly analogous to the scale of chemical elements and color."[242]

---

[240] Nakeseko, Kazu. "Symbolism in Ancient Chinese Music Theory," Duke University Press: *Journal of Music Theory*, Vol.1, No. 2, Nov. 1957, Pgs. 147–180.
[241] Danileou, Alain. *Op. Cit.*, Pg. 43.
[242] *Theosophy,* Vol. 42, No. 4, February, 1954, Pgs. 175–179.

Sharry Edwards, Inventor of BioAcoustics, defined emotions associated with pitches. When an ancient culture created music primarily in one key (such as C or F), then the culture exhibited the emotional qualities associated with those musical notes.

www.JillsWingsOfLight.com – Art Galleries

144

Emotions and Pitches[243]
By Sharry Edwards

- C - Self power, ego, self-directed, leader, physically motivated, difficulty self-directing and self-empowerment issues
- C# - Champion of justice, fair play, stubborn, secretly hard on self, hard on others as a cover and can be defensively sarcastic
- D - Self approval, expects reciprocation, caretaker, organizes, lacks self-approval, complains, analyzes and fixes people/things/issues
- D# - Information brokers, difficulty sharing emotions
- E - Self approval issues, uses words first to convey messages and meanings, likes to be appreciated, self-sabotages and needs to be needed
- F - Planner, sees flaws in the plans of others, procrastinates or is a workaholic, difficulty integrating perceptions and actions
- F# - One who carries out plans, works on unimportant things, doer, intuitive about the needs of others, shares and loves wholeheartedly, avoids important tasks or ignores everything
- G - Game player, likes to mix and manage the physical aspects of life, has problems prioritizing physical issues, motivated by future events and easily depressed
- G# - Wants to make a difference, likes to help and satisfy others, spreads self too thin, lack of confidence, hands on, time conscious and sways from egotistical to lack of self-esteem
- A - Spiritual, takes care of the needs of others, has problems prioritizing non-physical issues and tends to rely on what they think you mean (acts from within self)
- A# - Highly intuitive, others are more important, give a great deal physically and emotionally, likes mental games and is hurt easily
- B - Link between self and universe, martyr, needs harmony and balance, think they deserve things but do not know how to get it without appearing selfish

---

[243] www.nanovoice.org

When a population tuned to a specific note, people exhibited characteristic emotions as described in the chart above, *Emotions and Pitches.*

Chinese Music

How would ancient Chinese music sound? Many liken it to the distinct pleasant effect of exclusively playing the black keys on a piano. Groups of notes, used in songs, created sounds similar to major and minor chords, but generally avoided half notes.

Musicologist Curt Sachs described Far Eastern music differently. He agreed the musical pitches were easy to listen to, but the quality of singing was so unusual that people in the West disliked the Eastern music. Even though the music only used pleasant intervals, the singing was nasal, compressed, explosive, high pitched, often ventriloquist–like and full of glissando.[244]

According to Lois Elson, those rare people who heard ancient Chinese singing described it as "most torturing." The nose and throat created droning and hideous sounds. Likewise, the Chinese who were accustomed to their own music found Western, classical music disturbing. They politely noted, "Our melodies were not made for your ears, or your ears for our melodies."[245]

Resonance

Resonance is illustrated with this example: Two violins – in close proximity – are tuned exactly the same. As a string on the first violin is played, a field of sound energy is produced, that triggers the other violin's matching string. The matching string on the untouched violin vibrates, producing the same frequency as the plucked string, without being struck.

When exposed to a multitude of frequencies, an energy system singles out those that are resonant. The matching string absorbs energy. It is as if wormholes transfer energy to the same frequency wave in a nearby location. When the string's fundamental frequency is exposed to the same vibration – the string receives energy. *Resonance occurs when a system absorbs energy.*
Resonance not only occurs with two notes of the same pitch, but with octaves and certain intervals.

---

[244] Danileou, Alain. *Op. Cit.*, Pg. 137.
[245] Elson, Lousi. *Op. Cit.*, Pg. 74.

Rhythm did not command a major role in ancient Chinese music. Sachs believed that most percussive instruments in ancient China kept time, rather than creating elaborate rhythmic patterns.[246]

Ancient Chinese music had no place for staccato, accelerando, crescendos or anything that aroused passion and unrest. Emotions were stirred with single sounds, rather than melodies. Even today, oriental flute players are expected to enliven a single tone with interesting vibrato.

A Chinese melody could be shared by different instruments; one instrument may sound the first note and another instrument create the second one. Yet, a third musical device produces the next note of the melody. This practice was said to expand the mind. I have personally used this technique in my music; it produces a sublime feeling.

Similar to what we learned in the chapter on Atlantis, the position of the musician and the direction of the sound were crucial. Instruments associated with the direction west would be located in the western portion of an orchestra, while instruments associated with the south were located in the southern area of the musical ensemble. Instruments that resembled a "tattooed box" – that was struck by a wooden mallet decorated with special symbols, were situated at the corners of musical ensembles. An instrument was northeast of the musicians and played at the beginning of the music. It used a mallet that had a *tchu*, or owl symbol, which evoked profound moral concepts. Another "box", used as an instrument, was placed in the northwest corner of the musical ensemble. This instrument had the stamped symbol of a sleeping tiger, representing man's power over other creatures. This decorated box had six pegs that each created tones when struck. It was used at the close of a musical piece. When playing one of the symbolic instruments, the musician experienced the energy that it represented. For example, one musician felt like a powerful sleeping tiger, adding this energy to the musical mix.

The Chinese music revealed the "wisdom of the heart." The meaning of words and the speaker's intent were interchangeable

---

[246] Sachs, Curt. *Op. Cit.*, Pg. 138.

with musical sounds. The energy of the musician was absorbed into his music. A musical performance radiated the musician's degree of honor and connection to the Divine. The playing of an instrument was often associated with meditation – it was a prayer and the silent repose within one's heart.

According to legend, Master Wen of Cheng was unwilling to express tones on the zither until his "heart was prepared." Music would display his heart energy along with the instrumental sounds. He would not play a note until he perfected his own energy.

After Wen refined his internal energy, he played the instrument for his master and reportedly:

- When he plucked the *shang* string and the eighth semitone, a cool wind sprang up and the trees bore fruit.
- During autumn he strummed the *chiao* string and the second semitone. A gentle breeze arose and the shrubs showed their splendor.
- When it was summer he plucked the *Yu* string and the eleventh semitone and it then snowed and the rivers froze.
- At winter time he plucked the *chih* string and the fifth semitone. The sun came out and the ice melted under the warmth.
- At last, he played the *kung* string with the other four strings. The weather tuned immeasurably beautiful in the newness of spring.[247]

The forces of music, nature and the heart (the energy of one's values and feelings) are connected. Modern author, Victor Wooten, echoed this theme. "Music and Nature are the same thing and it is in everyone's best interest to become their ally."[248]

Musical vibrations were believed to affect people's emotions, morals, habits and physical health. One ancient Chinese writer advised that singing strengthened the spine. Another taught that a special type of singing cleared the eyes and ears, while balancing blood and vital energies. Mental and physical sickness were

---

[247] Danileou, Alain. *Op. Cit.*, Pg. 107.
[248] Wooten, Victor. The Music Lesson: A Spiritual Search for Growth through Music, Berkley Books, NY, 2006. Pg.112.

considered musical problems, as if the person had lost his inner harmony.

Musical Instruments

It is believed that one of the early emperors invented eight kinds of instruments, grouped by energy or activity:

1. Love the people
2. The black bird
3. Preserve the trees
4. Cultivate the eight different grains
5. Chant the celestial doctrines
6. Celebrate the merit of the sovereign
7. Imitate the virtues of the Earth
8. Recall the memory of all existing things

Again and again, music is associated with an energy or consciousness.

The ancient Chinese enjoyed hundreds of instruments. Throughout thousands of years, royal courts exchanged gifts of musicians with other countries. By receiving gifts from other countries, a variety of new instruments were introduced into China. Some important Chinese instruments included:

- The *zither* had strings representing the elemental energies and a string sounding the *kung*.
- There were 12 varieties of pipes, mouth organs and bells. Percussion sounds came from tapping and rubbing stones.
- The musical instrument called the *sheng* had 24 pipes with one *yin* and *yang* pipe for each of the twelve months or zodiac signs.
- The *cheun* instrument used thirteen strings with twelve strings devoted to the zodiac signs and one for the *kung*.[249]

The Chinese divided their instruments into eight groups according to material of composition:

- Tanned skins (drums)
- Stone

---

[249] Thirteen in antiquity did not denote a misfortunate number, but the sum of twelve attributes of God.

- Metal (similar to choir bells, not big church bells)
- Baked clay (whistles)
- Silk (used for strings)
- Wood (percussion instruments)
- Bamboos (used for flutes and pan pipes)
- Gourds

A Modern Fretless Zither [250]

The Chinese observed that some stones created pleasing musical sounds when struck with hard wooden mallets. Named *kings,* these stones were grouped according to mineral types and appearance. Their value increased if a set consisted of stones of the same color and composition. If the set of stones included five colors and produced "balanced energy," their value rose. The Chinese claimed that the stones produced sounds that blended beautifully with the human voice. Confucius experienced "ecstatic bliss" when he heard the stones for the first time. [251]

Sometimes instruments were equated with a special purpose. A large bell at court announced that someone had a complaint; a drum was used for national communications, a small bell for small business, a tam–tam for an individual misfortune and a tambourine announced when a crime was to be appealed. [252] This tradition has

[250] http://en.wikipedia.org/wiki/Zither
[251] Elson, Louis. *Op. Cit.*, Pg. 78.
[252] Elson, Louis. *Op. Cit.*, Pg. 67.

its roots in the time of Yu the Great – founder of the first Dynasty about 2200 BC.

Yin and *Yang*

The ancient Chinese classified energy into two opposing forces: *yin* and *yang*, such as life and death, male and female, and black and white. Associating a tone with masculine or feminine seems strange, but such differences are easily perceived in male and female voices. The singing of *yin* or *yang* is clearly evident with birds, as the male creates special sounds to woo the females.

Nature was always the inspiration for the Chinese musical system. For example, various reed pitch pipes were fashioned to sound like the male and female sounds of the phoenix – creating *yin* and *yang* sounds. The male bird sang ascending notes and the female voiced descending tones. To match these unique complimentary sounds, the Chinese used vocals in descending scales, while playing instrumental ascending scales. Music replicated the "songs of Mother Earth."

Yin and *yang* notes were measured from the original *kung*. If you play a C and move five Western notes above, a G is produced, which creates an interval of a fifth. By counting four descending notes from C, a G is obtained, creating an interval of a fourth. The relationship of 3/2 or going up a fifth makes a *yin* sound. Progressing down a fourth, a 4/3 interval, creates a *yang* feeling. Depending on the intervals between notes, they become either *yin* or *yang*.

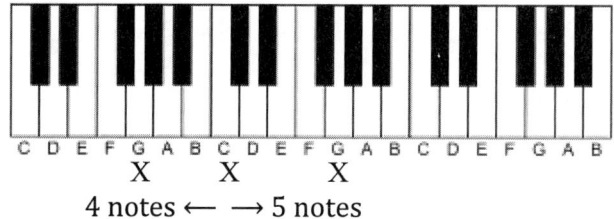

4 notes ← → 5 notes

**Moving *up* to G from C
produces an Interval of a Musical Fifth,
while going *down* from C to to G
produces an Interval of a Fourth.**

It is easier to imagine the opposite energetic feelings of tones by visualizing them in a zigzag pattern rather than a straight line.

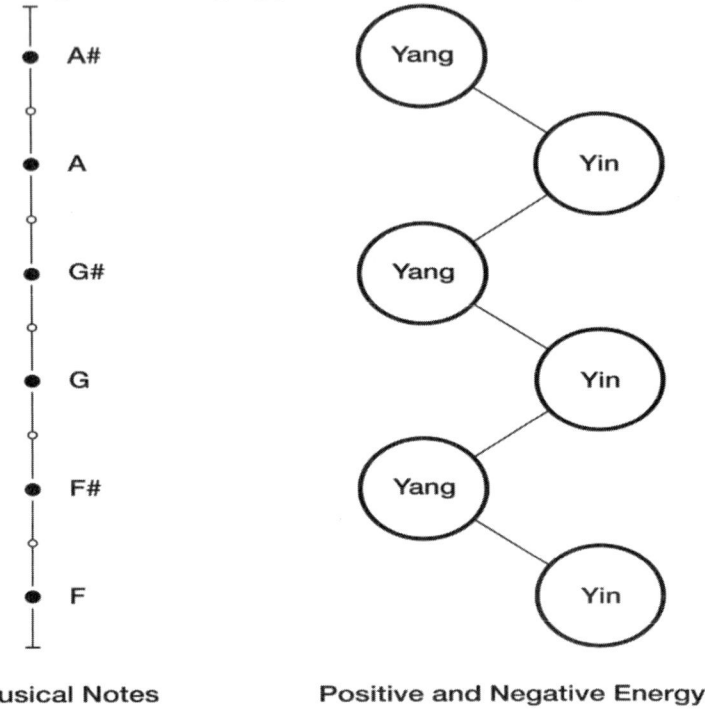

Musical Notes   Positive and Negative Energy

Chinese assignment of Yin and Yang within a Musical Scale

The Chinese believed that neighboring notes create feelings that seem to oppose each other. Likewise, a major (happy or "up" sounding chord) feels the opposite of a minor chord ("downward" or sad sounding). The difference between these two musical patterns is just one half–note, but it makes a dramatic shift in the mood of the chord.

In Ancient China it was widely accepted that energy empowered certain tones during specific time periods. The environmental energies, at certain times, transferred subtle energy to select scale tones within a twelve note chromatic scale configuration. Six notes were considered *yin* and six were considered *yang*. The scale's sequential notes were alternately considered masculine and feminine, representing the *yin* and *yang*.

152

Each Chinese musical selection was classified as *yin* or *yang*. Today people notice gender feelings in distinctive musical selections. For example, *The Star Spangled Banner* is perceived as *yang* or masculine, while *Silent Night* sounds *yin* or feminine.

The Chinese understood duality; our world is full of love and joy – and also sorrow and hatred. Rather than seeking only positive feelings, they sought balance and harmony. One method to achieve this was to listen to balanced *yin* and *yang* sounds in music.

Musical Astrology

Astrology was an integral part of ancient cultures. Just as all early civilizations believed in the mystical – they also believed in the power of the heavens. At its essence, astrology is created by celestial frequencies. According to David Tame, astrology began in ancient times via fascination with the cosmic tone (*kung*).[253]

The Chinese carefully observed that a particular tone expressed easier, louder and more beautifully during a certain time of the year. That tone became associated with that season. The *kung* and its octave were divided into twelve lesser tones. Each tone was a divine aspect of the master tone. Each of the 12 scale tones was associated with a zodiac sign, because it balanced the prominent subtle feelings during a particular zodiac time of year.

Danielou described the ancient links between music and astrology: "The Chinese scale of fifths reflects astrological correspondences and terrestrial influx, provided one knows the hierarchy of its intervals. In ancient times Zheng Xuan details, 'In the same melody, the prime, the third, the fifth, the sixth (notes of the scale), are chosen independently because of their connection with diverse constellations and consequently, with heavenly spirits, Earthly spirits and manes.'"[254]

By changing the energy of the primary note of a song, the Chinese captured the desired energy.[255] For example, when a sacrifice was

---

[253] Tame, David. *Op. Cit.*, Pg. 37.
[254] Zheng Xuan, quoted by Courant. Danielou, Alain. <u>Music and the Power of Sound: The Influence of Tuning and Interval on Consciousness</u>, Inner Traditions: VT, 1943, Pg. 37.
[255] Listen to this at Ancient-Music.com

made to the heavens, the Chinese used melodies with a scale beginning on the *kung* and with the most predominant note as the *kung*. When the sacrifices were dedicated to Earth, the melody was transposed a fifth higher; a second interval higher was used for the sun and a sixth interval higher for the moon.[256]

Planets moving in an orbit create vibrations (celestial frequencies), which can be described as astrological influences. The waves of celestial movements interact with the vibrations within our bodies. In this way, we are connected to the stars. Ancient leaders perceived celestial energy by focusing on a star and sensing subtle changes in their feelings. In this way, they connected the stars and their feelings. This is an elegant example showing how everything in the universe has a vibratory nature – and helps us appreciate the special role of music – pure vibration, able to access divine energies.

www.JillsWingsofLight.com – Art Galleries

---

[256] Sachs, Curt. *Op. Cit.*, Pg. 122.

154

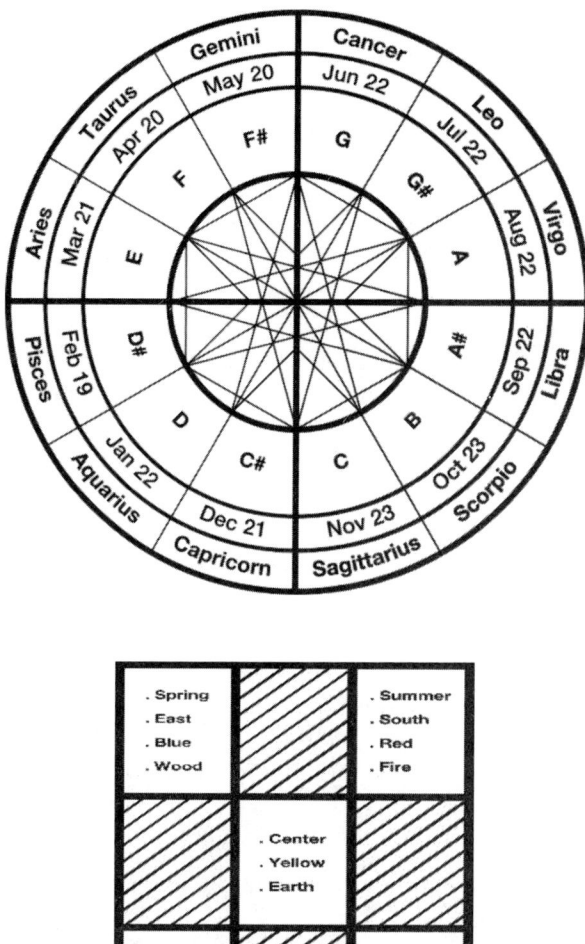

Ancient Astrological & Tonal Correlations[257]

Music and Other Relationships

Musicologist, Alain Danielou, depicted Chinese music as copying, combining and modifying energies found in nature. This elemental

---

[257] The ancient Chinese, if alive today, would alter these tones every 2,000 years as the stars in the zodiac move in space over time.

musical practice was not unique to China, but was used by musicians throughout the ancient world. Some of the best illustrations of this practice can be found in the Hindi histories. Danileou described Indian music that evoked the water element. He stated that although the Indian rain mode, "Megh–Mallar," does not sound like rain or thunder, one can feel rain in the air when it is played.[258] The famous Indian teacher, Paramahansa Yogananda, reported that Tan Sen, a Hindu musician, quenched fire by the power of his song.[259] CNN, (USA based news station), showed videos of fire extinguishers using only a subwoofer sound.[260] In a final example, Jesus walked on water – demonstrating mastery of the water element. The ancient Masters from China and around the ancient world, used sounds – not only to harmonize with elemental energy – but to control it.

The elements (wood, fire, Earth, metal and water) represent movement of energy. One energy either stimulates or diminishes another. For example, water puts out a fire, essentially "diminishing fire." Fire stimulates Earth; Earth augments metal, which builds water, which stimulates wood and this strengthens fire. One elemental order maintained the status quo and the other represented change. See the chart, *The Chinese Elements*.

www.JillsWingsofLight.com – Art Galleries

---

[258] Danielou, Alain. *Op. Cit.*, Pg. 123.
[259] Crowley, Brian & Esther. <u>Words of Power; Sacred Sounds of East &West</u>, Llewellyn Publications: Minn., 1991, Pg. 6.
[260] http://www.kulr8.com/story/28673486/new–fire–extinguisher–uses–sound–waves–to–put–out–flames

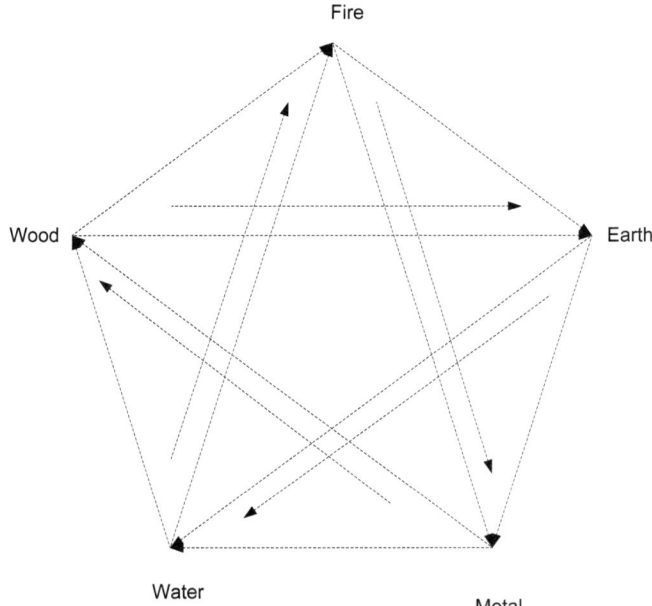

The outer arrows represent the creation cycle (water creates wood, that
is water energy has a tendency to transform into wood energy).
The inner arrows represents the control cycle (water controls fire, that is
water energy moderates fire energy).

Chinese Elemental Correspondences

Elemental energy was linked to musical pitches. The elements and
associated musical pitches were assigned numbers, creating
mathematical relationships between the elements and music.

Elemental Correspondences, Notes & Numbers[261]					
Element	Wood	Fire	Earth	Metal	Water
Pitch	F#	A	D	E	B
Number	3 & 8	2 & 7	5	4 & 9	1 & 6

[261] Nakeseko, Kazu. "Symbolism in Ancient Chinese Music Theory," Duke University
Press: *Journal of Music Theory*, Vol.1, No. 2, Nov. 1957, Pgs. 147–180.

As we have seen repeatedly, the Chinese correlated music with many aspects of life, such as the seasons, elements, directions, planets, colors and weather conditions. To illustrate, bells were associated with the direction west, autumn and metal. Percussion instruments represented north, winter and water. Each musical sound balanced the energy associated with it.

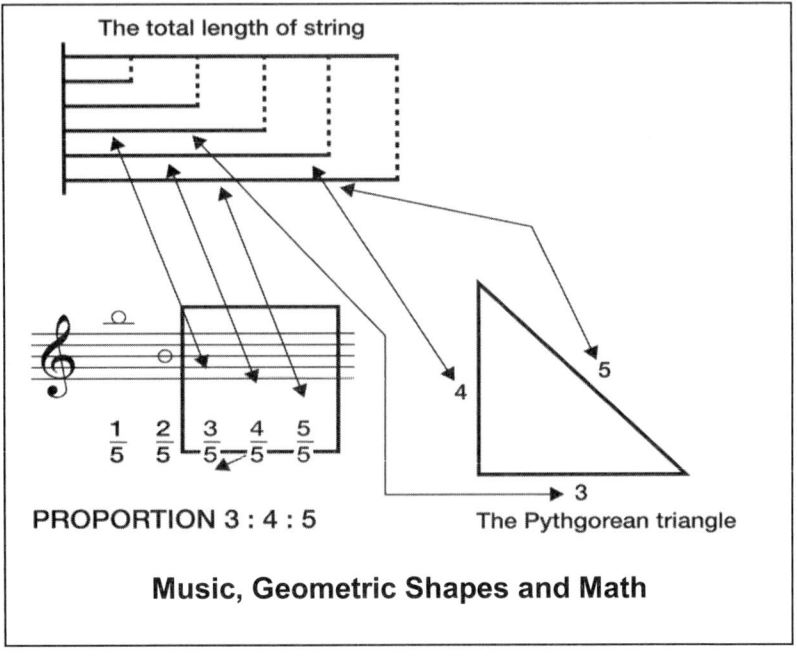

Music, Geometric Shapes and Math

Ancient people were sophisticated in varying their musical pitches for different energies – the ancient levitical singers at the Hebrew Temple had a "floating" tuning pitch. That is, the tuning pitch varied with the local air pressure, temperature and humidity.[262]

[262] http://musicofthebiblerevealed.wordpress.com/2014/03/03/what–was–ancient–israels–tonic–pitch–part–01/

A Multitude of Chinese Correspondences

Seasons	Spring	Summer	Center	Autumn	Winter
Instruments	Zither, lute	Gourd, mouth organ		Bells	Stones (percussion)
Notes[263]	E, F, F#	G, G#	A	A#, B, C	C#, D, D#
Notes of the Scale[264]	Third note of the scale	Fifth note of the scale	First note of the scale	Second note of the scale	Sixth note of the scale
Elements	Wood	Fire	Center of Earth	Metal	Water
Months[265]	1, 2, 3	4, 5	6	7, 8, 9	10, 11, 12
Colors[266]	Blue	Red	Yellow	White	black
Directions[267]	East	South	Center	West	North
Planets[268]	Jupiter	Mars	Saturn	Venus	Mercury

Musicologist, Rene Guenon, wrote that music was written to mirror cyclic patterns, such as seasons or astrological energy.[269] The first note of the scale changed each month, but the melodies remained the same. Different instruments were exclusively used during appropriate seasons and star alignments. This practice balanced China's energy, helping the people overcome challenging subtle energy, created by nature and by the heavens.

---

[263] Danielou, Alain. *Op. Cit.*, Pg. 52.

[264] Danielou, Alain. *Ibid,* Pg. 54.

[265] Nakeseko, Kazu. "Symbolism in Ancient Chinese Music Theory," Duke University Press: *Journal of Music Theory*, Vol.1, No. 2, Nov. 1957, Pgs. 147–180.

[266] From Grove's Dictionary of Music and Musicians (1954 edition).

[267] Danielou, Alain. *Op. Cit.*, Pg. 52.

[268] Sachs, Curt. *Op. Cit.*, Pg. 121.

[269] Danielou, Alain. *Op. Cit.*, Pg. 9.

Instruments made from natural materials (skins, wood, stones and reeds) not only mimicked the sounds of nature, but emphasized certain musical harmonics. Different instruments were exclusively played at certain times, further engineering the balancing effect of harmonics.[270] Wooden, metal, reed or percussive instruments sounded acoustically purer and louder during specific times and conditions (rain or dry, cold or hot). Instruments were subsequently connected to these times.

Numbers intimately linked to music. Notes in a scale were numbered, such A = 1 and B = 2, and so on. The even numbered *lu* (*Lu* are Chinese musical notes.) were feminine and odd numbered notes are masculine. Y*ang* energy corresponded to the number one and yin energy to the number two.

Numbers were primarily considered energy and secondarily used for counting. Every interval has an associated emotional feeling. This emotion is a form of energy and is linked to numbers. Below are some numbers with their characteristic energies:

- One ~ The great source
- Two ~ Earth or feminine
- Three ~ Heaven
- Five ~ Heaven and Earth

One and *two* reflected *yin* and *yang* energy, but *three* held these two elements together. Likewise, a coin has two sides, but the edge connects the two halves. In this way, a coin has three sides, a "trinity," composed of positive, negative and neutral energies.

Sounds have long been used by indigenous tribes to create sacred space, and uplift the subtle feelings of an area. Singing the proper sound – in the appropriate direction – creates sublime energy. Ancient people associated sounds with the directions on the compass, such as:

- East ~ eee   Associated with the Spiritual body
- South ~ aye   Emotional Body

---

[270] "According to the Chinese Five Element Theory, the root of Chinese acupuncture, five elements compose nature and human beings. These five elements are wood, fire, Earth, metal and water. Each resonates with a season, chakra and one of the eight extra–ordinary meridians." Tama-do.com, Fabien Maman.

- West ~ uuu   Physical Body
- North ~ ooo   Mental Body

The Chinese associated music and tone with concepts such as morality and noble virtue. The scale notes relate to virtues such as benevolence, righteousness, propriety, knowledge and faith. In a striking modern day analogy, Sharry Edwards[271] has developed a personality profiler comparing voice tones and character traits.

Chinese music was associated with one's soul. Towards the end of their lives, Confucius and his followers wandered in extreme poverty and starvation. One disciple asked how they could sing when famished. Confucius replied, "The wise man seeks, by music, to strengthen the weakness of his soul."[272]

Large Orchestras

Orchestras were sound bridges between the macrocosm and the microcosm. Lower pitches (within our hearing range) belonged to Earth. Tones played much higher than we can hear, the Music of the Spheres, were believed to be created by angels and gods. Energy travels on the waves of sound among the realms of the gods, our ancestors and the living. For example, Kwei, Emperor Shun's chief musician, played the stones to summon ancestors who had passed on.[273]

Every note made on Earth invoked a tiny bit of cosmic energy. Higher octaves of a note were believed to reach the realms of Heaven. Each musical note connected the country with the divine. Since each musician could "download" a little bit of divine energy, huge orchestras were assembled to amass this powerful energy. The huge Asiatic chorus sang the same notes in unison. The ancient book, *Yellow Bell,*[274] described sympathetic resonance and the underpinnings of the arcane idea, "so as above, so below." When celestial music was heard on Earth, it uplifted its listeners.

---

[271] nanovoice.org
[272] Elson, Lousi. *Op. Cit.*, Pg. 68.
[273] Medhurst, W. H. The Shoo King, Shanghai, 1846, Pgs. 10, 33. Translated by Walter Gorn Old, London, 1904, Pgs. 20, 46.
[274] Yellow symbolizes wisdom.

Celestial music transferred powerful healing energy from heaven to Earth.

The size of the orchestra also displayed the power and rank of its owner. In the Chou Dynasty (1122–1255 BC), the emperor sponsored laws to limit the number of musicians that lesser dignitaries could retain. High dignitaries had a maximum threshold of only 27 musicians, while the ordinary noble man was capped at a maximum of fifteen musicians. There were also restrictions on the physical arrangement of performing musicians. The higher noblemen were allowed to arrange their musicians in a square shape, while the ordinary nobleman could only place his musicians in a straight line. When an emperor conquered a territory, a large standing orchestra was established in the new land, to anchor the emperor's influence and power.[275]

Reportedly, ancient Chinese concerts were orchestrated with as many as 10,000 participants. Each performer's music captured a measure of divine energy, firmly anchoring the strength of the country. The more people involved, the greater the celestial energy that the dynasty invoked. Citizen participation in music developed and uplifted the society. This provided national strength and protection from without and within. Can you imagine the spectacle such a performance would be to all who experienced it?

The *Yellow Bell* claims, "In 110 BC... the Festival Orchestra boasted of more than ten thousand musicians that were divided into nine groups, playing simultaneously upon 300 different kinds of instruments."[276] In 58 to 75 AD the Han Dynasty described many orchestras: one for religious ceremonies, another for the archers, and one for banquets and the harem. There were 829 musicians in these groups plus an additional military band.[277] The T'ang dynasty in 618 – 907 AD boasted of fourteen orchestras, with each having 500 to 700 players. As late as 1897 in the Korean court, 772 musicians were employed.[278]

---

[275] Sachs, Curt. Op. Sit., pgs. 149–154.
[276] Yellow Bell, by Chao–mai–pa. Mulcahy, Pat. Esoteric Harmonics, Tuning to the Occult Scale of Sound, AstroQab Publications: 2009, Pg. 67.
[277] Sachs, Curt. *Op. Cit.*, Pg. 149.
[278] Sachs, Curt. *Ibid,* Pg. 150.

The idea of large powerful orchestras to access divine energy was wide spread in many cultures. During the reign of King David, from the *Bible,* there were four thousand musicians in the temple.[279] Jericho's city walls – that protected the Jews' enemies – tumbled after many musicians circled the city, playing for seven days[280] (playing the note G and/or performing in the key of G with musical fifth accompaniment).

The End of an Era

In 245 BC the emperor commanded all books written and revised by Confucius be burnt. Only works on agriculture were spared. A large number of people who hid books were put to death. All old musical instruments were destroyed and new instruments made according to the emperor's standards alone. Many of the ancient Chinese traditions were irretrievably lost at this time.[281]

Today, the ancient reverence regarding music in the Far East are forgotten by most. The popularity of orchestras has long declined in China, Japan and Korea.[282]

The final powerful Chinese dynasty, the Chi'ing Dynasty of 1644 –1912 AD, fell after the ancient traditional music was silenced. Western musicians became a permanent element of royal music, replacing the exclusive diet of the ancient Chinese music. David Tame observed that when destructive music appears in a society, it does so quickly, gaining widespread popularity in a decade or so, bringing swift changes in morals and lifestyles.[283]

Just as the long traditions of China were irrevocably lost at the start of the 20th century, the unique five–based music – that underpinned all that was China – was mostly silenced, probably forever.

---

[279] 1 Chron. Xxiii.5. Engel, Carl. The Most Ancient Nations: Assyrians, Egyptians and Hebrews with Special Reference to Recent Discoveries in Western Asia and in Egypt, Murray: London, 1864, Pg. 311.
[280] Hebrews 11:30
[281] Elson, Louis. *Op. Cit.*, Pg. 69.
[282] Sachs, Curt. The Rise of Music in the Ancient World, East and West, Dover Publications: Mineola, NY, 1943, Pg. 152.
[283] Tame, David. *Op. Cit.*, Pg. 189.

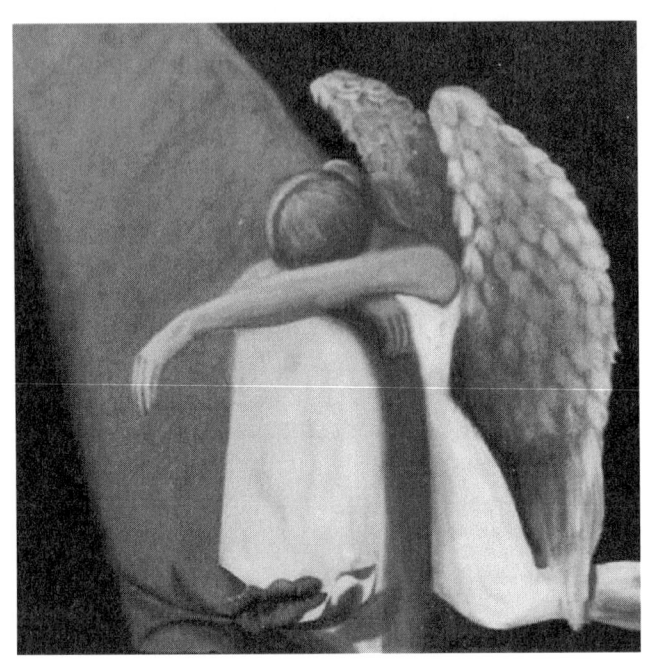

www.JillsWingsofLight.com – Art Galleries

Chapter Seven

Ancient Egyptian Music
3200 to 664 BC

Early Egyptians descended from various North African peoples that settled in the Nile Valley starting around 5000 BC. The primitive settlers were drawn to the land that became known as Egypt because of riches in: game, fish, stone, copper, gold and flax. Most important, was the fertile Nile plain that was enriched each year when the life–giving river overflowed its banks. The Egyptians were able to live comfortably with these plentiful resources, as evidenced by their ability to maintain a great civilization for thousands of years. The earliest Egyptian histories begin about 3200 BC with the Scorpion King who united the independent northern and southern kingdoms. The first dynasty was documented by the first Pharaoh, Menes/Narmer. Historians speculate that he also integrated the warring kingdoms of the north and south Nile Valley – this time through marriage. The kings of the southern kingdom, known as the White Kingdom, were recognized by their cylindrically shaped crowns. The kings of the northern territory, called the Red Kingdom, displayed a crown decorated with a curling cobra. When the two kingdoms combined, both shapes were merged into one crown.

The Egyptians wrote volumes of scrolls, comprehensively documenting Egyptian life. However, they were curiously silent on some important subjects, such as pyramid construction, the mummification process and details concerning their music. The secrecy that the Egyptians maintained for such critical areas doubly emphasizes the importance that they assigned to these things. Music, similar to the death rituals and monumental burial tombs (pyramids), was counted among the greatest secrets in

Egyptian society and was closely protected. The secrecy surrounding Egyptian music has long made it difficult to gain a deep understanding of it. Even more challenging, has been to trace how music evolved over the long tenure of a powerful nation. Only after intensive study has a clear picture of Egyptian music slowly crystallized. Archeological finds of musical instruments, which did not perish over thousands of years, provided some insight. However, drums and instruments constructed of "soft" materials have disintegrated by modern times.

There are other means to uncover ancient Egyptian musical secrets. Neighboring counties documented Egyptian musical practices, such as the Persians and the ancient Greeks. Some indigenous people of Egypt have long preserved ancient customs under a thin veil of Islam. Finally, musical customs are reflected in ancient Egypt's art, architecture, religion, healing practices and daily activities. We will explore all of these avenues to reach a thorough understanding of Egyptian music.

Music is Everywhere

Music was incorporated into almost every facet of Egyptian life. Music was used as a tool to enhance education, strengthen the fortitude of the army, obtain favor of the gods and much more. Music was used to strengthen everything the Egyptians deeply cared about. Today, knowledge and studies are separated into categories, such as biology or religion. Yet, the ancient Egyptians used music as a common denominator throughout many fields of knowledge. Music was a constant thread that bound all things together.

By the conclusion of this chapter, the prominent role played by music across all aspects of life – sculpting and maintaining harmonious subtle energy structures will be evident. Music, a potent form of subtle energy, was studied deeply by the Egyptians, particularly the sound patterns and rhythms of beautiful music. The mathematics underlying the music was studied and associated with an assortment of desirable things. These same mathematics, derived from harmonious music, were then used repeatedly in art, architecture, religion, hieroglyphs, dance and magic. Beautiful music was woven into all aspects of the Egyptian society.

Music was sophisticated, even in the early years. Hieroglyphs depict musical instruments 5,000 years ago and earlier.[284] Even as long ago as the first dynasties, huge musical ensembles performed concerts and royal family members were often musicians, enhancing the status of music.

In an example of using music in a way that we do not today, Egyptian children were taught songs with a certain "species" of music – established by the government – to aid learning hieroglyphs.[285] Perhaps singing "alphabet–like songs" made memorization easier. In addition to helping learning capabilities, music was used to mold a child's character. Certain sounds were thought to develop specific personality qualities. For example, calming music would encourage a peaceful nature. Children might learn different songs depending on their personalities, much like a Hindi guru gives a devotee a unique mantra today. The Greeks reported that the Egyptians took great care to guard the music their children listened to, insuring that they were exposed to pure and "good" music. No doubt the royal heirs to the crown listened to war–like music. The Egyptians were a fierce society that often made war against their neighbors. Victory in war was valued above all else in the Egyptian leaders.

Egyptologist, Moustafa Gadalla, documented ancient practices still used by the current indigenous people of Egypt. Gadalla reflected, "Maintaining harmony in the universe requires that the world in whole and parts, are all in tune. Therefore, the sound that man creates in music, singing or dancing (vibrating the body) can either strengthen or imperil the equilibrium of the world."[286] The proper music strengthened the Egyptian world. The stability of the society was maintained and the strength of the rulers was reinforced – evidenced by the long reign of Ancient Egypt. As we have seen – and will see repeatedly – music is integral to civilizations in a virtuous cycle. Powerful music that is fitting to, and characteristic of, a society helps build and maintain that society – which in turn

---

[284] Gadalla, Moustafa. Egyptian Harmony: The Visual Music, Tehuti Research Foundation: Greensboro, NC, 2000, Pg. 29.
[285] Heline, Corinne. Healing and Regeneration through Music, New Age Bible and Philosophy Center: Santa Barbara, CA, 1943, Pg. 53.
[286] Gadalla, Moustafa. Egyptian Rhythm: The Heavenly Melodies, Tehuti Research Foundation: Greensboro, NC, 2002, Pg. 155.

insures that the nation's music is protected and continuously seeded back into its people. The Egyptians did this better than almost anyone else, hence their long reign as a powerful and stable civilization.

Music was used to increase work productivity in a surprising number of occupations. The custom of singing at work was common to every occupation.[287] As late as the 1900s, Egyptian sailors sang when starting out on their voyage, sang again if there was danger, and then enjoyed another song after the danger had passed.[288] The Egyptians sang as they sowed, harvested, wove, fished, tended flocks, carried heavy loads and labored.[289] Scenes of music and clappers (who kept rhythm), depict music energizing workers. Singing in rhythm makes it easier to perform a chore by helping workers move in sync. In 1995, researchers from the University of Illinois showed that music boosted morale, significantly enhanced work performance and reduced stress. In one well documented example, work output performed by clerical staff increased by 14 percent with music.[290]

The strength of the Egyptian army was always at the top of the list of national concerns. Drawings of percussion units in Egyptian armies depict musicians invigorating and encouraging bravery. All over the world, martial arts instructors have used sounds to strengthen warriors and intimidate opponents.[291] A 2009 study at Brunel University (UK) showed a physical benefit of exercising to music, as this reduced the oxygen required while doing vigorous activity.[292] Music can quicken the muscle building process.

Music was a critical tool used in agriculture, fishing and other occupations. For example, "In farming, dancers and musicians

[287] Engel, Carl. The Most Ancient Nations: Assyrians, Egyptians and Hebrews with Special Reference to Recent Discoveries in Western Asia and in Egypt, Murray: London, 1864, Pg. 244.
[288] Elson, Louis. Curiosities of Music: A Collection of Facts Not Generally Known regarding the Music of Ancient and Savage Nations, O. Ditson Co., 1908, Pg. 9.
[289] Engel, Carl. Op. Cit., Pg. 244.
[290] Leeds, Joshua. The Power of Sound: How to be Healthy and Productive using Music and Sound, Healing Arts Press: VT, 2001, 2010, Pg. 120.
[291] Scott, Cyril. Music: Its Secret Influences throughout the Ages, Samuel Weiser: London, 1958, Pg. 162. Reprinted in 2013 by Inner Traditions.com
[292] Leeds, Joshua. Op. Cit., Pg. 117.

identified with what was planted. They danced to music around newly planted crops. The higher the leap, the taller the corn was supposed to grow."[293] Subtle energy created by music and movement, follows the direction of the dancer. (An object in motion possesses kinetic energy.[294]) Layne Redmond documented priestesses who used rhythms to "quicken the life in the fields," and even make childbirth easier.[295]

Plato credited the Egyptians with taming fish and land animals with sounds. He described that they lured fish into their nets with a special type of singing.[296] Today in Egypt, one can watch people "charm" snakes. Perhaps this art extended to other animals and fish.

Elements of Egyptian Music
~Instruments~

The ancient Egyptians enjoyed worldwide fame for their masterful instrumental performances. There are paintings of large orchestra performances with a wide variety of reed, stringed, percussive and flute instruments. Flutes were generally played by men, while tambourines were used by women. There were pipes, double pipes, trumpets, cymbals and drums. Drums were correlated to a man's energy, and the drum was used in Egypt's martial music. They played stringed instruments such as the lyre, harp and *cithar* (similar to a guitar). Older instruments dating back to the Old Kingdom include harps, end–blown flutes and clarinets. The oldest Egyptian harps date back 4,500 years, with a new version, the arched harp, appearing in 2613 BC.[297]

---

[293] Gadalla, Moustafa. Egyptian Rhythm: The Heavenly Melodies, *Op. Cit.*, Pg. 169.

[294] Kinetic energy is defined as the work needed to accelerate a body of a given mass from rest to its stated velocity. Having gained this energy during its acceleration, the body maintains this kinetic energy unless its speed changes.
http://en.wikipedia.org/wiki/Kinetic_Energy

[295] Redmond, Layne, When the Drummers were Women: A Spiritual History of Rhythm, Three Rivers Press: NY, 1997, Pg. 69.

[296] Aelian's description of how the Thrissa fish of Lake Mareotis "was caught by singing to it, and by the sound of crotala (clappers) made of shells…" and how "dancing up, it leapt into the nets spread for the purpose, giving great and abundant sport." Hickman, Hans. *Orientalische Musik* and *Musikgeschichte in Bildern,* Agypten, Leipzig: Germany, 1961.

[297] Manniche, Lise. *Ibid,* Pg. 26.

Curt Sachs, famed musicologist, concluded that these instruments were tuned to octaves, fourths and fifths.[298] Given the number of holes present in many flutes, they may have been pentatonic (containing five notes in a scale), similar to Chinese modes. Other flutes have seven holes, but historians debate which notes were created from those seven openings. Perhaps they produced five notes of a scale plus octaves of the primary note.

A *sistrum* is a musical rattle made of brass or bronze with a handle and a U–shaped metal frame, resembling a bell. There are small rings of thin metal that softly clank and jangle when shaken. The *sistrum* evolved from the old ritual of cutting papyrus stems and using them like rattles. The *sistrum,* a descendent of the ancient shaman's rattle, was a sacred instrument in the earliest Egyptian times. *Sistrums* were shaken to avert the flooding of the Nile and to frighten evil spirits and enemies. Bells were used to intercede with the gods in neighboring regions and to drive away negative spirits.[299]

Redmond expounded on the blessings associated with the sounds of the *sistrum*: "Their rhythmic rattling aligned one's consciousness with a deity."[300] The instrument's sounds strengthened vibratory connections with individual gods. For example, the goddess Hathor shook this rattle to enhance spiritual development of an initiate; one's heart softening to receive the goddess energy.[301] The *sistrum* was primarily used by women in the priestess classification.[302] *Sistrums* are still used in the rites of the Coptic and Ethiopian churches.[303]

---

[298] Gadalla, Moustafa. *Op. Cit.*, Pg. 29.
[299] Heline, Corinne. *Op. Cit.*, Pg. 56.
[300] Redmond, Layne. *Op. Cit.*, Pg. 65.
[301] Redmond, Layne. *Ibid,* Pg. 109.
[302] Engel, Carl. *Op. Cit.*, Pg. 223.
[303] http://en.wikipedia.org/wiki/Sistrum

Nefertari holding a *sistrum* in her Abu Simbel Temple[304]

Musical Practices

Harmony was not a major focus in Egyptian music; but melody and rhythm were important elements. Silent time beating was done with gestures, specifically by waving a circle formed from the thumb and forefinger, or patting a hand on the knee. In the Old Kingdom, pictures of "chironomists" appear. There is debate as what chironomists did in a musical ensemble, but they appear to be singing or miming to musicians. With defined hand gestures, the chironomist may have dictated pitches and intervals – similar to a musical director. Perhaps the chironomist was visually representing the subtle energy of the music. Similar hand positions in other ancient cultures stimulated various meridians and subtle energy channels throughout the body. In another culture, Tai Chi poses, create characteristic energy flows in the body. Perhaps the chironomist's hand positions directed energy through their bodies to amplify the effects of the music.

The Egyptians tuned in two ways: the divisive process and the up– and–down system that were described earlier on page 140. In the up and down method, they tuned up a fifth, down a fourth, then up

[304] Images from *Wikipedia,* http://en.wikipedia.org/wiki/Sistrum

a fifth and so on. The frequency difference in scale notes created from these two tuning methods was the Egyptian comma.[305] The difference between a fourth and a fifth is nine Egyptian commas.

Some ancient Egyptian scales used three notes (1/3rd tones) in the pitch range of two of our notes. At other times, scales had 1/4th tones, creating even smaller intervals. Listening to ancient Egyptian music demanded awareness of greater subtly than modern music requires. People developed keen awareness of fine energy by listening to notes that were extremely close together. Developing the ability to discern these tiny vibrational differences improved their intuition and psychic abilities.

Composer Cyril Scott related that the Egyptian 1/3rd tones primarily influenced emotional energies, calming them and purging gross emotions.[306] The Egyptians balanced their energies by calming down with their beautiful music. According to Scott, this stabilizing presence contributed to Egypt's remarkable duration of 3,000 years as a powerful nation. Prior to this time, feelings associated with survival were more predominant. After listening to 1/3rd tones for thousands of years, the desire for positive and harmonizing feelings became strongly set.

The Egyptians closely studied the mathematics underlying music. Ratios found by combining notes that sounded pleasing were used in other ways to create harmonic energy. For example, the harmonic mean[307] between the numbers 1 and 1/2 equals 2/3. The arithmetic mean[308] between the same numbers equals 3/4. The Egyptians valued a balanced and harmonic world, therefore the ratios of 1/2 and 3/4 were important. Important mathematical ratios found in music were used in the proportions of hieroglyphs, drawings, building dimensions and other surprising places. They believed these musical intervals created visual harmony as well as pleasing sounds. In another example, these ratios were used to calculate the design of frets on their ancient instruments, so all musicians produced unified, pleasing and harmonic sounds.

---

[305] The ratio of 8/9 is equivalent to nine Egyptian commas.
[306] Scott, Cyril. *Op. Cit.*, Pg. 154.
[307] The harmonic mean averages rates.
[308] The arithmetic mean derives the central tendency of a sample space.

Gadalla, an indigenous Egyptologist, described the tetra chord as the basis of ancient Egyptian music. A tetra chord spanned the interval of a fourth[309] and each tetra chord contained two whole notes and one semitone. The distance between neighboring notes determined the gender and mode of the tetra chord. One semitone was designated as the energy center.[310] These chords were arranged to create various mathematics and feelings. Each mode consisted of two tetra chords and two energy centers. (In ancient times there were many scales, unlike today when we use only one. The pitches and number of pitches could vary from song to song. Sometimes these scale–like constructions were called modes.)

Gadalla believed the Egyptians favored the Dorian mode. The feeling of this scale can be heard, by playing all of the white notes on the piano starting with D. One unique attribute of this scale is that its intervals are symmetrical in both directions, providing a vibrational balance.[311] The Egyptians would favor this scale for its symmetrical mathematics. The early Greeks also favored the Dorian scale. Herodotus (500 BC), the Greek father of history, said that he came from a Dorian province on a Greek Island. He described the Dorian's ancestors as Egyptians who brought with them Egyptian music and instruments.[312]

Egyptian musicians used many unique ways to perform music. Drawings from this period show Egyptian singers cup their hands over their ears. This custom was found in ancient China, as well. This enables the singer to better hear his own voice and notice greater details of its sound. With this practice, a singer can make his voice fuller and "creamier" by controlling the harmonics of his sound syllables – by throwing his voice into specific harmonics (the smaller after ripples of a sound). Some Egyptian musicians performed blindfolded to amplify the "metaphysical effects of music." By shutting off vision, other abilities such as hearing and intuition were amplified. This strengthened a musician's connection with his music. With greater focus he could improve

---

[309] An interval of a fourth is created by playing notes, four notes apart on our pianos. A fourth is 22 Egyptian commas or 498.11 cents.

[310] Gadalla, Moustafa. Egyptian Rhythm: The Heavenly Melodies, *Op. Cit.*, Pg. 181.

[311] The pattern of whole and half notes (between E and F, and B and C) is symmetrical in both directions – ascending and descending.

[312] Engel, Carl. *Op. Cit.*, Pg. 154.

his performance. In some drawings, you can see muscle contractions of the forehead, bridge of nose and the sides of the mouth. When these muscles are tightened, the singer is making a high–pitched nasal sound.

The Egyptians believed that music came from the gods and amassed their gods' strengths. Merit (*Netert* in Egyptian) was the Goddess who personified music. She established cosmic order with gestures. Plato elaborated, "Their music must originally have been the work of a god or a god–like being. The Egyptians attribute many forms of music to Isis."[313]

Michael Hayes wrote that the Old Kingdom's pantheon of eight gods – four male and four female – represented notes within the octave. Many songs were formatted to incorporate the number eight, which was associated with the God Thoth. The Egyptians called this number "the rhythmic number of the universe." By incorporating Thoth's number eight, into various aspects of music, the Egyptians honored and linked to Him. For example, all Egyptian songs had eight musical phrases. The theme of using the number eight continued with eight types of graduated vocal music ranging from talking and singing words to wordless musical vocalization.[314] The eighth form of vocal music is called *layali,* in which one sang the repeated syllables, *ya, leal* and *einy* during the music.[315] The Egyptians carefully designed music to incorporate many different numbers that linked to gods. Like a plumbing system in which water flows into many faucets, heavenly subtle energy forces were tapped by various musical techniques.

The Egyptians also communicated with the gods via vowel sounds. They carefully studied vowel sounds and used them to connect to planetary gods, as if the vocal sounds were a direct line to a god on a planet. (Some people think their target was extraterrestrials.) Musicians acted as bridges between the spiritual and Earthly worlds.

---

[313] Plato, Book of the Laws (656)
[314] Gadalla, Moustafa. Egyptian Rhythm: The Heavenly Melodies, *Op. Cit.*, Pg. 163.
[315] Gadalla, Moustafa. *Ibid,* Pg. 164.

Historian Schwaller de Lubicz[316] discovered the Egyptian wordless "vocal formulas" that were used in rituals. "Sacred or magical language is not a succession of terms with definite meanings... the excitation of certain nervous centers [causes] physiological effects [which] are evoked by the utterance of certain letters or words, which make no sense in themselves."[317] Confirming this, Asklepios, the ancient Greek god of medicine, is credited with saying, "As for us, we do not use simple words but sounds filled with power."[318]

Not only did the Egyptians scrutinize subtle impacts of sound, they also used sound to access spiritual realms. They believed there were seven heavenly realms, represented by seven tones of one scale. (Today we have seven or eight notes in a scale, depending on if you count duplicate notes. The first and last notes in our scale today are the same, just an octave higher or lower.) The eighth realm represents the human, and the ninth dimension is the realm of a person's spiritual Siamese twin (of the opposite gender that experiences what that person does). A musical comma represented the vibrational difference between a person and their twin spiritual soul. They employed twin 24–note octaves correlating to the 24 hours of the day, one octave to tune a person and the other to tune his spiritual twin.

> A folksong describes a person as a musical instrument:
> "My Singer, from that Earthen drum,
> What sweet music you bring
> From the Earthen drum of my body."
> Redmond, *Ibid*. Pg. 57.

Balancing Opposing Energy

The Egyptians observed positive and negative energies and sought to balance them; sound was essential in this balancing work. For example, the vibrational sound of a word was believed to be the same *energy* as what the word symbolized.[319] Today, you can

---

[316] R.A. Schwaller de Lubicz in his book, Sacred Science. In this quote he refers to the Corpus Hermeticum.
[317] www.cymascope.com/Egypt
[318] Cymascope.com from John Reid.
[319] Gadalla, *Op. Cit.*

observe specific shapes created on metal plates – containing sand or fine metal powder – after being exposed to a specific sound. This process is called Cymatics, named by Swiss physicist, Hans Jenny. The same sound always creates the same shape – they are inseparable. Ancient people placed sand on drums and gongs; they then exposed the instrument to a specific sound (vibration) and eventually a shape formed in the sand (this worked when the sound has a coherent vibrational energy – this obviously does not work with every possible sound). They correlated the shape with the sound that produced it. Ancient sages believed that each sound had its own subtle impact. In fact, many ancients constructed their languages – so that the shapes/sounds used for things – were a sampling of the energy of what they were talking about. To further illustrate this point, sometimes a word was reversed to create its opposite energy. *Akh* means spirit. *Hka*[320] (*Akh* spelled backwards) signifies a corpse.[321] In contrast today, our new words are entirely symbolic – not the energetic representation of a thing or its energy.

Ancient sages noticed that simple mathematics – such as a ratio of whole numbers – creates pleasant sounding intervals, whereas complex ratios create disharmony. In an example: going up an octave (the most harmonious of intervals) makes a simple ratio of 1/2. The next most pleasing sound is created by the interval of a fifth, which has an underlying ratio of 3/2. In contrast, a complex ratio such as 19/23, creates disharmony.

Similar to the Chinese Taoists, the Egyptians balanced polarity with music. They examined the mathematics that created notes and intervals, and then calculated tones to balance them. Balancing energy was a key activity in the pursuit of enlightenment, or raising their total (physical, mental and spiritual) energies. When they combined different sounds, they felt uplifted if the mathematics of the sounds combined into one – it was believed this maintained stability or balance. In an example, if one string vibrated at 240 cycles per second and another at 360 cycles per second, then the ratio of these strings to each other is 240/360 or 2/3. The 3/2 interval multiplied by the 2/3 interval equals one,

---

[320] Vowels are an approximation of sounds. The consonants were written and vowels were not.
[321] Gadalla, Moustafa. Egyptian Harmony: The Visual Music, *Op. Cit.*, Pg. 48.

showing a reciprocal relationship. Reciprocal notes balanced polarity, which the Egyptians believed kept everything in equilibrium.

Polarity was also balanced by alternating instruments, playing a melody with a constant drone, and by exchanging responses between a lead singer and chorus. Harmony can balance positive and negative forces, creating an unmistakable sense of equilibrium.[322] Similarly, rhythm stabilizes opposing energy. A loud beat followed by a soft one resembles a heartbeat or the rhythm of one's breath. A cycle of tension and release is created – representing a cycle of opposing energies.

Ascending and descending scales also balance each other. According to Scottish composer R. J. Stewart, "Chanting descending scales carried inner power outwards, while ascending scales carried consciousness inwards."[323] Music rose in pitch to higher dimensions and captured spiritual energy.[324] A descending scale pattern then brought this energy back to both the singer and listener, balancing energies of Heaven and Earth.

The Egyptians copied vibrational patterns found in the heavens. For example, the Egyptians believed (correctly) that a planet's orbit was elliptical, with two evenly spaced internal energy centers. The sun is located at one of these points (foci). Musical practices, dance choreography and architecture mimicked this balanced shape. The Egyptian musical scale had two energy centers (the first note of each tetra chord and there were two tetra chords in a scale). Balancing polarity in musical terms was accomplished by giving equal emphasis to the two foci, and also by alternating emphasis between them (like inhaling and exhaling).[325]

---

[322] Gadalla, Moustafa. *Ibid,* Pg. 36.
[323] Stewart, R. J. The Spiritual Dimension of Music: Altering Conscious for Inner Development, Destiny Books: VT, 1990, Pg. 101.
[324] This can even be accomplished by imagining the sounds – although the energy would be more subtle.
[325] Gadalla, Moustafa. Egyptian Rhythm: The Heavenly Melodies, *Op. Cit.*, Pg.157.

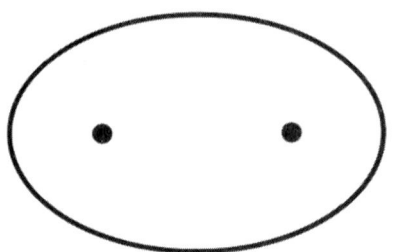

Balanced Polarity of a Planet's Orbit

We now leave Egyptian musical practices and move to the role of music within other areas of Egyptian life.

> Kepler admits that Egyptian secrets inspired his scientific discoveries. "Johannes Kepler (1571–1630) rediscovered – from Egyptian sources – that the orbit of a planet/comet about its sun has an egg–shaped path (ellipse). Each planetary system is balanced only when the planet's orbit is an egg–shaped plane with two foci. Similarly, Egyptian traditions follow the same pattern. All aspects of their thinking and society can be reasoned to egg–shaped characteristics – including music." Gadalla, *Ibid.* Pgs. 32–33.

Music permeated all Areas of Egyptian Life

~Art~

The Egyptians understood that subtle energy, or microscopically tiny vibrations that may be manipulated if properly handled, accumulates and influences emotions and even the physical world. Sound energy or vibration is particularly effective in adapting and influencing subtle energy. The Egyptian subtle energy practices can be observed in their art. They highly valued the calm emotional state that is reflected in their art. They were not interested in perfectly duplicating physical appearance in their art – rather they sought to create an ambiance they idealized. These feelings would be present in their music as well. Music would reflect calm, reinforce peace and tranquility.

Egyptian art – once perfected – did not change for thousands of years. Plato reflected, "The pictures and statues made ten thousand years ago are not better or worse than what they make now."[326] In contrast, today's artistic styles change from artist to artist, making wide-spread changes in art trends in as little as a decade or two. The main point of Egyptian art and music was to preserve strength by maintaining harmonious vibrations constant. Creativity was NOT tolerated!

As a world power, the Egyptian military regularly plundered neighboring nations. Other nations gave tribute to the Egyptians; they were at the top of the food chain. Their motto might have been: "If it is not broken, don't fix it." Likewise, music and art were strictly regulated by the government. Innovations were punishable by law.[327]

To validate this point: During the 26th dynasty, when Egypt was threatened by Assyria, the Egyptians made a concerted effort to copy art thousands of years old.[328] They even brought back archaic phrases used in their language from earlier, powerful times. Coincidently, the Assyrian threat diminished, but later on foreigners from Babylonia and Greece brought new influences, disrupting attempts to regulate subtle energy. With the loss of ancient vibratory patterns, stability waned and the decline of the civilization followed.

Constraints for art, music and writing were consistent throughout the entire 3,000 years of Egyptian dynasties – with one exception. Pharaoh Akhenaten broke with tradition for a brief seventeen year rule. Not only did he change the worship of gods to a monotheistic religion, but musicians and artists were given freedom – for the first time. The art produced during this period proved to be Egypt's best, according to many today. In his time, Akhenaten's behavior was scandalous and dangerous. All of his temples and monuments were defaced or destroyed after his death to erase the dangerous, new vibratory energy that he invoked.

The fact that Akhenaten gave artists and musicians freedom, does not mean that he undervalued music. In Akhenaten's "Great Hymn

---

[326] Baldawy, Bridgid. Mozart the Dramatist, New York, 1988.
[327] Elson, Louis. Op. Cit., Pg. 11.
[328] From the time of the Pharaoh Sneferu

to Aten," Pharaoh Akhenaten closely linked devotion, food and music. He depicted that the gods created the world for the king, who returned food back to the gods as an offering. The only people involved in this cycle were the Pharaoh and his musicians.[329]

Astrology

Egyptian paintings reflect the relationship between music and the heavens. Several paintings depict a series of red colored circles located above musicians. Some suggest the red spheres are musical notations, yet others believe them to be planets – connected to a musical scale.[330] In another example, the temple of Denderah, dedicated to the Goddess Hathor (Goddess of Music and Fertility), displays many drawings of musicians. Hieroglyphics on the wall read: "The sky and its stars are singing in you," again reflecting the relationships between the heavens and music.

The positions of stars were important to the Egyptians. To illustrate, the position of stars greatly influenced the location of temples and their building dimensions. The three pyramids in the Giza Plateau mirror the three stars in the belt of Orion.[331] Temple builders recorded where particular star-light shone on the ground throughout the year. Temples were then built so that at special times (such as the first day of summer, fall, winter and spring) the starlight would shine on the altar. In a final example: air shafts inside some pyramid chambers of the king and queen, aligned with important stars, such as Sirius, Orion or the Pole star.

The Egyptians charted the course of stars in the heavens and identified the subtle effects of each celestial body's movement. Festivals were scheduled to take advantage of favorable energy cycles resulting from star motions in the sky. Archaic societies believed that the movements of the planets created subtle vibrations that influenced them. These vibrations would be

---

[329] Manniche, Lise. *Op. Cit.*, Pg. 92.
[330] Manniche, Lise. *Op. Cit.*, Pg.12.
[331] Interview with Ani Williams, aniwilliams.com. Mattson, Jill. <u>Ancient Sounds Modern Healing</u>, Wings of Light: Oil City, PA., 2009, Pgs. 121–130.

replicated in music. Harmonizing with such heavenly music elevated and protected a civilization.

Death Rituals

The incantations of wordless planetary–based chants[332] ensured the pharaohs' safe arrival and a prime spot in the after–life.[333] Loyal subjects performed what later became known as the "Song of the Seven Greek Vowels," a mystical chant that harmonized the pharaoh's body to the seven spheres of the universe and the gods that ruled them.[334] The "magic lyre invoked the astral waves of the seven planets."[335] In another ceremony – to capture the astral planetary energy and embed it into a mummy – the Egyptian Hierophant[336] magically sounded seven notes (linked to the seven known celestial bodies in our solar system), in a three beat rhythm that smoothly flowed together.[337] The three–beat rhythm pattern correlated with their use of 1/3rd tones. The music was repeated to create a subtle energy effect: a charmed circle around the deceased's body.[338]

To aid the pharaoh after death, the priests generated powerful vowel intonations, gradually shifting the pitch until maximum acoustic excitation occurred in the acoustically–enhanced King's Chamber. At this point, two priests maintained the frequency while two others dropped their pitch by a small margin, thus creating dramatic beat frequencies that entrained brain waves. These sounds were to massage the pharaoh's soul, elevating his energy. Another priest recited magical spells. The Pharaoh would have great access to the higher spirit world if his energies were pure and uplifting. This elaborate ceremony was to

---

[332] Listen to this at www.Ancient-Music.com.

[333] Egyptologist Lise Manniche credited planetary music to the religious sect of the Egyptian Gnostics. Gnosticism refers to diverse, religious movements in antiquity believing that the material cosmos was created by an imperfect God and a supreme God existed. http://en.wikipedia.org/wiki/Gnosticism.

[334] Manniche, Lise. *Op. Cit.*, Pgs. 12–13.

[335] Godwin, Joscelyn. The Mystery of the Seven Vowels: In Theory and Practice, Phanes Press: MI., 1991, Pg. 70.

[336] A hierophant is a person who brings people into the presence of that which is deemed holy. A hierophant is an interpreter of sacred mysteries and arcane principles. http://en.wikipedia.org/wiki/Hierophant

[337] Ternary (from Latin *ternarius*) is an adjective meaning "composed of three items." http://en.wikipedia.org/wiki/Ternary

[338] Godwin, Joscelyn. *Op. Cit.*, Pg. 70.

help the pharaoh's spirit travel to the stars, via the star shafts of the pyramid.

The Egyptians communicated with the deceased by first calling out his name – gaining his attention. By mentally or physically calling the name of a deity, a part of the deity's consciousness is compelled to come. As prescribed in *The Book of the Dead*, loved ones chanted names of deities to help the deceased unite with gods. They also encouraged the deceased to be fearless, pure of heart and exhibit virtues. This elevated their energy in order to cross over to the highest energy plane possible in the afterlife.

The King's Chamber sarcophagus was highly resonant, partly due to its high quartz content. The sarcophagus rings like a bell when struck (albeit a low frequency). Acoustics engineer John Reid theorized that the pharaoh's casket was engineered to resonate at the frequency of a baby's heartbeat.[339] The vibrating sarcophagus sound became part of a rebirth ritual.

The vowel sounds associated with the "planets" known at the time of ancient Egypt are listed in the table **Vowel Sounds associated with the Planets**. In the table below, the planets on the left are closest to Earth; moving towards the right the planets progressively get further away, according to the Egyptian beliefs.[340]

<table>
<tr><td colspan="9"><h2>Vowel Sounds associated with the Planets[341]</h2></td></tr>
<tr><td>"Planet"</td><td>Moon</td><td>Mercury</td><td>Venus</td><td>Sun</td><td>Mars</td><td>Jupiter</td><td>Saturn</td></tr>
<tr><td>Vowel</td><td>Ei</td><td>I
(ee)</td><td>A
(ah)</td><td>Au</td><td>E
(eh)</td><td>O
(oh)</td><td>U
(oo)</td></tr>
</table>

---

[339] cymascope.com
[340] However, Venus is closer to Earth than Mercury
[341] Godwin, Joscelyn. *Op. Cit.*, Pg. 70. She reports different notes for the planetary notes associated with the planets: A, G, F, E, D, C and B.

The Egyptians believed that the planets nearer to the Earth revolved at a swifter speed. The moon was the fastest moving, producing the highest pitch. Saturn was the furthest away from the Earth and created the lowest pitch. Today, the sounds of the moving planets can be derived from their masses, orbits, velocities and relative positions.

The Egyptian esoteric studies, called the mysteries, were restricted to priests and pharaohs. The ultimate experience combined music and the rite to create a trance that induced an out–of–body experience to transport one's consciousness to other dimensions – reportedly similar to what souls experienced after death. This "initiation" provided a taste of immortality, showing the contrast of sublime heights and negative energy in the afterlife. This experience was to encourage the priests to be virtuous, as they believed the energies of their afterlife were created while living.

A form of this rite to separate the soul and body continued on in the Jewish Kabbalah tradition. Perhaps the Israelites got this tradition from Moses, who grew up as Egyptian royalty. Precise meditations, tonal patterns and chanting practices were followed, enabling the soul to leave the body to convene in the "other world" at a special location with loved ones. Variations in the chanted sounds or visualizations changed the time, location or dimension into which the soul passed. Precise sounds and visualizations were vibratory keys to inter–dimensional travel. Importantly, the proper sounds were needed to return to the right time and place. Varying the procedure could result in death, or said differently, the soul getting permanently lost in time and other dimensions.

Music and Time

Dio Cassius, a Roman historian, suggested that the seven planetary tones were responsible for the week being divided into seven days.[342] The Egyptians separated the week into two periods with two distinct energy focuses. They identified which days had more energy for a person to draw upon, increasing the chances that activities on that day would be successful. More activities were scheduled when energy was most concentrated. Gadalla described the weekly energy focuses in this way: "The concentrated

---

[342] Roman History, Book XXXVII, Sections 18 and 19

activities towards both ends of the week (with two centers of activity – one more prominent than the other) correspond to an elliptical form similar to Kepler's first planetary law." (See page 177 and 178 earlier in this chapter regarding "Balanced Polarity of a Planet's Orbit") The first four days can be compared to a tetra chord and the remaining three days, plus Saturday, create a second tetra chord.

Days of the Week and Energy Focuses

First Tetra Chord	Second Tetra Chord
Saturday – Not a good energy day	Wednesday – Not a good energy day
Sunday – light activity – Evening has concentrated activities	Thursday – Highly active
Monday – Light activity	Friday – Highly active – Evening has concentrated activities
Tuesday – Not a good energy day	Saturday – Not a good energy day

Gadalla, who was born and raised in Egypt, indicated that the silent majority of the Egyptian Baladi people still honor the association of days of the week with abundant, positive energy for specific things. Many current Hindu people have similar beliefs. They perform certain functions on schedules, such as marriages on Friday evenings. They even associate mundane functions, such as the best time to cut hair, with the position of the stars, seasons and time of day.

Dio Cassius[343] documented the correlation of each day to the Egyptian diatonic musical scale. Two explanations of this are

---

[343] Roman History, Book XXXVII, Sections 18 and 19

listed in the footnote.[344] Gadalla printed a 24–hour system connecting tones with every hour in a week.[345] Each hour of every day, the Egyptians musically balanced and harmonized their energies using this tonal system.

Each day of the week was associated with a specific planet. Each planet carried a characteristic energy that was stronger on that day. For example, Venus carried the feminine energy and that of love, whereas Mars was equated to masculine energy and war. Venus day would be an excellent one to be with your beloved, as Mars day would be better to fight or attack an enemy. The subtle energy of the planets is reflected in the names of the weekdays, for example, Saturday was equated with the planet Saturn and Monday with the Moon.[346]

www.JillsWingsOfLight.com – Art Galleries

---

[344] Dio Cassius, Roman History, Book XXXVII, Sections 18 and 19. "Apply the 'principle of the tetra chord (constitutes the basis of music) to these stars, the whole universe is divided into regular intervals, in the order they revolve, beginning at Saturn, omitting the next two, name the lord of the fourth, and passing over two others reach the seventh, go back and repeat the process with the orbits and their presiding divinities in this same manner, assigning them to the days, and the days will be musically connected with the arraignments of the heavens. This is one explanations, the other is: Begin at the first hour and count the hours of the day & night, 1st Saturn, 2nd Jupiter, 3rd Mars, 4th Sun, 5th Venus, 6th Mercury, 7th Moon, (the order of the cycles which the Egyptians observe). Repeat this, covering the 24 hours & the first hour of the next day, which is the Sun. Carry on the operation through the next 24 hours, the 1st hour of 3rd day is the Moon, and if you proceed similarly, each day will receive its appropriate planet.'" Gadalla, Moustafa. Egyptian Rhythm: The Heavenly Melodies, Tehuti Research Foundation: Greensboro, NC, 2002, Pgs. 24–25.
[345] Gadalla, Moustafa. Egyptian Rhythm: The Heavenly Melodies, Op. Cit., Pgs. 26–27.
[346] Heath, Richard. Matrix of Creation: Sacred Geometry in the Realm of the Planets, Inner Traditions: VT, 2002, Pg. 27.

185

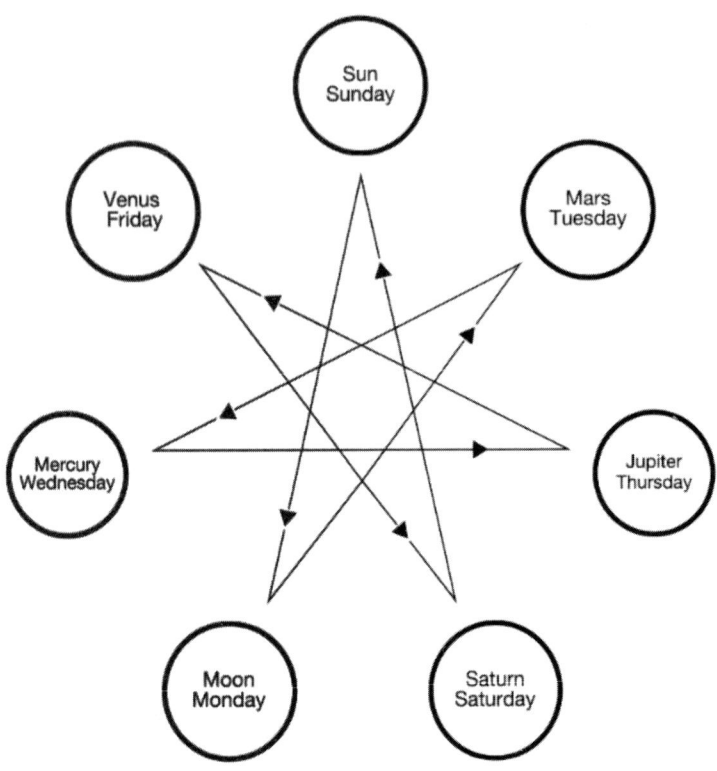

Days of the Week and associations with Planets[347]

The Egyptians divided the year into three seasons of four months each. Each season's music used designated tetra chords exclusively. Measuring their year with the movement of the sun, not the moon, each month had 30 days, and 5and 1/4days were added to complete a year. The Egyptians were aware that a year was comprised of 365 days and a partial day. Today, we balance this partial day by having a leap year in which we add one day to our calendar every four years. The ratio of 365.25 to 360 is 1.014 and is called a *buk–nunu*. This increment is equal to one third of the Egyptian Comma. (Recall: the difference between the divisive and up–and–down methods of creating scales was a comma.) Also, the difference between a person's fundamental frequency

---

[347] Heath, Richard. <u>Matric of Creation: Sacred Geometry in the Realms of the Planets</u>, Pg. 27.

and their *ka* or etheric double was also a comma. The *buk–nunu* also determined the distance between some holes in wind instruments and frets on stringed instruments. In this way, time and music are interwoven – and they have deep mathematical ties!

The Pythagoreans and ancient Chinese described a comma differently. They noticed that if you took a pitch up many octaves, not only did the frequency double but somehow increased a little bit more. This little discrepancy was called a *comma*. This phenomena was disturbing to ancient sages, as they were expecting mathematics representing natural phenomena to be simple and balanced. Some went so far as to credit this discrepancy with an "error" in nature. They believed octave creation and the time period for a year should reflect simple mathematics (no fractions). Ancient Chinese and Greek sages connected their definition of a *comma* with the *buk–nunu* (the time–measurement that a year varied from 360). They expected a year to be described by simple mathematics, just as they expected an octave to be a simple doubling of a frequency. They believed that the exact percentage that a year was off (or differed from the whole number of 360) was equal to the number of frequencies that seven octaves were off. Once again they believed music and time were related.

The musical scale used today, the equal temperament scale, avoids this messy mathematics by defining an octave as the doubling of cycles per second of a given note. There are twelve notes in our modern scale and each is 1/12 of the octave. This pattern is not found in nature, therefore ancient sages would not have approved of it.

Architecture and Egyptian Music

Egyptian architecture and musical intervals often used the same proportions. Architecture has been referred to as "frozen music," because one can observe the same "vibrations" found in music that he sees in architecture.[348] For example, musical intervals are created from ratios that can also be reflected in the dimensions of a building.

---

[348] Gadalla, Moustafa. Egyptian Harmony: The Visual Music, *Op. Cit.*, Pg. 136.

An Egyptian Mastaba[349]

Certain ratios were believed to create special energy. Room dimensions displaying these ratios created the same special subtle energy. For example, two quantities (a & b) are in the golden ratio, if their ratio (a/b) is the same as the ratio of their sum to the larger of the two quantities (a + b)/a. See following illustration.

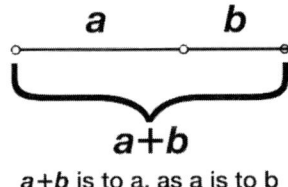

a+b is to a, as a is to b

The Golden Ratio[350]

Even in the early history of Egypt (5000 to 2575 BC) hundreds of tombs, called mastabas, were built according to harmonic proportions. In 1880 historian Auguste Mariette counted 800 mastabas near Abydos that were built with the proportions of 5/8 (the ratio associated with the musical interval of an augmented fourth and the Golden ratio.)[351] Many other structures also

---

[349] From mastaba, Wikipedia
[350] http://en.wikipedia.org/wiki/Golden_ratiov
[351] A golden rectangle has side lengths in the golden ratio, approximately 1:1.618. A distinctive feature of this shape is that when a square section is removed, the remainder is another golden rectangle; that is, with the same proportions as the first. Square removal can be repeated infinitely, in which case corresponding corners of the squares form an infinite sequence of points on the golden spiral, the unique logarithmic spiral. http://en.wikipedia.org/wiki/Golden_rectangle

incorporated the golden proportion,[352] such as the height–to–base dimension of the great pyramid of Cheops.[353]

The Egyptians sometimes used the Fibonacci[354] series of numbers (see footnote for more information) in the dimensions of their buildings 4,500 years ago (Fibonacci was credited with the discovery of this pattern, but he was born in 1179 AD). The Fibonacci numbers also determined the proportions of people in drawings, reflecting the proportions that already exist in the body. Drawings survive with these dimensions marked. Fibonacci relationships are evident in proportions within hieroglyphs as well. This series of numbers was also used to create musical scales.

Many dimensions and proportions found in the ancient Egyptian temples correspond to harmonious musical intervals, such as octaves, fifths, fourths, thirds and sixths. When the Egyptians embedded ratios of musical intervals into their building designs, they believed that the buildings radiated the energy of the associated musical interval. For example, in the temple of Horus, the ratio of one chamber's width to height is 2:3, the ratio of a musical fifth. The ratio of another chamber's height to width is 3:4, the ratio of a musical fourth.[355]

The resonant pitch of a room can be determined by playing music in it and observing which tones are richer and enhanced. Sharry Edwards[356], pioneer in the study of Bioacoustics, relates room shapes to the sounds they enhance. For example, when singing in a

---

[352] Two quantities are in the golden ratio if the ratio of the sum of the quantities to the larger quantity is equal to the ratio of the larger quantity to the smaller one. The golden ratio is an irrational mathematical constant, approximately 1.6180339887. http://en.wikipedia.org/wiki/Golden_ratio. Gadalla, Moustafa. Egyptian Harmony: The Visual Music, *Op. Cit.,* Pg. 58.

[353] Merrick, Richard. Interference: A Grand Scientific Musical Theory, Merrick: TX, 2002, Pg. 30.

[354] The Fibonacci numbers are a series of numbers in which any two neighboring numbers equals the next number in the series. For example, 1, 1, 2, 3, 5, 8… Forms in nature are often equated with these numerical patterns.

[355] Antoine Seronde. Rediscovering Music in Architecture of the Ancient Egyptian Temple, Quoted from www.aniwilliams.com.

[356] More information about Sharry Edwards: Mattson, Jill. Secret Sounds ~ Ultimate Healing: Your Personal Guide to a Better Life using Sharry Edward's Revolutionary "Secret Sounds," Wings of Light: Oil City, PA, 2011, available at www.jillswingsoflight.com & www.SoundHealthOptions.com.

square room, a C will increase in volume. Other notes in a square room will not.[357]

www.JillsWingsOfLight.com – Art Galleries

---

[357]Mattson, Jill. <u>Secret Sounds Ultimate Healing: A Personal Guide to Better Life Using Sharry Edwards' Revolutionary "Secret Sounds,"</u> *Ibid.*

190

Musical Characteristics linked to Geometrical Shapes and Dimensions

Pitch	Harmonic Scale Ratios	Musical Interval	Dimensions of the Room
C	1	Unison	Square (1)
D	9/8	The Egyptian representation of you and your soul (Spirit twin)[358]	18 x 16
E	5/4	Major Third	10 x 8
F	4/3	Fourth	8 x 6
G	3/2	Fifth	6 x 4
A	5/3	Major Sixth	10 x 6
B	15/8	Not a significant interval	30 x 16
In between B and C		Not a significant interval	Circle

In some temples, the sequence of enhanced notes from neighboring rooms forms a musical scale. As one walks the length of the temple, the dominant harmonic rises in pitch. According to Ani Williams, gifted harpist, at one end of the Abyddos temple the lower tones sound stronger. As a person moves through the temple, energy stirs the root chakra, which rises through the major chakras until it reaches the crown chakra.[359] By walking the length

---

[358] The 9th dimension represents the home of your spiritual twin. The number 8 is associated with Thoth. 9/8 is associated with 9 Egyptian commas.

[359] Ani Williams interview, Mattson, Jill. Ancient Sounds Modern Healing, Wings of Light: Oil City, PA., 2009, Pgs. 121–130.

of the temple, one entrains to the resonant subtle energy – to softly be transported to a specific state of consciousness.

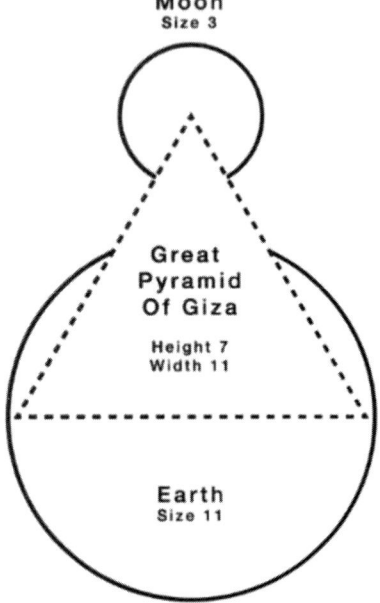

Moon
Size 3

Great Pyramid Of Giza

Height 7
Width 11

Earth
Size 11

The Pyramid Height = 11/2 +3/2 = 14/2 = 7[360]

Numbers displayed in nature were sacred and incorporated into the framework of extraordinary buildings and in the floor plan of temples and gothic cathedrals. The numeric energy of gods, music and energies was veiled in buildings, preserved to teach us in later times about ancient understandings. The geometry (dimensions) of a building creates subtle energy that intermingles with the energy of the occupants, affecting their thinking and feelings. Listeners got a double dose of "sacred geometry" energy from not only the building dimensions, but the music produced with an identical framework.

The designers of the Great Pyramid knew the dimensions of the Earth and the moon as shown in the drawing entitled "The Pyramid Height." Not only did the Egyptians place literally millions of huge blocks of stone to conform to precise geometrical and astronomical alignments, but they were precise about their

---

[360] John Mitchel

measurements and building dimensions. The red granite sarcophagus in the King's Chamber of the Great Pyramid was hollowed out to such accuracy that its external volume is exactly twice its internal volume. Engineer Christopher Dunn, a modern tool maker, believed the ancient Egyptians used an ultrasonic tool bit capable of vibrating at a rate thousands of times faster than a pneumatic drill.[361] This ultrasonic tool could effectively penetrate the granite because the sound it produces vibrates the quartz within the crystal, making it pliable. Current day researcher, Larry Hardee, described a process to make drilling of hard stones – such as granite – easier and more precise.[362] The key is matching a drill bit to the resonance of the stone.

In 1974, Phyllis Schlemmer,[363] internationally known psychic, described through channeling the construction of the Great Pyramid: "The pyramid's function was to bring energy to the planet and to rejuvenate cells. Building construction was done 'with the benefit of vocal sound tuned to crystal, with the sound of OM.'"[364] Schlemmer and Dunn both believed that sound played a key role in the monumental and precision building techniques.

The movement of subtle energy was a consideration in ancient building design worldwide. Naturally occurring energy currents were enhanced in sacred buildings. Pointed rods on the roofs of ancient temples tapped into lightning and the electric current from the air. Many cathedrals have wells in their basements, connecting them with the deep underground. Temples were often located on *ley* lines of magnetic subtle energy Earth currents, and above fissures and underground caverns. The Old Testament described life–giving energy streams beneath their temples that flowed to the four corners of the Earth.[365] These are some of the ways that energy currents were enhanced in sacred buildings.

---

[361] Hayes, Michael. The Hermetic Code in DNA: The Sacred Principles in the Ordering of the Universe, Inner Traditions: VT, 2004, Pg. 65.

[362] larry@phatatech.com and www.phatatech.com

[363] Born in 1929

[364] Godwin, Joscelyn. Atlantis and the Cycles of Time: Prophecies, Traditions and Occult Revelations, Inner Traditions: VT, 2011, Pg. 287; and Schlemmer and Jenkins. Only Planet of Choice, Pg. 171.

[365] Salverte as quoted form Thomas Milner's Gallery of Nature, as quoted in Michell, John. The Dimensions of Paradise: Sacred Geometry, Ancient Science and the Heavenly Order on Earth, Inner traditions: VT, 2008, Pgs. 14–15.

According to ancient historian, Freddy Silva, the ancient temples inspired pride in people by their grandeur. "The temples served as an insurance policy in times when people lost sight of the fact that they too are gods."[366] Throughout the world, ancient texts refer to temples as living entities, where people are "transformed into gods, into bright stars." The Gothic churches in Europe are often referred to as female.

Moving Large Objects with Sound Energy

Numerous legends of the ancient world (Mexico, Bolivia, Peru, and Egypt) portray sound being used to build cities and monuments. Huge blocks of stone were reportedly moved by employing instrumental music, whistling or singing.[367] There are many examples. A Mayan legend – about the pyramid at Uxmal in Yucatan – claims that builders whistled special tones and heavy blocks moved into place.[368] Chaldean priests lifted great stones at Baalbeck with melodious chants. At Tiahuanaco in Bolivia, stories describe ancient builders using trumpets as key building tools. Legends portray the walls of Thebes being built by Amphion's lyre. Other stories depict Stonehenge builders using drums, songs and *symbols* for construction means. Translations of Babylonian tablets reveal records of the widespread use of sound to lift heavy objects. The explorer, Hernando Cortez from Spain (born in 1485), was given wings made from bird feathers from American Indians. Two golden gongs were mounted above the wearer's chest[369] and when they were struck with a padded mallet, the gong sound supposedly allowed the wearer to fly like a bird. The Cortez ship's records showed that these objects were loaded on the ship for Spain; but on arrival, the golden gongs disappeared.

Eyewitnesses testify that Indian monks levitate with special sounds combined with concentration.[370] *YouTube* features videos

---

[366] http://invisibletemple.com/books.html

[367] Hayes, Michael. *Op. Cit.*, Pg. 77.

[368] Bierhorst, John. The Mythology of Mexico and Central America, Morrow: NY, 1990, Pg. 8.

[369] The kings gong was roughly 10" X ¼" thick solid gold, the queen's gong was about 8" X 1/8."

[370] Andrews, Shirley. Lemuria and Atlantis: Studying the Past to Survive the Future, Llewellyn Worldwide: Woodbury, MN, 2008, Pg. 149.

of Tibetan monks levitating.[371] Author, Andrew Collins, described accounts of travelers in Tibet who witnessed large stone blocks levitate to the sound of musical instruments. These photos have been published.[372] A German article describing the Tibetan levitation process said: "We know from the priests of the Far East that they lifted heavy boulders up on high mountains with the help of various groups of sounds. …the knowledge of the various vibrations in the audio range demonstrates to physicists that a vibrating and condensed sound field can nullify the power of gravitation."[373, 374]

Bruce Cathie, in *Acoustic Levitation of Stones*, described a 1939 eye witness account by Dr. Jarl, a Swedish doctor, as recorded in a German magazine.[375] This article described where each singer and instrumentalist (mostly drums and horns) stood, what direction each musician faced, the measurements of the instruments (example: how wide and deep the drums were), and the harmonic science that enabled boulders to float to the desired spot. In addition to numerous instruments, about 200 monks stood behind the musicians – ten deep – appearing to focus on moving the stone.[376]

Legends tell of Atlanteans lifting large stones by sonic levitation. They purportedly linked arms around a boulder to be moved, while dancing (creating rhythms by stamping their feet), using percussive instruments (like cymbals or drums) and chanting (to the pitch of the rock). The stone sat above a circular hole that was dug for this purpose. Sound vibrations filled the hole, building up energy under the stone to catapult it up. The singers used their

---

[371] http://www.youtube.com/watch?v=pV4bO7i6xrs,
http://www.youtube.com/watch?v=A7ZabuaPm6E,
http://www.youtube.com/watch?v=H7EI3NqkSfY,
http://www.youtube.com/watch?v=C8eOXoOHjxU
[372] Hayes, Michael. *Op. Cit.*, Pg. 77.
[373] Swedish engineer Olaf Alexanderson wrote about this phenomenon in the publication No. 13. Excerpt from "Anti–gravity and the World Grid" edited by D. H. Childress, Ch.8, *Acoustic Levitation of Stones* by Bruce Cathie, Pgs. 213–217.
[374] www.bibliotecapleyades.net/ciencia/antigravityworldgrid/ciencia_antigravityworldgrid08
[375] www.bibliotecapleyades.net/ciencia/antigravityworldgrid/ciencia_antigravityworldgrid08
[376] Hayes, Michael. *Op. Cit.*, Pg. 118.

mental strength – to focus on the pitch of the rock – to amplify the sound waves to lift the heavy stone.[377]

Edgar Cayce, while in a trance, described the building of the pyramids. He related that stones may be made to float in air with chanting and song. He indicated that this practice was used in the building of the Great Pyramid, much in the same manner that the Druids of England set stones in circles at a later period.[378]

The Egyptians describe lifting rocks with sound. A rectangular stone was covered on four sides with wet papyrus (a reed). A specially carved, wooden rod was used to strike the uncovered stone face and then it was removed. The vibrations – from striking the stone – continued to build and increase in the rod and at the maximum intensity the rod was again placed on the exposed stone. The energy from the rod vibrated the stone. These vibrations "altered the neutral center aether flow by stimulated kindling and caused *temporary levitation*."[379]

Throughout time, many legends describe other energy sources used to lift huge stones. Theories suggest that the Ark of the Covenant (originally in the possession of the Egyptians) may have been used to construct Egyptian monuments – by lifting heavy building stones. Perhaps Moses took the Ark (perhaps an antigravity device) when the Israelites fled Egypt. When the Pharaoh discovered that Moses had taken the treasure, he sent troops to recover the device; Moses escaped, using the relic to part the Red Sea for the Jews.[380]

In a modern account, Edward Leedskalnin built a Coral Castle for his lost love in Homestead, Florida. Leedskalnin cut and moved huge blocks of coral by himself, using only hand tools. In this area of Florida, the coral can be up to 4,000 feet thick. Each section of the wall is eight feet tall, four feet wide, three feet thick and

---

[377] Andrews, Shirley. Atlantis: Insights from a Lost Civilization, Llewellyn Worldwide: MN, 1997, Pgs. 160–161.
[378] Godwin, Joscelyn. Heaven and Earth: Mysticism in Music from Antiquity to Avant Garde, Inner Traditions: VT, 1987, Pg. 3.
[379] http://www.keelynet.com/gravity/deckcorr.htm
[380] Briar, Robert, Ph.D. Professor of Egyptology, Long Island University. *The History of Egypt*, the Teaching Company: VA, 1999. Audio CD: Lecture 32.

weighs more than 58 tons.[381] The coral weighs 125 pounds per cubic foot. Leedskalnin boasted that he knew the secret of how the Egyptians constructed their pyramids. He reportedly sang to large blocks to lift them. He placed his hands over the stone to be levitated and sang a particular scale until his hands felt a response from the stone. The sound that produced the strongest vibration was sustained and the rock levitated.[382]

Larry Hardee of New York describes how he lifts rocks with sound by vocalizing the fundamental frequency of the rock. "My methods are more advanced than Leedskalnin's, as I'm using a computer and digital electronics for precision control."[383] Hardee disclosed, "Most folks don't have this ability due to lack of personal power required to do this, but in ancient times I theorize that environmental energy was higher and people weren't disabled with calcified pineal glands due to fluoride poisoning. Not to mention the insulating layer formed in the skin by modern diet practices that prevent the body from utilizing the ever–present energy all around us."[384]

In 1981, the famous scientist John Keely wrote that tones from a violin could start an engine and that discord could stop it. Recently, sonic levitation was used in a space shuttle to hold a glass in suspension. Due to the lack of gravity, less intense sound was required.[385] In another modern day example, Viktor Schauberger wrote that by rapidly stirring sand, air or water to create a vortex, the aether flow through the neutral center could be enhanced to produce levitation.[386]

Ideas abound, explaining the vibrational power of sound and music to move heavy objects – to create huge buildings. Perhaps the Egyptians employed a variety of these sonic levitation techniques. As the reader well knows, the Egyptian's incredible building accomplishments remain deep mysteries and perhaps they always will!

---

[381] www.coralcastle.com
[382] Leedskalnin, Edward. His book: http://www.leedskalnin.com/Leedskalnins–Writings–MAGNETIC–CURRENT.html
[383] larry@phatatech.com and www.phatatech.com
[384] larry@phatatech.com and www.phatatech.com
[385] Andrews, Shirley. Atlantis: Insights from a Lost Civilization, Op. Cit., Pg. 162.
[386] http://www.keelynet.com/gravity/deckcorr.htm

Healing

The Egyptian papyri describe miraculous healings. Surrounding countries frequently referred their sick people to the priests and physicians of Egypt. Even Egypt's enemies touted her healing prowess. For example, documents at Kahum discuss Egyptian medical treatments in 2500 BC.

Healing from herbs was combined with subtle energy procedures. Medicine, religion and magic were inseparable in the healing process. For example, healing work was done in the temples and all physicians were also priests. The magician induced physical changes with sorcery, contrasting the priest's service of being an intermediary with the gods. The supernatural is called *magic* by a sorcerer, a *miracle* from a religious perspective, parapsychology from another viewpoint.

Medical papyri describe treatments for a wide variety of illnesses: removing bone fragments, setting broken bones and treating trauma. The *Ebers* papyrus[387] includes words to recite to strengthen a remedy. Some procedures used holy water, as churches do today. In some cases, the Egyptians used medicine and surgery like we do today. The extent of Egyptian knowledge of the human body is not well known but clearly embalmers were knowledgeable of anatomy, as they removed organs during the mummification process, storing them in coptic jars to remove moisture from the cadaver.

The Egyptians worked with a person's subconscious mind to release hidden emotional traumas – employing methods of catharsis. Emotional problems were linked to physical illness, much as we link anxiety to an ulcer today.

The Egyptians sought optimum states of consciousness. Author Redmond confirmed, "The Greeks copied the mind/body techniques of the Egyptians to achieve expanded consciousness. These are similar to many of the Hindu Yogic practices."[388] "Dream rooms" in the Dendra Temple were designed to induce dreams that reveal personal instructions for healing.

---

[387] http://www.cancercenter.com/Ebers Papyrus
[388] Redmond, Layne. *Op. Cit.*, Pg. 105.

Each brain hemisphere specializes in different activities: the right being more creative and the left analytical. Not only do the brain hemispheres have different functions, but they operate in different rhythms. The right brain may be operating in alpha while the left brain creates beta brain waves. States of intense meditation or creativity can create whole–brain functioning that is associated with heightened mental capacities. Ancient practices – such as drumming and chanting rhythmic patterns while gazing at geometric figures (like tantric combinations of Hindu mantra and yantra[389]) also engage whole brain functioning.

Chanting in a prescribed rhythm was a key component in medical procedures.[390] Rhythm from rattles and drums can produce a trance state; Egyptian music induced *emotional* trances.[391] They refined their music so that it accomplished precise purposes. Egyptian trance was not like the trance of the Indians, who strove to experience *Samadhi[392]* and spiritual bliss. The Egyptians had many purposes for their trances.

Music and dance were also used for healing and to restore inner balance by bringing a person back into "tune."[393] Sound–tuning in the body has been scientifically proven to heal. In three virtually identical experiments conducted in Canada and Russia, diabetic rats with dysfunctional pancreases were exposed to the sound waves of healthy pancreases from new born rats. Within weeks, ninety percent of the diabetic rats' pancreases were functioning normally and blood sugar levels normalized.[394] Once again the

---

[389] Yantras are symbols, processes, machinery or anything that has structure and organization, such as geometric figures. They are used in Eastern mysticism to balance the mind or focus it on spiritual concepts. The act of wearing, depicting, enacting and/or concentrating on a yantra is held to have spiritual, astrological or magical benefits in the Tantric traditions of the Indian religions. http://en.wikipedia.org/wiki/Yantra

[390] Gadalla, Moustafa. Egyptian Rhythm: The Heavenly Melodies, *Op. Cit.*, Pg. 164.

[391] Scott, Cyril. *Op. Cit.*, 158.

[392] *Samadhi* in Hinduism, Buddhism, Sikhism and yogic schools is a high level of concentrated meditation. The consciousness becomes one with the experienced object. The mind becomes still or one–pointed. In Buddhism the mind becomes still but does not merge with the object of attention, observing and gaining insight. In Hinduism, *samādhi* can also refer to the complete absorption of the individual consciousness in the self at the time of death.

[393] Gadalla, Moustafa. Egyptian Rhythm: The Heavenly Melodies, *Op. Cit.*, Pg. 182.

[394] Desaulniers, Mary, Ph.D. www.suite101.com/writer articles.cfm/mdesaulniers and Luckman, Sol. *DNA Monthly*, "Conscious Healing," "Potentiate Your DNA," www.phoenicregenetics.org

healthy vibration was used to overcome disease; stronger positive vibrations balance and heal us.

The Egyptians transferred subtle energy with resonance[395] in ways that modern man would not even dream of. For example, the Egyptian physician papyri document that a poultice of an ostrich egg helped heal a cracked skull. The shape of an ostrich egg is similar to the shape of a skull. They believed the egg carried the energy of its oval shape, and that subtle energy transferred between like shapes. The subtle energy vibrations emanating from the elliptical shape of an ostrich egg were believed to "tune" a broken skull (where the skull's normal overall frequency was disrupted). Perhaps the "subtle energy skeleton" of the egg transferred energy to a skull to reform its egg shape, healing the concussion.[396]

Author Richard Merrick explained another way this might happen: the later harmonics (13th through 16th harmonics) in the harmonic series get increasingly smaller and denser (higher pitches get closer together). Merrick believed tiny sounds and their harmonics are present as an egg is created in nature. He believed that certain harmonic sounds mold the newly forming egg shell. Merrick likened this process to cymatics – which we have visited before – a phenomena where sound creates shapes in matter.

In another example of subtle energy transference between surprising things, a lame person's foot was wrapped in a deer hide. Recall that deer are fast and fleet on their feet. The Egyptians are attempting to transfer the deer's ability move quickly and with agility to the lame foot.

Shapes were believed to contain beneficial subtle energy. Symbols create energies that a sensitive person can detect; the Egyptians wore amulets for protection. The Eye of Horus amulet strengthened one's health, whereas the scarab beetle subtly radiated the energy of continued existence. (The scarab beetle procreated asexually. Also, parts of beetles' bodies do not decay –

---

[395] Energy triggers like energy. Plucking the G string on one violin will cause the G on a nearby violin to vibrate. Energy transfers between like tones, octaves and to a lesser extent with some intervals such as a fifth. Resonance occurs with all types of vibrations or waves.
[396] Merrick, Richard. *Op. Cit.*, Pg. 219.

creating continued existence.) The ankh, a cross with a loop on the top, represented eternal life as well as the male and the female polarity. Sometimes it represented the ear, signifying the receptivity of the mind to receive divine inspiration. (In Egypt and Sumer, the words "ear" and "mind" were synonymous.[397]) The ankh amplified energy and thought. When it was held by the loop, it transmitted energy, and when held by the stem, it received energy. For this reason, the ankh was used only with the highest integrity, lest one's negativity return in amplified form. According to author Shirley Andrews, the priests and priestesses of Atlantis used the ankh for meditation, out of body travel, healing, shaping life and communicating with extraterrestrials.[398]

The Eye of Horus   **The Scarab Beetle**   **The Ankh**

Author Jerry Decker wrote that shapes, like telephone lines, emanate characteristic energy. "Shape power geometries are routinely used in the protective rings of ceremonial magic, the construction of amulets and talismans as well as the sigils (signatures) of various demonic or angelic entities. These patterns produce correspondences (resonances) to establish contact with the desired entity or influence. By stimulating shape power geometry, you literally evoke or call forth the influence, just like making a phone call."[399]

The labyrinth is another ancient use of subtle energy created from shapes. By walking the maze, a person tunes into the subtle energies created by the labyrinth's shapes and directions. These subtle energies resonate with one's mind, emotions, thoughts and body to stimulate health and spiritual growth. These mazes were used in ancient times all over the globe: China, Peru, England, the

---

[397] Redmond, Layne. *Op. Cit.*, Pg. 91.

[398] Andrews, Shirley. Lemuria and Atlantis, Studying the Past to Survive the Future, *Op. Cit.*, Pg. 116.

[399] Decker, Jerry, in introduction for Davidson, David. Shape Power: A Treatise on How Form Converts Universal Aether into Electromagnetic and Gravitic Forces and Related Discoveries in Gravitational Physics, Rivas Publishing: Arizona, 1997. Pg. xiii.

United States and many other places. The nave at the Chartres
Cathedral in France has a labyrinth inlaid into the floor.

Entomologist Phil Callahan discovered how insects and a few
plants use geometric shapes to receive and transmit
electromagnetic and acoustic sound waves.[400] Nature uses subtle
energy emitted from shapes in many ways.

Corinne Heline, Christian mystic and author, wrote that many
countries correlated shapes and sounds: "Every sound emanates a
certain color and takes on a definite form. Conversely, every form
gives forth a sound: that sound is its keynote. Everything, from
molecule to man and from plants to solar system, possesses a
keynote of its own. The sum total of all of these notes makes up
the music of the spheres."[401]

Dr. William Tiller of Stanford University, wrote about frequencies
within our bodies: "Each atom and molecule, cell and gland in our
body has a characteristic frequency at which it will absorb and
emit radiation."[402] In other words, each part of your body has a
signature frequency in which it will send and receive vibrations.
This corresponds to colors and tones that can amplify or sedate
energy within a body. Colors and tones were used for healing
purposes.

Many people have difficulty imagining that colored light creates a
physiological effect, but medical research verifies this is the case.
In an example, in some types of neonatal jaundice, blue–light
therapy is applied to the infant's skin to cause a chemical reaction
in the blood circulating under the surface of the skin, effectively
lessening bilirubin levels.[403] In another case, an ultraviolet light
generates the production of vitamin D. The human body also
produces vitamin D when exposed to sunlight. Additionally, full
spectrum light exposure helps those with seasonal affective

---

[400] Decker, Jerry. *Ibid,* Pg. xi.
[401] Heline, Corinne. *Op. Cit.*, Pg. 8.
[402] DelVecchio, Kimberly. "*Samvahan* Vibrational Medicine," *Healing Springs,* # 25, April
– May, 2005.
[403] Bilirubin is the yellow breakdown product of normal heme catabolism. Heme is found in
hemoglobin, a principal component of red blood cells. Bilirubin is excreted in bile and urine
and elevated levels may indicate certain diseases. It is responsible for the yellow color of
bruises, urine and the yellow discoloration in jaundice.

disorder (SAD), a condition believed to be caused by insufficient light exposure through the eyes to the hypothalamus and to the pituitary gland, which helps regulate the endocrine system.[404] These are some ways in which colors subtly affect the body. Likewise, the color of an Egyptian amulet also influenced subtle energy.

One of the foundations of color healing is that chemical elements radiate subtle frequencies correlating to certain colors. Color transfers information via octave resonance. For example, the prevailing corresponding color wave of hydrogen is red and that of oxygen is blue.[405] Each organ also has sympathetic resonance with a color wavelength. The liver is believed to radiate energy that is an octave below red, the pituitary green, the spleen violet, the circulatory system magenta, and the lymphatic system yellow.

When a particular organ or body system is underactive, its energy has decreased. To activate the problematic organ, an energizing color is projected onto the skin near the organ (or sometimes on the entire body). If a system is overactive (for example, a fever), the remedy is the opposite; a depressing color is used. Everything on the red side of the color spectrum is more or less stimulating, while the blue spectrum portion is sedating.

Sometimes healing and magical spells were written on papyrus and placed in water. A person drank the "magical" potion. Jacques Benveniste,[406] a French immunologist, showed that water "remembered" the vibration of something even when no molecules of the original substance remained. This evidence gives credence to the Egyptian healing procedure of drinking water exposed to special written words.

The Egyptians were opened minded about healing. They considered healing through: emotions, the subconscious mind, prayers, herbs, dance, amulets, colors, shapes and last but not least – sound and music.

---

[404] http://www.dinshahhealth.org
[405] http://www.dinshahhealth.org
[406] March 12, 1935 – October 3, 2004

The Bible and Egyptian Magic

The *Bible* described the power of Egyptian magic. Below is an excerpt from the *Bible, Exodus* 7:

Verse 8 The Lord said to Moses and Aaron, Verse 9 "When Pharaoh says to you, 'Perform a miracle,' then say to Aaron, 'Take your staff and throw it down before Pharaoh and it will become a snake.'" Verse 10 So Moses and Aaron went to Pharaoh and did just as the Lord commanded. Aaron threw his staff down in front of Pharaoh, and it became a snake. Verse 11 Pharaoh then summoned wise men and sorcerers, and the Egyptian magicians also did the same things by their secret arts. Verse 12 Each threw down his staff and it became a snake. (In Egypt, snake charmers today still use ancient "magical" secrets. They can paralyze a snake – making it straight like a staff.)

Verse 19 The Lord said to Moses, "Tell Aaron, 'Take your staff and stretch out your hand over the waters of Egypt – over the streams and canals, over the ponds and all the reservoirs and they will turn to blood.' Blood will be everywhere in Egypt, even in the wooden buckets and stone jars." Verse 20 Moses and Aaron did just as the Lord had commanded. He raised his staff in the presence of Pharaoh and struck the water of the Nile and all the water was changed into blood. Verse 21 The fish in the Nile died and the river smelled so bad that the Egyptians could not drink its water. Blood was everywhere in Egypt. Verse 22 But the Egyptian magicians did the same things by their secret arts.

The *Old Testament* continues, "Then the Lord said to Moses, 'Tell Aaron, 'Stretch out your hand with your staff over the streams, canals and ponds and make frogs come up on the land of Egypt.'" Verse 26 So Aaron stretched out his hand over the waters of Egypt and the frogs came up and covered the land. Verse 27 But the magicians did the same things by their secret arts; they also made frogs come up on the land of Egypt.

Not only Moses, but the Egyptian magicians turned sticks to snakes, water to blood and created frogs using words, sticks and their hands.

Hieroglyphs

The Egyptians used words to transfer or receive subtle energy from the realms of emotional, mental and physical vibrations. The energies of word, vowel and consonant sounds were carefully studied.

Gadalla implied that language and music were not once as separate as they are today: "For the ancient Egyptians, music and language were two sides of the same coin. The written symbols ("letters") are sonic pictures, i.e. each spoken letter has a specific vibration (pitch), just like a musical alphabet."[407] Many ancient languages, including Egyptian, have been referred to as "languages of light." Ancient people believed that everything in our world had a vibration. For example, the vibration of a stick or a feeling could not be heard – but they possessed vibration none the less. They believed that within sound waves there would be an equivalent sound for everything in their world. Their words were not just symbolic, but energetic thumbnails of the real thing. In modern times, the association between a word and the thing it describes is mainly symbolic. The ancient energetic associations with the sound of a word have dissipated in modern languages. (Some of the links still remain in most languages – what the English instructors call *onomatopoeia* – such as what the *buzzing* of bees or the *hiss* of a snake conjure up – the sound of the word as it is pronounced, makes the sound that the actual object makes or is.)

Not only did ancient people believe that there was vibration within music, art and spoken words, but also in physical shapes. They considered shapes found in nature "sacred," producing tiny vibrations that softly tuned viewers to harmony with the Earth. Since God created Earth, sacred geometric energy was considered divine energy. In an example the shape entitled Vesica Pisces is formed during an eclipse – as one celestial sphere overlaps another. It is considered "sacred geometry" because of this connection to nature. The energy of this 2–D shape is associated with positive things. It is the basic motif in the Flower of Life and an overlay of the Tree of Life symbols. On its side, it resembles a fish and is associated with Jesus Christ. Ancient people believed

---

[407] Gadalla, Moustafa. Egyptian Rhythm: The Heavenly Melodies, *Op. Cit.*, Pg. 82.

that even gazing at sacred geometry would bring (tiny packets of) positive energy to you. Some said that shapes emitted tiny sounds or energies below our hearing that were uplifting and harmonizing.

This same idea was woven into the selection of the shapes used for hieroglyphs. The proportions of the hieroglyphs were often prescribed from sacred geometry and number patterns found in nature (such as phi or the Fibonacci numbers). Likewise as we have seen earlier, their musical scales used these same patterns. In this way, the visual presentation of Egyptian words emitted harmony. There was a reason for each precise shape of each hieroglyph,[408] according to Egyptologist, Gadalla: "The proportions of these symbols must be analyzed harmonically, as to the relationship between sound and physical form, and the metaphysical significance of each symbol."[409]

Diodorus of Sicily,[410] a first century BC historian, stated: "The Egyptians' writing expresses the intended concept by the significance of the objects it copied. For instance, they draw a hawk, which signifies everything which happens swiftly, since this animal is practically the swiftest of winged creatures."[411] The energy portrayed was subtly transferred to all swift things.

Author Freddy Silva suggested that the Egyptian hieroglyphs created subtle energy in the subconscious mind. "As metaphors of the world above and below, they were also used to raise a person's awareness. This was achieved by encoding the glyphs to unlock information buried in the subconscious mind."[412]

The Egyptian language was written so that it could flow in any direction: up, down, left or right. It could create aesthetic symmetry. The same is true for music, as melodies ascend and descend. Pitches and rhythms flow back and forth. Both can create symmetry.

---

[408] Gadalla, Moustafa. Egyptian Harmony: The Visual Music, *Op. Cit.*, Pgs. 96–97.
[409] Gadalla, Moustafa. Egyptian Harmony: The Visual Music, *Op. Cit.*, Pg. 98.
[410] Diodorus Siculus
[411] Diodorus of Sicily in Book I as quoted by Gadalla, Moustafa. *Ibid,* Pg. 95.
[412] Silva, Freddy. Secret in the Fields: The Science and Mysticism of Crop Circles, Hampton Roads: VA, 2002, Pg. 147.

Magic Words

Magic was a central theme in ancient Egyptian life; the mystical and supernatural were entirely *real* to people of these times. "Magical words" were powerful tools. The Egyptian priests were famous for their spells, achieving acclaim even in the historical writings of their enemies. In dynamic contrast, reciting a spell today would be ridiculed and compared to an imaginative child saying "hocus pocus" or "abracadabra." Interestingly, in ancient Hebrew, the word "abracadabra," (a magic word), means "I create what I speak." In another way of viewing this: sound creates form in matter.

The Egyptians kept tedious records of what tiny effects were produced from words (sound vibrations), and related the energy of the words to colors, smells, shapes and materials. The Egyptian priests acted like scientists – observing, refining and documenting subtle energy effects to enhance their magical spells.[413] This knowledge was a highly prized possession of the Egyptian priesthood.

Magical words, rhythms and tones were critical in casting spells. Notice that the word "spell" also means the writing of letters in the correct order. Incanting magic words included speaking letters in the correct order to produce a special subtle influence. Each word that we pronounce can be considered a "spell."

Although modern man has lost the knowledge of the subtle power potential of words, he is on the verge of rediscovering this information. Sound can project patterns on physical matter, as documented by:

- Scientist Clarence Miller's[414] photographs of unique shapes created by vowels
- Masaru Emoto's photographs of frozen water crystal shapes – affected by words
- Scientist Chaldini's invention of putting sand on a plate and vibrating the plate with sounds to produce images in the sand

---

[413] Scott, Cyril. *Op. Cit.*, Pg. 162.
[414] Miller, Dayton, Clarence. <u>The Science of Musical Sounds</u>, Mc Millen Co.: NY, 1916.

In the videos of Swiss physicist Hans Jenny, a metal plate with sand on top of it is vibrated by sound. The sound waves travel to the edges and return, intersecting other vibrational lines. Nodal points are created at intersection points and the sand is pushed away where the vibrational energy is greatest. In the areas of low vibration, the sand accumulates. In this way, shapes were formed in the sand. Musical intervals create patterns, when vibrating sand. The patterns become more elaborate as the pitch is raised.

In 1787, German physicist Ernst Chladni published experiments showing geometric forms created by sound waves. With a violin bow, he vibrated the edge of a metal plate that had sand on it. The plate was bowed until it reached resonance – at which point the sand formed geometric patterns – these patterns showed the nodal or intersection regions of the resonant sound waves passing through the metal plate. Today, these patterns are often called cymatic images, a term coined by Swiss physicist Hans Jenny.

The CymaScope machine translates the sounds of intervals, two notes played together, into 2–D shapes. On the CymaScope website[415] (found in the footnotes) there are pictures of images formed from sounds produced by intervals equating to golden ratios. These "sound" images look like primitive organisms, perhaps representing a connection between sound and life.

As seen in Emoto's work, the vibrations of words subtly influence the shape of matter. The Egyptians believed that words were sources of miniscule energy. Words were dissected into smaller units of sound (vowels, phonemes and consonances) and each individual sound carried its own tiny force. Special sounds (repeated many times) unlocked the door to higher states of consciousness and produced desired energy. According to Gadalla, the Egyptians developed an extremely precise use of consonants and vowels to accomplish highly specific acts of white magic.[416]

Transformation was achieved through sounds and specific words. The god Thoth (also known as *Tehuti*, "the Divine Tongue") was

[415] cymascope.com
[416] Tame, David. The Secret Power of Music: The Transformation of Self and Society Through Musical Energy, Destiny Books: VT, 1984, Pg. 276.

the keeper of the "Words of Power". He obtained strength by properly using pronunciation and intonation. Words of power produced a "three dimensional matrix that resonated aether" (perhaps tiny vibrating strings – as in modern physics) to create reality in matter. In an example, the Goddess of Magic, Isis, healed her child of a fatal scorpion bite by using specific words of power to expel the poison and reestablish the child's life force.[417]

Gadalla emphasized that words were further enhanced by a healer's voice quality. "By pronouncing certain words or names of powers, in the proper manner and tone of voice, a priest or physician could heal the sick."[418] Dr. T.C. Singh, head of the Department of Botany at Annamalai University, conducted scientific experiments on the effects of prayers on plants. In one experiment with live bacteria, people cursed, *via prayers and chants*. The cursed bacteria died at the end of the day. The control group of bacteria (prayed for) thrived.[419] Bill Sweet published the book, *A Journey into Prayer: Pioneers of Prayer in the Laboratory: Agents of Science or Satan?* describing the thousands of scientific studies done on prayer and plants by Bruce and John Klingbeil. These studies showed the results of prayer, or subtle thought and emotional energy, directly impacting plants.

According to researchers Brian and Ester Crowley, special words, pronounced correctly, provided nourishment for the hungry, created health and provided protection.[420] Specific sounds tempered the rain, wind, storms, rivers and seas. In an example, Jesus walked on water and a storm obeyed His command. With His words, He fed 5,000 people with only a small amount of food. His divine consciousness was part of the miracle, but so was his voice. The *Bible*[421] tells that Joseph, Mary and the young Jesus

---

[417] Decker, Jerry, in introduction for Davidson, David. Shape Power: A Treatise on How Form Converts Universal Aether into Electromagnetic and Gravitic Forces and Related Discoveries in Gravitational Physics, *Op. Cit.*, Pg. xiv.

[418] Gadalla, Moustafa. Egyptian Rhythm: The Heavenly Melodies, *Op. Cit.*, Pg. 182.

[419] Heline, Corinne. Music: The Keynote of Human Evolution, New Age Bible and Philosophy Center: Santa Monica, CA, reprinted 1986, Pg. 123.

[420] Crowley, Brian & Esther. Words of Power; Sacred Sounds of East & West, Llewellyn Publications: Minn., 1991, Pg. 110.

[421] Bible: Mathew 2:13–15

fled to Egypt to avoid King Herod. Perhaps Jesus learned from Egyptian priests.[422]

The *Bible* states, "The Word was in the beginning and that very Word was with God and God was that Word."[423] The Christian God is associated with a word. Thoth, the Egyptian god of the moon, magic and writing, also spoke creative words that formed the spiral patterns found in nature.

All Egyptians had two names, one was a secret, only known by the person's mother and the goddess Isis. A person's real name was considered a direct energy connection to that person. In a curse, a person's name was used to transfer negative energy to him – via its sound. Therefore, the real name was hidden to prevent an enemy from using it in voodoo–like curses. Likewise, the Navajo Indians gave every child a secret name. They used their secret names in emergencies, such as in an invocation to the wind to prevent storm damage to their crops.[424]

In ancient Egypt, a person's public name was also significant. This name could describe the energy of the god he aimed to please and emulate. The symbolism of the name and its sound directly influenced the person. It was a direct subtle energy line to the god or what the name represented. The sound of the name was a tiny energy essence of the god.

The Egyptian names of things were thought to represent the energy of the object that the word represented. For example: *Neb* meaning gold, the perfect end product, the goal of the alchemist master. *Ben* (neb spelled backwards), meaning stone. The primordial stone, which was to be transformed into gold in Hermetic magic, therefore it was the opposite of the perfected (gold).[425] (Other examples: *Hetep* – stillness and *Ptah* (*Hetep* sounded backwards) – rearranging, forming. The energy of the word's sound was the same energy as the object to which the word

---

[422] The Bible described Joseph and Mary fleeing from their homeland to Egypt when Jesus was young.

[423] Bible, John 1:1. Lamsa, George, translated from the Aramaic of the Pershitta.

[424] Heline, Corinne. *Op. Cit.*, Pg. 88.

[425] Gadalla, Moustafa. Egyptian Harmony: The Visual Music, *Op. Cit.*, Pg. 48.

referred. [426] To express an opposite meaning, sounds of a word were simply reversed.

The Egyptians and the work of David Oates share a common fascination in reverse speech. Oates came to a different conclusion than the Egyptians regarding reverse speech. In 1984, Oates observed a damaged tape deck that played backwards. Surprisingly, he recognized words.[427] This tickled his curiosity, causing him to study this phenomenon. Oates' claim is that, on average, once in every 15 – 20 seconds of grammatically correct conversation, a person produces two related sentences, a "forward–spoken" message that is heard consciously, and a "backwards" message unconsciously embedded in the person's speech.

One explanation for this could be the tendency of the brain to perceive meaningful patterns in random noise (the reverse speech), but Oates believes it is far more. Oates claims that backward speech is always honest and reveals the truth about the speaker's intentions and motivations. People are not conscious of their subconscious thoughts; they hide unwanted issues. The subconscious mind stores this energy/thought somewhere and Oates contends that the reverse voice is one such location.

When we have a bad gut feeling about a communication with another, we may be subconsciously receiving an incongruous message. California State University published a paper finding that the brain is able to decode reverse speech;[428] on some unconscious level we interpret these hidden messages. Perhaps this is a method that we use to intuit things.

Magic's potency was based on spells, rituals and the energy of the magician. The Egyptians had rules for spells. A spell began with the words "*peret herou*," meaning "that which comes forth from the voice" or "the word is the deed." The sounds, intent and energy of the words were active ingredients in spells.

---

[426] Gadalla, Moustafa. *Ibid,* Pg. 47.
[427] The speed of the reverse speech also plays a factor in finding hidden messages.
[428] http://www.reversespeech.com/faq.htm Q 16

Magic rituals included things such as:

- Burning incense – this creates an aroma that subtly influences feelings and thoughts.
- Creating subtle energy structures with sound. For example, the Egyptians sang while moving in a circle around their sleeping spots. This subtle sound barrier wouldn't stop a person, but it would stop an insect or small animal, providing protection from small creatures such as scorpions.
- Using subtle energy ingredients from things such as colors, sounds, rhythms, shapes and objects.
- Creating a trance/altered state from sound and plants.
- Following Isis' instruction for singers – use their voice to carry energy out of their hands.
- The sound of a god's name contained a little packet of his strength. Each god was associated with the energy of a number and music using that number in some fashion. When the number was in the invocation, it strengthened the magic, intensified the spell, and ensured the spirit's presence.[429]
-

-

www.JillsWingsofLight.com – Art Galleries

---

[429] Channam, Talal, Ph.D. The Mystery of Numbers: Revealed through Their Digital Root, Create Space: South Carolina, 2011. Pg. 43.

Historian Layne Redmond described the purpose of ancient rituals and compared them to today's psychology: "There was no prayer without ritual, and the simplest ritual a libation of wine and sprinkling frankincense in the flame. Ritual behavior was a means of focusing the mind. The process of invoking the goddess through ritual and prayer, often accompanied by the powerful music of flute and the frame drum, was a means of visualizing what was hoped for. The use of creative visualization in contemporary therapeutic practices as a means of programming thought processes is very much the same technique."[430]

In summary, Egyptian magic was the careful use of subtle energy, often in the form of sound. The tiny packets of energy that we would not bother to notice today were studied, used and accumulated until there was sufficient energy to make a difference in a person's world. Likewise, music was the greatest tool to manipulate and accumulate subtle energy for the stabilization of the country. Music was a tool to study subtle energy and direct it in powerful ways, incorporating vitalizing energy into every facet of Egyptian life.

The End of a Great Civilization

The great culture of the ancient Egyptians officially began its decline in 332 BC when Alexander the Great conquered Egypt and native Egyptians lost the independent rule of their country. Rulers from other countries steered Egypt into further decline.

Composer Cyril Scott believed that the Egyptian civilization sought knowledge, which is easily equated with power; their love of knowledge morphed into love of power and selfishness.[431] Scott related that the decline of selfless attributes began in the priesthood, creating negative energy that eventually tumbled the great Egyptian civilization.[432]

Near the end of their powerful reign, Egyptian sacred music lost its prominence, especially when foreign governments assumed power. They neither understood nor respected the Egyptian music

[430] Redmond, Layne. *Op. Cit.*, Pgs. 116–117.
[431] Scott, Cyril. Music: Its Secret Influences throughout the Ages, *Op. Cit.*, Pg. 164.
[432] Scott, Cyril. Mu, *Op. Cit.*, Pg. 164.

and its harmonizing principles. At Egypt's demise, the sacred music was relegated to trivial purposes.

www.JillsWingsofLight.com – Art Galleries

Chapter Eight

Ancient Music of India
3102 BC to 483 BC

Little is known about the early settlers who lived in the Indus River Valley (modern India). Historians mark the Indian civilization beginning about 500 BC in the Indus Valley; yet recent discoveries push back the origin thousands of years. The sophisticated and well–planned cities of Harappa and Mohenjo Daro outshine the development of ancient cites in Egypt and Mesopotamia. At the archeological sites, no differences in social class can be discerned. The Harappa culture's origins and ultimate fate is unknown and their writing is completely indecipherable.[433]

Before written history, legends describe six semi–divine kings who reigned in India, each named Manu. They governed during three time periods, called the Ages of Gold, Silver and Copper. Legends of Golden Ages are found in Hindu, Greek and Asian texts. A Golden Age is a time in which harmony, stability and prosperity reign. It was a time in which mankind did not work for food. People lived to a very old age, maintaining youthful appearance, eventually dying peacefully. Their spirits remained to guide those left behind. In this global mythology, the Golden Age is the first in a sequence of four Ages of Man, followed by the Silver, Copper, and then the present age (Iron), which is a period

---

[433] http://listverse.com/2013/04/12/10–mysteries–that–hint–at–forgotten–advanced–civilizations/ 10 Mysteries That Hint At Forgotten Advanced Civilizations, Hestie Barnard Gerber, April 12, 2013.

of decline.[434] Legends describe that spiritual awareness decreased by about 25% with the passing of each age; the current Iron Age having little to no spiritual energies or information available to its people.[435]

An ancient written account describes the leader, Manu Vaivaswate, one of the divine kings in the Hindu legends, washing his hands in the river. A fish came to him and asked for protection from bigger fish. Manu saved the fish's life and, in exchange, the fish revealed to Manu information about the upcoming flood that would sweep the Earth. Manu built a wooden ark and boarded it along with seven wise sages, known as the Rishis. After the flood (~3102 BC) Manu embarked from the ark to the land now called India, while the Rishis became the stars of the Big Dipper. At this time, written history begins and archeological finds show that villages developed along the rivers. Two story houses and kilns for pottery were found dating to this time. For the sake of comparison, Fu Xi lived around 2850 BC in China and the first dynasty commenced in Egypt in 3100 BC.[436]

Spiritual author, Elizabeth Clare Prophet, attributed some influences on Hindu music to the ancient Lemurians; author Cyril Scott credited the origins of ancient Indian music to Atlantis. "The characteristics of Indian music are not those of sound volume but subtlety... Manu, the Ruler, counteracted the black magic prevalent among the Atlanteans.... He forbade playing existing music in India, the effects of which had proven so disastrous in Atlantis. He inaugurated a new scale and science of mantrams, so that the new race might respond to the higher vibrations and reach the mental plane. These mantrams were handed down by the Indian priests through the centuries."[437] Many of these musical customs are still revered today.

---

[434] Plato in Cratylus (397 e) recounts the golden race of humans who came first. http://en.wikipedia.org/wiki/Golden_Age

[435] Satya Yuga – Golden Age, Treta Yuga – Silver Age, Duapara Yuga – Copper Age.

[436] Bauer, Susan. The History of the Ancient World: From the Earliest Accounts to the Fall of Rome, W. W. Norton Co: New York, NY, 2007, Pgs. 30 –35.

[437] Scott, Cyril. Music: Its Secret Influences throughout the Ages, Samuel Weiser: London, 1958, Pg. 154. Reprinted in 2013 by Inner Traditions.com.

Hindu music originated, in part, from recitation of Indian religious texts – the *Vedas* – dating from 4000 BC.[438] The *Old Testament* was likewise a musical script according to expert musicologist Ernest McClain.[439]

The musical chanting of religious texts helped people to refocus their concentration – away from physical – to spiritual issues. The shift created a spiritual tone, which helped people worship and made them open to the religious sects.

In the ancient Sankrit language, three words describe sounds: *nada, sruti and swara.* The ancient Hindus communicated great detail regarding sound – emulating its power and importance.

Sanskrit Words for Sound
Nada[440] The Sanskirt root *nad* means "to sound" or "to reverberate." *Nada* is: • Primordial sound, the pervading sound that animates the universe • A general word for musical sound • Vocal sound that flows along the body channels •
Swara is one of the seven notes of the Indian scale within an octave. Unlike Western notes, the seven *swaras* are general scale steps with pitches varying by increments of *srutis.*
Sruti are minute pitches, representing subtle differences between musical notes. The *sruti* are closer together than the closest notes in Western music. There are two to four *srutis* between each neighboring note in Western music. There are a total of 22 *srutis* in one octave in ancient Indian music.

---

[438] The four books of the Vedas are the most sacred texts of India, containing over 1,000 hymns. These holy books preserve poetry, invocations and mythology in the form of sacrificial chants dedicated to the Gods. Great care was taken to preserve these texts, which were passed down by oral tradition.

[439] McClain analyzed and compiled musical selections by decoding the Bible. See Bibal.com.

[440] *Nada* is also the root of the word *nadi,* meaning: "to flow" or "river." *Nadis* are the subtle nerve channels in which life energy flows throughout the body.

Four Hindu religious texts comprise the *Vedas*.[441] The oldest, the *Rig Veda*, dates back to 4000 BC. It was recited in a monotone, but later developed higher and lower pitched accents. Another portion of the *Vedas* centers on sacrificial ceremonies, suggesting *veena* instrumental accompaniment.

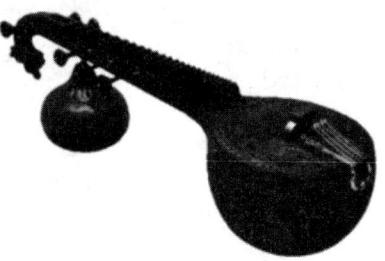

The Indian *Veena* Instrument[442]

Later, the chants included two main notes with two accents each. These became the first tetra chords (sets of four notes). The musical application of the third portion of the *Vedas* displays the foundation for today's Indian music. Three more notes were added to the original tetra chord, resulting in the first scale of seven notes. Musical arrangements of these seven notes became the first ragas.[443]

A raga is similar to a mode. A raga uses a series of five or more musical notes, which produce a specific feeling no matter what order they are played in. The musician improvises with these notes, but also follows in depth instructions that ensures his music delivers the prescriptive musical benefit and feeling of the raga.

In the original *Veda* text the seven tones (*swaras*) were called *Sadjama–grama*. As the chanting of the religious doctrines grew more sophisticated, so did the music. The Indians "flattened" the original *swaras* to create additional notes called the *Madhyama–grama*. This scale now had thirteen notes. Scales were built with the other twelve notes as foundations, collectively forming 13 scales called *murchanas*. To further illustrate this, one scale would

---

[441] The four parts of the *Vedas: Rig, Sama, Yajur* and *Atharvana*

[442] http://en.wikipedia.org/wiki/Veena

[443] According to Sakuntala Narasimhan in *"Invitation to Indian Music."*

start on the first note of the original scale, and a different scale had the second note of the original scale as a base and so on. Likewise in Western music, we also have a scale on each available note. We have a scale starting on C, C#, D, D#, E and so on. In the 17th century, the Carnatic musician and author, Sri Venkatamakhin, recast existing Indian scales into the 72 *Melakarta* Scheme, which is used today.

During the 12th and 13th centuries AD, the music of India separated into two distinct styles: North (Hindustani) and South (Carnatic). Northern India experienced invasions from Asia Minor, with crusaders spreading *Islam*. Muslim rulers introduced musical changes. Northern India's music was also influenced by Arabic and Persian music, resulting in a new style of music, called Hindustani music (meaning the "Music of India"). The Southern music, called "Carnatic," maintained the old traditions.[444]

Stories from around the world describe ancient musical traditions, unfortunately the practices or performances are near extinct. We cannot hear what their music sounded like – with the exception of a few masters performing ancient Hindu music. These musicians escort us to the ancient past to experience magical music. I have been honored to meet two of these world renowned masters, Sri Swamiji and Ali Akbar Khan.[445]

Sri Ganapathy Sachchidananda Swamiji, or simply Sri Swamiji, of India, uses music to heal the body and elevate the soul. Millions seek his musical gifts to uplift physical, spiritual and emotional energies. Sri Swamiji teaches, "*Nadopaasana* (worship of Sound) is a great spiritual science. Our scriptures declare *Nada* (sound) as *NadaBrahma,* meaning that sound is the supreme power. When devotedly meditating on sound, the doors of the divine open, helping the aspirant merge to be one with the supreme Lord."[446] Sri Swamiji continues: "There is an intimate relationship between

---

[444] www.dattapeetham.com, *Swamiji's Music* by Bill Osmer
[445] Ali Akbar Khan (1922 –2009), was a Hindustani classical musician of the *Maihar gharana*, trained by his father, Allauddin Khan. He came to America in 1955 and popularized Indian classical music in the West. He established a music school in Calcutta, the Ali Akbar College of Music, California and a branch in Basel, Switzerland. Khan composed many classical *ragas* and film scores. Khan was nominated for five Grammy Awards and received India's second highest civilian honor, the *Padma Vibhushan*.
[446] Dattaretreat: To Follow Him is to Follow His Words! Jan. 17, 2011.

music and God, but only when 'Nada' (sound) is approached with reverence and devotion."[447]

Absorbing music can be a sublime path to enlightenment, perhaps "the easiest way to attain salvation"; Ancient people described sublime music as an elevator to heaven. Ancient sages underscored this point, and said, "God is nothing but personified music."

Ethno–musicologist, David Reck adds, "In India, it is said, the universe hangs on sound. Not ordinary sound, but a cosmic vibration so massive, subtle and all–encompassing that everything seen and unseen (including man) is filled with it. The ancient seers practiced yoga and austerities to tune themselves to this cosmic sound, to make it vibrate in their spinal columns, hearts and brains."[448]

Like a great antenna, Sri Swamiji consciously connects with divine energy. Forces flowing into the master musician subtly massage the listener with beneficial energy transmissions.

"I do not claim to heal. The Lord heals. I am only the instrument," Swamiji confessed. "Some Higher Force takes care of my process, once I decide to heal through Music."[449] Sri Swamiji's musical transmissions help listeners across different backgrounds, cultures and religions. Sri Swamiji describes the openness of music: "Music is no religion, yet it is all religions. It has no caste, creed nor discrimination."

I have heard Sri Swamiji in concert a number of times. Even with high expectations, I was not prepared for these extraordinary experiences. At one concert, I quickly fell into a deep trance, becoming completely immobile. When I "awoke" I felt renewed and refreshed (but didn't remember the concert). At another concert, I experienced acupuncture–like needles at *nadi* intersections in my body – releasing energy blocks. Next, purified energy swirled into my body through the top of my head. Some of

---

[447] Dattaretreat: *Ibid,* Dec. 2, 2011.
[448] Reck, David. Music of the Whole Earth, Schribers & Sons: NY, 1977.
[449] http://www.dycusa.org/nadaprasara2003/moreinfo.asp

the claims of antiquity seem like faerie tales, but after Sri Swamiji's live concerts, I realized that music is more powerful than even I had imagined.

The responses, of attendees to the concerts, vary widely. I have seen people slumped over in a trance. Many were excited about internal healing sensations. Others were commenting on which songs they liked best, as if the music was a "regular" concert.

Sri Swamiji's live concerts incorporate frequencies to balance the weather and appeal to astrology; frequencies detect and adjust the audience's needs and deliver the most potent treatment. Concert attendees receive diverse benefits: physical healing, spiritual guidance and experiences of bliss/divine love.

Sri Swamiji reveals what music means to Him: "Music is my language and expression. Music is my soul and religion." The ancient sage, Plato, would agree as he said, "Music has privileged access to the soul."[450]

Sri Swamiji annually tours the world, usually visiting Canada and the United States in early summer. His schedule is posted at Dattapeetham.com. *You Tube* videos of his concerts are available; however, the energetic experience is much stronger in a live concert.

Sri Swamiji[451]

---

[450] Thaut, Michael. Rhythm, Music and the Brain: Scientific Foundations and Clinical Applications, Routledge: NY, 2005, Pg. 27.
[451] http://www.dattapeetham.com

Vibrations Connect Us

Sri Swamiji teaches that each vibration in the universe originates from the same source. Vibrations differ only in pitch, rhythm and degree of force. According to Swamiji's website, vibrations turn into atoms that generate life. Many of these tiny vibrations become audible when massed together. Similarly, our voice is a composite sound created by smaller sounds within our bodies.

Sri Swamiji relates: "The entire universe is immersed in *Nada* (sound). There is *Nada* in everything around us. There can be no movement without *Nada*. There is nothing in this universe that is free from the influence of *Nada*." Sound vibrations have a steady, subtle and powerful influence on everything.

A universe of subtle sounds influences us continually – though we are unaware. Plants and animals receive and interpret unheard vibrations. They anticipate approaching weather conditions, while man is often unconscious of these warnings. We live in a sea of vibrations; we are not conscious of many of the frequencies that surround us.

Vibrations transmit the conditions of one person to another – often unconsciously. For example, you can sense when someone is angry before a word is spoken. Likewise, when a person coughs in an assembly, many others are stimulated to do likewise. The vibration of the cough is subconsciously copied from one to another. The same thing happens with yawning, laughter, excitement and depression. The subtle energy of man interacts with his surroundings, according to the law of sympathetic resonance.

The observable results of sound depend on matter's density. Thoughts and emotions are more malleable than bones. However, even a bone fracture heals quicker when exposed to the "right" vibrations. An ultrasound advertisement reads, "Broken bones heal with lightning speed thanks to a device that bombards the body with low–intensity sound waves. Take off casts by using ultrasound for 20 minutes a day."[452]

---

[452] http://www.unexplainable.net/artman/publish/article_1802.shtml

Quickly, we observe the impact of sound on our feelings. Sounds are received by the ears, but also by receptors under the skin and through bone conduction. Sounds passing through bones either charge or discharge the nervous system.[453] It takes longer to notice, but bones conduct a wider range of frequencies than our ears can. Bones conduct waves from 10 hertz to 100,000 hertz, as compared to the 20 to 20,000 hertz that we hear with our ears. Many of us cringe when we listen to a recording of our voice. This is because bone conduction is more effective at transmitting lower frequency sounds to the brain, which means that we perceive our voice as being deeper than what it is.

Focusing on music creates a "turning away" of one's attention from the visible to the invisible world.[454] Music gets under your skin and is experienced internally.[455] Being invisible, it does not easily reveal its significance. It has the power to bond, attract, heal, arouse and charm. Music stills our thoughts, provides emotional cleansing and can help a person feel fulfilled by creating purposeful, intense feelings.

According to author David Burrows, music can bring people together. "Seeing separates things and sorts them out, but hearing connects the group as vision cannot."[456] Author William Benzon echoed this theme, "With music, individual brains are coupled in shared activity."[457]

Music conveys heartfelt feelings more powerfully than words. Sounds provide more detailed information and feelings than words can describe. Once or perhaps twice, a person will read a book, visit the same art gallery or attend a play. He ingests the experience and moves on. Yet, with music, he may endlessly delight in hundreds of sessions, listening to his favorite songs. In this way, one gets a much higher dose of vibrational energy from music.

---

[453] www.dattapeetham.com, "Swamiji's Music," Bill Owen
[454] Burrows, David. Time and the Warm Body: A Musical Perspective on the Construction of Time, Brill: Boston, MA, 2007, Pg. 71.
[455] Burrows, David. *Ibid,* Pg. 70.
[456] Burrows, David. *Ibid,* Pg. 83.
[457] Benzon, William. Beethoven's Anvil, Music in Mind and Culture, Basic Books: NY, 2001, Pg. 23.

An ancient Indian story relates a conversation between the sage Markendeya and King Vajra. "Once upon a time, a king, desirous of learning sculpture, went to a wise sage and asked to be taught the art. But the teacher said, 'How can you know the laws of sculpture, if you do not know painting?' 'Teach me painting, Master,'" said the disciple. "But how will you understand painting without the knowledge of dance?" "Instruct me in the technique of dance, O Wise One," requested the royal student. The teacher continued, "But you cannot dance without knowing instrumental music." "Let me know the laws of instruments," prayed the king. The guru replied, "Instruments can only be learned if you study the art of singing." "If singing is the fountainhead of all arts, I beg you, Oh Master, reveal to me the secrets of vocal music."[458] Sound is far more powerful than we perceive it to be.

Sri Swamiji's Methods

To gain real insight into the power of ancient Indian music I constantly invoke the modern master Sri Swamiji – who embodies the wisdom and power of music though the ages. Swamiji instructs: When ill, the body's rhythm and tone are out of order. How does one identify which frequencies, rhythms or harmonies need tuning? How does a person select appropriate musical nourishment? Sri Swamiji shares a few secrets, "I walk into the audience to discover clues of people's suffering." With intuitive powers he analyzes the physical, emotional and mental needs of the audience. Sri Swamiji may use a tall, thin crystal to enhance his analysis; the crystal resonates with the frequencies emanating from the audience.[459] With closed eyes, Sri Swamiji sees varying colors dancing out of the crystal. The crystal amplifies his perception of the audience's auras, revealing the crowd's needs. The audience's mental, physical and emotional frequencies correlate – through octave resonance – with the colors that Sri Swamiji sees. Sri Swamiji uses this information to select music to best benefit the audience. Sri Swamiji sends energy to correct the audience's issues through the same crystal. This pre–healing event prepares the audience for the concert.

---

[458] Deva, Chaitanya. An Introduction to Indian Music, New Delhi Publications, 1992.
[459] Crystals play a vital role in transmitting energy, both with radio transmissions and also among meditators who use crystals for balancing and calming effects. Crystals also represent, resonate and harmonize the five elements: Earth, air, fire, water and ether/spirit.

Sri Swamiji considers many factors before selecting music for an audience. He:

- *Selects pieces* to alleviate specific ailments.
- Uses *pitches, intervals and rhythms* to strengthen chakras and for multifaceted impacts.
- Selects *ragas* to balance elemental energies.
- Considers the audience's average level of consciousness (and composite frequency) and selects music depending on the listeners' average evolution. Sri Swamiji *gradually* raises a person's overall frequencies. Too much, too quickly, can present integration issues.
- Balances the incoming influences of the energy from the planets and celestial sources. Challenging astrological energies are mitigated with properly timed and composed music.

Swamiji's Mother by Jill Mattson

Swamiji revealed, "I attune man to God through belief and music. After that, the body consciousness vanishes gradually and then the affliction ceases to be experienced and exist." We give energy to whatever receives our attention. Why not give our attention to heavenly music? Elevating our aspirations eventually will elevate ourselves.

Nuero–scientist, Dave Eagleman, argued that the strength of the subconscious mind often trumps conscious thought.[460] Swamiji's music purifies the listener's subconscious mind, transforming unseen negative energy. Music can sooth the nerves, creating peace and stillness of mind. Physical issues improve with a healthy subconscious mind.

The intent and *strength* of the musician amplifies the power of his music. The musician's consciousness mingles with his sounds. "I know the precise form of healing that is to be accomplished through music. I firmly set my attention, becoming determined to heal. I am my own master." Swamiji exclaimed.

During his concerts, Sri Swamiji's energy voluminously increases before he walks on stage. Like a Sumo wrestler getting "pumped" before a fight, Sri Swamiji focuses his benevolent intention and consciousness until its power peaks.

During a concert Sri Swamiji uses special music to harmonize elemental energy within people. "I am both a servant and master of nature. I recreate the sounds of elemental energy from nature. I then give the audience a dose of the required energy they need for balance." Animals, plants, and minerals have healing energy that we can connect with through the vehicle of music.

Most physical pain comes from energy retardation and discordant (incorrect) frequencies. In a blockage, energy is converted into heat in the cells and is perceived as pain. Special Indian songs, alter energy flow to clear blockages, alleviating pain. The body's immune system normally eliminates attacking viruses and germs. Sound can strengthen the immune system and weaken unwanted frequencies of germs and viruses.[461]

The listener's role in healing, rivals the importance of the musician. One's intent, belief and receptivity affect the outcome. When people pay insufficient attention to music, they decrease its impact. "To get the most from healing music," Swamiji advises,

---

[460] Eagleman, David. "Secret Life of the Mind: The Subconscious Knows Things that your Conscious Mind does not," *Discover*, 9, 2011, Pg. 50.
[461] When the body's immune system is weak, it has lost its "vitality and confidence" (Confidence is located within each cell. The brain is not the sole source of consciousness.)

"Listen and energetically merge with the performer." This greatly amplifies the concert experience.

Impact of Hindu Music

Cyril Scott described the ancient Indian priests as contemplative. Their awareness of subtlety increased with meditations and mantras until they invoked *samadhi* – a super conscious trance. "In that state of trance they heard the 'music of the vision,' but they made no effort to translate it into Earthly sound."[462] Scott hinted that by perceiving great subtlety, one may access the famed "music of the spheres."

Scott reflected on the impact of the Hindu quarter tone (today a half tone is the smallest division of a note): "Because the Hindu quarter tone is so subtle, it subtilized the mind, inducing a contemplative trance. The outcome was more than acquisition of knowledge, but wisdom, for wisdom is subtilized spiritualized knowledge."[463] Scott correlated the perception of micro–tones to the ability to grasp the deeper subtle meanings beneath words. Many credit Hindu music for the Indian mastery of meditative techniques.

Indian music lacks the energizing sounds of Western music. The Indian culture lacked these attributes as well, according to Scott. Their music accentuated dreamy and meditative qualities, encouraging obsessive spiritual desires.[464] Many attributed their lack of industrialism and material sophistication to the influence of their music. Recently, Western music has increased in popularity in India. Simultaneously, the material sophistication of India has also increased.

The *Om* and Spiritual Silence

Hindu sounds are divided into three categories: 1.) Sounds of the physical world, 2.) Heartbeat and 3.) Silence,[465] which is

---

[462] Scott, Cyril. *Op. Cit.*, Pg. 154.
[463] Scott, Cyril. *Ibid*, Pg. 155.
[464] Scott, Cyril. *Ibid*, Pg. 155.
[465] The ancient Hindu people classified silence as a sound.

represented by the sound *om (aum)*.[466] Just as the Chinese revered the *kung*, the cosmic note of creation, the sound of *om* in Hindu tradition is equally revered.

According to Hindu teachings, chanting *om* increases consciousness; this brings forth energy from higher dimensions of reality. David Tame pointed out that the sound of *om* creates energy, when he said: "Descending in frequency from the realms of pure spirit into the arena of time and space, the *om* shapes and organizes primordial matter–energy; it causes atoms to coalesce, thus manifesting in physical matter."[467]

Church bells and Chinese gongs were also designed to expand our consciousness. The Aztecs blew conch–shell trumpets to evoke this divine and uplifting energy at dawn. Tibetan spiritual music also embraced the concept of a cosmic *om* sound.[468] The Logos[469] was a revered sound in Christianity (In the *Bible* the "Logos" is a word, a sound). Many cultures used certain sounds, such as the *om* sound, to harmonize and increase the vitality of their people's subtle energy systems, leading to greater health, intelligence and emotional control.[470] Clearly, the original cosmic sound of creation rang across the globe.

Sri Swamiji described one method of chanting the o*m* sound: "Chant it prayerfully, not rhythmically. Breathe deeply and then slowly pronounce the three sounds within *om*; (aa, oo, mm). Close your mouth when pronouncing the prolonged *m* sound. On your in–breath, notice how the sound has a purifying effect."[471]

A second method of chanting *om* comes from the ancient Egyptians. While in meditation, breathe in through your nose until your lunges are full, then breathe out your mouth. Open your eyes every several minutes to keep awake and then slowly close them.

---

[466] Crowley, Brian & Esther. Words of Power; Sacred Sounds of East &West, Llewellyn Publications: MN, 1991, Pg. 142.

[467] Tame, David. *Op. Cit.,* Pg. 171.

[468] Tame, David. *Ibid*, Pg. 226.

[469] "The Word was in the beginning and that very word was with God and God was that Word." Bible, John 1:1. Lamsa, George, Bible translated from Aramaic of the Peshitta.

[470] Listen to this at www.ancient-music.com

[471] Listen to this at www.Ancient-Music.com

Chant *om* for a minute or so and then chant it silently imagination.[472]

The Sanskrit language differentiates between audible and cosmic sounds. Both the Chinese and the Hindu believed that this inaudible sound elevated a soul and influenced society.[473] They devised spiritual practices to improve their hearing of subtle and high pitched sounds. Some uses of the *om* sound were believed to attune the soul to these "sounds of silence."

Spiritual leaders have long revered silence as evidenced in Hindu and biblical sources:

- "Silence is the altar of God."[474]
- "Be still and know that I am God."[475]
- "When we go into the inner chamber and shut the door to every sound that comes from life without, the voice of God will speak to our soul, and we will know the key note of our life."[476]
- "My Soul charged me to listen for voices that rise neither from the tongue nor the throat. Before that day I heard but dull and naught save clamor and loud cries came to my ears. But now I have learned to listen to silence, to hear its choirs singing the songs of ages. Chanting the hymns of space and disclosing the secrets of eternity."[477]

Focused, inner listening amplifies the sounds of our heart, circulatory and respiratory systems – our subtle chorus of inner sounds. Mystics profess that as one journeys towards enlightenment, a series of subtle, internal sounds may also be heard in quiet meditation. During meditation, people have professed to hear:

- Pounding of the sea's surf
- Humming of bees
- Tinkling of soft bells

---

[472] Listen to this at www.Ancient-Music.com
[473] Tame, David. *Op. Cit.*, Pg. 172.
[474] Autobiography of a Yogi is an autobiography of Paramahansa Yogananda (1893 – 1952) first published in 1946.
[475] Old Testament, Bible
[476] Hazrat Inayat Kan. Music of Life, Omega Publishing: New Lebanon, NY, 1983.
[477] Kahlil Gibran

- Chirping of crickets
- Babbling water of a brook
- Rumbling of thunder
- Roaring of a lion
- Blowing of a conch shell
- Gong of a big drum
- Strings of a harp
- Tone of a flute
- Sound of bag pipes
- Absence of all sound[478]

The *Bible* also refers to inner hearing, perhaps found in silence. "And I heard the voice from heaven. Like the sound of many waters, like the sound of loud thunder, the voice I heard was like the sounds of harpers playing on their harps."[479]

The ability to perceive these subtle inner sounds and receive associated benefits can be developed by patiently listening to silence. The Sufis believe that listening to these inner "sound currents" that include sounds that are not of the Earth, attune us to cosmic, uplifting forces.[480]

Correlations between Emotions and Music

Music historian Danielou reported that the Hindu sages defined musical energy: "The notes and chords of music have exact equivalents in every category of existence. Only the knowledge of such correspondences allows understanding of the real meaning of sounds and enables us to use them rationally as a means of evocation (of gods and higher spiritual energy)."[481]

Both ratios and feelings are linked to musical intervals. For example, a major third, such as the notes C and E, creates the ratio of 5/4. This interval creates a peaceful and loving feeling. Yet

---

[478] Van Dyke, Deborah. Traveling the Sacred Sound Current, Sound Current Music: Bowan Island, BC, Canada, 2001, Pg. 147.
[479] Bible, Revelations 14: 2
[480] Godwin, Joscelyn. Heaven and Earth: Mysticism in Music from Antiquity to Avant-Garde, Inner Traditions: VT, 1987, Pgs. 60, 61.
[481] Danielou, Alain. Music and the Power of Sound: The Influence of Tuning and Interval on Consciousness, Inner Traditions: VT, 1943, Pg. 87.

another musical interval, E+ and G+, leaves people feeling full of wonder or heroism,[482] creating the ratio 81/64. We can evoke an emotion with a sound. To illustrate this, combining the second and third notes of the ancient Hindu scale, adds a tinge of sadness, while adding sharp notes creates the feeling of arousal.

A study proved that the emotion correlated with an interval and the same feeling expressed by words, both create the same feeling. Researchers concluded, "The acoustic code for communicating emotions across music and speech is more similar than previously thought. The clearest correspondence occurred in the communication of sadness.[483] The minor third was the most common interval used to convey sadness in speech."[484] Musical intervals create a universal feeling and language. The Indians correlated notes with colors, emotions and God–like qualities.

Notes, Colors and Emotions[485]

Hindu Notes[486]	Notes Of the West	Colors	Emotions	Attributes of God
Sa	C	Red	sacred, ground, sky	God, the One
Fa	D♭	Brown	Sad, tender, shy, lovely, peaceful	God, we are mindful of
Ra	D	Orange	Vital, confident, commanding, honest	God, the all powerful
Ba	E♭	Tan	Sustenance, resignation, wonder	God, who provides

---

[482] E+ is a higher pitch than E, but lower than F. It is in between the half steps E and F.

[483] Curtis, Meagan and Bharucha, Jamshed. "The Minor Third Communicates Sadness in Speech, Mirroring its Use in Music." *Emotion*: Vol. 10, No. 3, 335–348. Tufts University, MA, 2010, Pg. 345.

[484] Curtis, Meagan and Bharucha, Jamshed. *Ibid*, Pg. 346.

[485] Information from Ron Bracale

[486] Western music uses seven notes within an octave. Likewise, Indian music also has seven *swaras* (notes). Each *swara* is identified and named by its position in the scale: *sa, ri, ga, ma, pa, dha* and *ni*. This is similar to do, re, mi, fa, so, la and te used in Western music.

Notes, Colors and Emotions[487]

Hindu Notes[488]	Notes Of the West	Colors	Emotions	Attributes of God
Ga	E	Yellow	Calm, joyful, content, compassion	God, our joy
Ma	F	Green	Feminine, passive, romantic, creative	God, the creator
Cha	F#	Black	Intensity, friction, mystery, surprise	God, our teacher
Pa	G	Blue	Masculine, active, fullness, clarity	God, our protection
La	Ab	Gray	Expectation, appealing, arousing	God, on whom we await
Dha	A	Indigo	Heroic, noble, restless, playful, brilliant	God, who fulfills
Ti	Bb	White	Beauty, hope, delicate, affectionate, purity	God, our Love
Ni	B	Violet	Bold, sensuous, childlike, desire of desires	God, our only desire
Sa	C	Red	Complete, abandoned, free, spiritual	God, the One

Certain chants create energy that is characteristic of a god, such as peace or joy energies. The chanters repeat phrases, called mantras, which are equated with virtues. Each time the singer chants, he creates a bit of this God–like attribute within. He acquires this

---

[487] Information from Ron Bracale, www.bracalemusic.com

[488] Western music uses seven notes within an octave. Likewise, Indian music also has seven *swaras* (notes). Each *swara* is identified and named by its position in the scale: *sa, ri, ga, ma, pa, dha* and *ni*. This is similar to do, re, mi, fa, so, la and te used in Western music.

habitual attribute with musical repetitions. Words and sounds are used to summon great celestial beings. Chanting a god's name strengthens one's contact with the god – like connecting with a subtle energy source.

Astrology and Music

The ancient Indians used seven notes in their scale, corresponding to the seven main celestial objects[489] known at that time. The seven heavenly objects were included within the twelve signs of the zodiac.[490] Later they adopted two more notes, which linked to the nodes of the moon.[491] These nine notes also related to the nine groups of consonants and vowels in the Sanskrit alphabet.[492] The Hindus link notes, vocal sounds, planets and other correspondences.[493]

Scales, created from notes associated with planets, were used for special purposes. For example, in the case of terrestrial music, the scale begins on the note C. Celestial music starts on E. Music for metaphysical purposes begins on F.[494] With proper selection of scales, music amplified prayer, connected the listener to the heavens, improved the collective feeling of a local place and enhanced intuitive pursuits.

Swamiji's *Twelve Signs of the Zodiac* CD provides balancing energy for zodiac challenges. He even specifies the time to listen – for optimum benefits – as he said, "It works during sleep. When you are awake it works only 20%. It has a low sound, working like a tranquilizer."[495]

Music and Time of Day

It is reported, that when an ancient Hindu musician played "night" music during the day, great psychics saw clouds of darkness form around him. (Dark subtle energy is equated with negative energy.)

---

[489] The seven main planets were known in antiquity before the arrival of telescopes.

[490] Danielou, Alain. *Op. Cit.*, Pg. 65.

[491] *A node is the point at which the orbit of the moon cuts the ecliptic.*

[492] Danielou, Alain. *Op. Cit.*, Pg. 81.

[493] *and the use of the 9/12 ratio (a musical interval)*

[494] Danielou, Alain. *Op. Cit.*, Pg. 65.

[495] http://itunes.apple.com/us/album/12–tunes–for–zodiac/id565050304
dattaretreat@yahoogroups.com

In contrast, when music was played at the proper time, dark subtle energy disappeared and the aura lightened. Using clairvoyant vision as a guide, the Hindus modified their music throughout the day to brighten a person's aura. Musicologist Danielou reflected on this: "One who sings knowing the proper time remains happy. By singing ragas at the wrong time, one becomes impoverished and sees the length of one's life reduced."[496]

Musical Timing

- Ragas, using sharps or the 2nd, 3rd or 6th notes of a scale are played after dusk and dawn.
- Major chords are best during the evening and midnight hours.
- Nighttime melodies create the feelings of minor keys. Most ragas with flats belong to the quietest hours – midnight to the heat of day.

Fabien Maman described various subtle energies received throughout the day; as energy changes so should harmonizing music:

- Between midnight and midday people receive cosmic energy/vitality.
- Sunrise is a potent time for cosmic energy and the best time to learn.
- From midday to midnight, the Earth gives energy. Everything on Earth and within us is active during this time. This is the time to move.[497]

Maharishi Mahesh Yogi elaborated, "At every level of creation is a frequency. One frequency melts into the other. This is how evolution takes place. The night comes to an end and the dawn begins. At dawn, inspiring freshness comes and there is a different frequency in the atmosphere. At midday, there is another big change in frequency; at midnight, there is a different frequency.

---

[496] Danielou, Alain. Northern Indian Music, Praeger: NY, 1968.
[497] Maman, Fabien. Raising Human Frequencies: The Way of Chi and the Subtle Bodies, Tamo–Do Press: Boulder, CO, 1997, Pgs. 46–47.

This cycle is perpetual, and because everything is a frequency, there is sound at every change."[498]

Hindu Music

Hindustani classical instruments include: the *sitar, sarod, tanpura, sahnai, sarangi,* and *tabla.* Instruments commonly used in Carnatic classical music include the *vina, mrdangam, kanjira,* and violin. The use of bamboo flutes, such as the *murali,* is common to both traditions.

Three categories of classical Indian instruments (string, wind and percussion) are associated with energies of the Trinity[499] – three forms of cosmic energy. The Trinity also has been referred to as harmony, melody and rhythm.[500]

Musical pitches in Indian music are typically limited to the three–octave–range of the human voice. Music emphasizes melody and rhythm, rather than harmony.[501]

The *Tanpura*, 1735[502]

The *Tabla*

[498] *Maharishi Grandharva–Ved.* Vishwa Vidya Peeth, Mahararishi Nagar, Age of Enlightenment Press: India & Livingston Manor, NY, 1991.
[499] In Christianity, the Trinity refers to God as three elements: Father, Son and Holy Ghost.
[500] Tame, David. *Op. Cit.*, Pg. 173.
[501] Crowley, Brian and Esther. Words of Power; Sacred Sounds of East &West, Llewellyn Publications: MN, 1991, Pg. 142.
[502] http://en.wikipedia.org/wiki/Indian_classical_music and http://en.wikipedia.org/wiki/Tabla

Pitch and rhythm are related. Most simply, a rhythm is a pattern of beats. The pitch of the beats varies – as a snare drum is higher pitched than a bass drum. So depending on the source of the beats, the pitch changes. Likewise, each pitch or musical note has a beat. Every note has a subtle pulse; you can hear this with low bass tones.

A raga, defined earlier, is a group of notes creating a feeling, like a personality. Medieval musicologists even classified ragas as male or female, husband, wife or offspring. A raga provides guidelines for improvisation. For example: "The *sa* (root note of the song) may be played at any time. The fourth note of the scale *(ma)* can only be played when descending and must be omitted during ascending. The fifth note of the scale *(pa)* is always approached by a glissando from the seventh note of the scale *(ni)*."[503] The first note of the scale note (the *sa*) and the fifth note (the *pa*) cannot be modified, while the remaining five notes each have two variations – flats and sharps.

The Chinese stressed individual tones, but the Indians emphasized relationships between scale notes and the *sa*. **The sa is constantly played throughout the raga.** Many Indian instruments play the *sa* along with the melody. The musician listens carefully for minor pitch differences. The continual sounding of the *sa* makes it easier to play in tune, as all intervals relate to the first. The continual playing of the *sa* gives the listeners large doses of this frequency – tuning the audience. This practice is found in other musical systems. In Byzantine music, the constant *sa* is called *ison* and in ancient Greek, it is called *mesa*.

Danielou correlates Indian modes with the star scape. One Indian scale, the *Ga Grama*, whose root note is F, corresponds to the platonic year, a 26,000 year cycle measured by the rotation of stars. The twelve constellations of the Zodiac create an imaginary belt in the heavens. When the sun's plane crosses the equator on the first day of spring, we observe which of the twelve constellations is behind the sun. Currently the sun appears to be located between Pisces and Aquarius on the first day of spring.

---

[503] As described by Ali Akbar Khan. Quoted from "An Introduction to USTAD Ali Akbar Khan and His Music."

The sun's apparent position in the Zodiac moves in a slow "apparent" backwards motion when viewed on successive vernal equinoxes. This movement is called the precession of the equinoxes. The sun's apparent position moves a little bit west in a constellation when observed on the same day each year; it takes an equinox sun approximately 2,150 years to transit one of the twelve constellations on its 25,800–year jaunt around the Zodiac.

Danielou and many ancient traditions believe that our solar system orbits around "the great central sun", and this movement creates a vibration. The *Ga Grama* raga captures this celestial vibration.

The same *Ga Grama* scale also corresponds to sacred geometry and the numerical properties of the pentagon;[504] its intervals link to the golden ratio of the pentagon.[505]

Yet again, we find numbers are connected to music:
- Hindu notes represent numbers. For example, the first note of the scale is linked to the number one, the second note of the scale corresponds to the number two and so on.
- Musical intervals mirror numbers as well. The interval of a fifth is expressed as the ratio of 3/2.
- Rhythmic beats also reflect numbers. For example there are four beats in a unit of time.
- The length of musical phrases can also reflect numbers. For example, one phrase is 30 seconds long, and the next is 60 seconds, creating a ratio of 1/2.

In ancient India each number is associated with a feeling. Similar to the ancient Chinese music, even–numbers equate to feminine energy and odd–numbers musically create male energy.[506] Numbers of greater importance are the smallest numbers. For example, two carries the greatest feminine energy, with four carrying less. Songs were created to reflect auspicious numeric patterns and capture high doses of divine energy.

---

[504] Danielou, Alain. *Op. Cit.*, Pg. 70.
[505] Danielou, Alain. *Ibid,* Pg. 70.
[506] McClain, Ernest. The Myth of Invariance: The Origin of the God's Mathematics and Music from the Rg. Veda to Plato, Nicholas–Hays: ME, 1976, Pg. 4.

Rhythm

A powerful secret ingredient of Hindu music is its elaborate rhythmic patterns. Few realize that rhythm patterns have a great impact on our thoughts, feelings and physicality.

Logically, one can understand the impact of a drum beat on one's heart rate, but the influence is much greater and more far reaching than we have ever imagined. This section will highlight research studies, demonstrating the broad impact of rhythmic musical patterns.

Short Western rhythmic patterns are significantly different than ancient Hindu ones. In modern music, rarely are there more than four beats in a rhythm pattern. Common patterns only have three or four beats. For example, an entire Western song will have a rhythm pattern of three notes, and each beat is the same length of time. In contrast, a raga uses long rhythmic patterns, which can vary from 3 to 128 pulses in length. These beats are varied and organized into many rhythm patterns. A song may have three beats, then two, then 1.5, then four and so on. These pulses can speed up and slow down. A typical Indian rhythm pattern may have 27 beats – divided into five sections.

Researcher Jeff Strong noted that complex rhythmic patterns activate specific parts of the brain.[507] Each rhythmic pattern produces a different response. Strong documented over 600 rhythms that correspond to a variety of physical responses. They can be used to relieve problematic symptoms, such a rhythmic pattern to help you sleep and one to energize you. Occasionally, Strong documented that different people can respond to the same rhythm in a slightly different way.[508]

For thousands of years the Chinese diagnosed disease by accurately measuring one's pulse – an internal body rhythm. The ancient Chinese found three hundred health problems were associated with pulse beat patterns.[509] The polygraph or lie detector test, measures body rhythms. When a person is lying,

---

[507] Such as the reticular activating system that controls sensory input.
[508] Leeds, Joshua. *Op. Cit.,* Pgs. 223–224.
[509] Hall, Manly. The Therapeutic Value of Music including the Philosophy of Music, Philosophical Research Society: Los Angeles, CA, 1982. Pg. 20.

there are changes in heartbeat, respiration and perspiration – especially in the palms. The ancient Chinese created a form of a lie detector. If a person chewed raw rice and was guilty, the salivary glands were blocked and the rice remained dry.[510] The complex and often lengthy rhythmic patterns of Hindu music are designed to alter your consciousness, mood and spirituality. Likewise, musicians use melody and harmony to do the same thing. Studies have shown that the greater the music's complexity, the more energy the brain needs to decipher it.[511] According to scientist Michael Thaut, a musical system that avoids complexity on one level allows intricacy on another.[512] For example, classical music uses harmonic complexity but short beat patterns; the raga embraces complexity in the rhythmic structure, but it is not harmonically complex.

The brain relentlessly searches for patterns. Continuous noise can be tiring because people unconsciously expend energy trying to categorize the sound patterns. Novel complex sound patterns create new neural pathways in the brain, as novel beat groupings are deciphered.

Scientist Michael Thaut studied rhythm deeply. He identified some powerful impacts:
- Rhythmic stimulation affects motor control, speech, physiology and behavior.[513]
- Rhythm can enhance learning, perception and language.[514]
- Rhythm creates a sense of predictability in our minds and bodies.[515]
- Rhythm influences our attention, memory, executive function and physical response.[516]

Thaut reported that, "Brain research shows impressively that sensory experience changes the brain."[517] Encoded patterns of

---

[510] Hall, Manly. *Ibid,* Pg. 21.
[511] Leeds, Joshua. The Power of Sound: How to be Healthy and Productive using Music and Sound, Healing Arts Press: VT, 2001, 2010, Pg. 153.
[512] Thaut, Michael. *Op. Cit.,* Pg. 14.
[513] Thaut, Michael. *Ibid.* Pg. 84.
[514] cf. Galaretta et al. 2001
[515] Thaut, Michael. *Ibid.* Pg. 9.
[516] Thaut, Michael. *Ibid.* Pg. 84.
[517] Thaut, Michael. *Ibid.* Pg. 16.

beats alter the brain. In fact, the brain feeds on them. For example, a rhythm makes us tap our fingers and feet,[518] which triggers the brain's movement–center that controls the lip and tongue. In another study, scientists measured the positive effect of saying rosaries and yogi mantras, (each containing a rhythmic element) that stabilized blood pressure.[519] Rhythms affect us physically.

Drumming induces brain wave synchronization, affecting both the right and left hemispheres of the brain. Andrew Neher, an author who gathered psychological research to formulate alternative explanations for psychic events, showed that rhythms can entrain both brain hemispheres to alpha or theta brain wave states, which correlate to certain states of consciousness.[520]

Rhythm can coax portions of the brain to take over for damaged areas – for stroke and Alzheimer's patients. Schlaug, a Harvard Medical School researcher, proved that music and rhythm can rewire the right brain hemisphere, making it similar to the left. Music stimulates more parts of the brain than any other human activity.[521]

During trauma the body becomes disorganized. Normally each part of the body works together, but in trauma, the systems go in different directions, losing rhythmic and body coordination. When health is out of order, body rhythm is out of order. Sufi master Hazrat Inyat Khan[522] elaborated: "When the rhythm in the body is disturbed it can lead to illness, because it disturbs the whole mechanism, which depends on the regularity of the rhythm. If a person suddenly hears something that causes fear, his rhythm is broken and his pulse changed. Every shock a person receives breaks his rhythm. Once the rhythm is broken, it is most difficult

---

[518] Suzanne Hanser, Chief of Musical therapy at Berkeley College in Boston, Weintraub, Karen, Karen. "Music can Heal Mind, Body and Soul." *USA Today*, Nov. 29, 2011.
[519] Leeds, Joshua. *Op. Cit.*, Pg. 129.
[520] Redmond, Layne. When the Drummers were Women: A Spiritual History of Rhythm, Three Rivers Press: NY, 1997, Pg. 173.
[521] Mannes, Elena. The Power of Music: Pioneering Discoveries in the New Science of Song, Walker & Co.
[522] Khan, Inayat, Hazrat (1882 –1927) was the founder of Universal Sufism and the Sufi Order International. Hazrat was born into a family of musicians in 1882. He came to the West to introduce classical Indian music and Sufi ideas.

to get it right again…. The rhythm should be regained in a gradual process."[523]

Hazrat Inayat Khan reflected on rhythms that we experience in everyday life, "Life is rhythm. At every stage this rhythm changes the nature and character of life. One rhythm is mobile, another is active and the third is chaotic. The mobile rhythm is creative, productive and constructive. This rhythm power can provide inspiration and peace. The advanced stage of the active rhythm can create success, accomplishment and maturation: the source of joy and fulfillment. And the third rhythmic stage, the chaotic rhythm, is the source of failure, death, disease and destruction: the source of all pain and sorrow."[524] Khan divided a human life into three major rhythm patterns, defining rhythmic cycles for spiritual development and personal growth.

The rhythms of the heart change with positive and negative emotions. For example, anger and frustrations are associated with erratic heart rhythms.[525] When feeling positive, the heart rhythms exhibit a stable sine–wave like pattern, and the heart's powerful electromagnetic field becomes more organized and efficient.[526] This wave pattern is linked to enhanced health, relaxation, emotional balance, mental clarity, intuition and improved cognitive performance.[527]

Mickey Hart, drummer for the Grateful Dead band and author, who described the impact of drumming on our physical bodies, elaborated, "Within the body itself the main rhythm is laid down by the cardiovascular system, heart and lungs. The heart beats between sixty to eighty times per minute, the lungs fill and empty at about a quarter that speed. But again these are the most obvious

---

[523] Khan, Inayat, Hazrat. The Music of Life, *Op. Cit.*, Pg. 264.
[524] Khan, Inayat, Hazrat. *Ibid*, Pg. 100.
[525] http://www.wakingtimes.com/2012/09/12/the–heart–has–its–own–brain–and–consciousness
[526] Correlates of physiological coherence include: increased synchronization between two branches of the autonomic nervous system, greater balance in the parasympathetic activity, increased brain–heart synchronization, increased vascular resonance and entrainment between diverse physiological oscillatory systems.
http://www.wakingtimes.com/2012/09/12/the–heart–has–its–own–brain–and–consciousness
[527] http://www.wakingtimes.com/2012/09/12/the–heart–has–its–own–brain–and–consciousness

bodily rhythms. From the vibration of a single cell to the slow peristalsis of our intestines, our internal machinery is all moving in a complex dance whose synchronization is carefully monitored by the central nervous system, which then reports on the state of internal rhythms to the midbrain."[528]

Research by the Heart Math Institute discovered that the nerves within the heart [529] enable it to learn and make decisions independent of the brain. The heartbeat influences the higher brain centers of perception, cognition and emotional processing.[530] The heart's pumping sends wave information to the entire body. Body rhythms communicate in a manner similar to Morse code – a system of long and short pulses.

Rhythms constitute a "signature" of each person's energies. Drummer Layne Redmond disclosed: "Scientific studies have shown that our moods, emotions, thoughts and bodily processes are rhythms of chemical energy. The Puerto Ricans call the fundamental rhythm that marks how we talk, walk and interact, *tumbao*. It is an expression of the totality of our personality."[531] Taking this idea further, musicologist, Rene Guenon believed that the rhythmic patterns were responsible for ancient cultures' social issues.[532]

Redmond described major events as rhythmic patterns. "Major events like birth, marriage, pregnancy, illness, separation or death are stressful partly because they break our familiar rhythms. People experiencing grief or depressions seem to be painfully unable to create and maintain organized patterns of rhythm."[533] In clinical settings, rhythms uplift patients. According to researcher Dr. C. Blair, of Toledo University, "Rhythms interrupt

---

[528] Hart, Mickey. Drumming at the Edge of Magic: A Journey into the Spirit of Percussion, Harper Collins: New York, 1990, Pg. 121.

[529] Numerous studies and books describe the relationship between the heart and the nervous system, such as The Nervous System and the Heart, edited by *Gert J. Ter Horst*, Humana Press: NJ, 1999. Michel Van Zandijcke, http://brain.oxfordjournals.org/content/124/3/637.full

[530] http://www.wakingtimes.com/2012/09/12/the–heart–has–its–own–brain–and–consciousness

[531] Redmond, Layne. *Op. Cit.*, Pg. 171.

[532] Danielou, Alain. *Op. Cit.*, Pg. 9.

[533] Redmond, Layne. *Op. Cit.*, Pg. 174.

entrenched patterns of the autonomic nervous system, release trapped emotions and allow for positive re–patterning."[534] In music therapy, initially the rhythm, mood and timber of the music match the patient's mood. Gradually the beat changes to transfer the listener to a desired state. We can engineer rhythms to create emotional, mental and physical stability.

Early Indian music copied nature's rhythms. Any rhythm found in nature was believed to emulate God's vibrational energy, as God created nature. Related, the Indians mimicked rhythmic patterns of animals, such as running camels. The tempo was established by the animal's speed and gait. The sharper the attack of the foot, the less time it spent on the ground. A staccato sound resulted from the quick speed at which the animal's foot hit and released from the ground. By listening to Hindu rhythms, one can entrain to the healthy and uplifting energies found in nature.

Ancient wisdom held that nature sang the music of the Earth. "The winds tuned to certain rhythms and also the beat of the waves. The tides also have their rhythm, coming in on major keys and going out on minor ones. The combined sound of everything on Earth[535] composes a harmonic chord which is the keynote of our planet."[536]

The energy of time creates rhythms, which occur in long segments – such as the seasons as well as a wide variety of other unsuspected places. There is rhythm in our cells, growth, emotions, music and languages.

The rhythms in ancient Indian music were designed to uplift one's health, emotions, spirituality and state of mind. In summary, ancient Hindu healing rhythms can impact us deeply and on many levels.

---

[534] Dr. Blair, Christine. "Vibrational Self–Healing," *Holistic Health Networker,* Fall, 2012.
[535] Corrine wrote that keynote of the Earth was F, which correlates to the color green, the most prolific color on Earth.
[536] Heline, Corinne. Healing and Regeneration through Music, Rowny Press: Santa Barbara, CA, 1943, Pg. 9.

Chakras, Elements and Ragas

Ancient people believed that subtle energy was crucial for life and health. This fine energy entered the body through the chakras that act like funnels or filters. Over time, negative energies create sluggish subtle energy flow – like mud, clogging the chakra; certain sounds liquefy the "mud." Clearing these blockages creates health on many levels.

The table on *Chakra Blockages* shows emotional and physical problems that result from chakra imbalances and blockages.[537]

Chakras receive and discharge *large* amounts of subtle energy. They connect to the smaller *nadis*. Subtle energies travel on the "energy subway system" (the *nadis)* to nourish the body's organs. This flow amplifies or sedates organs and body systems, and clears problematic energy blockages.

According to the Hindus there are 72,000 larger nerve branches in the human body. The subtle energy system, described in most all ancient cultures has not been mapped, but the Hindus believe that 72,000 *nadis* are energetic pathways that correspond to nerve branches.[538] Each *nadi* vibrates at its own frequency.[539] Listening to the appropriate rhythmic pattern entrains the body's rhythmic patterns, which is associated with health. Sri Swamiji adds that each *nadi* also has a rhythmic pattern, which when disturbed causes disease. The Indian 72 *melakarta* scales correspond to 72 categories of *nadis* found in the astral body.[540]

Fabien Maman adds that chakras reduce the high frequencies of the surrounding subtle energy to a lower frequency, which the physical body can use. This energy is then distributed through the three major systems of the body: the acupuncture meridians (*nadi*), the nervous system and the blood circulatory system.[541]

---

[537] Hero, Barbara. Lambdoma Unveiled: The Theory of Relationships, Strawberry Hill Farm Studios Press: Wells, ME, 1992. Pg. 135.
[538] www.DattaPeetham.com
[539] www.dattapeetham.com, "Swamiji's Music," Bill Owen
[540] The first 36 *melakarta* scales include a perfect fourth. The second half features an augmented fourth (4+). The tonic and fifth note of the scale are consistent in all 72 scales.
[541] Maman, Fabien. Raising Human Frequencies: The Way of Chi and the Subtle Bodies, Tamo–do: Boulder CO, 1997, Pg. 19.

Acupuncture meridians and the nervous system receive and transform energy. Once an energetic message circulates through the chakras, meridians, nervous system and blood, it becomes a tiny neuro–peptide receptor that records messages. Neuro–peptides each have different frequencies, just like musical notes.[542]

Chakra Blockage		
Chakra	**Physical dysfunction**	**Emotional Dysfunction**
Crown	Sensitivity to pollutants, chronic exhaustion, epilepsy, Alzheimer's Disease	Depression, obsession thinking, confusion
Third Eye	Headaches, poor vision, neurological disturbances, glaucoma	Nightmares, learning difficulties, hallucinations
Throat	Sore throats, neck aches, thyroid problems, tinnitus, asthma	Perfectionism, inability to express emotions, blocked creativity
Heart	Shallow breathing, high blood pressure, heart disease, cancer	Fears about betrayal, co–dependent, melancholic
Solar Plexus	Stomach ulcers, digestive problems, chronic fatigue, allergies, diabetes	Oversensitive to criticism, need to be in control, low self–esteem
Sacral	Impotence, frigidly, bladder and prostate problems, lower back pain	Unbalanced sex, emotional stability, feelings of isolation
Root	Osteo–arthritis	Mental lethargy, "spaciness," incapable of inner stillness

Science confirms that cells communicate via tiny, energizing frequencies. Dr. Bauer, one of the foremost experts in the field of

---

[542] Maman, Fabien. *Ibid,* Pg. 19.

electro–medicine, elaborated: "By sending out the proper frequency, proper waveform and current... we tend to change the configuration of the cell membrane... Cells that are at sub–optimal levels are stimulated to 'turn on' and produce what they are supposed to."[543]

Chakra ragas can improve health problems. For example, one raga vibrates a chakra and that in turn relieves asthma. Another raga clears a chakra that intakes subtle energy to resist colds.

In Indian Ayurvedic medicine, subtle energies are categorized into aether (space), air, fire, water and Earth. The Hindus believed that the elements combine in different ratios when each body system is healthy. Proper music creates proper proportions of energy. Ragas that relate to a specific element also resonate with a certain chakra and organ. For example, the colon is influenced by the air element. Ragas associated with the air will balance the colon's energy. The sounds will be expansive, like air and feel soft and warm.

Chakra Ragas

Chakra	Element	Name of Raga
Root	Earth	*Vagadhisvari*
Sacral	Water	*Kanakanji*
Solar Plexus	Fire	*Vachaspati*
Heart	Air	*Curukesi*
Throat	Ether	*Visshudd*
Third Eye	Light/Telepathic Energy	*Kamvardhini*
Crown	Thought, cosmic energy	No raga identified

Major chakra openings are located on both the front and the back of the body. Chakras on the front, *take in* energy and the back chakras *discharge* energy. Exceptions are the root and crown chakras, in which energy only flows one way. Sharry Edwards

[543] "Research Behind Acoustic Brain Entrainment," Pg. 9. www.neuroacoustic.org

postulated that the pitches for chakra intake and discharge have reciprocal relationships. The pitch of energy entering the body is balanced by the pitch of energy going out. For example, the energy going into a chakra might be X and the energy going out might be 1/X. When combined, these energies cancel each other out (like multiplying reciprocals equals one) providing a balancing effect.

Barbara Hero, mathematician, musicologist and author, also believes chakras absorb and transmit energies. She thinks that the frequency shifts to its reciprocal as it leaves the air and enters the chakra and denser matter within the body. Hero made her conclusions based on contemplation of the Pythagorean Lambdoma chart. She created the chart *Colors: Absorbed and Transmitted.*[544]

Chakra Colors Absorbed and Transmitted							
Notes	C	D	E	F	G	A	B
Color Absorbed	Red	Orange	Yellow	Green	Blue	Indigo	Violet
Color Transmitted	Green	Aqua	Blue	Violet	Magenta	Orange	Green

The ancient Hindu juggled this amazing maze of music–body correspondences to create prescriptive ragas. Many ragas are found at Sri Swamiji's websites and/or on *You Tube*. Many prescriptive ragas are included in Appendix A. The "Purposes of Ragas" is a sampling of ragas and their specific benefits.

---

[544] Hero, Barbara. Lambdoma Unveiled, Strawberry Hill Farm Studies Press: ME, 1992, Pg. 140.

Purposes of Ragas	
Name of Raga	**What it Does**
Nilambari	Alleviates sleeplessness
Bilahari and Kedaram	Creates energy for martial arts
Sri Raga	Aides digestion
Sama Raga	Improves mental abilities
Dwijavanti	Calms nerves
Bhupala and Malayamaruta	Gives invigorating energy
Sri Swamiji's bhajanas	Arouse kundilini energy

Musical Number

I have not discovered the musical number of the Indians nor the Egyptians. Although I have recovered nuggets of information from each musical system, I do not have all of their details and secrets. Further research will reveal their musical numbers and the reasoning for their musical practices. In an example, Sreeni Nambirajan, in his book, *The Mystic Citadel of 22 Srutis Music,* surmised that the Sumerian and Hindu sages, living in close proximity, cross pollinated their music and math into one puzzle, as some practices only make sense when combined. Nambirajan proposed that combining the mathematics behind several ancient systems and creating music with these techniques will provide extraordinary spiritual and health benefits.[545] The knowledge and benefits of calculating the vibratory patterns in music has just been birthed and is definitely in its infancy.

Conclusion

In the late 1880s to the early decades of the 1900s – in England, much of Europe and Russia – the system of aristocratic caste (nobility and monarchy classes) fell. Prior to that change, Europe and Russia stopped using musical scales that correlated to nature's

---

[545] Nambirajan, Sreeni. The Mystic Citadel of 22 *Srutis* Music, Maharashtra, India, 2010, nambi@22sruti.com, http://www.22sruti.com.

energies, adopting equal temperament scales, never widely heard on Earth before.

The equal temperament scale has been described as aural caffeine; it helped make people industrious. The Industrial revolution thrived, perhaps due in part to people no longer listening to the sounds found in nature. We disconnected from nature and were unaware that industrial waste was poisoning our Earth.

At the same time in India, the traditional style of music endured. Today ashrams are scattered throughout the country still teaching the old spiritual path. Many believe that the Hindu ancient music prolonged time honored practices in India, such as the ancient caste system. In the last forty–to–fifty years, the Indians adopted the equal temperament scale and they listened to Western music extensively. Concurrently, Indian success in building a modern industrial society leapt forward. Long respected Indian traditions have suffered; modern problems have widely escalated in India. In her defense, India has persevered longer than most any other culture in maintaining a spiritual society.

In conclusion, the ancient Hindu healing music is still practiced today, providing a rare glimpse into the fabulous past of ancient healing music. Remarkable Hindu rhythm patterns create powerful healing energy, demonstrating the vast power of music – far beyond entertainment. Music gives us great gifts when we believe in its potential and learn how to select and listen to the appropriate musical energy.

www.JillsWingsofLight.com – Art Galleries
249

www.JillsWingsofLight.com – Art Galleries

Chapter Nine

Ancient Greek Music
600 BC to 100 AD

In the 9th century BC, Greece was comprised of small independent states. During the 6th century BC, Athens, Corinth, Sparta and Thebes dominated the region. At the beginning of this period, around 500 BC, Athens became a democracy, fueling her strength and power. The democratic model led to a golden age for Greece, culminating with Alexander the Great's reign – during the zenith of Greek power. The Greeks fell from this position of dominance, with Rome annexing Greece in 146 BC. Greece's Hellenistic culture endured until the widespread practice of Christianity toppled it.

How important was music to these ancient Greeks? Music pleased the gods and was used by them to accomplish miraculous feats. For example, the son of Zeus (the "Father of Gods and men" in Greek mythology) used a golden lyre to build Thebes – by moving the stones into place with his music. Orpheus, the master–musician, played so magically that he soothed wild beasts.[546] Hundreds sang praises every day to the god Apollo, the god of light, truth, healing, music and poetry. The Greeks believed that music controlled their weather, the growth of plants and the flow of streams.[547] Music was powerful stuff! Plato said: "Music gives a soul to the universe, wings to the mind, flight to the imagination, charm to sadness, gaiety and life to everything."[548] In essence, man is a song of God. The quality of emotion embodied within

---

[546] Graves, Robert. The Greek Myths, Moyer Bell: Mt. Kisco, New York, 1955. Pg. 30.
[547] Heline, Corinne. Healing and Regeneration through Music, New Age Bible and Philosophy Center: Santa Barbara, CA, 1943, Pg. 60.
[548] Heline, Corinne. Ibid, Pg. 28

music was believed to not only have psychological, but even supernatural powers.

It is not surprising that music was omnipresent at the Pythian and Olympic Games; musicians were awarded wreaths – worn like a crown.[549] Surprisingly, athletes were introduced *after* the musical competitions.[550]

The prominent objectives of Greek music were to impact character, personality and emotion. Plato wrote, "Music is an art imbued with power to penetrate into the very depth of the soul, imbuing man with the love of virtue."[551] The Greeks valued the virtues of its citizens and music facilitated this. Plato made musical study mandatory – when he could – to instill values in the young. Music was not a luxury, but a critical component of developing people on a multitude of levels.

Musical History

The Greeks credited Egypt and the Asian countries of Phrygia and Lydia (both located in what we call Turkey today) with inspiring their musical system. Not only did early musical techniques come from Phrygia, but Phrygia's musical heritage is embedded in Greek mythology. Phrygian King Midas, who had the "golden touch," was tutored in music by the god Orpheus (who charmed all living things – and even stones with his music). Also the Phrygian satyr created the instrument, the *aulos*, a reed instrument with two pipes, using the hollowed antler of a stag. Later, this satyr lost a musical competition with the Olympian god Apollo who then flayed him alive. The Phrygian mode sounded fierce and was associated with war in ancient Greece. The Greek Lydian mode is similar to a minor scale today, but without the sadness; it contains a few quirky elements of surprise. (A mode is a pattern of intervals used in a song, similar to a scale, but the mode was known for the melodic feeling that it produced.) Phrygia and Lydia acknowledged the impact of Egyptian music on their systems, both pointing to Egypt as the original inspiration.

---

[549] Heline, Corinne. *Ibid,* Pg. 62.
[550] Elson, Louis. Curiosities of Music: A Collection of Facts Not Generally Known regarding the Music of Ancient and Savage Nations, O. Ditson Co., 1908, Pg. 22.
[551] Heline, Corinne. *Ibid,* Pg. 28

The Greek musical system is modal. A mode is a selection of notes that is used to improvise a song. A mode produces a characteristic feeling. Modes select notes outside of conventional, modern Western music. There can be thousands of cycles per second in the span of an octave; today's musical system picks only twelve frequencies to be the notes that we hear on our pianos. The reader does not need to understand the details of how modes and scales are constructed; the point is, the ancient Greeks enjoyed a greater variety of pitches than we do and they were selected for targeted benefits.

Differences between Modes & Scales

Name for Note Set	Number of Notes	Intervals	Instructions
Modern scale	7 notes	5 whole notes & 2 half notes	Musicians use all available notes
Chromatic Scale	12 Notes	12 half notes	Musicians use all available notes
Mode	A handful of notes (usually 5 – 7 notes)	Each mode has a variety of intervals, such as 1/3, 1/4, 1.25/1	Musicians use only prescribed notes of the mode to create a specific feeling

The earliest Greek music was composed by Grecian tribes and presented a diverse musical landscape. Each region created songs for special occasions and handed them down throughout the generations.

Like many other civilizations, early Greek music recreated sounds sung by Mother Nature. These songs were called *nomoi*, a word that translates into law or nature. In early times a Greek man, named Alcman, "invented verses and melodies" and "composed the voice of partridges."[552]

Most early songs used just four notes to accompany hymns.[553] Later, music was used to enhance other art forms, such as theater, dance and poetry reading. This music copied the metered accents of verses.

The Classical Greek period of music had its beginnings in the 6th century BC. At this time a multitude of tribes ranged in the region today called Greece; each had their own separate music – handed down from elders. In the Greek Classical period, the music of the various tribes intermingled to such an extent that the entire region was combined into one – as Greece. The music was still forming, but the die was cast from the diverse tribal beginnings. There is reference to great musicians of this period, but little has survived that describe the early Greek music. Information about the musical influence of Pythagoras (570 to 495 BC) and other famous philosophers does survive, although it is difficult to completely understand. Hundreds of years after Pythagoras's death, the contributions of Plato and Aristotle, both members of the Pythagorean Mystery School, defined Greek classical music. This chapter describes critical aspects of this music originated by these people.

Just as we use medicine today to fix a malady, music was selected to resolve a problem. It was categorized according to its purpose: prayers or hymns for the gods, dirges to express grief,[554] *paeans* to convey triumph or gratitude,[555] *dithyrambs* to honor the god Dionysus (the god of wine and fertility) and *normos* (musical poetry).[556] Musicians performed at meals to honor the gods, for healing, for special occasions and to enhance education. While performing music dedicated to the gods, the performer reportedly experienced attributes of a god, thus transforming himself.

---

[552] Comotti, Giovanni. Music in Greek and Roman Culture, John Hopkins University Press: Baltimore, 1989, Pg. 18.
[553] Elson, Louis. *Op. Cit.*, Pg. 20.
[554] *Dirge* – Funeral hymn or lament, a slow mournful composition or poem
[555] *Paean* – A song or lyric poem expressing triumph or thanksgiving. It is usually performed by a chorus, but some are done by an individual. Paean means, "Song of triumph, any solemn song or chant." "Paean" was also the name of a Divine physician.
[556] *Normos* – Lyric poetry or rhythm patterns with long and short beats

Music was not written down. Similarly, Plato wrote that the best philosophy (and music) should not be written. Plato's teacher, Socrates, never wrote anything down. Demonstrating this idea, the lengthy story the *Iliad*, was sung from memory. That is quite a feat! Reading the *Iliad* requires only mental energy without deeper integration on other levels. To memorize something, one repeated it enough times until the information entered his subconscious mind. Now the information automatically was available in his thoughts without prompting. The information became part of him. Plato pitied those who learned by reading and shamed the Egyptians for inventing writing, which opened the door for humans to grow lazy at the expense of deeper understanding.[557]

Consistent with this idea, Greek musicians adhered to guidelines and parameters for improvisation. Improvisational guidelines allowed the musician to feel each musical phrase, incorporating the sounds into his being and integrating its deeper meaning. Musical standards were comprehensive. There was no tolerance for changing the tuning, character or rhythm of any song.[558] For example, embellishments such as vibrato and sliding tones were considered the "enemy of melody."[559]

Songs could be played at different times, but the words, rhythms and music were adjusted depending on the setting or function of the music.[560] Special music was played in the morning; another selection was chosen for the evening. The music celebrating spring varied from that heard in the fall.

The early Greeks did not employ harmony in the sense that we do today; at most, a melody line in the Greek music was accompanied by the same note or an octave of it. Pythagoras (570 to 495 BC) advocated that a melody should be accompanied by another note, four or a five notes away, as is common today.[561] Other intervals

---

[557] Recall the phrase, "I know it by heart." This is something that is memorized and now influences you on a deep level. Likewise for music, guidelines for improvisation allowed people to be more attuned to the music than by merely replicating written notes.

[558] Comotti, Giovanni. Music in Greek and Roman Culture, John Hopkins University Press: Baltimore, 1989, Pg. 16.

[559] Ptolemy and Aristotle

[560] Comotti, Giovanni. *Ibid,* Pg. 7.

[561] Pythagoras 570–495 BC, Plato 428–347 BC, Aristotle 384–322 BC

were considered dissonant. This harmonic structure was used until the early Middle Ages.[562]

Instruments

The Greeks grouped musical instruments into categories. Instruments with equal string lengths (lyres and *citharae)* were in one category while instruments having different string lengths, such as harps, were classed differently. Winds and percussion were in other categories. The ancient seven string lyre, current during the lifetime of Pythagoras, had four of its seven strings fixed, tuned to an octave (which is two notes), a fourth and a fifth. The Greek musician adjusted the other three strings according to which mode was used.[563]

Flutes were popular. An able flute player could make good money – as could an accomplished instrument maker. Use of brass instruments was not widespread, even though other ancient cultures believed that brass instruments massaged and stimulated the subtle energy of the physical body. A forerunner of the brass instruments was the conch, a sea shell with a cut opening as a mouthpiece. Early versions of the trumpet used long metal tubes – up to 1.3 meters long – with a bone mouthpiece and a bell shape at the end of the tube. There were no valves, so the instrument played only one root tone and naturally occurring harmonics. This precursor to our trumpet was essential to the military, providing commands. The United States military still uses a form of the trumpet call, called "reveille," which is played to wake soldiers and call them to duty. The Greeks talked about "breathing brass to kindle fierce alarms" and painted a few brass instruments on vases. Music historian, Comotti, wrote that unlike other ancient peoples, the Greeks' percussion instruments were rarely used, except for the rituals of Dionysus cults.

Each instrument was employed for a targeted benefit. For example, the lyre and the kithara were used to evoke reason and linked to the worship of Apollo, the god of reason. The kithara was a more sophisticated version of the one stringed lyre and has

---

[562] http://www.justintonation.net/primer2.html quoting from
http://www.music.sc.edu/fs/bain/atmi02/pst/index.html
[563] Ferguson, Kitty. The Music of Pythagoras, Walker and Co.: NY, 2008, Pg. 63.

evolved into the modern day guitar. A double–reed instrument known as the *aulos* was said to arouse passion and was connected to Dionysus, the god of ecstasy. Pipe instruments, such as the pan and syrinx flutes, created a rustic sound and were associated with the god, Pan. The pipes were played to inspire frivolous behavior.[564] The Syrinx was named after the mythological nymph who was changed into a reed in order to hide from Pan. These instruments were a group of pipes gradually increasing in length. Sound is produced by blowing across the top of the open pipe (like blowing across a bottle top).

Pythagoras' concept of *monochordum mundi* suggested that the simple instrument, the monochord, created vibrations that linked the planets, stars and Earth. The position of the frets marked the star paths.[565]

Healing with Music

The ancient Greeks were adept at healing with music. Modern healing music instructor, Fabien Maman, correlated the musical components of modes, rhythm and timber to the endocrine glands, chakras and organs. According to Maman: "Each mode, whether it is Greek, Pentatonic or Hindustani, has a melody which activates a different function in the body and the consciousness. Intervals have an affinity for different endocrine glands, internal organs and chakras, which are sensitive to the rhythm and quality of the instrument."[566]

Author, Danielou, and musicologist, Muhammad Hafid, describe ancient musical therapies that use a specific musical scale for each disease. Hafid warns that small differences in pitch make a huge difference in outcomes.[567] Music historian, Curt Sach, cited numerous written examples reflecting the Greeks' belief in the

---

[564] Hall, Manly. The Therapeutic Value of Music including the Philosophy of Music, Philosophical Research Society: Los Angeles, CA, 1982, Pg. 65.
[565] Hall, Manly. *Ibid,* Pg. 54.
[566] Maman, Fabien. The Role of Music in the Twenty–First Century, Tamo–Do Press: Boulder, CO, 1997, Pg. 38.
[567] Danielou, Alain. Music and the Power of Sound: The Influence of Tuning and Interval on Consciousness, Inner Traditions: VT, 1943, Pg. 8.

healing power of music, "Athenaios[568] (a great orator in the 2nd to 3rd century BC) writes, 'persons subject to sciatica would be free from attacks if one played the pipe in the Phrygian harmonia over the part affected.'"[569]

The Greeks had an entire genre of music devoted to healing, called *paean* music (translates to healer). At first, a *paean* was a medicine dance and later it evolved into a chorus dance in honor of Apollo, the healing God. The paeans expanded and eventually included modes, special songs and techniques. An iconic source, *The Iliad*, described a *paean* that *"banned"* the plague. Centuries later in Sparta, the governing board appointed a musician to organize *paeans* for physical ailments.[570]

Aristotle[571] described "mystic melodies" that caused people to fall into a frenzy – reminiscent of African witchdoctor dances – for purification of negative emotions.[572] The Greek word, *katharsi,* means healing through purification. A troubled soul listened to dark emotional music to experience a cathartic release.[573] This healing method assumed that physical illness resulted from accumulated negative emotions. Aristotle stated, "If insanely overwrought persons listen to enthusiastic melodies that intoxicate their soul, they are brought back to themselves again, so that catharsis takes place exactly like a medical treatment."[574]

In further examples, legends describe the Greek god Orpheus as a musical messenger, whose music stilled troubled minds, enabled flowers to bloom, and calmed the waters and wind.[575] Likewise in the *Old Testament*, David's song and harp soothed the madness of Saul. Proper music can be restorative according to Hippocrates, the father of medicine, who instructed people with mental health

---

[568] *Athenaeus Naucratita* was a Greek rhetorician and grammarian, flourishing about the end of the 2nd and beginning of the 3rd century AD.
[569] Sachs, Curt. The Rise of Music in the Ancient World East and West, Dover Publications: Mineola, NY, 1943, Pg. 253.
[570] Sachs, Curt. *Ibid,* Pg. 267.
[571] Aristotle. Politics 8:1340 b. 8
[572] Sachs, Curt. *Op. Cit.*, Pg. 253.
[573] Comotti, Giovanni. Music in Greek and Roman Culture, John Hopkins University Press: Baltimore, DL, 1989, Pg. 40.
[574] Sachs, Curt. *Op. Cit.*, Pg. 253.
[575] Heline, Corinne. *Op. Cit.*, Pg. 29.

issues to listen to temple concerts to lessen their problems.[576] In Rome, the temple priests and physicians used music to induce health up until the country was entirely converted to Christianity.[577]

An ancient story relays how music was used in surprising ways, even to prevent crime and resolve mental health issues. A young man was partying all night, listening to music in the Phygrian mode, which was known to incite violence. In the early morning, this young man saw a girl that he loved sneaking out of the home of his rival. He went into a rage and prepared to burn her house down, killing all those inside. Pythagoras was star gazing and observed this man's rage and preparations to destroy lives. Pythagoras intervened and talked the man into listening to a song with tranquilizing "spondies" (rhythmic pattern used in the verse of a song). The young man's madness was immediately calmed and he went home in an orderly fashion.[578]

In a modern day example, Michael Riversong, a school teacher, experimented with playing the Greek modes on his harp to autistic children experiencing "behavior episodes." He found that the Lydian mode calmed the students within minutes. He encourages people to experiment with songs in the Lydian mode and offers music samples freely at the web site in the footnotes.[579] In another example, in 19th century France, troubled children were exposed to uplifting music, reporting successful changes in behavior.[580]

Rhythms were associated with the physical life form and functions of the body. The music's speed and rhythm were also a diagnostic consideration. A fast meter was thought to be too nervous for some, while a slow tempo may be overly effeminate and passive for others.[581]

---

[576] Tame, David. The Secret Power of Music: The Transformation of Self and Society Through Musical Energy, Destiny Books: VT, 1984, Pg. 156.
[577] Tame, David. Ibid, Pg. 156.
[578] James, Jamie. The Music of the Spheres: Music, Science and the Natural Order of the Universe, Copernicus, NY, NY, 1993. Pg. 32.
[579] http://www.biblicalbards.org/music/AutismKit/AutismKit.html; http://www.biblicalbards.org/music/rivcharity.html
[580] Heline, Corinne. Ibid, Op. Cit., Pg. 28.
[581] Sachs, Curt. Op. Cit., Pg. 265.

Socrates believed that orderly and suitable rhythm patterns led to a virtuous life.[582] Plato defined rhythm as "the moving image of eternity," far more than the beat of the drum. E. John Blacking, from Berkeley University, looked beneath a civilization's actions to perceive their rhythmic patterns, "Music is a mirror that reflects a culture's deepest social and biological rhythms: it is an externalization of the pulses that remained hidden beneath the business of daily life."

Pythagoras read poetry, such as Homer (the author of the *Iliad* and the *Odyssey*), to patients in order to cure disease.[583] This may seem ridiculous at first glance, but the rhythmic patterns of the verse were thought to entrain and restore natural body rhythms. In Homer's classic work, each line complied with a complex set of parameters, with each line featuring two beat patterns comprised from one long and two short syllables.

Michael Thaut responded – to the idea of rhythms influencing people – from a scientific viewpoint. "In Plato's educational view (now understood within a biological framework) music trains the senses, body and mind. The arts connect and exercise brain function and the physical world through aesthetic perception and expression. This is in principal no different than the studies of reading, writing, arithmetic or physics."[584]

Pythagoras' Lambdoma

A prized theoretical tenant of the inner circle of Pythagoreans was the Lambdoma numeric table. This mathematical tool was believed to reveal fundamental secrets for many aspects of our world – and primary among these – for our purposes, were the power and interactions of sound and music. The Lambdoma diagram represents a pattern of frequencies and their resulting harmonics (think of harmonics as after ripples in sound following a root note). Important ancient leaders believed everything had vibrations with harmonics (some the ears cannot detect), therefore, the Lambdoma displayed the harmonic patterns relating to

---

[582] Comotti, Giovanni. *Op. Cit.*, Pg. 94.
[583] Hall, Manly. *Op. Cit.*, Pg. 62.
[584] Thaut, Michael. Rhythm, Music and the Brain, Scientific Foundations and Clinical Applications, Routledge: NY, 2005, Pg. 37.

everything. The Lambdoma was like a periscope of a submarine – from which you could view the world above – that could not be otherwise seen. The Lambdoma was also thought to show the numeric patterns of subtle energies, such as thoughts, words and prayers. The Lambdoma was ancient man's idea of a hologram: a 2–D diagram that could be projected to interface with everything. Further, by applying sound to the Lambdoma, one could transfer subtle energy between disparate things.

Ancient tales suggested that the Lambdoma table originated in Atlantis; later it surfaced in ancient Egypt and sparked interest later still in ancient Greece. The Lambdoma diagram is attributed to Pythagoras, who spent 20 years studying in ancient Egypt before starting his famed Mystery School. The Lambdoma chart, and its uses, were a prized secret of his Mystery School.

The secrets of the Lambdoma held allure for philosophers, geniuses and spiritual masters throughout the ages. This mathematical template was prized by the ancients and its significance was cloaked in secrecy. Currently, the concept of the Lambdoma matrix is relatively unknown, and is not cited in most dictionaries.

www.JillsWingsOfLight.com – Art Galleries

The Lambdoma Matrix

Start on the Lambdoma's bottom corner, the 1/1 block, notice the sequence of numbers running along the edge up and to the right (2/1, 3/1, ...) and then notice the reciprocal of these numbers (1/2, 1/3, ...), running along the left edge.

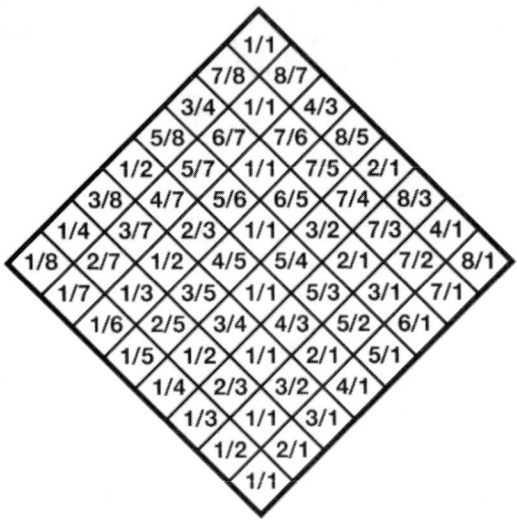

At first glance, the Lambdoma chart is a pattern of numbers, reflecting mathematical properties or operations. One can insert any number, N, in the two "1/1" corner positions of the Lambdoma, and create a numeric table according to its guidelines. The right axis represents 2N, 3N, 4N... (Multiplication table) and the left axis represents N/2, N/3, N/4... (Division table). The Lambdoma is a multiplication and division table made up of whole numbers and whole number ratios. If you were to take the Lambdoma diagram and fold it diagonally along the center 1/1 line, each ratio that touches its counterpart has a reciprocal relationship (1/2 & 2/1, 1/3 & 3/1, 2/3 & 3/2 etc.). The numbers of the touching squares, when multiplied, equal one. Tones with a reciprocal relationship have a balancing effect. The Lambdoma is a table of numbers that mirror each other in this way.

Ratios that are less–than–one, occur on the left side of the diagram; they progressively descend in magnitude as you move diagonally up and to the left. Ratios that are greater–than–one, are on the right side of the diamond and ascend in value.

When you insert a new integer number into the 1/1 position – all numbers generated in the table are in perfect harmonic proportions, making this table useful for architects and designers. The first six Lambdoma positions mirror ratios of shapes in crystallography and calculations of chemical elements, chromosome numbers and plant structures.[585]

The Lambdoma matrix includes ratios found in the heavens. A ratio is formed by comparing the number of orbits completed in the same time interval (by two planets). For example, the 2:3 ratio occurs when Pluto completes two orbits in the time it takes Neptune to complete three. Ratios are also formed by numbers that represent the lowest and highest points of a planet's orbit around Earth, and the closest and farthest points of an orbit around the Sun. In the 1600s, scientist Johannes Kepler found that the movement of the planets creates a scale resembling the Lambdoma chart, made from simple, whole numeric ratios.[586] In Kepler's book *Hermonices Mundi, the Five Books on Musical Harmony,* he calculated the angles of the planets (as measured from the sun) from their extreme positions in elliptical orbits during a twenty–four–hour period. A system of simple intervals emerged, sixteen in all, which are musical consonances or intervals with whole number ratios (two of the intervals were not whole number ratios).[587]

The Lambdoma matrix mirrors patterns found in nature, the study of chemistry, art, geometry, music and other disciplines. The Lambdoma chart also bears mathematical relationships to Diophantine equations[588] and the Farey series,[589] (for those interested read brief descriptions of these in the footnotes); it also reflects the work of Isaac Newton and scientist Georg Cantor.[590]

---

[585] Levarie and Levy. <u>Tone: A study in Musical Acoustics</u>, Oberlin Printing: USA, 1968. Pg. 30.
[586] Godwin, Joscelyn. <u>Cosmic Music: Musical Keys to the Interpretation of the Universe,</u> Inner Traditions: Rochester, VT, 1989, Pgs. 111–112.
[587] Godwin, Joscelyn. *Ibid,* Pg. 117.
[588] An algebraic equation with two or more variables whose coefficients are integers, studied to determine all integral solutions.
[589] The Farey sequence of order n is the increasing sequence, from 0 to 1, of fractions whose denominator is equal to or less that n, with each fraction expressed in lowest terms.
[590] Quote from Lambdoma.com. Georg Ferdinand Ludwig Phillip Cantor (1845–1918) was a German mathematician, born in Russia. He is known as the creator of set theory, a fundamental theory in mathematics. Cantor established the importance of one–to–one

Using the theory of sympathetic resonance (energy transference between special notes), the Lambdoma diagram displays relationships across an amazing range of things, creating bizarre connections. For example, advocates say that it shows subtle energy relationships between the shapes of crystallography and intervals in a Byzantine hymn, or the relationship of one's horoscope to colors. Hermann Hesse won the 1946 Nobel Prize with his book, *The Glass Bead*. The book, about the Lambdoma's principle of organizing harmonics, described the intellectual manipulation of many concepts. The book suggested that the Lambdoma could be a "Transcendent Universal process leading to an experience in consciousness of the Unity of the Cosmos."[591]

The Lambdoma pattern, can be used to create musical modes or scales.[592] Any number representing the cycles per second of a frequency, may be placed in the 1/1 position. For example, let's say we insert the number one in this slot. Then the numbers on the right edge will be 2, 3, 4, 5... and the numbers running along the left edge will be 1/2, 1/3, 1/4, 1/5... and so on.

The rest of the chart can be filled in following the same pattern as in the above in figure. One axis of the Lambdoma can represent the harmonic cycle, while the other suggests the notes of a scale. Barbara Hero invented a musical instrument to play Lambdoma frequency patterns.[593]

As we saw in Chapter One, at some level, everything vibrates; therefore, everything has a frequency or said another way – waves that can be counted. A sound wave produces harmonics (think of them as after–ripples of a sound wave, the sound waves combine making new waves – the harmonics). All vibrational energy creates harmonics according to ancient wisdom. One can insert a frequency in the 1/1 position in the Lambdoma chart and calculate the frequency of its harmonics. In this manner the Lambdoma is a "one size fits all" diagram for all sound waves. The ancients

---

correspondence between sets, defined infinite and well–ordered sets, and proved that the real numbers are "more numerous" than the natural numbers. Cantor's theorem implies the existence of an "infinity of infinities."

[591] http://www.glassbeadgame.com

[592] www.Lamdboma.com

[593] www.Lambdoma.com

believed that the Lambdoma could reveal the harmonic structure of many things (in addition to sound waves), even things with no seeming connection other than harmonics. In other words, the sages believed that this pattern applied to all – not just sound waves. Remember everything has a wave nature. This is what this book is about and why music and sound matter so much!

People have used harmonic sounds to accelerate the growth of plants, speed the rate of composting (low sounds), imitate dolphin sounds (high harmonic frequencies) and so on in an amazing variety of applications.[594]

Impact of Greek Music

Pythagoreans believed that good music was made partially audible by divine, cosmic sound. This divine music, often called Music of the Spheres, created influential vibratory blueprints that matter and emotions adhered to. An expert on ancient music, Ernest McClain, reflected: "To both Greek and Hindu the scale is essentially a falling form."[595] Rudolf Steiner agreed that the ancient musical pattern primarily descended in pitch, which helped man incarnate into duality with increasing identification with matter. It was as if the falling musical forms, descending in pitch, allowed man to identify with lower ranges of sound that corresponded to the dense material world.

According to Steiner, Greek music enabled people to identify with matter to a greater extent. With greater attachment to physicality, they perceived the world primarily in a *physical* way.[596] The phrase, "I'll believe it when I see it," emerged as the spiritual world faded due to lack of emphasis. In contrast, earlier civilizations saw the world through the *spiritual* lenses of their culture.

Greek art reflected their deep love of physical beauty. Their sculptures and paintings revealed realistic and beautiful forms. Their gods had flaws, but their statues displayed physical

---

[594] Hero, Barbara
[595] McClain, Ernest. The Myth of Invariance: The Origin of the God's Mathematics and Music from the Rg. Veda to Plato, Nicolas–Hays: ME, 1976, Pg. 14.
[596] Godwin, Joscelyn. *Op. Cit.*, Pgs. 191–205.

perfection and beauty. The Greeks' athletic contests and heroic deeds also glorified the physical aspects of man.

The Greeks, seeking beauty, were revolted at the aging deterioration of the physical form. In stark contrast, the Hindus were engrossed in thoughts of heaven and neglected life on Earth, including their own physicality. If the music of the Greeks was to increase their consciousness of physicality, it certainly achieved that objective.

Greek music gave its listeners numerous important influences. In its earlier history, the ancient Greeks identified with groups that governed themselves independently. The Roman historian, Publius Cornelius Tacitus (55 – 120 AD), affirmed this: "The Cheruss do not experience themselves as individuals, but as members of the tribe."[597] Not only their identity, but their security and success depended on the group's abilities and performance. Tribes have common physical characteristics, as well as stereotypical personalities. After experiencing the ancient Greek music, members expressed themselves more as individuals.

According to Cyril Scott: for the very first time – beginning during the Greek era – subtle energy from music *began* to develop individuality, helping people break away from group identification. Greek sound patterns (musical modes) enabled people to balance tribal personality characteristics and develop unique individual attributes. According to Scott, "The music of the Greeks used elemental energy to solidify personalities. It was even more: it was the reduction of the human passions to concrete personalities."[598]

The Musical Number

To review: Lemurian music encompassed the energy of the number *nine*. Atlantean music revolved around the number *seven*. Sumerians used the configuration of the number *six* in their

[597] Publius Cornelius Tacitus (55 – 120 AD), _De Origine et situ Germanorum Germania_. Steiner, Rudolf. Reading the Pictures of the Apocalypse, Anthroposophic Press: USA, 1919 and 1993, Pg. 79.
[598] Scott, Cyril. Music: Its Secret Influences throughout the Ages, Samuel Wisner: NY, 1958, Pg. 169. Reprinted in 2013 by Inner Traditions.com.

musical systems. The Chinese created their music with patterns of *fives*. The Greek system is built with tetra chords, a series of *four* notes.

The energy of four is the most practical of the numbers. When a person's name or birthday correlates with the number four, he is expected to be practical, detail–oriented, organized, stable, orderly, systematic, methodical, precise, reliable, punctual, dependable, trustworthy, perseverant and hard working.[599, 600]

The ancient Greek philosophers correlated the number four to many significant things. In nature there are many flowers with four petals. The Greeks associated seasons, directions (north, south, east and west), elements (air, fire, water and Earth) and basic tastes (sweet, sour, bitter and salty) with the number four.

It is revealing, that the Chinese had a proclivity for the number *five* and they found five elements and five directions and so on, while the Greeks counted *four* of the very same fundamental quantities. The culmination of their reverence for the numbers five and four respectively was reflected in the music systems that were based on these magical numbers.

The Number Four in Crop Circles [601]

The same interval pattern can be found across the globe, with the Navajo Indians, located in the USA. They embrace four "songs," four directions, four colors and four sacred mountains.

---

[599] http://www.spiritual–numerology.com/numerology–number–meaning/numerology–meaning–of–number–4.html
[600] Negative "four" energy is characterizes as rigid, judgmental, stubborn, too detail–oriented, bossy, overly cautious, too serious and lacking flexibility.
[601] http://www.hypermaths.org/cropcircles/chapter4/ Used with permission – Peter Sorensen http://cropcircleconnector.com/Sorensen/circles/1999/main.html

Greek Tetra Chords

Historians disagree on the basic tenants of the Greek musical system. The Pythagoreans transmitted secrets orally, lest their written materials fall into the hands of self–serving people. Officials of the early Catholic Church burned as much information on the Greek, Pagan and Egyptian music as they could get their hands on. Many of the remaining documents that escaped demolition were flawed. The Greek's limited historical papyri and remaining fragments described their musical terms, however, often the words changed meaning over time. Shifting the meaning of terms made clear understanding elusive. Documents describing Greek music vary from one ancient Greek writer to the next – and likewise among today's musicologists.

According to musical historian Danielou, documents explaining Greek music were mainly written by Boethius and other European authors who did not completely understand the Greek musical complexities. The Arabs and the Turks (who maintained their ancient music) shed better light on the Greek musical system. With this warning, our description of Greek music will continue with the best available information.

In this section we will show that the Greeks created their music based on mathematical patterns – particularly numeric patterns observed in nature. Further, the Greeks sought to produce correspondences linking the subtle energy of the music with many important things – also like other ancient cultures. This section is quite detailed, involving difficult musical and mathematical concepts. For the reader who does not want to struggle through these technical sections – it is sufficient to understand that the Greeks used music for prescriptive purposes, rather than entertainment values.

A tetra chord is a musical structure formed by *four* consecutive notes. It can also be created by dividing a string into *four* parts. The first and fourth notes of a tetra chord create the ratio of 4/3 or a perfect *fourth*.[602]

---

[602] When an interval sounded neither major nor minor, it was deemed "perfect."

The Greek musical system arranged how intervals fell within tetra chords. Next in complexity, two tetra chords combined to create a distinctive mood and was called a mode. A musician improvised exclusively using the notes prescribed by the mode. Modes resemble our scales. Today's major and minor scales were each originally one of these modes.

Tetra chords were used in a prescriptive way for their emotional influences. One ancient writer claimed that a tetra chord was "soft" if the distance between the two notes with the highest pitches was relatively large. Listening to these sounds "narrowed and softened" the soul.[603] "Hard" tetra chords "expanded and stimulated." (Hard intervals today are a combination of the first note in a scale and one of the following: second, third, fourth, fifth or seventh notes of the scale.[604]) Tetra chords were used like medicine for personalities.

The mathematics used to create tetra chords could be quite complex. For example, when two intervals of a perfect fourth are connected, a total of seven notes are created (C – D – E – F and F – G – A – B; the F note is shown twice). The 7 notes are: C, D, E, F, G, A, and B. This set of notes is one note short of an octave (we might call this set of notes a scale, they would have called it a mode).

As people naturally love the sound of an octave – the Greeks later added an eighth note (to the system above), to complete the octave. Although they enjoyed the harmony of the octave, a new problem arose: With this extra note, the last tetra chord was no longer a perfect fourth and sounded dissonant. To correct this, Pythagoras added an additional note in between the two tetra chords. By doing this, two tetra chords each made a perfect fourth interval and created a mode that spanned an octave.

---

[603] Sachs, Curt. *Op. Cit.*, Pg. 212.
[604] Soft intervals are thirds and sixths.

Two Methods of creating Greek Modes with Tetra Chords

- C+D+E+**F** & **F**+G+A+B   no 2nd C to make the octave
  tetrachord   tetrachord

(the 1st tetra chord's last note and first note of the 2nd tetra chord are the same, F)

- C+D+E+**F** & **G**+A+B+C   we have a 2nd C in this mode,
  tetrachord   tetrachord   creating the octave, C_1 and C_2

(The note F is considered to be in between each tetra chord)

The Greeks eventually dropped the first method of creating modes with tetra chords in the table above, as they favored modes that spanned an octave. A problem arose with this method. Pythagoreans expected this mode would be symmetrical. Pythagoreans believed the world was composed of numbers – expressed as frequencies (somewhat similar to string theory). Pythagoreans believed musical mathematics were the foundation for the material world. God was thought to be a mathematician and simple ratios were divine attributes. Similarly, recall that the ancient Sumerians worshipped gods as simple whole number ratios.

In the second method of creating a mode in the table above, the two tetra chords were the same size, and Pythagoreans expected to divide the note F (the whole tone in between the two tetra chords) in half. Splitting the F in half created a complex ratio. Pythagoras expected a simple ratio, 1/2. The disappointed Greek philosophers named the "symmetry plus a little bit left over" a "schism," meaning split or crack. The Greeks associated this "crack" with an error of nature and it was philosophically paralleled to negative energy within music.[605]

Ancient Greek musical theory categorized tetra chords into three *generas*. Much of the Pythagorean information was destroyed or kept secret – so historians are left guessing about the reasoning for the *genera* system. Musical scholars often overlook the *genera,* because they do not appear to have much significance, but that is far from the truth.

Generas

Enharmonic –used tetra chords with major third and two microtones (about a quarter tone). In an interesting sidebar, at this time Japan used a scale that was the exact counterpart of this enharmonic structure.[606]

Chromatic – had tetra chords with a minor third and two semitones. This *genera* was reputed to be the "sweetest" for expressing grief.

Diatonic – included a seven note mode using five whole steps and two half steps separated from each other by two or three whole steps.[607]

Ancient music expert, Richard Merrick, formulated a brilliant conclusion regarding the purpose of the *genera* system. Merrick wrote that the Greek *generas* created intervals that formed golden ratios in different note locations. He proposed the golden ratio that creates phi is at the root of Pythagoras's reason for creating the *genera* system. The sounds that create phi are linked to numeric patterns within nature. Nature was considered a divine gift. Each different phi location in the mode, created a unique musical remedy.

What does phi have to do with the music? The golden ratio (or phi) equates to 1.618033... In music this refers to 1.618... cycles

---

[605] Merrick, Richard. Interference: A Grand Scientific Musical Theory, Merrick: Texas, 2009, Pgs. 22–23.

[606] Sachs, Curt. *Op. Cit.*, Pg. 209. Curt Sachs believed that the enharmonic tetra chords evolved into the Dorian structure.

[607] http://en.wikipedia.org/wiki/Diatonic_scale

per second. When certain notes combine they create a wave that is 1.618... cycles per second. This number is not rounded off. An interval that creates phi emulates pushing/pulling sensations; the effect feels like it needs to be resolved, as if it is incomplete. Similarly, at the end of an inhalation, one feels the need for movement and the exhalation. The feeling of movement, created by the phi interval, is strategically placed in Greek music.

Golden Ratio

Two quantities are in the golden mean (or ratio) – if the ratio of the sum of both of the quantities – to the larger quantity – is equal to the ratio of the larger quantity – to the smaller one. In the simplest case: A = 1 and B = 0.6180. A/B = 1.6181; A+B/A = 1.6180/1 = 1.6180 (golden ratio)
https://commons.wikimedia.org/wiki/File:Golden_ratio_line.svg

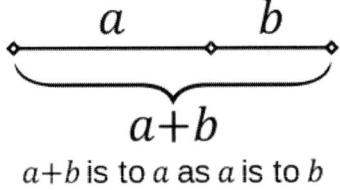

$a+b$ is to a as a is to b

Why is Phi Important?

Phi was extremely important to the Greek sages, but why? The number phi is significant, because of the number of times and places that it appears in the macrocosm and the microcosm of our universe: from the simplest algae to the largest tree, from the nautilus shell to the unfolding of a fern, from the shapes seen in distant galaxies to proportions found in our bodies. Here is a small sampling: The distance from the finger tips to the wrist as compared to the finger tips to the elbow creates the golden ratio and phi. The distance from the knees to the waist, as compared to the waist to the top of the shoulders, creates the golden proportion. The distance from the knees to the waist, as compared to the feet to the knees, also equals the golden proportion. It's certain that the Creator of the Universe saw special meaning in phi; He probably designed it into nature for us to discover its secret and ultimately benefit from it.

To summarize: the ancient Greeks linked phi, nature, music, shapes and emotional energies. This idea is also prevalent in many other ancient musical systems. For readers who are satisfied with this level of discussion on phi – and don't want to bother with mathematical explanations – skip to the next section, *Personalities and Character*. If you are interested in the mathematical details, please read on.

Many ancient philosophers revered the five pointed star. Did they fancy the shape or was there a deeper meaning? The golden ratio and phi are found in numerous ways in the pentagram. Nature likes this shape, as seen in examples such as the star fish and seeds that form a five pointed star in a horizontally sliced apple.

"All proportions of the pentagram express the golden ratio or phi. If a pentagon surrounds a pentagram, as shown below, phi is in the ratio of the sides of each of them, i.e. AE/AB, AB/BD and BD/CD."
Hypermath.org

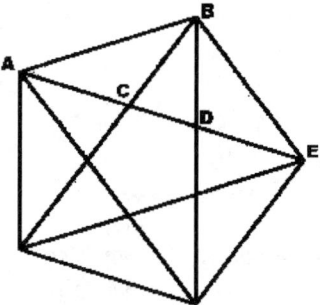

Phi, the Pentagram and Pentagon

Phi emerges in the orbits of Venus and Earth, around the sun. Venus' orbit creates a shape – similar to a pentagram that is full of phi ratios – in the path it traces across the sky every eight years. When a ratio of Venus' and Earth's orbits is taken, phi is the result.

Venus traces a Pentagram in the Sky

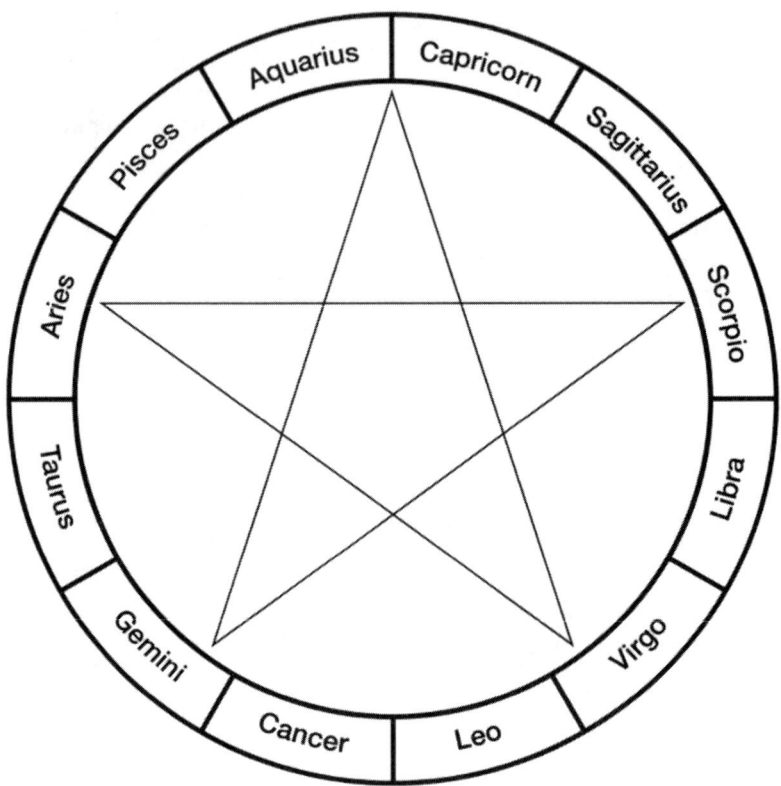

In eight years, Venus "apparently" stands still in the sky five times. These points of inflection in its orbit, trace a five pointed star in the heavens (a pentagram). These motions occur over a span of 584 days. The ratio of this measurement (584 - called the Venus Synodic Period) – when compared to Earth's year - equals a ratio of Fibonacci numbers that create phi.

Phi Exists in Planet Orbits			
Planets	Phi Ratios	Fibonacci Numbers	Phi = 1.6281...
VSP/EY	= 584/365 ("a"/"b")	8/5	1.600
VSP + EY	= 584 + 365/584 = (a+b/a)	13/8	1.625
EY/VSD	= 365/225	5/3	1.622

Venus' Synodic Period = VSP   Earth's Year = EY
VSD = Venus Sidereal Period[608] (225 days)

Phi or the Golden Mean

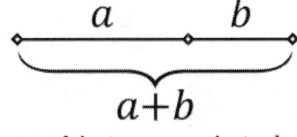

$a+b$ is to a as a is to b

The ratio of two consecutive Fibonacci numbers (0, 1, 1, 2, 3, 5, 8, 13...) creates approximations of the Golden mean or phi.

Crop Circle containing Phi repeatedly[609]

---

[608] https://en.wikipedia.org/wiki/Orbital_period. The sidereal period is the cycle that it takes an object to make a full orbit relative to the stars. The synodic period is the time interval that it takes for an object to reappear at the same point in relation to two or more other objects, e.g., when the moon, relative to the sun, as observed from Earth, returns to the same phase.
[609] Nick Kollerstrom, Nick. Crop Circles, The Hidden Form, Hypermath.org, Chapter 5, www.hypermaths.org. http://www.axve02.dsl.pipex.com/cropcirc/FrontPage/FrontPage.htm Thanks to Peter Sorensen for the photo[609]

Phi in a Crop Circle[610]

Merrick believes that the energies found in sound waves that combine and form phi are different that sound energies within harmonics. Harmonics resemble smaller "sound after ripples" following an initial sound. Different amounts of energy flow into each ripple. Brass, string and reed instruments create different amounts of energy in various ripples. This is why a C on a violin sounds different (or has different timber) than the same C on a trumpet. If more energy falls in a higher pitched harmonic, then that note has a higher pitched feeling to it. (Like the sound/feeling of a violin versus a trumpet.)

There are sixteen harmonics that result from an initial sound (as represented in the Lambdoma diagram). The harmonic pattern starts with pleasant sounding intervals and becomes increasingly dissonant. When compared to the root note, each harmonic creates a ratio, such as 1/1, 1/2, 1/3, 1/4...

The Fibonacci numbers are found extensively in nature: such as in the mathematics that create a spiral sea shell and in the design of many flowers. In this number series, the sum of any two adjacent numbers equals the next number in the series (0, 1, 1, 2, 3, 5, 8, 13...). *The ratios between adjacent Fibonacci numbers approximate phi.* As the numbers get larger the ratios get closer

---

[610] Thanks to Peter Sorensen for the photos[610]

and closer to phi – one approximation being a little more and the next less, but they never reach the exact phi value.

Phi is anti–harmonic, according to Merrick. It *kills resonant vibration*, and because of this it also facilitates the flow of energy between different harmonics.[611] When two notes create phi, the resulting energy is different than that from other intervals. "The phi ratio is mathematically imbedded within the sounds that are devoid of harmonics, sounds that we might label as "pure". (Pure sounds do not contain the rich complexity of musical sounds. Two examples are bubbling and whistling water.) Such pure sounds contain the all–important phi ratio and create sonic scaffolding that we believe organized, structured and triggered life…"[612, 613]

Merrick states that intervals that form phi lesson or dampen most vibrations. Recall that two waves interacting in close proximity combine. If the peaks of the waves collide, then their frequencies are added to create the new combined wave. If the peak of one wave collides with a trough of the second wave they cancel each other out, or reduce the resulting wavelength. When two waves (notes) create phi, all resulting fractional waves cancel out and allow the energy of whole ratio sounds (harmonics) to vibrate sympathetically. When two musical notes are in close proximity and combine, the primary root notes combine; each note's harmonic partial notes, also combine. Some musical intervals create energy, such as the energy of the fifth. Other intervals, such as phi, diminish energy.

Merrick applied the understanding of phi in nature to the *generas*. In tetra chords the locations of intervals that created phi varied.[614] For example, in the key of C, the golden ratio in an averaged– *genera* tetra chord is created from pitches in between B & C, and E & F. Next, Merrick averaged all of the phi locations for all individual *generas* and modes.

There are astonishing similarities between the *genera* modes and a five pointed star. "The tetra chord *genera*–average of one golden

---

[611] In contrast to a destructive, "anti–harmonic" phi interval, the interval of a major 6th is the least destructive wave pattern of all intervals. This is indisputable science.
[612] CymaScope website
[613] Merrick, Richard. *Op. Cit.*, Pg. 108.
[614] Merrick, Richard. *Op. Cit.*, Pg. 30.

section nested inside another golden section is the same as that found in the intersections of a pentagram."[615] Merrick links the average location of phi in music to the pentagram, the symbol so revered in ancient Greek mystery schools.

Merrick discovered another relationship. The ratio between the bottom and middle intervals of *genera* versus the middle and top intervals is almost 3/2, close to the ratio created by a musical perfect fifth.[616]

In the figure, **The Five Platonic Solids**, one can see how two tetrahedrons fit together to form an octahedron.[617] Five octahedrons could be put together to make a dodecahedron or an icosahedron.

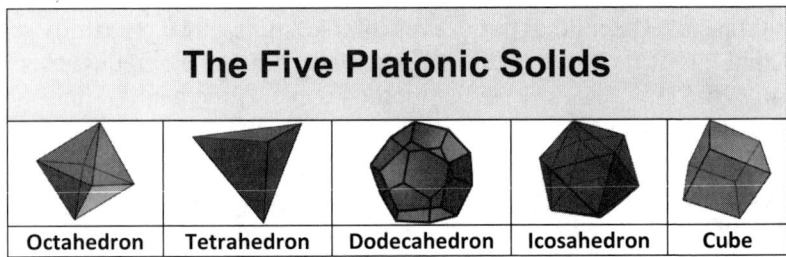

The Five Platonic Solids				
Octahedron	Tetrahedron	Dodecahedron	Icosahedron	Cube

Merrick convincingly related the shape of a dodecahedron to a musical tetra chord. To the Greek philosophers, a tetra chord was the auditory version of tetrahedron shape. Each Greek mode included two tetra chords (and also two tetrahedron shapes). Just as two tetrahedron shapes combine to form an octahedron shape, two musical tetra chords also form a sound comparable to the shape of an octahedron.[618, 619] Merrick continued to correlate the five Greek male modes to the combination of 5 octahedrons that form a dodecahedron. He even showed how the pentagram shape is contained in the octahedron. Merrick believed that Pythagoras built the *genera* system to copy the pentagram's golden ratios.

---

[615] Merrick, Richard. *Ibid,* Pg. 28.
[616] Merrick, Richard. *Ibid,* Pg. 28.
[617] These shapes are found in carbon allotrope molecules of soot and graphite. Carbon is the most stable element in the universe. Merrick
[618] Associated with air
[619] Associated with fire

Merrick's complex mathematical explanation will not be covered here, but is available in his book, *Interference*; a free download is available at Interference.com. By equating geometry and Platonic solid shapes with music, Merrick discovered a link between ancient Greek music and geometric shapes.

Merrick also believed that the *generas* form five male and five female modes, which are linked to the five perfect Platonic solids.[620] Five Greek modes were classified as male: Ionian, Aeolian, Locrian, Dorian and Hyprodorian. Each mode, when converted to a shape, created a dodecahedron.[621] Another five modes, the Phrygian, Hypophrygian, Lydian, Hypolydian and Mixolydian modes, created feminine feelings and related to an icosahedron shape.

Sacred Geometry & Greek Music	
Musical Balance	**Geometric Balance**[622]
2 tetra chords = octave	2 tetrahedrons = octahedron
Can divide an octave with a golden ratio	Can cut octahedron with a golden ratio
5 male modes	5 octahedrons = dodecahedron
5 female modes	5 octahedrons = icosahedron

Merrick drew attention to the placement of intervals that create phi within each *genera* and mode. These two groups of five modes were paired to produce male–female feelings or ethos, and created

---

[620] Merrick, *Op. Cit.*, for the quote, Pg. 28. The sides, edges and angles of the Platonic solids are congruent and fit perfectly inside a sphere.
[621] Associated with aether
[622] Merrick, Richard. *Op. Cit.*, Pg. 30.

ten musical modes. Each *genera's* mode had a positive (male) and negative (female) golden ratio. "The Pythagorean concept of *ethos* is a tug–of–war between two golden ratios, pulling emotions positively or negatively, or up or down." [623] A tetra chord combination was like a recipe of sound energy that influenced character in a particular way.[624]

Platonic Solids, Phi and Tetra Chords

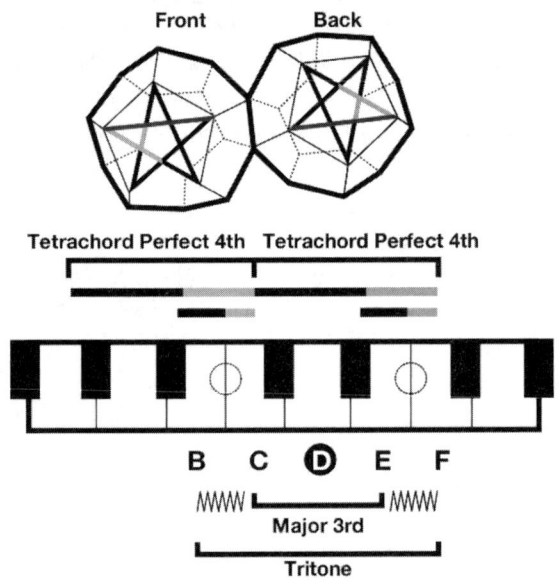

Dodecahedron showing Pentagram in Faces.
Pentagram Proportions in an averaged Tetrachord.
Golden Ratio locations in the Cracks between the Keys
Tritone Functions as a Harmonic Spring.[625]

The important point is that the Greeks used math to create music, featuring ratios and patterns found in nature. Like many other ancient musical systems, the music was not only connected to

---

[623] An octave is constructed by two tetra chords of a perfect fourth and two intervals called *leimmas*, meaning "left over" or dieses – indicating a shortened semitone. When the five whole tones and two *diesis* semitones of the Pythagorean disjunctive scales were subtracted from an octave yet another small fraction occurred called a comma. A comma plus a *diesis* produced a slightly larger semitone called an *apotome*. Levin 1994. Merrick, Richard. *Op. Cit.*, Pg. 24.

[624] Merrick, Richard. *Ibid*, Pg. 30.

[625] Illustration from <u>Interference: A Grand Scientific Musical Theory</u>, Merrick. *Op. Cit.*

numbers, but had a variety of other correspondences, such as with emotions and shapes.

Merrick connected the human psyche with music: "The implications of this are staggering. If the Greek philosophers were right, then the human psyche must be organized geometrically something like an octahedron or octave in music with the two counter–posing golden ratios at work inside our brain. Perceiving music would then be a matter of physically matching musical harmonics to identical proportions built into the structures of our brain!"[626] Merrick hinted that the brain structure and shape of the skull reflect waves and create frequency patterns, like modes. Waves hitting differently shaped skulls produced phi at different locations in the brain, which then could influence our individual personalities.

Throughout antiquity to modern times, others have had similar ideas. An ancient Vedic sage, Sarngadeva, related anatomy to musical sound production.[627] This mirrors Merrick's ideas. In the book, *Face Reading*, Richard Wagner connected the shapes of parts of your face, such as the size of your nostrils, to personality characteristics – reminiscent of how the lines on one's palm represent a personality.[628]

As we have seen, sand on a cymatic drum is moved around by sound waves. The sound vibrations travel to the edge of the surface and then reflect back inward again. Depending on the frequencies, wave vibrations combine at certain points, creating areas where sand accumulates and areas with no sand. This process can create images in the sand. Think of the body as a cymatic instrument. Internal waves reverberate throughout our body; they bounce off the edges of our body structures and reflect back – creating different combinations of frequencies (reinforced waves and canceled waves) that correlate to specific emotions and states of mind.

---

[626] Merrick, Richard. *Ibid,* Pg. 30.
[627] Shringy, R. K. and Prem Lata Sharma, *Sangita Ratnakara of Sarngadeva,* Vol I, Munshiram Manoharial: India, 1991.
[628] Wagner, Richard. Face Reading: Quick & Easy, Llewellyn Publications: MN, 2012.

Personalities and Character

We will now leave Merrick's technical explanations of how the ancient Greek modes influenced feelings and see how other historians explained the same concept. The Greek idea that music affects the nation's character had its roots in China, India and Egypt. About the 5th century BC, the Greeks attempted to come up with "perfect scales," such as Dorian, Phrygian and Lydian modes. As you recall, a mode is like a scale. A scale is comprised of a smaller number of frequencies in–between an octave that are selected to be notes of the scale. Within an octave one could choose any of thousands of possible frequencies. Today we use the same method to select these frequencies; we select 12 frequencies to represent notes of a scale. In times past, the method to select notes varied. Each mode selected just a handful of notes – that when played in any order – created a unique and characteristic feeling. The mode was then used by a musician to improvise a song. Since the note selection was limited by the mode (and modes may have other guidelines too), a song in a mode sounded similar and produced the same feeling. Each mode had its prescriptive purpose, as if it were a medicine used by a doctor. This can be seen in Hippocrate's (460 – 377 BC) statement, "It is more important what sort of person has a disease, than what disease a person has."

The following shows some of the feelings associated with songs created by various modes.

- The Dorian mode inspired courage, self–esteem and respect for the law. The center of Pythagoras' system was the Dorian scale, the only mode that is symmetrical on either side of a center point.[629] The Dorian structure was considered "the scale" by many Greeks.
- The Phrygian mode developed repose, dignity and self–control.[630]
- The Lydian mode scale induced voluptuous and self–indulgent feelings.
- The Mixolydian mode was plain and tragic.

---

[629] A scale starting on D, using all white keys, is symmetrical (in terms of whole and half steps) in both directions.
[630] Scott, Cyril. *Op. Cit.*, Pg. 166.

Modes were given familiar names to the ancient Greeks, such as Dorian and Aeolian. Pythagoras named them after local tribes. Today, when people refer to a population in a particular location they conjure up a stereotypical personality. For example, a "New Yorker" clearly invokes different personality traits than a Midwestern or a German person. The same was true for the ancient Greeks and their stereotypes.

The following are descriptions regarding the personality types associated with Greek scales:

- The word Dorian comes from an ancient root that means "golden." The roots of "oak trees" were also called "*duir.*" The word "durable" comes from this ancient word. Dorian was a location and a group of people with Egyptian ancestry who were considered moral, upright and strict.
- Aeolian and Ionian modes were named after Greek tribes.
- Phrygian and Lydian were foreign nations. Phrygians were aggressive and wore distinctive hats.
- Ionians (our current major scale) were "straight shooters," reminiscent of today's stereotypes of plain speaking/straight forward people.
- Locrians (or Laconians) were remembered for their concise words and eccentricities.
- The original name of the Mixolydian mode was Lesbian – the people of that island were known as hard partiers – the association with anything else came from a poet named Sappho who came along much later and was mostly ignored until the late 1800s.

The Greek philosophers disagreed as to which modes were appropriate for what, although they all espoused direct connection between character and music. For example, Aristotle favored the Dorian and Lydian modes, but believed the Phrygian made people too excitable. In contrast, Plato approved of the Phrygian mode.[631]

Music affects our emotions as we dance to a lively beat or calm down with serene music. The ancient Greeks believed that music,

---

[631] Comotti, Giovanni. *Op. Cit.*, Pgs. 31, 40.

subtly intertwined with and altered subtle emotional energy. In other words, a steady diet of the same music becomes inbred in personalities, influencing character. Cyril Scott made this point powerfully with: "However horrifying this statement may seem to the orthodox, music is a more potent force in molding of character than religious creeds." [632] Music constantly entrains man so he feels certain emotions. With prolonged listening, emotional habits are formed and become part of one's character.[633]

Ethos is a musical energy, which can positively and negatively affect emotions.[634] Aristotle elaborated, "Emotions are produced by melody and rhythm: therefore, by music, a man becomes accustomed to feeling the right emotions; music has the power to form character. Types of music based on the various modes, may be distinguished by their effects on character: one, for example, working on the direction of melancholy, another of effeminacy; one encouraging abandonment, another self–control, another enthusiasm and so on thorough the series."[635] Not only does each mode produce a different effect, but that individuals can react differently to the same mode. Aristotle added that: "some modes make people sad and grave, like the so–called Mixolydian, others enfeeble the mind like the relaxed *aneimenas harmonias,* others produce a moderate and settled temper, which appears to be the peculiar effect of the Dorian: the Phrygian mode inspires enthusiasm."[636, 637] On a comical note about music and emotions, William Shakespeare jested, "If music is the food of love, play on."

Not just the intervals and modes, but pitch ranges (high or low pitches) created *ethos*. Comotti suggested that certain modes were characteristically tuned higher or lower. A low note was called soft and calm, while a high one was exciting.[638] In ancient Greece Ptolemy stated, "The same melody has an activating effect in the

---

[632] Scott, Cyril, *Op. Cit.*, Pg. 40.
[633] Scott, Cyril. *Ibid*, Pg. 40.
[634] Comotti, Giovanni. *Op. Cit.*, Pg. 32.
[635] Scott, Cyril. *Ibid*, Pg. 39.
[636] Sachs, Curt. *Op. Cit.*, Pg. 248.
[637] Metaphysics 8:5
[638] Aristolelian Problem 19:49

higher pitches and a depressing one in the lower keys, because a high pitch stretches the soul, while a low pitch slackens it."[639]

When someone hears majestic music he feels like a hero. Even a timid person can increase vitality and strength. He must listen to heroic music a multitude of times to create enough energy to become bold, but there is improvement with each auditory session. The effects eventually wear off, but if we listen to this music every day for a year – it now affects character. The dosage (listening time) of music needed to make changes in a personality varies per person.

Aristotle recommended changing music to match the evolutional level of the crowd. Higher evolved people benefitted from refined music; baser music should be given to coarser people.[640] An analogy is that babies need pureed food, but as they develop they can handle solid food.

What is a nation made up from? A nation is the accumulation of all of its individuals. In an analogy, if a nation is a brick wall, then each citizen is an individual brick. If music determines the quality of the bricks, then music is of utmost importance to the whole.

Each civilization's music gently builds people's stereotypical personalities. Our character eventually becomes ingrained in our genes. To illustrate this point Dr. T. Singh[641] reported that classical music helps plants grow up to two times their normal rate, with the sounds of the violin being the most life enhancing. What was significant with this study was that later generations of seeds (from plants in the original classical music studies) retained the improved growth characteristics. Music changed the plants' chromosomes![642] Likewise, ancient people related their music to their nation's characteristics. The double–edged sword of sound builds and erodes a civilization.

Just as a man selects protective clothing at appropriate times and what to eat when appropriate, he must discriminate what to listen

---

[639] Sachs, Curt. *Op. Cit.*, Pg. 248.
[640] Aristotle. Pol. 8.1342a.26 f, f
[641] Head of the Botany Dept. at Anamalia University
[642] Tame, David. *Op. Cit.*, Pg. 145.

to. Greece was serious about the impact of music on the nation's character. The Greeks observed that sound and music can destroy. Recall a singer shattering a wine glass or the walls or Jericho caving in from the sounds of the Israelites. The Greeks observed people's reactions to music. If an unnatural or depraved behavior resulted from a song, the music was banned. The Greeks protected their country from those who made these choices foolishly. If a composer created music determined to be detrimental to the public, the musician was fined or even exiled.[643]

Education

Plato credited the Egyptians with using music to influence their youth. Aristotle believed that education should not just develop the intellect, but also foster virtues.[644, 645] The Egyptians allowed nothing but quality music to be heard by their young people,[646] insuring the strength of future generations.

Melodies that young people were allowed to hear and perform were posted in the temples. Plato advocated limiting the music – including certain modes and instruments – for a child's listening.[647] This practice was extended beyond music. Artists and dancers were forbidden to deviate from prescribed standards.[648]

Researchers at Harvard University found that early musical training enhanced motor, auditory, verbal and non–verbal reasoning[649] in subjects. Scientist, Gottfried Schlaug proved that music strengthens auditory perception that in turn, relieves dyslexia and language deficits. A study conducted at an inner city day care, showed that three year old children who had voice and piano lessons for eight months, increased their spacial–temporal

---

[643] Hall, Manly. *Op. Cit.*, Pg. 7.

[644] Ferguson, Kitty. *Op. Cit.*, Pg. 118.

[645] Stewart, J. S. The Spiritual Dimension of Music: Altering Consciousness for Inner Development, Destiny Books: VT, 1990, Pg. 118.

[646] Engel, Carl. The Most Ancient Nations: Assyrians, Egyptians and Hebrews with Special Reference to Recent Discoveries in Western Asia and in Egypt, Murray: London, 1864, Pg. 234.

[647] *De Musica*, written by Boetheus, a widely used book in medieval times. Ferguson, Kitty. The Music of Pythagoras, Walker and Co.: NY, 2008, Pg. 118.

[648] Michell, John. The Dimensions of Paradise: Sacred Geometry, Ancient Science, and the Heavenly Order on Earth, Inner traditions: VT, 2008, Pg. 8.

[649] Leeds, Joshua. The Power of Sound: How to be Healthy and Productive using Music and Sound, Healing Arts Press: VT, 2001, 2010, Pg. 106.

IQs (necessary for mathematics) by a 47 percent mean.[650] Indeed, Plato intuited the value of music developing the intellect correctly!

In Plato's Academy, music was a preparatory course for philosophy. Much of Plato's work was based on the musical theories of Pythagoras – who believed that God built the universe by using numbers and ultimately music is numbers. Students studied math, physics, astrology, metaphysics and universal laws through music. Music was a core unit of natural science because of its extensive influence. Studying music unveiled the secrets of everything. The famed Egyptian Hermes said that when people knew "true" music, they knew the workings of everything.[651] The Greeks echoed this sentiment throughout society.

Silence in Pythagorean Schools

Pythagorean school initiates took vows of silence in their first five years of study to:

- Learn the reticence of speech
- Keep school secrets
- Learn to listen, not talk
- Strengthen nonverbal communication
- Become aware of how sound resonates in their bodies
- Find power in silence
- Pacify their nature
- Develop internal strength and increase spirituality
- Learn to think before they spoke
- Learn to be in harmony with their words… speak the truth
- Learn the power of words
- Increase awareness of sounds

There are many reasons why the Pythagoreans kept mute for five years, but an important theme was to increase their consciousness by noticing the relationship between energy and words. By focusing on listening, students learned what sounds were associated with specific mental states.

---

[650] Leeds, Joshua. *Ibid*, Pg. 107.
[651] Mulcahy, Pat. Esoteric Harmonics, Tuning to the Occult Scale of Sound, AstroQab Publications: Australia, 2009, Pg. 67.

Roman Music

The priorities of the Roman civilization were not at all the same as the Greeks. The Romans were practical people. They were farmers and warriors – not lovers of art as the Greeks were. Music was never a part of education for the young in Rome. Their first temples were to Mars, the War God. Perhaps they reacted to the Greek feminine admiration of beauty and sought the opposite quality – masculine power and strength.

The Romans had the desire for colossal effects, as we see in the Roman games. Roman statesman Seneca,[652] said that in Nero's time the chorus was larger than the audience. Flanks of trumpeters and flutists performed at the games, much like today's sports contests with the band in the bleachers.

One can understand the role of music in the Roman society by learning about the Roman victory parades. Trumpeters and singers led – playing triumphant songs. Members of the prestigious senate and magistrates followed. Animals (usually oxen for sacrifice), with garlands in their horns and accompanying priests, plodded behind. The musicians and flute players followed this group to assist with the sacrifice.

Wagons with spoils and captives were included. Tribute from foreign countries followed next. The captives' kings, leaders and their wives were chained and followed – sometimes awaiting their deaths. Musicians dressed as satyrs, crowned in gold, danced and added cruel jesting. Mimics (often men dressed as women) made fun of the prisoners with gestures and insults. Acting like cheerleaders, the mimics encouraged cruelty from the crowd.

Participants in the parade spread perfume. Four white horses, or sometimes elephants, pulled a flamboyant chariot carrying the highest ranking general. He dressed in purple, wore a garland on his head and his face was painted orange. The general's friends and family followed, dressed in white. A slave, carrying a richly

---

[652] Lucius Annaeus Seneca (often known simply as Seneca; ca. 4 BC– AD 65) was a Roman Stoic philosopher, statesman and dramatist. He tutored and advised Emperor Nero. He was forced to commit suicide for alleged complicity to assassinate Nero, the last of the Julio–Claudian emperors. He may have been innocent.

gemmed crown, followed the general; it was his duty to admonish the general by whispering in his ear that he was only a man.

This procession was followed by the entire army wearing laurels and sporting captured booty. The army sang and praised the general; sometimes they sang coarse verses and cracked vulgar jokes aimed at their general.

Buildings along the route were decorated. Banquets awaited the spectators. When they arrived at the Temple of Jupiter, the captives and oxen were killed, entertaining the crowd. After the parade, musicians escorted the general home, still singing his praises.

Rome was cruel – even in her rejoicing. This coarse use of music included: loud trumpets, a vile musical pantomime encouraging the crowd to jeer at captors before their deaths, sacrificial music for the killing of animals and opposing warriors. The rude songs of the army illustrated how Roman music glorified victory, power and brutality.

Music was used for warfare in many other ancient cultures. In the *Old Testament*, Joshua marched around the city of Jericho, beating drums and blowing trumpets for seven days. Finally, the Israelites gave a shout and the defensive city walls tumbled down.

The primary use of music in Rome was to instill courage and fortitude in battle. Brass instruments, short and long varieties resembling trumpets, the curved buccina horn and double pipes were among their battle instruments.

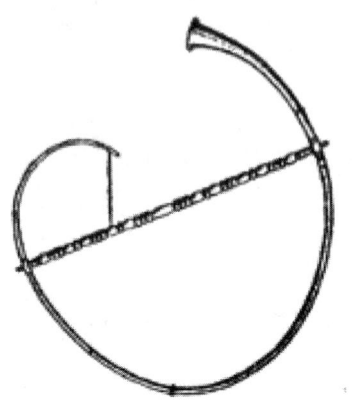

A Roman Buccina[653]   **A Double Pipe**[654]

Fall of Civilizations

The important Greek philosophers attempted to control music, but apparently their grip wasn't strong enough. Plato called for a return to the old parameters of music after he blamed the traumatic fall of Athens in 404 BC on unacceptable music. Plato's ideas about the role music played in their culture and Greece's musical history are reflected in his quote, "(Musicians) used high musical talent, showmanship and virtuosity... consciously rejecting educated standards of judgment.... Our music was once divided into its proper forms... It was not permitted to exchange the melodic styles of established forms. Knowledge and informed judgment penalized disobedience. There were no whistles, unmusical mob–noises or clapping for applause. The rule was to listen silently and learn; boys, teachers, and the crowd were kept in order by threat of the stick.... But later, an unmusical anarchy was led by poets who had natural talent, but were ignorant of the laws of music.... Through foolishness they deceived themselves into thinking that there was no right or wrong way in music, that it was to be judged good or bad by the pleasure it gave. By their works and their theories they infected the masses with the presumption to think themselves adequate judges. So our theatres, once silent, grew vocal, and aristocracy of music gave way to a

---

[653] http://en.wikipedia.org/wiki/Buccina
[654] http://en.wikipedia.org/wiki/Aulos

pernicious theatrocracy (when spectators rule the theater)... the criterion was not music, but a reputation for promiscuous cleverness and a spirit of law–breaking." [655, 656]

By about 100 AD Greek genres and modes were forgotten, leaving only one scale or mode, the diatonic. Microtones and their prescriptive scales had been abandoned, reflecting that the old music was discarded. By the third and fourth centuries AD these practices were long forgotten. The remnants of ancient Greek music were documented with written notes, a practice that would have been appalling to earlier musicians.

Plato believed that the rise and fall of good music was linked to the fate of its civilization.[657] In *Laws*, Plato reflected on popular tastes in music, "Through foolishness they deceived themselves into thinking that there was no right or wrong in music."[658, 659] "The introduction of novel fashions in music endangers the whole fabric of society."[660]

Aristotle also wrote about the importance of music, "Styles of music are never disturbed without affecting the most important political institutions."[661] ... "The behavior of a republic can have no greater stain than to abandon right and honorable music."[662, 663]

Music was an important ingredient that fortified or destroyed a civilization. This belief occurred across the globe and spanned many eras. Yet, modern man regards music as peripheral entertainment. Philosophers of antiquity would have considered such an idea irrational and suicidal. Author, David Tame summed it up, "From ancient China to Egypt, from India to the golden age of Greece we find the same: the belief that there is something

[655] Henderson, Isobel. "Ancient Greek Music" in The New Oxford History of Music, Vol.1: Ancient and Oriental Music, edited by Egon Wellesz, 1957, Oxford: Oxford University Press. Pg. 395.
[656] Plato. Laws, 700–701a. Cited in Wellesz, Pg. 395.
[657] Scott, Cyril. Op. Cit., Pgs. 174–175.
[658] Tame, David. Op. Cit., Pg. 189.
[659] Pythagoras 570–495 BC, Plato 428–347 BC, Aristotle 384–322 BC
[660] Rep 4.42b–c trans. cornford
[661] Scott, Cyril. Op. Cit., Pg. 39.
[662] Ferguson, Kitty. Op. Cit., Pg. 119.
[663] Aristotle quoted his teacher, Plato. Perhaps from his memory or a source now lost. Plato 428–347 BC

immensely fundamental about music; something which, they believed, gave it the power to sublimely evolve or to utterly degrade the individual psyche and thereby to make or break entire civilizations."[664]

Music creates a subtle vibrational foundation. People's thoughts and feelings conform to this blueprint. Cyril Scott declared that "People think that civilizations come first and its characteristic music afterwards. But an examination of history proves the truth to be exactly the reverse: an innovation in musical style has inevitably been followed by an innovation in politics and morals. And, what is more, as our study of Greece and Egypt will show, the decline of music in these two instances was followed by the complete decline of the Egyptian and Grecian civilizations."[665]

Ancient musical expert, Fabien Maman agreed. "It is the musicians of each culture who are the spiritual guides of consciousness. Their music opens the fields, announces and prepares the way for the re–sounding of the musical vibration which sets the tone of each civilization long before the masses are aware of any change."[666]

Modern day writer, Henry David Thoreau also equated a civilization's fate with its songs, "Even music can be intoxicating. Such apparently slight causes destroyed Greece and Rome and will destroy England and America."

Summary

"The soul of a people is revealed in its music,"[667] wrote author Heline Corrine. In retrospect, accomplishments within a civilization are evident. For example, the Egyptians built fantastic pyramids and were an enduring super power for 3,000 years. They sought knowledge, an admirable trait. The priests experimented with subtle energies as evidenced by the volume of hermetic magic scrolls and the *Book of the Dead*. However, one can acquire

---

[664] Tame, David. *Ibid*, Pgs. 13–14.
[665] Scott, Cyril. Ibid, Pg. 42.
[666] Maman, Fabien. The Role of Music in the Twenty–First Century, *Op. Cit.*, Pg. 30.
[667] Heline, Corinne. Music: The Keynote of Human Evolution, New Age Bible and Philosophy Center: Santa Monica, CA, reprinted 1986, Pg. 82.

knowledge for selfish purposes. Experiencing both positive and negative sides of character traits allowed people experiences that enabled them to develop emotionally. For example, one can fall in love, only seeing the good traits of his beloved. After time he deals with the negative traits of his partner. Only after that, can he learn the skills of a lasting love that can stand the test of time.

www.JillWingsofLight.com – Art Galleries

The Greeks did not share the objective of gaining knowledge, but rather sought to develop reasoning skills and beauty. The Greeks exalted reasoning skills eventually fell through excessive love of beauty, pleasure and focusing on the indulgences of the senses. The Greeks idealized beauty, the physical form and pleasures that could be found in music. At the end of their era, their music became effeminate, focusing on the sensuous. Deeply felt emotions were minimized, contributing to the decline of the civilization.

The Roman music energized the body, while creating health, courage and virility. Perhaps they were disgusted with the downfall of the Greeks and their fixation on love and beauty; the Romans subsequently chose a masculine goal in reaction. The Roman love of manliness, courage and sexual virility disintegrated into love of power, brutality and hedonism.[668] The Roman games encouraged brutality and focused attention on death, creating fear.

---

[668] Scott, Cyril. *Op. Cit.*, Pg. 177.

Eventually, this weakened their nerves, downgrading manliness into cowardice.[669]

Danielou noted that the major scale, which is the basis of current Western music creates feelings of industrialism, materialism, sensual egotism and hardness.[670] This scale became the staple of Renaissance music and influenced their civilizations accordingly. In contrast, Eastern music employed older scales from antiquity and they developed great meditation skills and deemphasized material life.

Purpose of Civilizations

Epoch	What they sought	Difficulties
Chinese	Balance & Harmony	Neglected Individuals and Industrialism
Hindu	Heaven & Meditation	Neglected Life
Egyptians	Knowledge	Short on compassion and emotional development necessary for Wisdom. Priesthood amassed knowledge for power (selfishness)
Greeks	Beauty of Physicality, Reasoning Skills	Voluptuousness, love of beauty and pleasure of the senses caused their downfall
Romans	Power & Strength, Practicality	Love of manliness & sexual virility disintegrated into love of power, brutality, sensualist and cowardice

---

[669] Scott, Cyril. *Ibid,* Pg. 178.
[670] Danielou, Alain. *Op. Cit.*, Pgs. 143–144.

Chapter Ten

Music of the Dark and Middle Ages
115 – 1400 AD

History and Remnants

In Europe, the Druid's influences can be traced back many thousands of years. When the last Ice Age retreated in Europe, local people began to erect megalithic buildings, such as Stonehenge. They excelled in astronomy and used mathematics in their building construction 2,000 years before Pythagoras was born.

Julius Caesar and other writers described the sophisticated spiritual system of the Celts and Druids. There were three types of "Druids": the Bards who sang the stories of the tribes, the Ovates, who were the healers and seers, and the Druids who were the philosophers, judges and teachers. With the triumph of Christianity over Europe, the Druids assumed occupations consistent with their expertise. For example, a Druid teacher became a Christian teacher.

Christianity's climb to dominance was sparked by the conversion of Roman Emperor Constantine I in 312 AD. After the collapse of the Western Roman Empire in 476 AD, invading Germanic tribes reigned; laws became virtually non–existent. The Christianized masses looked to the Church for guidance during this chaotic time. As hallmarks of Roman life dwindled, such as education, people relied upon the church for knowledge, as clergy were among the rare few that were literate and educated. The Catholic Church controlled information that people received, strongly influencing beliefs, attitudes and actions. In addition to "pagan" philosophies, many types of knowledge was suppressed, such as science and technology.

The customs and legends of Druids, Knights Templars and Pagans were preserved in the carvings on cathedrals, in stories and written records. Even St Patrick documented old Druidic laws in Ireland.[671] Remnants of ancient musical habits are woven throughout Druid and Pagan writings and customs. The ancient ideas of music, reminiscent of other parts of the world, were an integral part of life in ancient Europe's history. A few examples will be highlighted to confirm this. In Estonia, a small country near Finland and Russia, a week of twenty–four–hour–per–day singing is currently sponsored every five years, boasting of 500,000 singers, to empower their country – a definite throw–back to ancient times.

Author John Michell, who was inspired by Plato, described ancient Druid and Pagan musical practices. For example, thousands of years before Christ,[672] the British Isles conducted three perpetual choirs throughout the year, singing twenty–four–hour–days for weeks. At Glastonbury, Stonehendge and Llan Illtud Vawr,[673] 2,400 individuals committed to ceaseless chanting with at least 100 people singing simultaneously. The music varied with the seasons, the hour of the day and other cycles. Michell confirms that ancient musical practices of the East were also utilized in Europe, "The song that the elders sang at the perpetual choir was an astrological chant, pitched to the music of the spheres, celebrating the order of the heavens and guiding the ritual order of life on Earth. The temple was the central power station of the whole country, transmitting throughout the nation the current of the divine word, generated through the ceaseless activity of astrologers, priests and officials."[674]

---

[671] http://www.druidry.org/druid–way/what–druidry/brief–history–druidry
[672] In the Welsh Triads
[673] Near Llantwit Major in Glamorgan
[674] Tame, David. The Secret Power of Music: The Transformation of Self and Society Through Musical Energy, Destiny Books: VT, 1984, Pg. 281.

A circle can be drawn through the above three locations. Mitchell felt that, if the circle was completed, there would be ten temples with music echoing at all times, creating a powerful subtle energy ring. Mitchell suspected a further site fell on the circle at Goring–on–Thames where the remains of a temple were later discovered.[675] The practice of combining sacred geometry and sound is powerful indeed and reminiscent of ancient practices that are referenced in the lore of Atlantis.

The Dark Ages – Early Middle Ages

Historical books depict the Dark Ages as a period of cultural and economic deterioration that occurred in Europe following the decline of the Roman Empire. From 476 to 800 there was no Roman emperor in the West; furthermore, the years 500 to 1,000 were marked by frequent wars and urban life disappeared. At this time "barbarian invaders," including various Germanic peoples, formed new kingdoms in the area that is now Europe.

Twentieth century history books long taught that the Dark Ages continued until the 13th century. As more of the accomplishments made during this time have come to light, this date has been shortened by some, to conclude at 1000 AD. Today, some prefer not to use the term Dark Ages at all due to its negative connotations.

www.JillsWingsofLight.com – Art Galleries

---

[675] Michell, John. <u>City of Revelation</u>. Sphere Books, 1973.

Events in Dark Ages

Event	Approximate Year
Classical Greek music forgotten	115
Constantine converts to Christianity, which becomes Rome's religion.	476
The Eastern Roman emperor Justinian condemned all pagans to death.	529
Music is condemned by the church, except Plainchant.	576
Pope Gregory I, Bishop of Rome, organizes Plainchant music; (Gregorian chant.) He burns all information on ancient music.	590 – 604

Musicologist and medieval historian James McKinnon described this shadowy time, "Western society was in the worst state of its entire history. The cities had all but ceased to exist… There was no central government to speak of… the countryside was dominated by warring chieftains… The peasants were little better off than beasts of field… The people's religion was a hodgepodge of saints, relics and pagan superstition… Virtually no education took place outside the monasteries."[676] It was a dark time, indeed.

This dark period was marked by the Inquisition and hard living. Life's dark atmosphere blanketed the Earth like a charcoal mist. Cyril Scott, an English composer and writer, painted a picture in which the Dark Age was literally "dark." He described collective dark and muddy thought forms (they appear like a dense vapor when looked at clairvoyantly) that covered large sections of the Earth at this time. "In the Middle Ages these thought forms were,

---

[676] McKinnon, James. Antiquity and the Middle Ages from Ancient Greece to the 15th Century, Macmillian Press Limited: London, 1990, Pg. 17.

in part, responsible for the many and varied manifestations of cruelty mentioned in the chronicles of that period. They obsessed some of the inquisitors, for instance… After the Reformation (1517) thought forms played their part in inciting the various sects to persecute one another and resort to violent measures in order to repress so called heresy."[677]

When a person experiences a "melt–down," he may perceive inner stillness in his emptiness, similar to the "death" of a caterpillar that rebirths as the butterfly. During a person's low ebb, subtle changes occur that become obvious afterwards. The phoenix rises from the ashes, ascending out of the stillness – out of seemingly nothingness. The Dark Ages can be considered a void of social, emotional and intellectual progress, however, internally people changed, and this prepared the way for the Reformation. In the silence, the old musical norms of the Pagans and Druids were wiped clean, paving the way for the Renaissance music – the rebirth of creativity and inventiveness.

In the beginning of the Dark Ages almost all music was silenced. Similarly, before a war breaks out, music in that location literally stops. Likewise, Osama bin Laden outlawed music for all disciples – many of whom fought his terrorist wars and volunteered to be suicide bombers. The lack of music was followed by difficult years.

www.JillsWingsofLight.com – Art Galleries

[677] Scott, Cyril. Music Its Secret Influences throughout the Ages, Samuel Weiser: NY, 1958, Pg. 137. Reprinted in 2013 by Inner Traditions.com

When the Greek and Roman civilizations declined, the reverence for great musical secrets dissipated. In approximately 115 AD Alypius,[678] a vicar[679] of Roman Britain wrote, "Tis agreed of all the learned that the science of music, so admired by the ancients, is wholly lost and what we have now is made up of certain notes that fell into fancy or observation of a poor friar in chanting his mantims."[680] The once esteemed knowledge of the power of music entered a period that can be likened to a vacuum.

From 476 to 800 there was no Roman emperor in the West, leaving a void of organized civilization. German invaders conquered small areas, creating many warring fiefdoms. In 529, the Eastern Roman emperor Justinian[681] condemned all pagans to death. The pagans enjoyed a rich heritage of music. Author and musicologist, Layne Redmond, commented on the fate of the pagans and their music: "Music was frowned upon in private life as well as in worship. Actors, athletes and professional musicians could not be baptized. In the 6th century, Pope John III outlawed the tambourine."[682]

In 576, the Commandments of the Fathers, Superiors, Masters and the Synod (assembly of the church) decreed, that Christians were forbidden to teach their daughters singing, the playing of instruments or similar things because, according to their religion, it is "neither good nor becoming."[683] Music, save a little Plainchant, was mostly absent from early historical writings from the Dark Ages.

John Chrysostom, Archbishop of Constantinople, reflected on the attitude of the church: "Where the *aulos* (a Greek musical instrument) is, Christ is not." Instrumental music was cloaked as the enemy of Christ. The church heaped condemnation on all

---

[678] Alypius of Antioch was a geographer and a vicarious of Roman Britain, probably in the late 350s AD. He replaced Flavius Martinus after that vicar's suicide. His rule is recorded is *Ammianus XXIII* 1, 3. http://en.wikipedia.org/wiki/Alypius_of_Antioch
[679] A representative of the Pope in the Roman Catholic Church
[680] Scott, Cyril. *Op. Cit.,* Pg. 180.
[681] Justinian the Great, was Eastern Roman (Byzantine) Emperor from 527 to 565. During his reign, Justinian sought to revive the empire's greatness and re–conquer the lost western half of the classical Roman Empire.
[682] Redmond, Layne. When the Drummers were Women: A Spiritual History of Rhythm, Three Rivers Press: NY, 1997, Pg. 154.
[683] Redmond, Layne. *Op. Cit.,* Pg. 159.

musical instruments, dancing, musical theater and music from banquets, weddings and local songs. The music was deemed the "devil's rubbish."[684]

Some Pagan feasts included: gluttony, guests wildly dancing to music and the beat of the drums. The Christian church responded by forbidding the use of most music in Christian worship. All that was heard was the lone voice of acappella singing[685] the *Psalms*. This music was called Plainchant, which was a solo voice singing Christian texts without instrumental accompaniment. This was the only type of music allowed in early Christian churches.[686]

To make a listener receptive to spiritual thoughts, the Plainchant melody was kept pure and unaccompanied. It was believed to bring church members closer in harmonious relationships, relax the mind and help one forget outside pressures. Plainchant assisted the listener in obtaining a pious state of mind. The music was designed to calm the congregation.

The lone voice of a Gregorian chant (also known as Plainchant or plainsong) was named after Pope Gregory I, Bishop of Rome from 590 to 604 AD. Pope Gregory I simplified and cataloged Plainchant, and assigned music to be played at specific celebrations in the church calendar.[687] Services were rigidly structured to occur four times throughout the day – on the first, third, sixth and ninth hours.[688] One might say that the Earth got her vibratory doses on a schedule: intervals reflecting a 3, 6, and 9 pattern of time.[689] The church musical timetable was often set a year ahead of time with no room for spontaneity.

Pope Gregory was a violent enemy of pre–Christian culture and burned all ancient books, which explains in part why ancient musical techniques were lost. Burning the only available reference

---

[684] McKinnon, James. Antiquity and the Middle Ages from Ancient Greece to the 15th Century, Macmillian Press Limited: London, 1990, Pg. 81.
[685] Acappella singing is "in the style of the chapel" or singing without independent instrumental accompaniment. http://www.singers.com/a–cappella.html
[686] http://musiced.about.com/od/faqs/f/Plainchant.htm, Plainchant emerged as early as 100 AD.
[687] http://en.wikipedia.org/wiki/Gregorian_chant
[688] McKinnon, James. *Op. Cit.,* Pg. 89.
[689] The 3, 6, and 9 pattern encoded within the solfeggio tones avoids the golden ratio.

materials was not the best way to understand the complicated modal system of the Greeks. Gregory did create a musical modal form similar to the Greeks, but his work lacked understanding of how or why Greek music was performed. Although the modes kept their old Greek names, their notes changed. Music expert Curt Sachs reported that Plainchant lost the metaphysical correspondences that Saint Gregory thought he had discovered.[690]

The tradition of dictating musical rules continued, but without knowledge of why it was done. For example, mixing modes was considered a sin. "In spite of the permission given by King Louis IX to form an academy of music, the Parliament of Paris closed it on the grounds that musicians did not observe the ecclesiastical rules and were passing too frequently from one mode to another."[691]

According to Curt Sachs, the tangle of ever changing Greek names and meanings led to the medieval monks badly misrepresenting the Greek system. Although the scales were named after the Greek ones, they were altered. Under the reign of Pope Gregory, the number of modes, likened to scales, increased from four to eight:

- Mixolydian   musical notes of GABCDEFG
- Lydian   FGABCDEF
- Phygian   EFGABCDE
- Dorian and Hypomixolydian   DEFGABC
- Hypholydian   CDEFGABCD
- Hypophygian   BCDEFGAB
- Hypodorian   ABCDEFGAB[692]

Even though the Catholic Church adopted and expanded scales modeled after the Greek modes, later in the 15th century, they dropped all but two of the above scales, renaming them "major" and "minor". During this time, the earlier pentatonic scales of Asia evolved into the major scale, as well.[693] Once again, similar

---

[690] Danielou, Alain. Music and the Power of Sound: The Influence of Tuning and Interval on Consciousness, Inner Traditions: VT, 1943, Pg. 125.
[691] Fabre d' Olivet. Pg. 42. Danielou, Alain. Music and the Power of Sound: The Influence of Tuning and Interval on Consciousness, Inner Traditions: VT, 1943, Pg. 125.
[692] Sachs, Curt. The Rise of Music in the Ancient World East and West, Dover Publications: Mineola, NY, 1943, Pg. 238.
[693] Sachs, Curt. Ibid, Pg. 304.

musical matrices emerge simultaneously in different corners of the globe.

This modal music did not descend in pitch as the earlier musical systems from antiquity had, but developed upwards. This was a new musical innovation.

Gregorian chants are recognized by endless acappella notes. The melody features numerous intervals three and four notes apart. Leading tones, such as the 7th and 2nd note of the scale, are avoided. The musical sensations of pushing and pulling, as well as the feeling to resolve tones are avoided.

The singing of chants was a constant endeavor, as author and musicologist McKinnon explained: chanting was a full time occupation by many clerics – including their early childhood years. They memorized many chant repertories. The medieval cantor sang for hours every day.[694] The same chants were passed down through the generations orally.

In the 9th century, the Aurelian of Réôme, a Frankish music theorist, published a unified musical system called *Musica Disciplina,* based on eight modes and a crude notational system taken from an incorrect interpretation of the Greek modes by Boethius. [695, 696]

After the 10th century, melodies became more remarkable. Rather than the former endless chant that had little or no recognizable melodies, the word "amen" was added, which created a feeling of an ending – a resolution. Once a song had an ending, it begged for a beginning as well. Prior to this, the music could be likened to wind chimes that sing tirelessly while dancing in the breeze without any identifiable starting or ending.

At this time, musical notation also originated. The first written symbols were "neumes," a mark that recorded the number of pitches and indicated their relative direction. Neumes were signs

[694] McKinnon, James. *Op. Cit.,* Pg. 113.
[695] A 6th century Arabic to Latin translation
[696] Merrick, Richard. Interference: A Grand Scientific Musical Theory, Merrick: Texas, 2002, Pg. 42.

such as squares and shapes written above the text to give the singer clues about the pitches; if the neumes went up, so did the singer's pitch.

Around 1000 AD, further advancements were made in the notation of music. The words of chants were written to aid the singers. In the late 10th and early 11th centuries, a Benedictine monk named Guido d'Arezzo,[697] reduced the necessary time to teach a chant from a dozen to two years (with written words and notations). Guido added lines similar to today's musical staff, so the distance between the neumes were a more accurate reflection of the music. He even colored some lines. A yellow line represented the note C, red for F, and Green for B flat.[698]

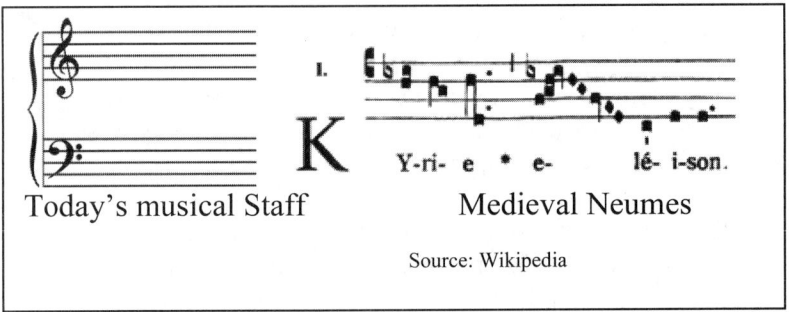

Today's musical Staff   Medieval Neumes

Source: Wikipedia

Musical Notations: Modern and Medieval

Guido d'Arezzo addressed the difficulties of memorizing the long church chants by inventing a clever method of teaching music, known as the "Guidonian hand," which made it possible for teachers to use their own hand as a "visual aid."[699] With this system, each new piece would not have to be memorized.

Guido d'Arezzo was heavily influenced by Muslim musical theories (the Arabs preserved the modes of the ancient Greeks) like those of Gerbert of Aurillac[700] of Spain. Guido reworked the church modes in his book, *Micrologus*. He also introduced the use

---

[697] Writings of Guido of Arezzo – 990 to after 1033
[698] Arnold, Joan. Medieval Music, Oxford University Press: Oxford, 1982. Pg. 37.
[699] James, Jamie. The Music of the Spheres: Music, Science and the Natural Order of the Universe, Springer–Verlag: NY, 1995. Pg. 82.
[700] Later becoming Pope Sylvester II, d. 1003

of two voices that sang different harmonious notes, a novel invention after hundreds of years of Plainchant. Cyril Scott stated that this harmony created coordination and cooperation.

Based on the ancient Greek theories, Guido proposed yet another new hexachord system for the church modes, known as the solfeggio scale, which has recently gained popularity as a spiritually uplifting scale. He named the notes of the solfeggio scale, using six syllables: *ut, re, mi, fa, sol,* and *la,* taken from the words of an old Latin hymn.[701] This jingle method of teaching music was used in addition to the Guidonian hand, making learning music much easier, as mentioned earlier. In a modern example, the 1959 movie *The Sound of Music,* the song *Do–Re–Mi* also uses a jingle to teach scale note names. Guido named the lowest octave note "*gamma ut.*" Eventually this was shortened to "gamut" to identify the entire range of octaves. The term "gamut" has since been used to describe a complete range of any spectrum, such as the range of visible colors.[702]

The primitive, folk music in Europe was based on harmony composed of intervals *three* notes apart. Likewise, Guido's solfeggio scale is encoded with numbers that are multiples of *threes.* When the Pythagorean skein[703] is applied to the cycles per second of the solfeggio frequencies, each note reduces to an arrangement of 3's, 6's and 9's.

Unlike the scales of his time, Guido's system used a type of tuning developed by Pythagoras, but with one really big difference: Guido's system *avoided* the tri–tone chord that created a phi interval, which was associated with the Egyptian mysteries and Paganism.[704] Guido's system spread throughout the monasteries of Europe. The phi interval (close to a diminished fifth/augmented fourth) was termed "of the devil" and was strictly prohibited by the Catholic Church.

---

[701] Engel, Carl. The Most Ancient Nations: Assyrians, Egyptians and Hebrews with Special Reference to Recent Discoveries in Western Asia and in Egypt, Murray: London, 1864, Pg. 364.
[702] Merrick, Richard. *Op. Cit.,* Pg. 42.
[703] Continually adding each digit in a number until you have a number from 1 to 9. For example 12, would be: $1 + 2 = 3$.
[704] Merrick, Richard. *Op. Cit.,* Pg. 42.

The Musical Number

The notes in primitive folk music in the European countryside, were composed by coupling musical thirds, both major and minor. When the intervals of three were stacked, they created larger patterns of sixes and nines. There was one exception: the jump of two minor thirds created an interval of a fifth. The intervals of the octave and the fourth were skipped.

At this time, melodic patterns of *threes* were common in the music of the North America Indians, Melanesians (New Guinea and surrounding islands), Africans, territories from Iceland to the Baltic States, and from Sweden to Spain.[705] In addition to the use of the *third* interval, notes were coupled in triplet rhythms – emphasizing the pattern of *three* in another expression. Local primitive music, constructed mainly from *thirds*, blossomed in spite of the fact that the Greeks and the Catholic Church considered this sound dissonant.

The number three – the most playful of all numbers – can be linked to traits of understanding, beauty, harmony, idealism, completion and growth. The following are characteristics of people having a *three* in their numerology: creative, socially active, artistic, positive, optimistic, playful, happy, fun–loving, inspirational, imaginative, motivating, enthusiastic and uplifting. They also often have great verbal skills.[706]

There are many important concepts associated with the number three: The Trinity (Father, Son and Holy Ghost) and symbolism of man, woman and child are key examples. There are three primary colors, Jesus spent three days in the tomb, and Jonah spent three days in the belly of the whale. Space is three dimensional (height, width and depth). People make three wishes and give three cheers.

---

[705] Sachs, Curt. *Op. Cit.,* Pg. 296.
[706] The difficulties associated with the number three are being cynical, disorganized, irresponsible, moody, emotional and vulnerable. People with this energy lack focus, discipline and may have difficulties handling money. They scatter their energies, lack direction and find it difficult to finish projects. http://www.spiritual–numerology.com/numerology–number–meaning/numerology–meaning–of–number–3.html.

The Number Three in Crop Circles [707]

From antiquity to the Dark Ages, the interval of a third was considered dissonant. However, by the year 1033, the interval of a major third was perceived to be consonant, and even minor thirds were tolerated. [708]

Later, Renaissance musicians (ca. 1500 and on) used the **1–3–5** chord as a staple of harmony. As people harmonized with a sound formerly considered dissonant, their energy modulated – reflecting this new vibratory influence. Populations grow accustomed to sounds and harmonize with them. Ancient sages believed that such harmonization transitioned people's consciousness and perceptions. As civilizations became harmonious with new intervals, their mental and emotional wavelengths and corresponding experiences changed.

In a modern day example, people have harmonized with a previously grating and scandalous sound, the interval of a seventh,

[707] Thanks to Peter Sorensen
[708] Gushee, Marion. "The Polyphonic Music of the Medieval Monastery, Cathedral and University," Gushee, Marion. Edited by McKinnon, Antiquity and the Middle Ages from Ancient Greece to the 15th Century, Macmillian Press Limited: London, 1990, Pg. 145.

which is used extensively in Jazz. (One contributing factor in this harmonizing is the use of **1–3–5–7** chords.) Jazz was originally deemed the music of the Devil, perhaps because of its blatant use of the "devil's tritone" (intervals that combined to create a number associated with Phi; the ancient Egyptians, Greeks and Pagans related this to curved patterns found in nature. Just as these religions were deemed enemies of the Church, so was their music. The devil was believed to be summoned through music, especially this interval). The pushing and pulling feel of the tritone was resolved by jazz musicians by sliding a finger a half step on a stringed instrument. These sliding movements created the outrageous sensual *ethos* of the music. Yet within a hundred years in Western societies, Jazz was added to the repertoire of elevator music and perceived as pleasant background music. It was no longer associated with scandal and the devil; it was not even considered naughty any longer.

The Music of the Later Middle Ages

The Middle Ages continues until the dawn of the Renaissance, which started in the 13th, 14th, or 15th century, depending on the region of Europe and other factors.[709] After 1000 AD, Europe's population increased greatly as technological and agricultural innovations allowed trade to flourish. Peasants gravitated into villages where they owed rent and labor to nobles and knights. This created a workforce that could be organized and controlled. Beginning in 1095 Western European Christians attempted to regain control of the Middle Eastern Holy Land from the Muslims in the Crusades.

Music continued to change and evolve. In the latter half of the tenth century, chant writers designed voice crossings with one musical line ascending, while the other moved downwards or in another direction. This was quite innovative, given the history of Gregorian chants and earlier papal directions – that only one tone was to be heard at one time.

---

[709] http://www.britannica.com/EBchecked/topic/380873/Middle–Ages

Events of the Middle Ages

Event	Approximate Year
Melodies were more remarkable. The word "amen" was added to music, creating beginnings and endings. Musical notations developed. Two voices were heard instead of just one. The solfeggio scale that avoided the phi interval was used.	1000
The interval of a major third is described as consonant and not shunned.	1033
In the Crusades Christians tried to gain control of the Holy Land.	1095
The monastery population also declined, but music grew in new choral establishments, providing career paths for musicians.	1200 – 1300
Black Death killed a third of the population in Europe.	1347 – 1348
New instruments used and musical groups roamed the country. Music became more complicated, featuring many instruments and singers at once. Paper became more readily available, allowing music to be documented and distributed.	1200 – 1400

Another novel technique mixed a tenor drone sound and a fast moving upper voice. Constant repetition of the same tone (such as a drone, mantra or rosary) influences the brain. This formulates energy patterns in the subconscious mind, facilitating organized thinking.[710] The Ambrosian chant of the Middle Ages created such energy.

---

[710] Scott, Cyril. Music Its Secret Influences throughout the Ages, Samuel Weiser: NY, 1958, Pg. 183. Reprinted in 2013 by Inner Traditions.com.

Middle Ages expert and musicologist, McKinnon, detailed evolving musical practices: 11th century musicians focused on pitch, but in the thirteenth century rhythm was the main concern.[711]

Leonardo of Pisa (1170–1250), also known as Leonardo Fibonacci, wrote about the flowering and branching patterns found in nature; he described a spiraling number pattern, in which the ratios between each number are the golden ratio. This numeric pattern was named the "Fibonacci numbers." This number pattern was considered sacred in antiquity and musical scales were created using these numbers.

As we have already learned, patterns found in nature were converted into numbers that reflected their geometry and used as cycles per second (frequencies) in music. The Fibonacci numbers are found extensively in nature: such as in the mathematics that create a spiral sea shell and in the design of many flowers. In this number series, the sum of any two adjacent numbers equals the next number in the series (0, 1, 1, 2, 3, 5, 8, 13…). The ratios between adjacent Fibonacci numbers approximate phi. Phi is a mathematical constant (1.61803399). This ratio is found in our bodies, the spiral of a seashell and in billions of stars in distant galaxies. *Nature loves this pattern, as it uses it again and again!*

In 1232 AD, Pope Gregory IX's musical doctrine became law. He described a philosophical cornerstone of the Catholic Inquisition; the use of the tritone was forcefully banned.[712] In 1234, two years after the Church acted on eliminating paganism… the law, entitled *Liber Extra…* banned the tritone from music.[713]

In the 13th century, each note of the old Plainchant was accompanied by a second line of music, like a shadow note that was a fourth or fifth apart. Towards the end of the 13th century, this second line moved freely and independently from the Plainchant melody. Shortly thereafter, musical pieces sported three

---

[711] Hiley, David. "Plainchant Transfigured: Innovation and Reformation through the Ages," Hiley, David. Edited by McKinnon, <u>Antiquity and the Middle Ages from Ancient Greece to the 15th Century</u>, Macmillian Press Limited: London, 1990, Pg. 122.
[712] Merrick, Richard. *Op. Cit.,* Pg. 43.
[713] Merrick, Richard. *Ibid,* Pg. 43.

singers, each producing independent lines of music. In 1285, a song with four independent voices was written in Paris.

Similar musical developments occurred spontaneously throughout the world, according to musical historian, Curt Sachs. Sachs documents that the same techniques, notes, intervals and other musical inventions become popular in faraway places at roughly the same time. For example, by the end of the sixteenth century, Chinese instrumental music was a fourth higher than the accompanying vocals. Likewise, the organum (a Plainchant with an added voice) of the early Middle ages used a melody that was accompanied in parallel notes a fourth lower. In a similar way, the Siamese played parallel fourths on their gong chimes.[714]

In the latter half of the 13th century, rhythms were recorded in groups of three, giving music a dance–like feel. Yet, local music (based on intervals three notes apart) was still considered the "enemy of the Church."[715]

Significant musical advancement was made from 1200 through 1300.

- New instruments included bowed string instruments similar to the violin. These were popular outside of the Church.
- Minstrels, "carolers," and troubadours introduced new musical career paths outside of the Church. Local roaming musicians dubbed as story tellers, errand boys and joke tellers – much like jesters – freely entertained the people.
- Italy's madrigal, a polyphonic melody with complex rhythms, flourished. The madrigal was often accompanied by words, perhaps to one's lover. This musical form was considered rustic or an unsophisticated genre.
- Motets, music with several choral parts, become popular in England, France and later in Italy. Motets often applied

---

[714] Sachs, Curt. *Op. Cit.,* Pg. 119.
[715] Page, Christopher. "Court and City in France: 110–1300," Page, Christopher. Edited by McKinnon, James. Antiquity and the Middle Ages from Ancient Greece to the 15th Century, Macmillian Press Limited: London, 1990, Pg. 208.

new lyrics to older music. Rhythmic variations became complex.

The Black Death occurred in 1347 to 1348 and struck down a third of the population across Europe. Controversy and heresy within the Church paralleled Europe's civil strife and peasant revolts. In addition, the monastery population also declined starting around the 1200s through the first several decades of the 1300s. It was during this time that music grew in new choral establishments, providing career paths for musicians.

In the 14th century, paper became more readily available, resulting in detailed documentation of historical records and hardcopies of written music. The musical notation system was now quite developed, similar to its form today.

As cultural and technological developments transformed the European society, the Middle Ages ended with the beginning of the Renaissance – about 1400 AD. The Renaissance further accelerated the stream of more complex musical forms and innovations.

Musical Shapes of Phi

Cymatics was described in the section on Egypt, showing how sound can create shapes in materials when correctly applied. This technique is not new, as evidenced by the "Chladni pictures" carved in stone in the Rosslyn Chapel in 1446. The Gnostic Ebionites (Ebionites are connected to the Essene mystery school, a precursor to modern Freemasonry), who built the Chapel, were similar to Cathars and Templars. Among Rosslyn's many intricate carvings is a sequence of 213 boxes with etched patterns embossed on the pillars and arches. The motifs on the boxes resemble sound patterns and images.[716] Many contain proportions equating to phi. During the period when ancient musical secrets were forbidden, sacred music was sometimes carved on the walls of chapels. The father–and–son team of Thomas and Stuart Mitchell, in 2005, matched cymatic images formed from musical notes to the

---

[716] Cymatic patterns or pictures are formed by placing powder upon a flat surface and vibrating the surface at different frequencies. The same frequency repeatedly creates the same image.

Rossyln carvings. In this way, the carvings served as a musical score. The Mitchells performed and recorded the music of the 213 cubes described above, called the *Rosslyn Motet.* Deepening the mystery, some of the 213 cubes are reminiscent of crop circle designs found around the world. Why did the Gnostic Ebonites, or perhaps extraterrestrials, draw attention to these cymatic pictures that geometrically displayed the golden mean and phi?

In the Rossylyn Chapel, underneath the cubes, are 13 angels and 8 Naga dragon–serpents. This pattern of images reflects the ratio of 13/8, the golden ratio. (Recall that the golden ratio kills vibration, yet facilitates the flow of energy. In sharp contrast, the major sixth is the least destructive vibration of all intervals.) The chapel's dimensions approximate ratios of 5/3, which equates to musical major sixes. Richard Merrick, musician and technology expert, suggested that these carvings preserve the harmonic principles that were forced into secrecy by the church.[717] These codes were hiding – in plain sight in a chapel – where no one would suspect them to be!

Merrick concluded, "Was the secret of the Rosslyn Chapel the interplay of 13/8 and 5/3 that is found not only in music but in the heavens as well? Were its master masons trying to tell us that the Naga dragon–serpents, symbolizing the Fibonacci series of numbers spiraling into the golden ratio, support the resonance (or enlightenment) of angels as they play their musical instruments on the pentagonal Star in the East?"[718]

The *Diabolus in Musica* – The Devil's Tritone[719]

The Church condemned the chord that expressed energy of the golden ratio, labeling it the Devil's Tritone or *Diabolus in Musica.* The Church even considered intervals close to phi (a sound in which energy is shared) as forbidden sounds

---

[717] Merrick, Richard. *Op. Cit.,* Pg. 65.
[718] Merrick, Richard. *Op. Cit.,* Pg. 65.
[719] Pictures of the piano form http://www.music–for–music–teachers.com/piano–keyboard.html

The Devil's Tritone is a chord, composed of three tones, each a minor third apart. Levarie and Levy noticed that the tension and dissonance in the tritone are the greatest of any combination of notes in the modern day scale.[720]

Today's music system only has numbers that approximate phi. The earlier scales were designed to "hit the nail on the head." Merrick described the fate of older scales that included the exact phi ratio. The older augmented 4th and diminished 5th intervals that created phi were rounded off. These separate notes became the same note in the equal temperament scale (F# = Gb).[721]

As a prerequisite to understanding the Devil's Tritone, Merrick located symmetry within a scale. The balance point of a diatonic scale[722] (see footnotes for definition), which can be heard by playing C to the next octave C on the piano, is the second note of the scale. (In the key of C, the center is D.[723]) When you go up or

---

[720] Levarie and Levy. Tone: A Study in Musical Acoustics, Oberlin Press: USA, 1968, Pg. 202.

[721] They balance around the equal tempered tritone at mid–octave. When you take the differences, they appear to balance asymmetrically due to the logarithmic curvature of pitch space (same as actual space), but in a logarithmic scale they are symmetric.

- Augmented fourth: $7/5 = 1.4$
- Mid–Octave = $2 \char`^ (1/2) = 1.414213...$
- Diminished fifth: $10/7 = 1.42857...$
- The 7:5 and 10:7 ratios are now inverses of one another with, one note an octave higher – Correspondence with Richard Merrick

[722] The diatonic scale includes five whole steps and two half steps for each octave, in which the two half steps are separated from each other by either two or three whole steps, depending on their position in the scale. This pattern ensures that, in a diatonic scale spanning more than one octave, all the half steps are maximally separated from each other (i.e. separated by at least two whole steps). The word "diatonic" comes from a Greek word that means meaning progressing through tones. Ball, Philip. The Music Instinct, London: Vintage: London, 2010, Pg.44

[723] "The super tonic or harmonic center D sounds consonant when played with the first note of the scale because it synchronizes with every one of the maximum resonance and maximum damping locations (Damping alters the sound of a musical instrument. For example, on guitar, damping is a technique where, shortly after playing the strings, the sound is reduced by pressing the right hand palm against the strings.) on the fundamental or open string. Imagine when a guitar string is first plucked, the string is stretched and must be warped a little to create the standing wave we hear as a musical tone. As the energy stabilizes into a stationary standing wave, the harmonics vibrate in a piggybacked fashion on the note of the fundamental (or open string). But there is only one harmonic that is perfectly synchronized with the fundamental and that is the ninth or major second (the ninth is an octave of the major second). The space–time matrix causes waves to form and dampen at the golden ratio or Phi intervals. These constant phenomena of nature causes the 1st and 9th harmonic partials to be synchronized, creating a twin center in the harmonic series at the ninth partial, around which all of the other harmonics balance or orbit. The harmonic

down on the notes of the C scale, the intervals are symmetrical if D is the center. Each half mirrors the intervals of the other half of the scale.

In the key of C, the Devil's Tritone includes the notes of B, D, and F; the balancing note in the C scale (which is D); and intervals of two phi ratios (B to D, and D to F). These notes are called the *Diabolus in Musica*. (See X's marked below the keyboard.) In the Devil's Tritone two adjacent intervals each approximate the golden ratio.[724]

The Devil's Tritone

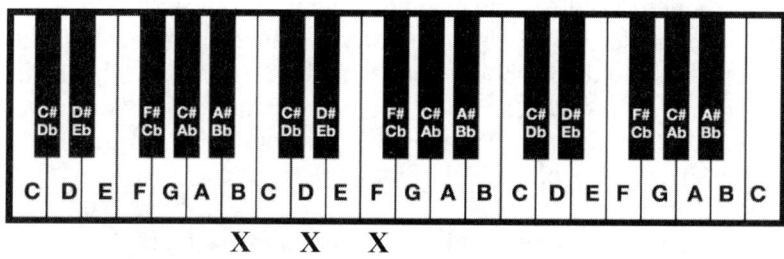

Merrick added, "As the force of symmetry and harmonic function in music, the tritone function oscillates around the golden ratios in

---

center, the ninth interval, exists in all living things. As a set of nested phi–spaced rings, it is centered on the navel. Seven rings spiral into the head (around the ear canal), then down the spine to the eighth ring centered on the solar plexus followed by a shift down to the navel for the ninth. The 10–12th rings then extend to the fingertips and goes concentric around the ninth/navel. In this way, the body resonates out of the brain, down the spine, and then gradually dampens down along the limbs, branching into fives before reaching silence (trunk, 2 arms and 2 legs).

In every solar system, the harmonic center is its sun. The system's fundamental frequency will then be the second orbiting planet, in our case Venus. Earth is the "leading tone" or lower half of the solar tritone just below one of the solar golden means located in the space between Earth and Venus. This is why Venus resonates as a pentagonal geometry with Earth..." My correspondence from Richard Merrick.

[724] "The golden mean up from G# lands between E and F while a golden mean down from G# lands between B and C. The golden means are in the cracks of the keys near B and F. In the key of C, B leads of pulls energy towards C. F leads energy towards E. The major third (C, E) and D and F oscillate back and forth across these two golden means, creating a feeling of energy rotating back and forth. Try it and see if you can't hear this switch from tension to resolution and back. In the more general case, the velocity of energy flow is greatest around these two golden means pulling all of the notes in an octave toward D and away from G# just like a magnet. Since our brain is structured in the same way, we can measure, predict and feel the direction of energy flow in music as if we were another magnet." My correspondence from Richard Merrick.

315

a diatonic scale, mending the gaps in an octave as if it were a musical sewing machine. When allowed, the tritone function will always reveal the symmetry of counter posing golden ratios."[725]

Merrick described the Church's efforts to eradicate anything related to nature's phi – the golden ratio – in this way: "During the Inquisition the church was bent on eradicating Paganism, the free natural study of harmonics and the center of the anti–harmonic campaign was the golden ratio revealed in music, termed the 'Devil in Music.'"[726] He goes on to say, "Under church law anti–harmonic agenda, suppression of the tritone in music was crucial. Cannon laws were passed to mandate rules for how to construct scales, how to handle voice leading, what was considered consonant and dissonant, how contrary motion should be handled, what notes should and should not be emphasized in rhythm, which rhythm patterns were acceptable and specific instructions for how music should be written. Tritone omission was the first principle – the foil, if you will, behind all of these rules."[727]

Merrick continued with the history of the suppression of the tone equating to phi or the golden mean: "The Church mounted a Great Crusade against the very cradle of civilization – the people who had discovered and preserved the ancient knowledge of harmonics. The Church knew that eradicating paganism simply could not be done without first eradicating free harmony in music."[728]

The Church intended to eradicate Pythagoreanism, Platoism, Mithraism, Egyptian Hermeticism, Zoroastrianism, the Hebrew Kabbalah and similar Gnostic teachings. The Catharas of southern France were executed or exiled, forced to roam the countryside as "gypsies." The Knights Templar, the primary keepers of the Babylonian and Egyptian mysteries, were hunted down and murdered by the Church on Friday 13, 1307.[729]

---

[725] Merrick, Richard. *Op. Cit.,* Pg. 49.
[726] Merrick, Richard. *Ibid,* Pg. 49.
[727] Merrick, Richard. *Ibid,* Pg. 49.
[728] Merrick, Richard. *Ibid,* Pg. 50.
[729] Merrick, Richard. *Ibid,* Pg. 49.

In suppressing the tritone, the medieval Church hid the golden mean that expressed itself in music. Merrick described the motive for the anti–harmonic campaign: "For if a perfect order were thought to exist in nature, immediate and present in everything, there would be no need for a separate creator, no need for the Church to intercede on behalf of God. People would simply seek the answers directly from the world around them and in their own inner most chamber as had always been the shamanic way of tribal cultures."[730] The golden mean was associated with a God in nature, a pagan concept counter to the Christian ideal of a pure Catholic God existing apart from nature.[731]

What is the impact of listening to the tritone or the phi sound? This sound equates to branching, spiraling and scaffolding patterns – found in nature. Perhaps it helps us to grow and develop new ideas and lift our energy towards God.

Summary

Beginning with the fall of Roman domination, this period continues for a thousand years, combining the Dark Ages and the Middle Ages. The Dark Ages produced a musical void – save a single unaccompanied voice in church music. Growth in music stagnated just as with almost everything else... this is probably a necessary incubation period as the ancient societies and civilizations disappeared and along with them their long lasting stability and culture – principal of which – in the author's view, was the musical structures. People remembered the importance of music, but lost the knowledge of why and how it was to be used. Although people attempted to steal the secrets of Greek music, they unknowingly created an entirely new system, different in all ways.

---

[730] Merrick, Richard. *Ibid*, Pg. 50.

[731] http://www.cymascope.com/cyma_research/biology.html. The cymascope website suggested that understanding the energy created by intervals helps us understand better the creative force of God: "Cymatic patterns created from stillness were geometric in shape, such as that of a dodecahedron.[731] Adjacent to these still air spaces were areas of dynamic vibration, which we could think of as the dynamic creative force of Source who many call 'God.' If this hypothesis is correct then it may be the reason that many people meditate in stillness to reach God within.

In this barren period people suffered in many ways: the poverty of peasants, the black plague, famine, Church persecutions, and inner Church corruption, all made living hard. Yet, in spite of this, resilient man created significant musical innovations. Music began to be written and performed, giving creative power to the composer. The musician no longer improvised, but became a master of performing written music. The interval of a third became consonant to people. Music evolved from a single thread of Plainchant to innovative and complex musical structures. Perhaps as a reaction to "thin" Plainchant (one lone voice), the reign of "thick" musical harmony began, with many notes played at once, creating intricate sounds. When this music is converted to numbers, it reveals complex numerical patterns. This complexity was mirrored in the accomplishments of communities in other areas of life; and thus the Middle Ages were left behind.

Humanity left what were golden eras for Rome and Greece and other ancient civilizations, that in some ways even rival modern achievements... and entered a dark period, a void; wandering in the desolation... but eventually rose and rediscovered the power of music – but not in the same way. Lost was the all–pervasive power that once existed when man was closer to the supernatural element in the universe – closer to his divine God. We leave our ancestral times behind as we begin to move into the modern era.

www.JillsWingsofLight.com – Art Galleries

Chapter Eleven

Classical Music
1400 – 2000

Classical music embodies a rich tradition of innovative musical creations, with distinctive and overlapping phases. In an unprecedented period, free of musical restrictions, creativity ran rampant. Innovations occurred at seemingly lightning speed. We begin this time period at the close of the Middle Ages and the dawn of the Renaissance.

The beginning of the Renaissance is dated differently in different locations – for various reasons. Generally speaking, the Renaissance spans the 14th to the 17th centuries, encompassing literary, artistic, musical and educational reforms. It started as a cultural movement in Italy in the late Medieval period and spread across Europe. Although the Renaissance contained intellectual revolutions, as well as social and political upheaval, it is best known for its artistic developments. The Renaissance era is somewhat different than the Renaissance musical period which lasted about ~1400 to 1600.

A steady parade of innovative musical developments marked the Renaissance music period: The scale we use today was being sculpted. New harmonic structures were presented to listeners. This music can be likened to a flower bud, about to bloom. The music of the Baroque period (1600 – 1750) featured exquisite mathematical patterns in music, complex harmony and melody innovations. Enthusiasts had never grappled with such complexity in music.

Continuing with our metaphor of a flower – the Classical music of this age represents the splendor and glory of a rose in full bloom. In fact, this entire musical gamut (ca. 1400 – 2000), is now referred to, by the layman, as simply Classical music. For the purposes of our book we are lumping all the above periods into what we are going to call *Classical Music* – the groupings reflected below are important subsets of Classical music. They are important in their own right for the developments and advances that occurred to shape Classical music during these eras. The mature bloom of the genre can be compared to the Romantic period of music (1815 – 1910), followed by outrageous experimentation with dissonant sounds in the Modern era (1900 – 2000).

Classical Musical Periods:
- Renaissance musical period (1400 – 1600)
- Baroque musical period (1600 – 1750)
- Classical musical period (1750 – 1815)
- Romantic musical period (1815 – 1910)
- Modern era (1900 – 2000)

History

Picking up where we left off at the end of the Middle Ages with the invention of the printing press, circa 1450, printed music was made tremendously more available and inexpensive. This development allowed greater numbers of musicians to enter the profession – resulting in more innovations and contributions. The cathedrals and aristocratic courts trained hundreds of musicians and composers. Musicians were highly sought throughout Europe during this time of relative political stability and prosperity. Music was increasingly freed from medieval constraints that blocked creativity of rhythm, harmony and form. Music quickly became a vehicle for personal expression – *something that was never allowed in the past.*

In the late 15th century, Bartolome Ramos de Pareja (1440–1522), a Spanish mathematician and composer, tweaked the tuning of musical 3rds and 6ths. He modified the third intervals by making them ratios of 5/4 and 6/5, instead of the complex Pythagorean 81/64 and 32/27 ratios. This small difference created a more pleasing sound. These harmonious tones increased the usage of the third interval, which had already become a popular sound.

In Venice, from about 1534 until around 1600, an impressive poly–choral style developed, with grand multiple choirs of singers accompanied by brass and string instruments. Prior music never featured such rich harmony and complex sounds.

Many of the Renaissance composers are relatively unknown. Opera arose at this time in Florence as a deliberate attempt to resurrect the music of ancient Greece.

Towards the end of the 1500s the system of church modes broke down entirely. Gioseffo Zarlino (1517–1590), an Italian music theorist, Franciscan monk and Renaissance composer, tossed the tetra chords out and replaced them with a 7–step Ionian scale; this became the precursor to today's major scale.[732] Zarlino later divided the octave into 12 musical half steps and emphasized triadic chords (a set of three notes that make two intervals which are a third apart). This is the model of today's modern musical system. This procedure was codified in 1592 and revised in 1622. Many musicians began to use it.

In 1550, Luther wrote scathing pamphlets about the Catholic Church in Germany, where many of the Renaissance composers lived. With the ensuing birth of the Protestant Church, the Catholic Church's iron grip on music weakened, which served as a prerequisite for more musical innovations and the resurrection of ancient musical wisdom. With musical restrictions mainly eradicated, Renaissance music paved the road for a parade of musical innovations. Music now contained:
- Several singers combined on each vocal part
- Choruses
- Ornate chants
- Canons – songs in which the melody is played at different durations. The child's song "*Row, Row your Boat*" is an example. Two and three part canons were now composed and played.

[732] Merrick, Richard. Interference: A Grand Scientific Musical Theory, Merrick: Texas, 2002, Pg. 52.

- A large variety of instruments
- Four musical parts, all playing different notes
- Primitive, folk and local music blended into formal musical structures
- City concerts beginning as early as 1480
- No general pitch standards

Monteverdi (who lived 1567–1643) initiated the transition from Renaissance to Baroque music. Baroque literally means "broke music." Monteverdi *broke* numerous canon rules of the church. He perfected two styles of composition: polyphony (numerous harmonious musical parts played simultaneously) and the basso continuo technique (Chords/figures were written under the music to be used to create an improvisational bass part.).[733]

Musicians revived ancient ideas of using music for beneficial purposes. A group of Florentine academics attempted to restore word–to–music relationships advocated by Greek philosophers – such as Plato – and published the *The Doctrine of the Affections*. This philosophy described beauty in painting, music and theatre, and was widely admired during in the Baroque era (1600–1750).[734] With this school of thought, a sound was a tangible embodiment of *Affekt:* an emotional state of being. It was believed, for example, that *lamento bass* expressed sadness, while a rapidly rising sequence of thirds produced the opposite – euphoria.[735]

In 1717, J. S. Bach was hired by Prince Leopold, a Calvinist who advocated freedom from religious musical traditions. Free of the church's constraints, Bach unleashed the power of the tritone. Bach's brilliant compositions legitimized the tritone, leading to its increasingly popular use.

---

[733] Basso continuo is a form of musical accompaniment used in the Baroque period. It means "continuous bass." All notes were not written. Underneath the music's melody the composer wrote figures, representing bass notes/chords that the musician used to improvise the bass part. http://simple.wikipedia.org/wiki/Basso_continuo

[734] Harnoncourt 1983; Harnoncourt 1988

[735] http://jan.ucc.nau.edu/~tas3/Baroqueideal.html

www.JillsWingsofLight.com – Art Galleries

Music evolved with different countries sharing their latest musical ideas. In England, France and Italy, musicians cross pollinated ideas, styles and sounds. Musical practices also moved across classes – from peasants to middle class, royal courts and finally to the church. For example, elite musicians were incorporating common folk melodies. This cross pollination had never occurred in earlier times.

Musical canons (different musicians repeating a melody line at different times, for example, think of the song "Row, Row your Boat") emphasized give and take. According to composer and author Cyril Scott (1879–1970), the canon's mathematical matching of notes developed the intellect, supporting the Age of Reason.[736] *The Age of Reason* was written by eighteenth–century American revolutionary, Thomas Paine. He criticized institutionalized religion and challenged the legitimacy of the *Bible.* Paine spread engaging ideas to a mass audience, inspiring many freethinkers of the nineteenth and twentieth centuries.[737]

---

[736] Scott, Cyril. <u>Music: Its Secret Influences throughout the Ages</u>, Samuel Weiser: NY, 1958, Pg. 183. Reprinted in 2013 by Inner Traditions.
[737] http://en.wikipedia.org/wiki/The_Age_of_Reason

Musicians were using scales similar to the ones used today. At this time, Far Eastern music also evolved towards the major scale.[738] Music historian Curt Sachs noted that music evolved in a similar manner in unconnected places around the Earth. He said, "The common development toward major–like and minor–like melodies from systems as different as the East Asiatic pentatonicism, Indo–Islamic and Greco–Roman modes and European and Ugro–Finnish thirds, suggests that there may be some imminent force at work, a force embracing all mankind rather than a merely a race or religion."[739] Sachs suggested that a "worldwide influence" (from the heavens?) inspired vibrational musical patterns for mankind and was responsible for similar musical constructions popping up simultaneously all over the Earth – over and over throughout time.

The collective unconscious, a term coined by Carl Jung, is thought to be the totality of humanity's expressions and thoughts.[740] Perhaps the idea that individuals could access this collective repository, explains the development of near identical musical styles in unconnected corners of the Earth.

Curt Sachs insisted that musical vibrations influenced art. "A close examination shows that musical invention precedes artistic accomplishments. As Europe attained the 'third dimension in music' (by using the musical third), its painters conquered the third dimension in space by means of perspective."[741] Cyril Scott agreed, suggesting that musical vibratory patterns penetrate art, architecture, dress, style and the emotional/mental attributes of a population. (Musical frequencies and artistic colors are mathematically connected. The cycles per second of colors can be lowered many octaves until they fall into the human hearing range. In this way, each color corresponded to a musical note. Said differently, colors are like an octave of music. Artists compose visual music – in the octave encompassing colored light.)

During the Middles Ages, the ancient secrets of the power of music seemed to disappear. The idea that societal upheavals were

---

[738] Sachs, Curt. The Rise of Music in the Ancient World East and West, Dover Publications: Mineola, NY, 1943, Pgs. 300–304.
[739] Sachs, Curt. Ibid, 305.
[740] http://en.wikipedia.org/wiki/Collective_unconscious
[741] Sachs, Curt. Op. Cit., Pg. 309.

associated with musical change also vanished. People did not fear the consequences of rapid and dark changes resulting from musical creativity – as innocents take risks of huge consequences. With restrictions on imaginative musical styles removed, musicians stretched way outside of existing boundaries. Likewise, the Renaissance time period came with unbelievably rapid changes, creating ripple effects on many levels well into the future.

The European chain of thirds, created different music than the fourth–and–fifth–based music of the past. The typical Western chord, then and today, is composed of harmony made from the 1st – 3rd – 5th notes of a scale, used together as a chord.[742] Many melodies included these same 1 – 3 – 5 patterns, sometimes adding passing notes.

In ancient times, musicians improvised within strict, established guidelines. Now music was composed by brilliant and gifted composers – with few restrictions. Musicians performed written masterpieces, as opposed to improvising within guidelines. Greater numbers – of less talented people – became musicians, took piano lessons or sang in a choir. Hundreds of years earlier these opportunities were virtually nonexistent.

Romantic music displayed a preoccupation with nature, and mystical and supernatural inclinations. This music also reflected national identity. Jean Sibelius' *Finlandia* represented the rising nation of Finland, struggling to gain independence from Russia. Likewise, Frederic Chopin's music portrayed Poland's struggle for freedom from tsarist rule.

At the turn of the century, composers such as Gustav Mahler and Richard Strauss pushed the boundaries of late Romantic symphonic writing. Composers showed relentless discontent with musical formulas and conventions. Simultaneously, the Impressionist musical movement evoked a dreamy mood, featuring rich and dissonant chord combinations, ambiguous tonality and chords that were larger than an octave. This musical

---

[742] First, third and fifth notes in a scale. For example, in the key of C, this would be C, E and G.

movement was spearheaded by Claude Debussy and Maurice Ravel.

In ancient times, music was maintained unchanged for thousands of years. Musicians, adding notes outside of parameters, were banished from their kingdoms, as leaders feared parallel societal upheavals resulting from the vibrational changes. Leaders clung to the "Good Old Days." Each song was formerly built on a mode or a scale, which may be considered the backbone of the song. Now, not only were dissonant notes used, but the type of backbone was rapidly changed in a mere minute of music.

In the twentieth century, the modern era music reflected a widespread break with traditional tonality. Pure musical dissonance was pursued and highlighted. There was no attempt to make the music sound pleasant in any way – the more outrageously nasty it sounded, the better. After the First World War, some composers returned to the past for inspiration and wrote works labeled neoclassicism. Igor Stravinsky and Sergei Prokofiev are stellar examples. Other modern composers recreated everyday sounds in their music. Representative is the "Machine Music" of George Antheil.

Not only was the pursuit of pleasant sounds discarded – but artists strove to invent the next new musical idea – challenging and changing every concept that music embodied. The changes were as rapid, as they were outlandish. In the beginning of the Renaissance period, musical changes *inched* outside of acceptable parameters. Now, lack of adherence to any former concept of music was flagrantly promoted. Ancient man would predict – accurately – that future changes would occur rapidly in society – at a pace never imagined in historic times.

Notes can have different frequencies in various ancient scales. For example, in one scale the note "A" equates to 432 cycles per second CPS (or hertz) and in another scale A is 440 CPS. Musicologist Danileou stated that people's behavioral habits change in response to the current frequency increase of the tuning note, resulting in huge societal changes.[743]

During the last 40 years tuning frequencies generally rose. Handel and Mozart considered that A was 422 CPS. In 1858 a French government commission, and in 1939 the London Agreement, A was set at 435 CPS.[744]

In 1955 A was established at 440 hertz. This was globally agreed upon, but twenty thousand musicians in France protested. Rudolf Steiner, an Austrian philosopher, fought for "*A = 432*" because of its energy influences.[745] In 1988 the Schiller Institute in Italy unsuccessfully launched a campaign to lower the world tuning pitch from 440 to 432 hertz. Why the fuss over only an 8 hertz difference (432 – 440)? Proponents of *A = 432* believe that this vibration resonates the heart chakra, while *A = 440* creates mental emphasis and greed.

Proponents of *A = 432* are not alone in chastising new musical trends. Changes in musical practices have always been discouraged by spiritual leaders, as the new vibrational system is believed to create greater distance from God.

Currently some orchestras tune to 444 hertz. In 1968 the Boston Symphony was tuning to an A at 476 cycles per second. By tuning a little higher, a musician produces a more brilliant sound than his rivals, which is helpful in musical competitions.

---

[743] Danileou, Alain. Music and the Power of Sound: The Influence of Tuning and Interval on Consciousness, Inner Traditions: VT, 1943, Pg. 41.

[744] Levarie and Levy. Tone: A Study in Musical Acoustics, Oberlin Publishing: Canada, 1968. Pg. 58.

[745] Many sacred geometry relationships correlate to a scale with "*A = 432,*" such as D becomes 144 hertz, as auspicious number in the Bible and other sacred traditions. The number 432 is found at numerous ancient sacred sites. Another coincidence is that 432 X 432 = 186,624. The classic speed of light is 186,400 miles/second, a difference of .001201. Saturn's orbits the procession ever 864 years (432 X 2). Bruce Cathie wrote books on anti-gravity and light harmonics for more than 30 years. He believes that the universe is based on harmonic series including numbers such as 72, 144 and 432.

327

The Equal Temperament Scale

In China, Zhu Zaiyu,[746] a prince of the Ming court, devised an ingenious method to calculate equal temperament chords in 1584. This idea shows up in Europe a year later, when Flemish Simon Stevin offered a mathematical definition of equal temperament. With equal temperament scales, an octave is subdivided into 1200 units. Musical historian, Ernest McClain, observed that earlier societies could not have used this scale, because they only worked with whole numbers, and this was beyond their mathematical abilities. From 1450 to 1800, most musicians switched to the equal temperament scale. India and parts of Asia held on to their older scales.

In early scales, the pitch for the *same* note was slightly different in each key. The piano had to be *re–tuned* with every key change.[747] The sound of each scale produced a slightly different mood. Bach wrote *The Well–Tempered Clavier* in all 24 major and minor keys in order to capitalize on those differences.[748] The arrival of the equal temperament scale made changing from one musical key to another easy. An important benefit was that musicians could now accommodate singers' vocal ranges – without re–tuning any instruments. This scale was widely used in the Baroque, Classical and Romantic musical eras.

Some liken the equal temperament scale to "aural caffeine," claiming that in the Western Hemisphere this stimulant influence spurred industrialization and modernization. After the introduction of the equal temperament scale, the industrial revolution began. The equal temperament scale is energizing, creating a restlessness and desire to be active. In contrast, the Eastern societies played

---

[746] Zhu Zaiyu, a prince of the Ming court, spent thirty years on research based on the equal temperament idea originally postulated by his father. He described his new pitch theory in his *Fusion of Music and Calendar* published in 1580. This was followed by the publication of a detailed account of the new theory of the equal temperament with a precise numerical specification for 12–TET in his 5,000 page work *Complete Compendium of Music and Pitch* (Yuelü quan shu) in 1584. http://en.wikipedia.org/wiki/Equal_temperament#History
[747] Powers, Cameron. Harmonic Secrets of Arabic Music Scales, http://www.gldesignpub.com/HarmonicSecretswithCDs.html, http://r20.rs6.net/tn.jsp?e=001j–Stqi2bZQsYh7hjXYZcBujFU28qGSrJJojjpm6VB.C.yb
[748] The misconception that Bach wrote *The Well–Tempered Clavier* to take advantage of equal temperament began with mistaken information written in the 1893 Grove Dictionary and still exists in many books.

older scales full of soft and calming sounds. These vibratory influences were compatible with their advanced meditation practices. The vast differences between the scale/modal systems used in the West – as opposed to the East – had monumental impacts on the divergent development of these societies.

When the equal temperament scale became "the accepted global scale," old scales disappeared. The practice of producing musical intervals that reflected nature or universal patterns was abandoned. People stopped harmonizing to patterns created in nature, distancing themselves from this source of inspiration. Yet, this dramatic change in the sound environment was barely noticed by the general populace. Once people stopped listening to vibrational patterns that harmonized with nature, they lost their vibratory connection with the Earth and then plundered and polluted.

The octave sounds harmonious, as if it is the same note, just higher. When one octave is doubled in our hearing range, the cycles per second also double. However, when the cycles per second are doubled many times to create numerous higher octaves, a new octave is not created. Ancient philosophers and musicians found this highly disturbing. One needs to add a few extra cycles per second to create the pleasing sound of an octave. The extra cycles needed to make the octave sound like a consonant octave, are called a Pythagorean comma. Ancient people believed that the behavior of sound mirrored what happened in nature.

In equal temperament tuning, the Pythagorean comma is deleted. The equal temperament scale is a compromised tuning scheme. It sounds equally good (or bad) in any key.

Music theorists, Kyle Gann and Cameron Powers, used this analogy to describe the impact of listening to the equal temperament scale: Modern Western listeners are like babies who have eaten only genetically modified foods (listening to the equal temperament scale). They have never tasted a real tomato (listened to scales copying patterns found in nature) and do not know what they are missing![749]

---

[749] Gann, Kyle. An Introduction to Historical Tunings by Kyle Gann. http://www.kylegann.com/histune.html

When the frequencies of octaves are graphed (in cycles/second and including the Pythagorean comma) a spiral shape is formed. Merrick summarized, "A temperament scale is analogous to cutting the natural spiral of pitch frequency, stretching it to fit within a perceived circular octave and the adjusting tones to sound less out of tune. In this way, musical scale temperament is nothing less than an attempt to close an infinite spiral into a closed circle."[750] Gone were the opportunities for man to entrain–to and travel–up this spiral shaped "elevator" – to "quicken" the spirit with sound.

In 1939 the equal temperament scale was adopted as an unprecedented, worldwide musical standard. This "sound matrix" united civilizations (East and West) in universal vibrational experiences. Further, today the East and West now extensively cross pollinate – sharing gifts of material sophistication and the development of meditative practices.

Famous Composers

This section describes "humanitarian gifts" bestowed by many Classical composers; the unique gifts listeners receive from each composer's repertoire are discussed. Also, the connections of the composer to ancient musical concepts are listed. Our discussion will not attempt to provide details on – widely available – "harmony and theory" that relate to the Renaissance period.

Cyril Scott examined music of the Renaissance period and its effects on people and history. He claimed that composers were inspired by "Masters"[751] who "whispered" music into their heads, allowing them to "hear" music with something other than their physical ears. Composer Stravinski reflected that his song, *The Rite of Spring*, was created by simply writing down what he "heard." Author Joscelyn Godwin believes that such composers intuit the sounds of archetypical energy found within the collective consciousness.[752] After such an experience, the composer wrote

---

[750] Merrick, Richard. *Op. Cit.,* Pg. 14.
[751] This is a being no longer in a physical body and possessing more advanced mastery of all energies.
[752] Godwin, Joscelyn. <u>Heaven and Earth: Mysticism in Music from Antiquity to Avant Garde</u>, Inner Traditions: VT, 1987, Pg. 14.

music according to his evolution and consciousness. The inspiration and the energy of the composer were combined in the final work. For simple illustration, a savage could never compose the delicate music of Chopin. A unique creation was formed – the final musical blend mingles with the listener's subtle energy. Each listener changes the music in his own personal way – it combines with his signature energy fields. Every individual has the possibility of an experience unlike anyone else – while listening to the same music.

www.JillsWingsOfLight.com – Art Galleries

During the Renaissance period, harmony was the most powerful practice – a new development. Harmony was created by using a standard chord over and over, with its root note changing pitch. The meaning of the word "chord" evolved from meaning any combination of notes played at once – to the first, third and fifth note of the scale played together. Ancient cultures powerfully objected to the use of the *third interval* in any construction of music, let alone making it a building block. Despite all the change, elements of ancient interval patterns still can be found in most songs; they are present as a series of chords based on the first, fourth and fifth note of the scale.

Handel

George Frederick Handel (1685–1759) was a German–born, Baroque composer who spent the bulk of his career in London.[753] He composed for royalty, producing music that mimics regal and uplifting emotions. Handel's emotional music was formal with added feelings of grandeur. This music fostered the love of ceremony and adherence to convention.[754] Handel's signature technique was using a series of imitated chords during a phrase, creating an echo effect. He reiterated the same melody in different positions and began it on various notes. This style was distinctively formal and created formal effects.

Scott described the impact of Handel's music: "Handel flourished in England during the era when Swift, Sterne and Smollett were writing their breezy obscenities and when reverence even for sacred things was an almost negligible quantity.[755] …and to the influence of Handel's music we largely owe the characteristics of the Victorian era, it was, in fact, his exalted mission to revolutionize the state of English morals: it was he who came to be responsible for the swing of the moral pendulum from the one of extreme laxity to the other of undue constraint."[756]

When complimented on his music, Handel replied, "I should be sorry if I only entertained people; I wished to make them better."[757] Clearly, Handel sought to compose music to uplift listeners, improving them on many levels.

Johann Sebastian Bach

Handel's musical constructions are free and easy going. On the other hand, listening to Johann Sebastian Bach[758] (1685–1750) was more demanding – due to complex harmonies and interweaving numerical patterns underneath his music. Different areas of the brain are engaged by the vibratory stimulus of such

---

[753] George Frederic Handel, 1685–1759, was a German–British Baroque composer who is famous for his operas, oratorios and concertos.

[754] Scott, Cyril. *Op. Cit.,* Pg. 50.

[755] Scott, Cyril. *Ibid*, Pg. 50.

[756] Scott, Cyril. *Ibid*, Pg. 47.

[757] Heline, Corinne. Music: The Keynote of Human Evolution, New Age Bible and Philosophy Center: Santa Monica, CA, reprinted 1986, Pg. 79.

[758] Johann Sebastian Bach, 1685–1750, was a German composer, organist, harpsichordist, violist and violinist whose sacred and secular works became famous.

complexity. In the act of listening, the brain must process interacting and complex harmonies, rhythms and melodies. This requires more mental energy than listening to a simple melody with little accompaniment. Bach's music was widely enjoyed in Germany and strongly influenced the German mentality.

According to Cyril Scott, the influence of Bach, consciously and unconsciously, developed potential composers in Germany; this is evident by the rich harvest of famous composers that followed him.[759] The mathematical ingenuity of his fugue–writing alone greatly expanded the listener's mental capacities. The listener must simultaneously process many musical lines and patterns of melodic, rhythmic and harmonic fronts. All fugues and cannons create energy that facilitates the exchange and assimilation of ideas. Bach was the master of these techniques.[760] Cementing this view is musicologist Corinne Heline, who believed that Bach's music united the "intellect with the soul."[761]

If the musical complexities written into Bach's masterpieces were not great enough, he added hidden patterns correlating to alphabets and words. One code to connect language and music was called the Boethian, which superimposed the Latin alphabet on the white keys of the piano. To do this in *English,* sequentially write the alphabet from A to Z on the piano keyboard, with each note receiving one letter. With this code, playing the piano can incorporate encoded hidden meanings from language. Using this system, Johann Sebastian Bach repeats the notes B – A – C – H in his last fugue.[762]

T. A. Smith, in *Honorific Canons,* described additional codes hidden within Bach's fugues and canons. Another method was to code the alphabet by assigning a sequential number to individual letters. So the letter A becomes the number one and the letter B transposes to two and so on. The numbers that result from the letters that compose words, were then woven into the music. One piece contained the name of Bach's organist, Walter. Its melody

[759] Scott, Cyril. *Op. Cit.,* Pg. 58.
[760] Scott, Cyril. *Ibid*, Pg. 58.
[761] Heline, Corinne. *Ibid*, Pg. 78.
[762] Silva, Freddy. Secret in the Fields: The Science and Mysticism of Crop Circles, Hampton Roads: VA. 2002, Pg. 296.

contained 82 notes, the numeric sum of W+A+L+T+E+R. That same piece contained twice the sum of J+S+B+A+C+H and fourteen (B+A+C+H) measures.[763]

Merrick pegged Bach as the foremost evangelist of the tritone in the Protestant Revolution. Prior to this time, the Catholic Church forcibly banned the use of this interval. Bach used tritone chords starting on lower musical notes and added more tritone chords in higher and higher note ranges. This created higher and higher levels of excitement and tension, prior to resolution. The sounds from multiple tritones were so appealing that other composers copied this technique.[764] Beethoven later built the tritone chord progressions into his music. Later still, Chopin and Schumann ran rampant with tritone arpeggios.

Scott expounded on how Bach's music impacts our energy: A fugue of Bach creates yellow (representing the mental energy of the intellect) and the second movement of *Mendelssohn's Violin Concerto* creates apple green (correlating to the emotion of sympathy). If a listener has yellow in his aura then the yellow produced by Bach's music will increase it, because "like attracts like." A listener without a grain of sympathy (not a trace of apple green in his aura) will be impervious to the influence of Mendelssohn's music.[765] That is, no energy will transfer from the music to his aura through resonance. Mendelssohn's music will not influence him, if he never felt sympathetic. If he did, however, the music would increase his capacity to feel sympathy.

Mozart

The Germans and Austrians were the first to be blessed with the musical nourishment of Mozart (1756–1791). Due to Mozart's amazing music, these gifts spread quickly. Musicologist, Fabien Maman, suggested that the music of Mozart[766] assisted people to integrate higher realms of subtlety. The music has small influences

[763] Smith, T. A. "Honorific Canons," Phoenix, AZ, Arizona University, 1997, www.2.nau.edu/
[764] Merrick, Richard. *Op. Cit.,* Pg. 59.
[765] Scott, Cyril. *Op. Cit.,* Pgs. 115–117.
[766] Wolfgang Amadeus Mozart, a German composer, lived from 1756 to 1791. He was an influential composer of the Classical era. He composed over 600 works.

on the physical body but deeply massages "higher subtle bodies" (spiritual and mental energies).[767]

Don Campbell's book, *The Mozart Effect: Tapping the Power of Music to Heal the Body, Strengthen the Mind and Unlock the Creative Spirit*, claimed that listening to Mozart was an easy way to boost IQ. Later two researchers, Frances Rauscher and Katherine Ky, conducted a study[768] and coined the term "The Mozart Effect." Students listening to a Mozart sonata experienced a nine point increase in subsequent IQ tests. The IQ increase was transitory. This is exactly what ancient sages would predict. Music does affect us in a variety of ways – but we must consider the dosage: you have to listen for extended times to make a lasting and obvious change.

In 1988, neurobiologist Gordon Shaw duplicated "synthetic" brain activity on a computer. Simulated nerve cells tended to use certain firing patterns and rhythms, perhaps reflecting mental activity. He decided to study neural activity by comparing it to music – so he converted the simulated nerve activity into sound. The resulting product was music, reminiscent of Baroque, New Age and Eastern styles. Since the brain activity correlated to music, he figured that music might also stimulate the brain by activating similar firing patterns of nerve clusters.

Mozart left clues regarding his involvement in esoteric circles that embraced ancient musical secrets. In Mozart's opera, *The Magic Flute,* he reflected Masonic (Hermetic) ideology beneath an innocent fable. Pressure still existed to hide ancient musical secrets, echoing back to prohibitions of the Middle Ages. These secrets were preserved in plain sight, such as the deeper meaning of an opera story, so the messages would endure and be rediscovered in better times.[769]

Mozart's piano sonatas incorporated the golden ratio. For example, in the *Sonata No. 1 in C major*, there are 62 measures in

---

[767] Maman, Fabien. The Role of Music in the Twenty–First Century, Tamo–Do Press: Boulder, Colorado, 1997, Pg. 41.
[768] Published in "Nature," Oct. 14, 1993.
[769] Frers, Ernesto. Secret Societies and the Hermetic Code, Destiny Books/ Inner Traditions: VT, 2005, Pg.160.

the Development and Recapitulation section and 38 in the Exposition.[770] The ratio of 62/38 is 1.63, close to the golden ratio. Mozart created the golden ratio from segments of time in his music.

Beethoven

Beethoven (1770–1827) was a crucial figure in the transition between the subset styles of classical and romantic music. His powerful development of feelings and moods with music, evoked great compassion. In an example, earlier music sharply contrasted loud and soft sections. One verse was loud and the second echoed with a soft reply. This created a prim and proper kind of feeling, as if everyone would only act according to expected behavior. Beethoven threw out the rules and gradually amped up the volume, producing a natural implosion of emotions. Not only did he replicate how our feelings naturally build, but he did so to extremes, reflecting the depravity of depression and the power of a painful cry. It is difficult not to re–live the suffering of others, while listening to some of his works.

Beethoven understood the deep healing impact of his music. He wrote, "Life resembles the vibration of the sound and the human is like the play of the strings… Whoever understands my music will free himself from the misery in which all others are entrenched."[771]

After listening to the great depths of Beethoven's music, a person gains the ability to understand another's pain. With understanding, we forgive – show compassion – and charity grows. Only *after* the music of Beethoven was widely enjoyed, did charities flourish in the 19th century. For example, education was permitted in prisons after people experienced the music of Beethoven – but not before. Scott added that the prostitute and the orphan, the sick and elderly – who perhaps have never even heard his name – in reality owe him most of all.[772]

---

[770] in the first movement
[771] Maman, Fabien. *Op. Cit.,* Pg. 42.
[772] Scott, Cyril. *Op. Cit.,* Pg. 69.

Beethoven expressed the entire spectrum of emotions in his music; this ability made him a great musical psychologist. According to Scott, his music created the energy of psychoanalysis, which appeared shortly thereafter.

www.JillsWingsofLight.com – Art Galleries

The Victorian age was full of prudishness and repressed feelings. The same people who highly prized proper etiquette, were also intolerant and unsympathetic. People of the Victorian period did not acknowledge grief, depravation, sickness and yearning in others or themselves. They suppressed passions that they were ashamed of. When emotions were suppressed, they were forced inward, which was detrimental to the nervous system. [773, 774] They desperately needed emotional outlets. Beethoven's music supplied this and far more.

Maman believed that Beethoven's music disturbs people and forces them to pay attention. His music improves all levels of a person's energy: physical, emotional and mental.[775, 776] Beethoven moved humanity forward with his bold dissonances, harmonies and structure.[777]

---

[773] Scott, Cyril. *Ibid,* Pg. 67.

[774] Scott, Cyril. *Ibid*, Pg. 64.

[775] Ludwig van Beethoven, 1770 –1827, was a German composer and pianist. He was a crucial figure in the transitional period between the Classical and Romantic eras in Western classical music. He remains one of the most famous and influential composers of all time.

[776] Maman, Fabien. *Op. Cit.,* Pg. 41.

[777] Maman, Fabien. *Ibid*, Pg. 42.

Subtle music requires more time to produce observable results than invigorating music. It is a general rule that simpler, straight forward and exhilarating music, has immediate effects. Scott reflected that Beethoven's music took about 100 years to reach the plentitude of its influence.[778]

Beethoven first introduced the seventh interval that was shunned in earlier music in Western Europe. Listeners were exposed to a somewhat dissonant sound, which induced such patterns elsewhere in their consciousness. Hector Berlioz, in his biography of Beethoven, said that the first time that Beethoven's music was played in the Paris Opera Hall, the consciousness of the audience opened and "exploded"; the audience received a new impulse, which it would never forget.[779]

Beethoven's composition master, Chrisian Neefe, was a known Mason and a member of the secret Illuminati.[780] Beethoven dedicated his piano sonata, *Opus 28*, to the known grand master, the Priory of Sion,[781] Joseph von Sonnenfels. Beethoven composed *Maurefragen*, meaning *Masonic Questions*, establishing another link to the esoteric school of thought.[782] Beethoven well understood ancient ideas regarding the power of music.

Chopin & Schumann

Chopin and Schumann belonged to what is called the Romantic period, by musical historians. These composers added to the experimental processes, in which music became more fragmented and varied. Music became a matter of personal preference. Unlike musicians in antiquity, a musician in the Romantic period could make a living, if his *unique* music was popular. We see the role of people selecting music that *pleased* them in creating the musical environment – not the prescriptive, rigid ways of the past.

---

[778] Scott, Cyril. *Op. Cit.,* Pg. 189.
[779] Maman, Fabien. The Role of Music in the Twenty–First Century, *Op. Cit.,* Pg. 30.
[780] Cooper, Barry. Beethoven, Oxford University Press: October 2008. Pg. 14.
[781] The Priory of Sion, a strictly secret and Hermetic sect, was made famous in the book and movie, Da Vinci Code. The ancient group believes themselves to be off spring of the married Jesus Christ.
[782] Merrick, Richard. *Op. Cit.,* Pg. 66.

According to Scott, the graceful and elegant music of Chopin[783] (1810–1849), awakened the desire for culture. His music sang like poetry and was enticing, leaving people hungry for more. As a result, women who had previously been perfectly content to be homemakers, joined societies for poetry and the refined arts. The emancipation of women began.[784]

During the Victorian era, "children were to be seen and not heard." They were punished for their natural energy – romping and making noise were not approved. Robert Schuman's music[785] abounded with innocence, tenderness, humor, questioning, fancifulness and dreaming, which resonated in the hearts of listening mothers. Schuman's music deepened the understanding of and improved the support for children. Scott reflected that the Montessori system was inspired by this vibrational influence.

Later, the post impressionistic artists, Van Gogh, Gauguin and Picasso, displayed childlike qualities in their artistic works, but this sense of the childlike spirit originated in music.

In Romantic music, a pianist would often display conflicting rhythm patterns. For example, the right hand of a pianist played five notes per measure, while the left hand ran at six notes per measure, creating a 5/6 rhythmic ratio. Pieces abounded with all kinds of unusual rhythmic ratios such as 3/2, 1/5, 2/5… and so on. Similarly, if you take a string and with your finger press down to make it shorter, making the string 1/5 shorter equals one note, and 2/5 of a string equals another note. Ratios were used to create notes, intervals and scales in earlier music. *These same ratios occur in rhythms.* Different intervals were linked to states of higher consciousness; it logically follows that complex rhythms produced similar experiences.

[783] Frederic Chopin, 1810 – 1849, was a composer, virtuoso pianist and music teacher. He was of French–Polish parentage. He was one of the great masters of Romantic music. All of Chopin's works involve the piano. They are technically demanding but emphasize nuance and expressive depth. Chopin invented the musical form known as the instrumental ballade and made major innovations to the piano sonata, mazurka, waltz, nocturne, polonaise, etude, impromptu and prelude.
http://en.wikipedia.org/wiki/Fr%C3%A9d%C3%A9ric_Chopin
[784] Scott, Cyril. *Op. Cit.,* Pg. 86.
[785] Robert Alexander Schumann, 1810 – 1856, was a German composer. He is regarded as one of the greatest and most representative composers of the Romantic era.

Redmond reported that not only does our brain attune to conflicting rhythms, but each hemisphere may operate in different rhythms. For example, the right brain can generate alpha waves while the left brain is in a beta state. Both hemispheres can also generate the same type of brain wave, but be out of sync with each other.[786] Redmond is suggesting that a ratio of two rhythms going on at the same time (like rhythmic patterns found in this music), may also be found in one's brainwaves.

www.JillsWingsofLight.com – Art Galleries

Wagner

Richard Wagner (1813–1883) was a German composer, conductor, theatre director and essayist – primarily known for his operas. Wagner's compositions featured complex, changing harmonies, which produced upward sonic movement that lifted the listener to new realms. Formerly, a song would be written in one scale. This pattern of notes was the backbone of the song. However, within the span of a minute, Wagner changed key signatures so many times that the listener became ungrounded, confused and seemed to float up with the ascending music.

Wagner's musical themes painted individual characters, places or ideas – making his music highly symbolic. Wagner was not afraid

---

[786] Redmond, Layne. When the Women were Drummers: A Spiritual History of Rhythm, Three Rivers Press: NY, 1997, Pg. 173.

of discord. His music expressed realism, negative feelings, pain and suffering.

Wagner's dissonant sounds would have terrified many ancient leaders. With flagrant disregard for rules, Wagner's methods were scandalous, but inspired freedom. The ever changing structure of his music gave people a feeling of being flexible and going with the flow, and this broke down barriers to unity.[787] Scott summed it up, "Wagner's music momentarily transported people to that exalted plane and rose to that state of unity of selfless and unconditional love."[788]

After noting that music can be used in positive and negative pursuits, Scott further noted the impact of Wagner: Wagner's feeling of elevation was powerfully combined with Strauss's nationalistic music by *dark forces* to arouse the Germans to intense nationalism. Hitler loved Wagner.

Strauss, Debussy & Grieg

Scott reviewed the influence of Johann Strauss (1825–1899), the "Waltz King" of Vienna.[789] Since the music of Strauss, European history is full of social changes, aimed at greater freedom and self–expression. Strauss used daring, unconventional harmonics and melodies. His music created feelings of exuberance; listeners aspired to break bonds that contained them and become free.[790]

Strauss's music was even more nationalistic than Wagner's. With this music, the German audience felt deeply sentimental about their country. His music also painted a grandiose portrayal of war and strife. According to Scott, this energy was used by the dark forces to help precipitate the war in Germany.[791]

---

[787] Scott, Cyril. *Op. Cit.,* Pg. 97.
[788] Scott, Cyril. *Ibid*, Pg. 98.
[789] Johann Strauss 1st, 1825–1899, was an Austrian composer of dance music and operettas. He composed over 500 waltzes, polkas and other types of dance music, as well as several operettas and a ballet. He was largely responsible for the popularity of the waltz in Vienna during the 19th century.
[790] Scott, Cyril. *Op. Cit.,* Pg. 103.
[791] Scott, Cyril. *Ibid*, Pgs. 102–103.

Claude Debussy (1862–1918),[792] a French composer, along with Maurice Ravel, created the new genre, called *impressionist* music. This music is known for its sensualism and avoidance of any key signature. Within listeners, Debussy's music inspired a refined, feminine sensuousness. Debussy also wrote "pure nature" music, displaying the realms of gnomes and faeries. The music of nature is characterized by its soft subtle qualities. Nature spirits sing, dance, bathe in moonbeams and shower in early morning dew, without the moral and philosophical thoughts that laden humans. They play in the breeze and laugh with the brook, creating an entirely different dimension than our familiar reality. Debussy's music makes us feel like we are joining the nature spirits in a lively dance. Edward Grieg (1843–1907), was a Norwegian composer and pianist. He also joined Debussy in using music to transport the listener to the realm of the faeries and angels.[793]

Claude Debussy was the grand master of the Priory of Sion for 33 years, between 1885 and 1918.[794] He fraternized with many well–known Rosicrucians, a group with a secret theology based on esoteric beliefs of the ancient past, which provide insight into nature, the universe, the spiritual realm and the ancient musical teachings.[795] He was keenly aware of the patterns of the tritone and proportions found in nature that were used in ancient music. Music once again embraced the old concept of mimicking sacred geometry. Merrick reflected, that Debussy's emphasis on the "pentatonic scale surrounded by the odd–even circularity of dual whole tone scales" is a musical allusion to an apple – a circle inscribing a pentagram.[796]

Stravinsky, Schonberg, Bartok & Schillinger

Modern composers of the twentieth century are renowned for their dissonance. Scott explained that discord can be destroyed by discord. Recall a singer belting out a high note and a crystal glass shattering. Imagine sound blasting a kidney stone to tiny bits.

---

[792] Claude–Achille Debussy, 1862 –1918, developed a highly original system of harmony and musical structure that expressed in many respects the ideals to which the Impressionist and Symbolist painters and writers of his time aspired.
[793] Heline, Corinne. Music: *Op. Cit.,* Pg. 80.
[794] According to the *Prieure* Documents
[795] Frers, Ernesto. *Op. Cit.,* Pg.171.
[796] Merrick, Richard. *Op. Cit.,* Pg. 67.

Likewise, dissonant music can shatter intense emotional discord. Scott said, "Only dissonances possess the power to alter the hard outlines of the mental bodies of conventional people and so render them more pliant and receptive to new ideas."[797] In contrast, beautiful music creates delicate vibrations that slip through the cracks of coarse and discordant emotions.

Although it is logical to think that dissonance only creates dissonance – which it indeed can – dissonance can also break unseen subtle energy forms through cathartic release. The hidden discord within is loosened and massaged, creating greater possibility of freedom. Whether it is intensified or released, is a result of whether or not someone – on a deep level – is ready to let go of negativity.

Stravinsky (1882–1971) was a Russian and later a naturalized French and American composer. Schonberg (1874–1951), an Austrian composer and painter, was also an expressionistic poet. Both artists created musical weapons of discord. This is typical of music belonging to the Modern period.

Art from this time also served this same purpose, using the power of unpleasant images, colors and forms to rattle the viewer's expectations. People were forced to view devastated individuals and experience their brokenness. Most viewers had many painful memories hidden deeply within and the image forced them to reflect on old wounds (and perhaps release the negative feelings), instead of bury them intact. This can be seen in Gauguin and Van Gogh; they produced harsh paintings of women and realistic renditions of the poor rather than portraits of beautiful and wealthy people.

Composer Bela Bartok's[798] (1881–1945) chromatic and rhythmic techniques used the golden mean in a variety of ways. For example, in his *Music for Strings, Percussion and Celesta*, the 89 measure movement is divided into two parts, containing 55/34

---

[797] Scott, Cyril. *Op. Cit.,* Pg. 136.

[798] Béla Bartók, 1881–1945, was a Hungarian composer and pianist. He is considered one of the most important composers of the 20th century and is regarded, along with Liszt, as Hungary's greatest composers (Gillies 2001). Through his collection and analytical study of folk music, he was one of the founders of ethnomusicology.

measures, creating the golden ratio. In fact, the Fibonacci numbers were frequently used in the timing within this music.[799] He goes so far as to structure any change in the music – such as volume, length of the theme, usage of mutes, numbers of notes and texture changes, according to the Fibonacci numbers and golden ratios. This is a novel way of using the ancient wisdom – in patterns of time.

Joseph Schillinger[800] (1895–1943) wrote music with successive notes following the Fibonacci intervals when counted in half step notes. He also copied the stock market curves from the *New York Times* on graph paper and translated the ups and downs into proportional intervals, creating a composition sounding like J. S. Bach.[801] He believed that other, unsuspecting parts of our world would reflect patterns found in nature, such as our economy.

Summary

As we have seen repeatedly – antiquity strictly enforced musical rules that served to carve out a unique direction and stability for a country. During the Classical period, the *popularity* of music dictated what sounds were heard rather than church officials or government. Rules were now created by mass consensus; the paying audience gave the musician the opportunity to make a living. In this period, for the first time, *when a musical style lost popular favor*, the culture transitioned with the rebirth of new music.

In summary, if the Dark Ages equated to stillness and a musical void, then Classical Music represented the "phoenix rising from the ashes." The grand scale of Classical Music with its diversity, power and mathematical formulations is mind boggling. The musicians daringly created diverse masterpieces without any fear of negative consequences. This music not only changed the world forever, but did so with lightning speed. Its influences endure to modern times.

---

[799]Lendvai, Erno. As quoted in Livio, Mario. The Golden Ratio: The Story of Phi, the World's Most Astonishing Number, Broadway Books: NY, 2002, Pg. 189.
[800] Joseph Schillinger, 1895 – 1943, was a composer, music theorist, and composition teacher. He was born in Ukraine and died in New York City.
[801] Livio, Mario. The Golden Ratio: The Story of Phi, the World's Most Astonishing Number, Broadway Books: NY, 2002, Pg. 193.

www.JillsWingsofLight.com – Art Galleries

Chapter Twelve

Modern Music
1900 to Present

The Blues and Jazz

By 1808, the slave trade had transferred almost half a million Africans to the United States. They came with strong tribal musical traditions.[802] African music was functional; it was used to enhance work or perform rituals. Old African musical traditions were kept alive at festivals, featuring African dances and drumming events, such as one that was held on Sundays at Congo Square in New Orleans until 1843. Similar musical events occurred in New England and New York.

Elements of African music merged into other musical genres. The Blues, reflected traces of European harmonic structure, plus the African call–and–response tradition. Essentially, the Blues is a mixture of the musical styles of Europe and Africa, along with the unaccompanied oral traditions of American slaves. Their single–line melodies were similar to slave "ring shouts." "Field hollers" expanded into solo songs full of emotion.[803]

American slaves, often treated poorly, received no freedom for individuality, education or creative expression. The early music they created was poorly documented, due in part to racial discrimination and the lack of literacy of African Americans at the time. Blues music emerged between 1870 and 1900, only after the

---

[802] Cooke, Mervyn, Horn, David G. *The Cambridge Companion to Jazz*, Cambridge University Press: NY, 2002. Pgs. 7–9.
[803] Ferris, Pg. 229. http://en.wikipedia.org/wiki/Blues#cite_note–45

Emancipation Act of 1863.[804] The Blues expressed hardships before, during and after the newly acquired freedom of the Africans. Blues music flourished in the 1920s and 1930s; it included elements of: spirituals, work songs, shouts, chants and rhymed ballads.

The term "the Blues" came from the term "blue devils," legendary beings that specialized in causing depression and sadness. Likewise, the Blues music reflected melancholy and sadness. Some churches branded the Blues music as the calling card of the Devil himself – and a sorrowful Devil at that.

www.JillsWingsofLight.com – Art Galleries

The words in Blues songs sound like "rhythmic talk," more so than a melody. Rhythms also reflected African speech patterns. The Blues conveyed a conversation, showing the depths of personal pain, cruel police, lost love, discrimination and hard times of African Americans. For instance, Blind Lemon Jefferson's song, *Rising High Water Blues,* described the Great Mississippi Flood of 1927:

> "Backwater rising, Southern peoples can't make no time
> I said, backwater rising, Southern peoples can't make no time
> And I can't get no hearing from that Memphis girl of mine."

---

[804] Lawrence W. Levine, *Black Culture and Black Consciousness: Afro–American Folk Thought from Slavery to Freedom*, Oxford University Press, 1977, Pg. 223.

Blues' lyrics express sorrow and depression; the music enables a cathartic release of pain. People who suffer stoically attract others who dish out punishment. A bully picks on someone who is broken, afraid – someone that he can clearly dominate. The painful emotions of African Americans had to be washed away to attract better treatment. The Blues helped this happen. Musical catharsis removed pain, making space for better energy. Like the Estonian song fests, the Blues music rebuilt the strength of the African American people.

www.JillsWingsofLight.com – Art Galleries

In the 1950s, the Blues made its mark on popular American music. By the 1960s, prominent white entertainers performed African–American music in the US and abroad. White audiences' interest in the Blues increased dramatically when bands such as Janis Joplin, The Animals, Fleetwood Mac, Jefferson Airplane, The J. Geils Band, The Allman Brothers Band, Led Zeppelin and The Rolling Stones performed classic Blues songs.

How far the Blues had come was highlighted in 1980, when Dan Aykroyd and John Belushi released the tongue–in–cheek film: *The Blues Brothers*. Acoustic guitarist Eric Clapton, who marked a comeback in the 1990s, prominently used standard Blues numbers. Blues rock performer Jimi Hendrix, a skilled guitarist, pioneered innovative uses of distortion and feedback. Even orchestral works

– such as George Gershwin's *Rhapsody in Blue*, *Concerto in F* and the second *Prelude* for piano – incorporated Blues techniques.

The Blues' format utilizes standard chord progressions, with the twelve–bar Blues chord[805] being the most popular. Standard Blues chords are based on the fourth and fifth notes of the scale with a seventh note added. The Blues' rhythm pattern has twelve beats and is made up of uneven – three note riffs, creating a "groove feel." Technically speaking, there is more syncopation (rhythmic deviations from the regular beat) in Jazz music than in the Blues.

The "Blue notes" are gradually lowered (like a major 3rd to a minor 3rd) to create Jazz's recognizable sound.[806] In ancient Greece, notes were also flattened to create a sad, calm or melancholy sound. The use of glissando, the gliding up or down in pitch and hitting every possible frequency along the way, also created some of the Blues' characteristic sounds. In contrast, this practice was not acceptable in ancient Greece.

The Blues usually featured a solo – unlike Jazz instrumental bands.[807] Although Blues music evolved to include bands, the first Blues solo player used only a slide guitar. Later, common Blues instruments included: guitar, bass guitar, piano, harmonica, double bass, saxophone, vocals, trumpet and trombone.

The Blues music influenced the development of Jazz, Country, Rhythm and Blues, Blue Grass, and Rock & Roll music. Jazz's roots are the same as the Blues, but Jazz evolved to include more variety – more styles and subgenres.

In its beginning, Jazz was considered scandalous, due in part to its sensuous sounds. Jazz was pegged as the "slippery slope to Hell." Initially, it pulled people deeper into physicality. Today, people are accustomed to Jazz music, as a result it no longer creates

---

[805] 1, 4 and 5 chords within a given key
[806] Cooke, Mervyn, Horn, David G. *The Cambridge Companion to Jazz*, Cambridge University Press: NY, 2002. Pgs. 11–14.
[807] Difference Between Jazz and Blues
http://www.differencebetween.net/miscellaneous/culture–miscellaneous/difference–between–jazz–and–blues/#ixzz3Qb4NYOuJ

scandalous sensuality nor is it associated with the fiery underworld. It is played everywhere as popular background music.

Research shows that jazz musicians – sharing improvisations back and forth – resemble what happens in our brains during a conversation. Jazz music activates brain areas that process the syntax of language.[808] MRI images of the brain having a conversation and the experience of listening to jazz are strikingly similar. *This strongly supports the idea that music is a universal language.*

Musicologist Berendt observed that Jazz features spontaneity with improvisation playing an important role.[809] The performer shares the creative role with the composer. Musicians improvise, using the structural format of the genre, but they can alter melodies, harmonies and tempo. The Jazz soloist is supported by other musicians providing a rhythm section and chords – outlining the song structure and complementing the soloist.

Merrick described Jazz as the stacking of tritone chords. These chords emphasize the "pulling" effect of energy.[810] Jazz employed and harmonized this feeling.

Jazz created signature rhythms such as the "swing." In swing style, the beat is divided in two, but reflects an underlying triplet feel. Downbeats are 2/3 of a beat long, while upbeats last only 1/3 of a beat in length. This forms a syncopated rhythm. "Swung" notes are played alternately – longer then shorter – than written.

Jazz quickly spread – or perhaps developed simultaneously to some extent – around the globe. Jazz forms are enjoyed in Australia, Azerbaijan, Brazil, Cuba, France, Germany, India, Italy, Japan, Malawi, Netherlands, Poland, South Africa, Spain, United

---

[808] Journal Plos One, March 12, 2014, quoted by Derrick News, Washington AP article, *Jazz study reveals link between music, language.*
[809] Berendt, Joachim E. The Jazz Book: From Ragtime to Fusion and Beyond, Translated by H. and B. Bredigkeit with Dan Morgenstern, Lawrence Hill Books, 1981, Pg. 371.
[810] For example, a dominant 7th chord (G7 in the key of C) combines with another tritone chord, starting on D and including the 7th note of the scale. This strengthens the pull towards C.

Kingdom and many other countries. Jazz is an important genre that influences people across the globe.

The Musical Number of Two in Jazz

People harmonized to the interval of a seventh, with Jazz's signature 1–3–5–7 chords. The seventh note of the scale and its neighbor, the octave (or 8th note) when played together, sound a musical *second*. Jazz featured a heavy diet of the second interval. The intervals of a seventh and a second were strictly shunned throughout antiquity due to their dissonant feelings.

Melodies define most Swing, Jazz, and Rock music. Jazz melodies incorporate sequential notes, which create an interval pattern of *twos*. The Jazz rhythmic patterns use hard and soft beats, which create a pattern of *twos* (or fours, which divide down to two). Jazz's *two–beat* rhythmic patterns, (melodies with *two* neighboring notes and the chord interval of *two* – created from the 7th and 8th note of the scale), create a dominant array of twos.

Number two is the most sensitive of all numbers. A "two" symbolizes balance, duality, opposites, choices, the subconscious and nurturing. Perhaps the number two's greatest association is with *duality*.

People with two in their numerology chart are gentle, subtle, cooperative, tactful, diplomatic, patient, sincere, harmonious, artistic, emphatic, intuitive, supportive, loving, humble and peaceful. They are considerate and sensitive to the needs of others. They are often the power behind the throne. [811, 812]

---

[811] http://www.spiritual–numerology.com/numerology–number–meaning/numerology–meaning–of–number–2.html

[812] Challenging issues associated with the energy of two are timidity, fear, low self–esteem, lack of self–confidence, depression, vulnerability and avoidance of confrontation and criticism.

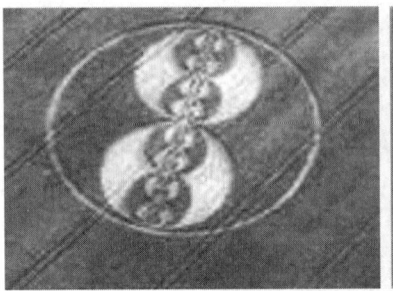

The Number Two in Crop Circles[813]

Rock & Roll Music

In the 1950s, the Blues scale that led to Jazz, mixed with folk music and a new sound was created – dubbed Rock & Roll. The phrase "rocking and rolling" originally described the movement of a ship on the ocean; by early in the twentieth century it described the spiritual fervor of black churches and it was also a slang term used to refer to sex. Typically, Rock features melodies in a chorus–verse format. Mostly, Rock is not improvised.

Rock typically highlighted the play of electric and bass guitars, and drums. Other important instruments include: acoustic guitars, synthesizer and keyboards – plus vocals. Brass instruments are sometimes used to strong effect (*Chicago*, Clarence Clemens, *Blood, Sweat and Tears* and so on).

The percussion sounds of Rock & Roll are loud. Deafening concert volumes produced a new dimension to musical effects and bursts of energy. The loud volume could sometimes cause hearing loss.

Although Rock & Roll's melodies resemble folk music, its rhythms are significantly different. Rock & Roll's 4/4 beat uses a snare drum back–beat on beats two and four. Rock & Roll's rhythmic tension builds – just as harmony and melody did in Classical music. A steady rhythmic beat creates patterns – just as intervals, harmonies and pitches do. Steady rhythms diminish any

---

[813] Used with permission – Peter Sorensen.
http://cropcircleconnector.com/Sorensen/circles/1999/main.html

feeling of confusion. As we correctly anticipate beat patterns, we build a sense of confidence or a comfortable feeling regarding what is coming next. We want to participate – tap our feet, sing along.

The speed of Rock & Roll rhythms is considerably faster in comparison to earlier music. It is among the fastest paced music throughout all of time. Similarly, changes are also occurring much faster in today's society than in ancient times. Indeed, the pace of change is unrivaled in history and the people of the modern world know this – as they wonder what will become of our species?

As the pace of music quickened, so did our brain waves that entrained to it. As Rock & Roll created faster brain waves, people exhibited consciousness associated with speedy brain waves. Simply stated, listeners sank deeper into the physical world.[814]

The fastest brain waves, gamma waves, support mental functioning, helping people operate in the physical world. These same fast brain waves can create a negative consciousness – associated with ADHD, depression, learning disabilities, or anxiety, high arousal, and stress. Beta brain waves are the next fastest brain waves, connected with normal waking consciousness. They can aide focus, memory and problem solving abilities. When these are not "balanced" they relate to anxiety, high arousal, inability to relax and stress. Beta brain waves are also coupled with ADHD, daydreaming, depression and poor cognition. The effect of beta brain waves creates an impact similar to coffee, energy drinks and stimulates.[815] Slower, alpha brain waves are linked to meditative states, allowing intuitive states of mind. Science has demonstrated that people utilizing even slower brainwaves, called theta brain waves, access greater intuition, tap internal and external knowledge, show improved creativity and consciousness.[816]

---

[814] Morris, Suzanne, Evans, Ph.D. (speech and language pathologist), *"Research behind Acoustic Brain Entrainment,"* Pg. 5. www.neuroacoustic.org.
[815] http://mentalhealthdaily.com/2014/04/15/5-types-of-brain-waves-frequencies-gamma-beta-alpha-theta-delta/
[816] Dr. Peniston and Dr. Kulkosky of University of S. Colorado, *"Research Behind Acoustic Brain Entrainment,"* Pg. 5. www.neuroacoustic.org.

Rock & Roll sometimes used advanced technology to add subliminal words and sounds outside of our hearing range – creating powerful subtle influences. Ancient leaders did not have the technology to subliminally influence their people in this way. They hid their secrets within other musical techniques and secretly influenced their people by controlling pitches, instrumentation and rhythms.

All musical genres can have positive and negative influences on people. Rock & Roll is no different. Rock has been credited with improving racial attitudes by opening up African–American culture to white audiences. Rock & Roll helped further the civil rights movement when teens enjoyed music by performers of both races. Songs were sometimes socially responsible. As African–American singers and musicians succeeded, their wider acceptance naturally grew. Think to the eventual popularity enjoyed by someone like Michael Jackson – amazing; such success driven by musical genius helped greatly elevate an entire race. (However, Michael's music would be more accurately categorized as Pop – a popularized form of Rock & Roll.)

Rock and Jazz deepen feelings associated with the senses, helping us enjoy physicality and gradually lead us away from spirituality. Each important Rock group had its own sound and unique gift. Each mini–style also had its own recognizable sound, with its own unique effect. For example, the Beach Boys with their breezy surf songs, enabled people to let their hair down and be more in the moment. Bruce Springsteen and the East Street Band painted portraits of the common man and added romance and zest to his plight. These dramatized emotions were not widespread in the 1930s and 1940s.

Subtle negative energy accumulates, becoming trapped inside the physical body. For example, if we worry, then negative energy amasses in our stomach. With enough worrying, an ulcer results. The subtle emotional energy bores a whole in our physical stomach. The feeling of negative emotions can create two opposing results. You either (subconsciously or consciously) augment your negativity or release it. In a unique way, Rock & Roll can enable cathartic release by resonating with buried feelings, vibrating and freeing emotional baggage with unnatural beat patterns.

www.JillsWingsofLight.com – Art Galleries

In antiquity, rhythms emulated patterns found in nature and the human heartbeat. Rock & Roll beat patterns are anything but natural. Put your hand over your heart while listening to fast and slow music. Watch your heart copy the beat. Tests demonstrate that some Rock music also creates negative effects on digestion and high blood pressure.

Studies by author, and amateur botanist Dorothy Retallack, documented the impact of musical genre on household plants:
- Three hours per day of Acid Rock stunted and damaged squash, philodendrons and corn – in less than four weeks.
- Plants exposed to soft, "pleasing" music leaned towards it and grew two inches taller than plants left in silence.

Twenty–first century spiritualist, Elizabeth Clare Prophet, preached that the Blues, Jazz and Rock & Roll music were of the Devil. Her objection stemmed from their unnatural beat patterns not found in nature. Prophet believed that being close to God results from harmonizing to patterns found in nature (since God created nature). She compared Blues, Jazz and Rock beat patterns to the jagged, African Voodoo rhythms that she credited with aiding the demise of Lemuria. Voodoo music is sensual and unrestrained. The syncopated Rock & Roll beat places the accent on the offbeat. With constant repetition, it has a hypnotic effect. Prophet believes that such music strengthens a "dark" type of individualism, which she calls a "lesser" god. A similar musical rhythm was used in the Dionysian cult, discussed briefly in ancient Greek music.[817]

According to Elizabeth Prophet, some Rock concerts spawned riots and injuries due to the influences of the music.[818] She condemned the jagged rhythms, hard noises and chaotic patterns for frazzling people's nerves. According to John Phillips of the Mamas and Papas, "By carefully controlling the sequence of rhythm any rock group can create hysteria in the audience. We know how to do it."[819] When the Rolling Stones played *Sympathy for the Devil,* violence often occurred. Mick Jagger reflected, "Something like that happens every time I play this song."

Prophet reflected that some ancient music increased energy in the chakras, sending it up the spine as part of the ascension process. Temples in ancient Egypt facilitated this upward flow of energy. Likewise, Hindu music is designed to serve the enlightenment process. In contrast, Rock and Jazz rhythms cause chakras to release energy, reversing the enlightenment process. This may feel good immediately as energy is released and the accompanying high is experienced, but in the long haul an overall loss of energy occurs. Soon afterwards, people desire to listen to the next jumpy song for another energy boost. This is not unlike why people drink the second cup of coffee to maintain the morning pick–me–up. Too much coffee gives us the jitters and frazzles our nerves. Prophet believed jagged rhythms also stress the nervous system.

---

[817] "The follower of Voodoo seeks to incorporate a LOA (lesser god) into himself by writhing and leaping through a dance, while drums bang out complex rhythms. When just the right rhythm is found for an individual LOA, the dancer takes it up, and the LOA enters his soul. His physical and mental powers are immediately heightened; he becomes god–like himself. Animals will often be sacrificed to appease the spirits...The religion is strictly Dionysian, and dances often end in wholesale copulation." Steele, John. *World of the Unexplained,* (Ripley Museum Inc., 1977), Pgs. 9–10.

[818] Prophet, Elizabeth, Clare. The Science of Rhythm for the Mastery of the Sacred Energies of Life: Uses and Misuses of the Word in the Music of the East and West, Cassettes, Church Universal and Triumphant: USA, 1978.

[819] *Saturday Evening Post,* 25, March, 1967.

Music such as Swing, Jazz, and Rock & Roll literally alters the heartbeat, giving listeners a jolt that kick–starts faster paced energy. This creates a heart rhythm that behaves like one on steroids. Rock's accelerated beat gave the heart a new form of aerobic exercise, not from physical exercise but from loud and unnatural rhythmic patterns. Listening to Rock & Roll rhythms can be likened to ingesting stimulants... an aural amphetamine.

The theme of individualism became popular – most evident beginning in the 1960s; think of Frank Sinatra crooning *I Did it My Way*. If this were played in ancient Egypt, Sinatra would have been jailed. Individual musical expression parallels individual expression in life. In ancient times, when the survival of the group was of paramount importance, individual expression was muted. Nowadays, individualism is in your face and highly respected.

Rock & Roll, Disco and Heavy Metal music primed the pump for rapid transitions; changes occurred in the twentieth and twenty first centuries at an accelerating rate. Speed and synthesis are characteristic of this music and reflect the pace of innovation and societal changes. The physical body of the dedicated listener, entrains to these accelerated rhythms. Accompanying these pumped–up frequencies, the personal computer, Internet, smart phones and wireless technologies turned the world upside down in a few decades. To demonstrate how the pace of our world snow balled: there are more negative stories in *one* big city's newspaper today – than someone would have known about in his entire lifetime 150 years ago. *Contrast these observations regarding the pace of change in modern times, with the stability of an ancient culture that endured for dozens of centuries.* The importance of music in the development and dynamics of a culture is immense – undeniable!

Rock & Roll greatly influenced lifestyles, fashion, attitudes and language during the 1950s, 1960s and 1970s. United Kingdom and United States Rock music served as the vehicle for cultural and social movements. How important was the music within the "hippie" culture? Can you imagine a gathering such as Woodstock without musicians being the primary draw? Impossible. The overall impact of Rock & Roll can be seen in the massive social, emotional and physical changes in society during this short period of time. Openness to new emotions and innovative music allowed people to accept changes going on around them.

This music inspired listeners to question societal values and seek truth. Rock music has been closely linked with the rebellion against social and political norms, such as consumerism and conformity. Inheriting the folk tradition of the protest song, Rock music went hand–and–hand with political activism and contributed to ending the Vietnam War. Listeners, such as "Flower Children," protested killing people in third world countries. They were not buying packaged nationalism, political rhetoric or materialism, rather they searched for truth and peace. There was a huge change in society as people stopped having blind faith in leaders and closely examined their values.

In the 1960s Rock music was associated with divergent views on sexuality – facilitating greater sexual freedom. Individual musicians produced music about aspects of romantic love. Sometimes the search for love and truth took a wrong turn as drugs presented themselves as an answer – one that included harsh disillusionment. Rock has long been associated with drug use; sometimes the experimentation was in the name of expanding consciousness, but often, it was just abusive and addictive.

In summary, the Blues, Jazz, and Rock & Roll genres depend upon innovative rhythms unlike those found in nature. The emotional content of this music is all over the board – with different styles adding unique emotional tunings. Fast music and high volume levels act like a jack hammer – ushering in the new everything. The rapid, pounding musical beats preceded the unceasing pace of change that helped drive societal changes unlike ever before. People opened up to greater individualism, with each successive musician providing new uprooting expressions to resonate to. All music provides positive and negative outcomes, but these genres changed so fast that both results occurred – almost instantaneously.

Impacts of Modern Music

When listened to intently – a serious modern song creates an emotional, mental and/or physical response. As we have documented, ancient people were well aware of this. For example, the medicine priest of the Navajo Indians would never use music, such as a Wind Chant or a Blessings Chant, for any other purpose than the song was intended for.[820] Today, people get high doses of music they enjoy without any thought to its purpose or impact. Ideally, deep within one's subconscious mind, there is an attraction to the appropriate genre, which is needed to release negative emotions or uplift one's energy – deeply influencing the body, mind and soul.

Many studies and observations point to the impact of Rock & Roll music. The *Wall Street Journal* reported on a study that measured key signatures and tempos of "Hot 100 Charts" from 1965 to 2009. The study assumed that songs written in minor keys, with a slower pace, were associated with sadness. During 1965–1969, 85 percent of hits were written in major (or happy) keys. That usage fell to 42 percent by 2005–2009. During the same time period the beats per minute dropped from 116 to 100.[821] This study measured emotional patterns by tempo, and major versus minor key signatures.

Prophet believed that Voodoo beat patterns – rhythms not found in nature – stimulated violence from Mother Earth. How could rhythms cause violent acts of nature such as volcanoes and floods? Some rhythms are associated with patterns in nature and within the human body. The heart has a rhythm, the movement of cranial–sacral fluid has a rhythm and there is the Circadian rhythm in the body.[822] The Earth also has rhythms – high and low tides, wet and dry seasons – its revolution around the sun. As much as unnatural rhythms take people's hearts out of sync, they also interfere with the Earth's rhythms.

---

[820] Hall, Manly. The Therapeutic Value of Music, including the Philosophy of Music, Los Angeles, CA, 1982, Pgs. 30, 68.

[821] Schaellenberg, Glenn, E., and Scheve, Christian. "Emotional Cues in American Popular Music: Five Decades of the Top 40." Wall Street Journal, Sat/Sun, June 9–10, 2012.

[822] A circadian rhythm is any biological process that displays an entrained oscillation of about 24 hours, which are observed in plants, animals, fungi and cyanobacteria.

All over the globe for thousands of years, ancient people performed rain dances. Without successes, this practice would have died out. Apparently it worked. How did the music precipitate the rain?

What do we know about the basics of rain? All air contains water; near the ground it contains an invisible gas called water vapor. When warm air rises, it expands and cools. Cool air cannot hold as much water vapor as warm air, so some of the vapor condenses onto tiny pieces of dust in the air and forms droplets around dust particles. When billions of these droplets accumulate they become a visible cloud. The droplets bind together and form even bigger drops. When they are large enough, they fall to the ground because of gravity.

Bigger and denser clouds, best allowed ancient shamans to release the precious water droplets. A fire in the middle of the rain–dance circle made hot air rise. Long ceremonies of dance and song also created heat. The rising warm air eventually cooled down and helped form clouds. The water droplets stuck to dust particles until they got too heavy or were shaken out, so they fell. Water droplets were vibrated with singing, drumming and dancing. This helped the water droplet overcome cohesion and release from the cloud.

People have long experimented with types of dances, rhythms, pitches and vowels sounds that were the most effective. Sometimes conditions felt more right for rain – such as prior to a full moon. This would be an excellent time for a rain dance. Even the color of their clothes or face paint would subtly add to the vibrational matrix. Rain–dancing was a practical art that was perfected over thousands of years by people who used the energy of music to enhance their lives.

A parallel may exist between rapid, pumping rhythmic beats and increased intensity of violent weather. This relationship appears to hold in patterns of tsunamis, hurricanes, tornadoes and earthquakes from 2000 – 2015. Waves from music combine with vibrations of the Earth; energies interact and build. It is thought that the aggressive and accelerated rhythmic pulses accentuate the energy of Mother Earth, which is subsequently released in frenzied storms and calamities.

People are being exposed to ever greater "silent" vibrations – both in quantity and strength. These "dark" waves bombard everything, zapping us like a microwave thaws frozen meat. From cell phone signals, satellite transmissions, wireless internet to electric current EMF, we are drowning in vibrations, becoming dulled in the process. We overlook subtle, natural and tender sounds that once were so important – the crickets and birds chirping. We are slowly becoming deaf to nature.

Scientist, Dr. Becker, studied our current dark vibratory diet (outside our hearing range). He reports: "All abnormal, man–made electromagnetic fields, regardless of their frequencies, produce the same biological effects. These effects, which deviate from normal functions, are actually or potentially harmful. They:

- Increase the rate of cancer–cell division and incidence of certain cancers
- Develop abnormalities in embryos
- Alter neurochemicals, resulting in behavioral abnormalities such as suicide
- Alter biological cycles
- Create stress in animals that, if prolonged, leads to declines in immune–system efficiency
- Alter learning abilities"[823]

The conversion from analog to digital recording methods created a new environment of distorted harmonics. The digital revolution is another subtle but huge change in our vibratory world. In nature we find only analog sounds. Digital vibrations are faster paced, containing a great quantity of information but with less detail. Analog sounds can be nourishing to bodily processes. Yet, the use of digital formats creates different effects. Digital is a powerful format to kill pathogens and viruses, while analog sounds mimic the internal body sound patterns.[824]

---

[823] Becker, Robert, Dr. Cross Currents, The Perils of Electropollution, The Promise of Electromedicine, Penguin Group: NY, 1990, Pgs. 214–215.
[824] Sharry Edwards, www.SoundHealthOptions.com

On the positive side, thanks to digital forms of information, far corners of the Earth sonically unite on a multitude of unseen levels. Radio, TV, MP3s and the Internet grant easy access to a multicultural sonic experience. Music from around the globe spreads with the push of a button. Travel is no longer necessary for cultural exchange, allowing ease of access to positive world influences. Composers from different cultures – that were formerly isolated – now easily connect and share musical ideas. In this manner, musical styles blend in Earth's huge, global, musical melting pot.

Historically, musical styles lasted thousands of years. Now they change in just one generation – or less. The rate of societal change has also kicked into high gear; just fifty years ago color TV was an exciting innovation – that seems trivial today. Nowadays the Internet, cell phones, tablets and personal computers have revolutionized our world and how we are entertained, how we get our news and interact with others. Once again, the sonic vibratory changes preceded the physical ones. When the music changes, its ripple effects always follow.

People get attached to music, particularly what they listened to during their youth; they resist listening–changes throughout the remainder of their lives. For example, some in the Eastern hemisphere listen to Beethoven's music and cringe as the harmony spoils the charm of the melody. Westerners listen to the Eastern melodies with notes closer together in pitch and perceive the music as sounding "off." People get accustomed to certain sounds. Further, they associate music with specific cultures, times, feelings or events. For example, we have an idea of what Chinese and Gregorian chants sound like, associating one with China and the other with the time period of the Middle Ages. In times past, once listeners "harmonized" with their music, a new sound seemed strange and unattractive. A radically new genre of music is not popularized until young people, who have not solidified their listening preferences yet, harmonize with it.

Musicologist, Victor Wooten, suggested that all types of music have beauty, but most people only like limited genres. The variable is not the beauty of a genre, but what the listener can relate to. According to Wooten, "All music, like all people, contains beauty and soul. For you not to recognize it is not Music's fault. It is you who does not recognize! There are millions of people who love this genre. Are all those people wrong?"[825]

Wooten felt that beauty can be seen in all things and in all people; these perceptions can improve the world.[826] By accepting the music of different cultures, we embrace diversity as well. Music can be used to create peace, just as the ancient Sumerians believed. Music from all over the world should be shared. If we love a country's music, we will more readily love the people, too.

There are numerous modern musical genres that are descendants of Blues, Jazz and Rock, such as Heavy Metal, Punk Rock, Pop, Country, Hip Hop and many other off shoots. In the interest of time, we have reviewed just a few genres to demonstrate general modern musical developments. Below, we touch on RAP, as it clearly leaves the musical pattern of twos behind. It will go down as an entirely new vibrational form – more like poetry – departing from music in most ways.

Rap Music

At the beginning of the 1900s, West African and Caribbean musicians were telling stories rhythmically; their tales were accompanied by a drum beat. These singing poets established the foundation for modern–day Rap music. Rapping essentially involves speaking in rhyming lyrics, usually set to a beat. The words of the "song" are like an accented conversation, not a melody.

Rapping first gained popularity in the USA in the 1970s as a street art, particularly among African American teenagers. In 1979, when the Sugarhill Gang released their breakaway hit, *Rapper's Delight*, Rap's audience began to swell. The new genre was not only composed of African American male rappers. White Rap bands such as the Beastie Boys were topping the charts.

---

[825] Wooten, Victor. The Music Lesson: Spiritual Search for Growth through Music, Berkley Books: NY, 2006, Pg. 56.
[826] Wooten, Victor. *Ibid,* Pg. 54.

Rap's rhythm provides structure and even security – as the sounds organize neatly into predictable patterns. It is like modern poetry – street poetry – with a beat.

Author and musicologist, Joshua Leeds described how Rap music entrains the listener into a trance–like state: "The primary elements of Rap are fairly slow, repetitive rhythms on a drum machine along with lots of upfront bass. This is sonic valium! The rhythm slows the nervous system. The preponderance of the bass does not energize the nervous system; rather it discharges energy. Add lyrics, wrapped in a periodic cadence. This style of speaking, along with the rock steady percussion, facilitates trance."[827] Rap helps inner city youth to "chill out." Rap represents those who resist authority and provides an outlet for personal conflicts.

Many are appalled at the lyrics of Rap, Heavy Metal and other modern genres. Equally, the ancient Hindus would be aghast at the "somebody–done–somebody–wrong" songs that people still enjoy... like the Country Western song, *It is Cheaper to Keep Her.* Hindu songs only reflect God and His Divine attributes. Once again, with the inexorable passing of time, the music pushes us further into physicality, creating the perception that we are entirely separate from God.

www.JillsWingsofLight.com – Art Galleries

[827] Leeds, Joshua. <u>The Power of Sound: How to be Healthy and Productive using Music and Sound</u>, Healing Arts Press: VT, 2001 and 2010, Pg. 103.

The vocal content of Heavy Metal and Rap music can be *cathartic* and shatter dissonant negative energy. Earlier, Cyril Scott suggested that only dissonant sounds are powerful enough to penetrate inflexible thoughts and ideas of conventional people – to make them receptive to new ideas.[828] Dissonant energies agitate and pull negative energies loose; this frees negativity from people's fields. On the downside, the singer or listener who is not ready to release the low ebbs of human emotions, may allow negative words to *enhance* his misery, anger and violence. At the very minimum, the negative energy is agitated before it gets a chance to pull free and release.

Excessively crude vocal content represents an unconscious and disguised call for unconditional love or help. The singer represents himself as coarse and indifferent, appearing not to care what anyone thinks. Someone who goes out of his way to portray that he "doesn't care," deeply wants someone to care. Angry words can be an unconscious cry for help. Perhaps humanity is longing for the return journey from individuality to the collective spirit. It feels good to do everything on our own, but we also desire companionship and union.

When I was a child, my neighbors were like an extended family. We lived in one another's pockets and thought nothing of entering each other's homes without knocking. Today, I do not even know my neighbors. Further, when I was growing up, most everyone was married by their early twenties. My children are in their 20s and 30s and hang out in "packs" of friends. It is rare when one of their gang gets married. Marriage rates were at all–time lows in 2011, with only 51 percent of the population participating. The average age that people marry keeps getting older as well. Currently it is 29 years for men and 26 for women. When my mother was young, a woman was considered a spinster at age 22. Has our society transferred from the two–energy (of a couple) to one–energy (of a single)? This (energy of one) is a major influence on the prevailing energies of our time.

---

[828] Scott, Cyril. Music: Its Secret Influences throughout the Ages, Samuel Weiser: NY, 1958, Pg. 136. Reprinted in 2013 by Inner Traditions.com.

When I was young, all sneakers were white and looked exactly alike. There were only several styles of furniture and dishes to choose from. With only three TV channels to watch, everyone related to the same entertainment. People didn't express their individuality with material things partly due to a limited selection of merchandise and entertainment. In today's world, with many more options to choose from, everyone expresses individuality to a far greater extent. It seems natural to do so. Choices have exploded.

Numerology patterns are mirrored in popular dances. A group or line dance was popular during the Renaissance. Later, waltzing couples was the "rage." Far later, Rock & Roll dances, such as the Twist, encouraged each individual to express himself while dancing alone. Dancing transformed from a group activity to an individual's personal expression.

www.JillsWingsofLight.com – Art Galleries

All indications point to the conclusion that these are the days of the "ebb tide" – when the energy flow of the human race halts its *involutionary* cycle into matter and reverses directions – to begin the *evolutionary* process – growing less connected to matter. Eventually we will be free of the material world; all will be spirit once again. Think of a stretched slingshot, pulled back to the furthest and tightest position... it is ready to strongly snap back – just as our souls are poised for their journey to become one with spirit again.

Rap's Musical Number of One

Rap rhythms create a steady pattern of *ones*. Rappers "sing" mainly *one* pitch. This creates a musical matrix of the number *one* – the most individualistic number. ...One is the loneliest...

The number one symbolizes beginnings, self, ideas, unity, gifts, seeds, potential isolation and initiation. The number one represents people with extraordinary leadership skills, ambition, drive, will power and courage. These people are unconventional, inventive, creative, original, pioneering and independent.[829, 830]

Rap's musical structure, based on the pattern of one, represents the pinnacle of duality – the outer most point that we can reach in our involution into matter; it signifies the greatest degree of individuality and the furthest point away from God possible. The energy of individuality is the epitome of the spirit's long journey to experience physicality.

The Number One in Crop Circles[831]

---

[829] http://www.spiritual–numerology.com/numerology–number–meaning/numerology–meaning–of–number–1.html

[830] Some of the difficult qualities of people associated with the number one are stubborn, dominant, impatient, concerned with status/appearance, selfish, egotistic, angry, aggressive, demanding respect/attention, pride and the need to feel in command.

[831] Used with permission – Peter Sorensen.
http://cropcircleconnector.com/Sorensen/circles/1999/main.html

New Age Music

"They will return again. All over the Earth, they are returning again, ancient teachings of the Earth, ancient songs of the Earth. They are returning again. My friend, they are returning. I give them to you, and through them you will understand, you will see. They are returning again upon the Earth." These are the predictions of Crazy Horse (1842–77), from the Sioux tribe of North America. In what form will the ancient songs of Earth return? One strong possibility is New Age music, which is defined by the feelings that it produces.

New Age music is the final stop on our trip through Modern music. It reverses the trends of identifying with the physical world, rather than a spiritual one.

New Age music consciously seeks to replicate many of the ancient musical techniques. It seeks to take its listeners on the return journey to greater connectivity with "spirit," be it God or developing psychic skills to receive spiritual messages.

This purpose driven–music provides targeted benefits of artistic inspiration, stress management and optimism. Ambient sounding New Age music aids meditation, massage, yoga and relaxation. It supports alternative healthy practices such yoga, guided meditation and chakra balancing.

The author creates multidimensional soothing music, with frequencies associated with vitamins and nutrients, stars and nature frequencies. Songs feature cathartic release of negative emotions and compositions that build positive emotions, reminiscent of ancient Greek healing techniques. Other pieces replicate numeric patterns found in nature and the cosmos; they immerse the listener in special sounds to improve energies of the body and mind. Emotions are soothed, tuned and released as the need requires.

Many beat patterns in New Age music intentionally copy rhythmic patterns of the heart, body processes, ocean wave patterns and other naturally occurring repetitive cycles. New Agers experiment with scales that begin on pitches other than 440 cycles per second (concert A), to observe which tonal patterns provide the most benefits. A few, such as harpist Michael Riversong,[832] are working with the ancient Greek modes used in ancient times for specific benefits, especially effective for children with disabilities.

The sounds of New Age music are generally ambient, modal and consonant. The pleasant, uplifting and calming melodies are often repetitive, creating a hypnotic feeling. It is not unusual for meditative pieces to last up to thirty minutes – dishing out a generous vibratory treat. Ancient music – without beginnings and endings – was also lengthy and calming.

Vocals often use ancient languages such as Native American, Sanskrit (now an extinct language) or Tibetan. Mystics claim that the vibratory sound patterns of these ancient languages connect our souls to higher energy sources. Vocals may feature lyrics based on mythology such as Celtic legends or the realm of Faerie.

New Age music often includes nature sounds and is even classified as environmental music. Musician Tom Kenyon "channels" songs featuring sounds not used in modern singing. He professes that he receives sounds of the spirit "ensouling" Mother Earth, and that the Earth needs these "songs" for health and balance. Further, Kenyon traveled the world many times, singing these unusual sounds and sprinkling the "Song of Mother Earth" over the planet in a grid like pattern. The ancient sages believed that the Earth was covered with a grid of subtle energy "veins," that were like little "rivers" that can be likened to our circulatory system. Kenyon suggests that singing on the "ley lines" all over the world brought vibratory nourishment to the Earth through these energy arteries.

Popular themes in New Age music include: space and the cosmos, wellness, harmony, dreams and journeys of the mind or spirit. Titles of New Age albums and songs are frequently descriptive, examples include: *Shepherd Moons* (Enya), *Straight a Way to Orion* (Kitaro), and *Symphony of the Stars* (Mattson).

---

[832] Free harp Music in Greek modes by Michael Riversong. Www.biblicalbards.org

The New Age music features a wide range of music, including Ambient, Neo Classical, Electronica, World Music, Celtic, Chill Out, Space Music and many others.

New Age music includes both electronic and acoustic instrumentation. Instruments used include: flute, Native American flute, piano, harp, acoustic guitar synthesizer, sampler, sequencer, computer, strings, nature sounds (bird song, whale song and waterfalls), folk and ethnic instruments such as the Hindu sitar, *tamboura* and *tabla*.

Crystal bowls provide a respite of rich harmonics – heard in sweeping and rolling sounds. Also, intoning healthy harmonics are Tibetan bowels made from metals, such as gold, silver and cooper (and alloys). (Ancient practices used sound vibrations produced from different metals for various subtle energy impacts.) Glissando sounds from bowls provide a smorgasbord of frequencies that a body may need. People place bowls on acupressure and meridian points, to maximize the vibratory effects throughout the body. Importantly, these sounds can offset the effects of our digital sonic poisoning.

A tuning fork creates one frequency, an exact cycle per second. There may be hundreds of cycles per second between a half note; our listening ears are deprived of many frequencies in between our closest notes. Tuning fork sets accurately replicate numbers used in geometry to express forms found in nature, and prized "healing" sound patterns, such as the Fibonacci numbers, solfeggio tones, *om* and planetary sounds. Tuning forks also enlighten aural fields and send energy into chakras and meridians. These precise frequencies can be found in new age music.

Fabien Maman revived the balancing seasonal energy concerts, characteristic of many ancient musical practices. Deval Premal, Krishna Das and Robert Gass revived and "Americanized" ancient mantras and chants.

In an interesting magnification of ancient sound processes, today's technology can *amplify* the ancient methods to improve body, mind and soul energies. For example, sounds made very close to the ear (so that a sound heard in one ear is not heard in the other) forces the two brain hemispheres to open up and work together to process these frequencies (each ear is working separately rather than in combo as is normally the case). This creates whole brain functioning, quickly teaching meditation, increasing IQ, and producing theta and delta brain waves. While in theta and delta brain wave states, the physical body rebuilds and repairs itself, renewing health. Today, this is done efficiently with New Age music and headphones, and Sound and Light machines!

In another project, biologist Dr. David Deamer, calculated the frequencies of the four DNA base molecules and used these pitches as a tuning system for music. In 1990 the soothing music was released and entitled *Sequencia*. In addition to amassing testimonials, claiming benefits from the music, Deamer's work also opened a path for science to study biology and DNA – using the clues of tiny unheard sounds.

New Age musicians often recreate ancient vibratory practices to take the "fast track" back to spirit – listeners paying attention to the subtle energy of the music and the spiritual world – leaving behind attachment to the physical world. We are finally seeing the turn of the long cycle of musical involution. Music has mirrored and indeed *driven* our long journey into matter and physicality – reaching its pinnacle (and low point for many) with modern music – particularly the latest incarnation in the form of Rap. New Age music is the first solid step taking us back to the long journey to rejoin God and leave the material world behind...

www.JillsWingsofLight.com – Art Galleries

371

Chapter Thirteen

...And so it Ends...
and so it Begins...

Musical Numbers

As the reader clearly appreciates, ancient sages understood God's creations through numbers. God left clues about himself as He surrounded us with His mathematical revelations – hidden in nature. As ancient man came to understand numbers, he was awed by their presence in the natural world.

Ancient man believed the universe was constructed by numbers, which *expressed* as sound and music. Among a myriad of mathematical designs, numbers correlated to stops on musical strings. Analogously, modern physicists and String Theory, suggest that strings (that vibrate in certain ways) are the foundation of the universe. The number patterns found in nature were incorporated into music, making numbers, music and nature interconnected and interchangeable. Numbers are the DNA of the universe.

Pythagoras said, "All is number." Numbers were valued far beyond a mere counting tool. The higher calling of mathematics involved the energy, deeply associated with numbers. The hidden power of numbers came from the linked energy. Numerology reveals remnants of this lost understanding. Arithmetic was the mundane and demeaning use of numbers; numbers possessed real power.

.

Numerical energies were believed to be the building blocks of creation[833] – each number manifesting something different! The unique energy of each number was correlated to items displaying the same number. For example, the energy of five was associated with flowers having five petals. Music with a signature pattern of five, contained the energy of five; this was one of the most important attributes of the music – the musical number – the number–energy that it generated, built up and transferred to mankind.

Ancient philosophers even correlated numbers to the celestial heavens. Astrologers assigned numbers to shapes, such as a *five* or *six* pointed star, made by transiting heavenly bodies. The path of Venus creates a five pointed star, while Mercury's movements trace a perfect six pointed Star of David.[834] Five would be associated with Venus, while six is linked to Mercury. An online free app (in the footnotes) displays the stars creating shapes in their orbits – drawing a variety of forms, flowers and heart shapes.[835]

Energies transferred, through resonance, on many levels: physical emotional and mental. For example, when ancient masters gazed at the constellation Aquarius, they noted what they felt, and that their feelings changed when they gazed at (and subtly connected to) other constellations. Aquarius star energy bestows the energy of difficulty, illumination and brotherly love.[836] When the sun's position at the vernal equinox is in front of the constellation, the

---

[833] Heath, Richard. Sacred Number and the Origins of Civilizations, Inner Traditions: VT, 2007, Pg. 1.

[834] Mercury traces this star between two successive conjunctions and its repetition of evening and morning stars. The circuit of stars and the sun present a numerical sequence created in part by the Earth's rotation. The movement of the moon and planets follow a different circuit, called the zodiac. These circuits are different because the Earth's axis is tilted.

[835] http://clixbits.com/planets/

[836] Esoteric Astrology, Alice Bailey, 1975. "...Our sun is now entering into the sign Aquarius; its three decanates, Saturn, Mercury and Venus, bring inevitable difficulty, illumination and brotherly love. In the spiritually developed man, in all outer affairs, Saturn controls and he finds himself in a state of chaos and trouble. But Mercury is becoming active, affecting the consciousness of the race. A steady illumination is taking place and light illuminates all problems – government and politics and the basic ideologies: light clarifies the material nature of the world through all the many branches of science; and enlightens education, philosophy and psychology."

wise sages believed that the masses absorbed the same subtle, but influential feelings, creating the "Age of Aquarius."

Ancient masters strongly desired to be "in sync" with the energy of "Heaven and Earth." One way they tuned to Heaven was to use the astronomical time periods of the stars as organizing principals in their world. For example, Saturn's cycle divides by the number seven, which could explain why early people assigned seven days to measure a week. Saturday is derived from the name, Saturn Day, which features a strong dose of this planet's energies.

Numerical energy was associated with the gods by the ancient Sumerians, Egyptians and others. Author and historian, Richard Heath, reflected that a god's character correlated to a specific number.[837] The god was closely linked to this number, and he was considered to be a master of its energy, which was associated with emotional strengths and virtues. Using a number in a variety of creative ways was one method of cementing a connection with a god and "downloading" his energies.

Ancient legends perceived the world through the lens of music. What is music at its deepest core? Music is essentially numbers, counting out: cycles per second, intervals, rhythmic beats, harmonics and time periods.

Music could emulate nature and the heavens, reflecting divine perfection and mathematical design. Special music harmonized the changing energy of the stars and seasons. When man vibrated in sync with Heaven and Earth, he was in harmony with God and all cosmic forces. Music was a prime vehicle to amplify such heavenly energies and the nurturing forces of Mother Earth.

There are many creative ways of instilling a number's energy into music. One can use rhythmic patterns, tuning notes, length of notes and timed sections of music. In a creative example, today's scale has seven notes, with the eighth note being an octave of the first note of the scale. The Lambdoma scale has eight notes with the "octave" being the ninth note. The ancient Chinese commonly

---

[837] Heath, Richard. *Ibid,* Pg. 133.

divided an octave by five notes. Dividing the octave into different numbers of notes, creates different "numerical feelings."

As we have already seen, music's hidden mathematical patterns, not listening qualities, were of supreme importance to ancient leaders. The music of a culture usually incorporated a *"signature"* number or energy. Notes, intervals and rhythms reflected this signature number. The signature number was musically used over and over again. The energy associated with the number was highly valued, becoming the foundation of the culture's music and resulting values.

As we have learned, the signature musical number of cultures varies throughout the ages, unfolding in descending numerical order: 9, 7, 6, 5, 4, 3, 2 and 1. The earliest number (9) was found in Lemuria (based on legend) followed by Atlantis (with 7), then Sumeria (6) and later China (5), Greece (4) and so on, up until Rap music's signature number of one. The number eight is missing, but perhaps future researchers may find it.

A common way to highlight a number in music was to use one interval predominantly. The chart, *Musical Numbers throughout Time*, on page 377, begins with intervals nine notes apart and decreases to intervals with the span of one note, as civilizations relentlessly created new musical genres. As intervals became closer together, different musical sounds were created. The new music produced fresh influences on many fronts: emotions, thoughts, physicality, brain waves and more. With the passage of time, people experienced greater individualism and lost abilities to sense subtle energies. It is a pivotal contention of this book that there is a connection between closer musical intervals and people becoming immersed in physicality.

In legends and obscure written documents, early inhabitants of Earth were described as highly evolved beings – not homo sapiens. They used a different range of the electromagnetic spectrum – a higher and broader range of frequencies – than we do today. Likewise, their music encompassed a higher range of vibrations – massaging the corresponding areas of their consciousness. They vibrated too quickly to be focused on the slower waves associated with matter and duality.

Today we have a world resonating with the lowest musical number (1) – reflected in predominant pitches, intervals and rhythms. Simultaneously, the churches of the world – from all religions – are fading, along with acceptance of the spiritual world. "Seeing is believing" reflects mankind's materiality. This inescapable trend – from the beginning of human legends – demonstrates the strong decline in spirituality and the transformation to being concerned only with the physical.

www.JillsWingsofLight.com – Art Galleries

Era	Number	Interval Patterns	Effect
Lemuria	9	**9** of our notes was the smallest interval	Linked to the Divine
Atlantis	7	**7** of our notes was the smallest interval	Connected to your Higher Self (Divine or Holy Spirit)
Sumeria	6	**60** based math, Musical system of **6's**	Linked with the Planetary Logos,* creating a spiritual experience
China	5	Uses a scale created from notes that are **5** notes apart.	Augmented the imagination
Greek Roman	4	Employed tetra chords – **4** notes in a sequence	Developed the personality
Dark Ages Middle Ages	3	Music was a series of **3**rds, Introduction of the 3rd as a staple of harmony in the 1–3–5 chord	Pulled the population out of the Dark Ages. Developed compassion, freedom, other feelings/values
Swing Rock and Jazz	2	Melodies are often **2** notes apart, 1, 3, 5, 7 chords (7th to an octave creates a 2nd interval)	Questioned government and established values, Rapid changes in society
Rap	1	**1** repetitive pitch	Individuality accentuated

* Planetary Logos is one of the seven highest spirits corresponding to the seven archangels in Christianity. http://en.mimi.hu/esoteric/planetary_logos.html

It is clear that musical numbers changed over time. The bird's eye view of music across the ages reveals sequentially declining intervals and numbers. The odds of this happening – an ever descending pattern of signature numbers from the earliest days up to modern times – cannot be due to chance. Who organized these declining numbers throughout history? Clearly, no human lived long enough to orchestrate this. The "Force" that drove this trend, knits global energies, religions and beliefs together into a beautiful tapestry.

In another curious observation, the same musical pattern emerged in many parts of the Earth, simultaneously. Did a person travel across the oceans to the "four corners of the world" and share the musical ideas? Or did the energy emanating from the Earth – subtly influence musicians around the world? Were the musicians in different locations inspired by an unseen force? Are there biological reasons explaining why people find a certain musical style attractive? Our sophisticated body releases endorphins, causing pleasure when it hears the musical elements it needs for harmony. On some unconscious level, does the body select our favorite songs? Could this be responsible for the overarching pattern?

It is peculiar, to say the least, that there is a logical sequence to the intervals and musical numbers that people harmonized to. The musical numbers from the beginning (9) to the present (1) correlate to all possible human emotions. Systematically, civilizations immersed in the energy of decreasing musical numbers; this enabled people to experience and master each number's energy. Likewise, all the colors contained in the rainbow merge to form dazzling white light.

In the chart "Emotions & Intervals," below, author Fabien McMann correlated musical intervals to emotions. A steady diet of one interval produces consistent and precise emotions. Listeners learn to master the correlating emotion. Ancient leaders understood this well.

Emotions & Intervals	
Fabien McMann	
Interval	**Quality**
Root Note	Mirror of oneself, immobility, rest, old memories
Second	First tension between two polarities, birth of movement
Third	Inner emotional and psychic life
Fourth	Awakening and at the same time paralyzing, stretching towards conclusion
Fifth	Reverse of the fourth, transmutation, the boundary between inner and outer space of the body, passage from inner to outer world, freeing the creative potential, most stimulating interval, factor of expansion, brings joy
Sixth	Total opening, gives feeling of offering yourself to the universe, contrary to the third that is contained completely inside, the sweetest interval
Seventh	Extreme tension that is resolved when the octave is played
Octave	Final resolution, reaching for the higher self, stability, linking past and future in the present, transformation

Another method providing a civilization a healthy dose of a particular frequency, is the note they tune their musical instruments to. A tuning note is featured predominantly in songs, giving listeners high exposure to its particular frequency and corresponding energies.

Today, we do not play music exclusively in one key, nor do we listen to just one note. In antiquity, most instruments were unable to transpose from key to key. In ancient China, the frequency of the tuning note was locked in place by the government. They regulated the specifications for making instruments – to precisely control the exact pitches an instrument produced. All music centered on the note that the civilization was tuning to. In days past, people absorbed concentrated and restricted diets of the musical number.

The ancient Hindu's tuning practices served two primary purposes – all aimed to tune instruments and the audience. Although musicians can tune their instruments in a few minutes, the Hindu musicians played a tuning note for at least 60 minutes at the beginning of a concert. A strong dose of the tuning note insures that the audience absorbs this pitch. The ancient Chinese practiced meditating to a tone for hours, producing a similar effect to listening to musicians tune their instruments for an extended time.

Modern day scientist, Michael Thaut, showed that sustained notes entrain brain waves, producing different states of consciousness. Thaut claims that reality is intimately connected to the state of consciousness and associated brain waves.[838] Some scientists emphasize that states of consciousness change in response to *vibratory* simulation (such as music).[839] Tuning to various notes alters our consciousness accordingly.

Science has shown that sound alters and entrains brain waves. Different brain waves are associated with specific states of consciousness. Putting this together, the energy of *musical notes* – on miniscule levels – entrains brain waves *and consciousness*. This is one more way we can understand how music and its numbers impact us.

Overtime pitches and rhythms changed – altering attributes of great civilizations. Although one's conscious mind is unaware of music's numerical patterns, they have a subtle and predictable impact; this is happening on a powerful subconscious level.

Sharry Edwards, inventor of BioAcoustics, identified emotions associated with pitches. When an ancient culture composed music primarily in one key (such as C or F), then the culture strongly exhibited the qualities associated with those musical notes. (See page 145.)

Over the years people tuned to various frequencies, stimulating different thoughts and emotions for them to "master." While we

---

[838] Tart, 1975
[839] http://web-us.com/thescience.htm

give attention to something, our subconscious minds simultaneously run "automatic" programs. In a similar way, one program can be featured on a computer screen, while others run in the background, such as virus protection. Likewise, when people have mastered an action, they no longer expend conscious attention to repeat it. A mastered skill can operate subconsciously, while one focuses on something new. As civilizations moved forward, people incorporated mental and emotional skills and no longer required special attention for them. They were ready for a new tuning note or more complexity within music!

This idea can be illustrated by observing that ancient China and India tuned to and "mastered" the notes of C and F (corresponding to balancing complementary colors). Their music mostly featured *one* melodic note with only *one* accompaniment note. In a new development, Renaissance people listened to complex chords with *three or more* notes (the first, third and fifth notes of a scale – like F, A and C). Earlier people did not listen to many notes at one time. Perhaps humanity was not ready to listen to complex chords until they had "mastered" the component pitches.

Energy is not static, but ever changing. And so it is with music and all of its influences. It slowly, but relentlessly changes, providing us with new vibrational challenges and opportunities for growth.

Music always leads the Way

So thus ends our ambitious journey, tracing the role of Music (with a capital M for its significance) throughout time. As the persevering reader has seen, we began at the very dawn of man – even before – as our predecessors entered into the material world. The earliest origins involved spirit moving to occupy matter – for *perhaps* the first time.

The reader now clearly appreciates that when spirit first entered the physical world, the vibrations of higher subtle energy were condensed, that is, lowered in frequency, so that a soul could inhabit a physical form and associate with matter. This process long continued, as man involved into matter to ever greater degrees. Ancient sages believed that the music of an epoch was deeply responsible for shaping their people and their worlds.

Initially, we had faerie–like creatures that were physically insubstantial and communicated exclusively by telepathy. They probably first lived in a place today we call Lemuria (Mu), the Mother Land. It is important to understand, however, that these beings were very spiritual and not like humans at all. They retained their close links to God and the Unity of All There Is, but they desired to experience the sensual: to smell the roses, enjoy the warmth of a sunny afternoon and to feel emotions. With the passing of many centuries, the people of Mu became more attached to matter.

Lemurians were clairvoyant and clairaudient - seeing and hearing far more than modern man. Everything vibrates and produces frequencies, much too subtle for us to hear today, but not for them. They could hear the harmonies of the night skies and the entire range of vibrational sounds from nature. They interpreted a broader range of the electromagnetic spectrum, perhaps more like dolphins. Since they were able to see and hear subtle energies, they saw the colors radiated by a healthy body and listened to the perfect harmony that it created. When someone got sick, they observed the beautiful colors of the body's energy darken and the body's sounds disintegrate into discord. The ancient Lemurians knew the connection between sound, light and physicality. This was not a mystical phenomenon; it was obvious to them. They saw it in plain sight. Ancient practices using sound and music were a "fall out" from seeing and hearing subtle energy impacts. Only when the clairvoyant and clairaudient abilities faded (many ages later), did these ideas become mysterious, then superstitious and finally ridiculous.

Today, healer and author Donna Eden, sees subtle energies radiating from the body. She has created a system where others can use movements, intent and techniques to restore healthy colors to the physical body, which translates into being healthy.[840] Sharry Edwards hears tiny sounds, so low in volume that only sophisticated equipment can detect and record such minute volumes. As a result of her special abilities, Edwards has founded BioAcoustics, a system to analyze sounds in the body, and employ carefully selected techniques to bring the body back into harmony,

---

[840] Intersource.net

which translates into being healthy.[841] Fables and stories describe the Lemurians doing similar things as Eden and Edwards.

We traced music from prehistoric caves and tribal shaman ceremonies through the great ancient civilizations... the Sumerians, Egyptians, Greeks, Hindus, Chinese up through the Middle Ages to modern times. Each culture had musical specialties or "flavors." Strict parameters defined the consistent *sound* of a culture's music. That is why we can easily recognize Chinese or Indian music versus Gregorian chant. The music of an epoch produced the characteristic "feel," reminiscent of a group or nation that lasted centuries and even millennia.

Earlier peoples embraced the supernatural. For most of our history – dating back hundreds of thousands of years – men believed in the supernatural as a fundamental aspect of the universe. Invisible, spiritual powers were very real to these people. There was not a division between the "real world" and the mystical world – they were completely integrated into ONE reality. Music influenced subtle energy in a way that nothing else could; as a result, it interacted with the spiritual and the nonmaterial realms. Shamans used music to enter different "dimensions" and retrieve information for healing and decision making. *Music was magic.*

...And music was much more. It worked on the emotional and intellectual components of people. Even further, special music and sound frequencies directly impacted the physical body and all of its parts. Sound power led to victory at war and enabled people to move massive monoliths. Music in its beauty, with an almost endless spectrum of vibratory energies, impacted: subtle energy, emotions, abstract intellects and physical bodies.

Sound vibrations are energy, just as much as your emotions, thoughts and physical body are forms of energy or function via energy... Energy constantly transfers between these levels. This is easily seen; recall that music readily makes us feel this way or that way... happy or sad... anxious or euphoric... brave, determined. Subtle, influential energy – disguised as music – has affected mankind for many thousands of years. Highly evolved musical

---

[841] SoundHealthOptions.com

systems could create an entire cultural matrix, selecting and maintaining desired behaviors and values. Ancient sages believed that the *music of an epoch was responsible for this process, slowly and carefully tuning the populations' thoughts, feelings and even physicality.* The music worked like a kaleidoscope, changing and blending the strengths and weaknesses of the group.

Recall that the Egyptians endured thousands of years – their music remained unchanged during this long span. Sometimes music morphed, but within parameters that maintained its critical aspects. The subtle energy foundation of music propped up cultural stability; it created and maintained the values system. For example in China, if two villages' scales sounded abrasive together, the villages acted in an abrasive manor towards each other, causing internal strife. A Department of Measurements insured that the length of instruments, such as a flute, were exactly alike across their vast territories to insure that all villages heard the *same* harmonious music. Properly controlled music kept citizens' behavior in line. This vastly overlooked historical influence was a major and crucial component in shaping a culture, and hence all of human history.

Fast forward to the 1960s and the birth of Rock and Roll. For the first time ever, young people rallied to a new beat and brought down the war in Vietnam. Think to Woodstock, flower children, "sit-ins" and peaceful demonstrations. The author is convinced that none of this could ever have happened without the energy and love and peace that the best of Rock created. ... Later the beauty faded with the arrival of Acid Rock and Heavy Metal.

The drivers of civilization throughout time were not only religion, science, war, drought and so on, as we have learned since grammar school... BUT included the physic, the nonmaterial, and the divine. Music has the unique ability to act in the physical and the metaphysical realms. The remarkable power of subtle energy and vibrational energy in the form of music, figured decisively in mankind's story.

Subtle Energy

Pliable water takes the shape of an ice cube tray when frozen. Subtle energy and associated thoughts, feelings and music are malleable and easily changed, much like the water. It readily conforms. With enough repetition, sheer volume and exposure to a uniform subtle energy, thinking patterns - and the resulting actions - of a civilization are shaped and cemented.

At first glance, this theory appears to be a leap of faith. Can music affect an entire culture? Yet, we all agree that music makes us *feel*. If we all consistently listened to the *same* music, we would have a society with many uniform feelings. Feelings are motivating forces that influence our actions and accomplishments; they can define the attributes of a culture.

Initially, we squirm at the idea that music affects physicality; isn't that an even bigger leap of faith? Recall the case of a person constantly worrying. This negative, subtle energy accumulates within the lining of his stomach. (The frequency of the emotion "worry" interacts with the frequency of the lining in the stomach.) Through sympathetic resonance, energy transfers on the same pitch, depositing the negative "worry–energy" in the gut. High enough doses of this bore a hole in the physical stomach, creating an ulcer. The subtle energy of "worry" (a nonmaterial thing), with enough volume, changed the physical shape of the man's stomach. Although we cannot see "worry", we can clearly observe its impact.

We cannot see quantum energy either. Matter is composed of quantum energy and it is constantly moving. Ancient man also believed in quantum energy, (although he gave it a different name: prana, chi, subtle energy…) and believed that it behaved like sound waves. Around 2,500 years ago, Democritus named the atom after the Greek word *atomos*, which means "that which cannot be split."

Medicine men, priests and magicians altered the energy that they could control – often through words, sounds, chants and music. They collected malleable vibrations that they could use to solidify energy in matter. Likewise, we put molten wax into a mold, while it can be shaped. With relentless applications of sound, gradual changes in matter are possible. Results are not quickly seen; they are easily overlooked. The challenge of manipulating subtle energy was to amass enough to alter physical matter. "Magic" words and spells did just this. The subtle energies of words, music, colors, oils and herbs were combined like ingredients in a recipe. Things were combined for their subtle energies, not their physicality. The mixed items are not logical, because they were chosen by how they felt or based on their "numbers," not for what they were. Shamans mixed a concoction of many sources of subtle energy to alter matter.

As science reveals theories and concepts of the quantum world, the universe seems weirder than we could have imagined. Often, the new studies describe phenomena that recall accepted ancient practices that we deem superstitious. For example, in the famed Schroeder's cat experiment, certain quantum particles do not appear, unless there is an observer present. A magician is an observer who expects subtle energy to behave in certain ways. His faith and will are part of the magic. As mankind lost more and more subtle awareness and stopped believing in his abilities to influence energies that could not be seen, this job became next to impossible. Magicians resorted to parlor tricks to keep up appearances.

As subtle energy channels closed, man's belief in the mystical was deemed superstitious. The understanding of ancient practices was lost as well. Recall that the Egyptians mended a cracked skull by sleeping with an ostrich egg near the head. I wondered, "How can the people who built the pyramids, be so ridiculous?" Years later, Sharry Edwards described tiny sounds emitted from shapes. Dan Davidson, in *Shape Power*, also described tiny energies radiating from shapes. Finally, when my son broke his arm, the orthopedic surgeon suggested a sound machine to lessen the healing time. Putting this all together, I deduced that: if the energy of sound helps repair broken bones and tiny sounds release from shapes, then subtle sounds coming from an ostrich egg (the same shape and size as a skull) could mend a crack in a skull. Turn the clock forward and I once again read the Egyptian ostrich egg treatment, but this time I understood it. They were using quantum energies to knit the crack in the man's skull.

Before giving medical advice, an ancient physician evaluated the patient, giving him a "Yes, I will try to heal him," or a "No, I can't help." Why couldn't there be a "We can try" option? The question wasn't whether or not the patient could be cured, but could he survive long enough to absorb enough subtle energy – where one only soaks up tiny amounts at a time? They were judging if a person could live long enough to ingest the necessary quantum energy.

Remember that the Egyptians changed their music every hour to "tune" to the changing energies of the day (early morning feels different than late afternoon). They also used a mirror set of musical tones to harmonize the "*ka*" body, (a person's energy fields located someplace else and an exact opposite energy set). Did the Egyptians understand quantum entanglement?

A physicist reads antiquity and infuses the laws of physics into his interpretation. A chemist understands when ancient people displayed a deeper knowledge of chemistry. A different interpretation is obtained according to the perspective of the reader. To crack ancient subtle energy secrets, one needs to be knowledgeable of numerology, music, quantum physics, altered states of consciousness, psychic abilities and more. Without this broad background, it is too easy to conclude all ancient people were primitive.

The Lost Subtle Energy Connection… and so it Ends…

We observed several historic trends. As time relentlessly moved on, the channels of information from subtle energy were diminished until man perceived himself as entirely separate from everyone and everything. Now he must take sole responsibility for his choices and actions. The power of music was credited with causing this to happen, at least in part.

Around the world, music formerly replicated sounds and patterns found in nature. Today electronic music, rap and heavy metal create an artificial sonic diet.

In another trend, Connections to "spirits" from other dimensions declined from being of utmost importance to mere superstition. Indeed, some ancient musical practices were designed to enable listeners to grasp greater subtlety in energy. These discriminating skills, perhaps psychic skills, were respected and valued. Today these abilities are considered weird or evil by many. Today we falsely believe that reality is only what we see, making subtle information immoral or deceitful. We read old manuscripts and conclude that ancient people were steeped in superstition and stupidity. Yet, they built pyramids that our technology cannot replicate today. They had knowledge that was lost: *The Lost Waves of Time.*

Musical secrets were shared with extreme caution, lest such powerful information get into the hands of unscrupulous people. Music was used for controlling people and their values, physical healing, personal development, getting food (rain dances for crops, gardening vibrations and aiding the hunt) and as a source of energy. Recall that when the demise of each civilization occurred, it coincided with the fall of the music. This fact, the Chinese Emperor knew well; he kept close observations of the purity and unchanging nature of Chinese music. This role was so important it belonged to the Emperor – highest authority in the realm! Now the widespread understanding of music is that it is entirely entertainment, and at best, a tool to sell movies and products.

The Lost Waves of Time is the story of how music worked through the ages – how it built and maintained and then destroyed and tore down – each great civilization. The point that I believe is unique in *Lost Waves* is that Music played a far greater role throughout time than any historian has ever recognized. And it impacted on every level. Music was crucial at pivotal points in time:

> ➤ To aid the original involution of spirit into matter – with spirit gradually losing subtle energy discrimination

- To impact *individuals* & *civilizations* – spiritually, emotionally, intellectually, creatively and physically
- To move people into greater individualism and duality
- To release individuals from group energies to become independent
- To "connect" people to nature and then gradually dissolving that link
- To develop subtlety, physical healing and provide practical benefits transformed to the belief that music is only entertainment
- And to reverse all of this to complete a cycle – the final evolution of spirit back to the One

Only as man became isolated from the spiritual – entirely material in focus – did the power of Music become lost to mankind. The **modern** student of music starts his study of the subject in the Renaissance time period – a mere 600 years ago. We have completely lost touch with eons of musical knowledge – to our huge detriment!

We have reached the nexus point in man's destiny. We are further from God and the divine than we have ever been. Look around you – can you doubt that this is so? So what happens next?

Today, many believe that we are staring into the abyss: environmental disaster, war, revolt and global upheavals, economic collapse... and yet some think that we are on the brink of re–capturing subtle energy for marvelous results. For example, scientists have discovered that the ears can detect subtle differences in patterns that the eye cannot. Our auditory system transmits neuron movement much faster than the rest of the brain; this process is significantly slower with vision.[842]

Science has recently learned that great subtlety can be heard. Space physicist Robert Wicks observed that sound condenses an incredible amount of information. A year's worth of field measurements, which would take months to analyze, becomes only two hours of sound on a CD. Audible patterns can be quickly discovered. In other situations pitches can be assigned to x–rays or

---

[842] Cowan, Ron. Sound Bytes, *Scientific American*, Feb. 17, 2015, Pgs. 45-47.

gammas rays, and converted into sound waves, so we can quickly grasp greater amounts of information and patterns within data. In other applications, tiny vibrations are converted to audio to quickly detect cancer cells or particles from space, according to Ron Cowen in *Scientific American*.[843] The use of sound to represent voluminous information and as a superb diagnostic tool is completely under–utilized.

We see modern man apply sound in a variety of useful ways. We can greatly expand on current knowledge and abilities by gathering ideas from ancient practices – for the good of all. It is time to put everything together.

And so it Begins again…

There is strong evidence that the trends may be reversing and that finally we are entering the "return to God" stage of the long road of involution and evolution of spirit and matter. The next step in this grand design is for the subtle energy to speed up again, quickening and preparing a soul to exit matter. After reaching the apex of involution, perceiving himself as a separate being and fully immersing in duality, a soul *evolves* back to unity – to the One – All That Is. This is the process ancient people called enlightenment.

As the soul evolves during the spiritual enlightenment process, it gains greater conscious connectivity to group energies, at first with the species' collective energy and then with other, higher energies as well. He now enjoys intuition, telepathy and other psychic abilities, while retaining what he learned in the physical realm. Yet he is different than when he started this voyage into matter. He now has the skills associated with being a mature individual; he has learned to take responsibility for himself and others, and to be his own master.

An individual abiding in positive energy elevates the collective unconscious energy – uplifting, to a surprising extent, the world around him. As we evolve, gaining greater consciousness, awareness and connectivity to other energy fields, music can

---

[843] Cowan, Ron. Sound Bytes, *Scientific American*, Feb. 17, 2015, Pgs. 45-47.

hasten our journey back home, connecting us to higher realms of existence. Thus ends the journey – once again where we began – but we have learned much and the wonder and glory of the One has increased. And so it ends... and so it will someday begin again... and the universe sings to the wonder of it all.

www.JillsWingsofLight.com – Art Galleries

Appendix A

Carnatic Ragas and Benefits

by Bill Olmer – www.dattapeetham.com

Ahir Bhairav – Gives free relaxed feeling, mitigates dust allergies and skin disease. Good for arthritic conditions.
Amrutavarshini – Alleviates diseases related to heat
Ananda Bhairavi – Suppresses stomach pain, reduces kidney problems, controls blood pressure
Bagesri – Helps in attaining Guru's grace
Bhairavi – Reduces anxiety, pressures, skin, disease and allergies
Bhupala – To awaken someone out of deep sleep
Charukesi Bhajan: Shantirastu Pushtirastu – Rejuvenates the mind, helping one to age gracefully
Desh – The suppression of the senses releases a neg ative force. Its energy gives serenity, peace, inner joy, right valor, universal love and patriotism
Dwijavanti – Quells paralysis and disorders of the mind
Ganamurte – Helpful in diabetes
Hansadhwani – Gives energy, aides thinking
Bhajan: Sambho Samba – Good for joint and back pain
Kindolam – Improves digestive power, cures stomach related disease
Kalyani Bhajan: Jai Jai Ganapathi – Gives energy and removes tension and acts as general tonic. Dispels the darkness of fear, gives motherly comfort and increases confidence. Recited with faith and devotion, it is believed to clinch marriage alliances. Many authentic reports exist about the raga's power to destroy fear in many forms: fear of poverty, of love, of power, of ill–health and of death.
Kapi – Releases depression, anxiety, absent mindedness
Karaharapriya– Curative for heart disease, nervous irritability, neurosis, worry and distress
Kedaram– Gives energy and removes tension
Keervani – Promotes meditation at mental and physical levels
Kokilam – Helps prevent stone formation, burning sensations, sleeplessness and anxiety
Madhuvarshini – Good for nerves, Cures diseases like slight headache, sleeplessness, and sinus problems
Madhyamavati – Clears paralysis, giddiness, pain in legs/hands and nervous complaints
Malaya Maruta – To awaken someone out of deep sleep

Maya Malava Gowla– Counters pollution, gateway to Carnatic music

Bhajan: Mayamalava gowla – Neutralizes toxins in the body. Practice it in the early morning, in the midst of nature to enhance the strength of the vocal chords

Mohana Bhajan: Ishapathisha – *Mohana* is present where beauty and love coexist. It filters out the ill–effects of desire for sex, anger and lust, cures chronic headaches, indigestion and depression

Neelambari – Gets rid of insomnia

Ranjani – Cures kidney disease

Rathipathipriya– Ads strength and vigor to married life, eliminate poverty, wipes out bitter feelings

Rohini – Cures back pain, joint pain

Sama – Makes mind sober, tranquil, induces good sleep. Good for world peace

Saramati Bhajan – Elevates from depressed state, cures crying and irritability in children, helps sleeplessness, itching, eye and ear problems, skin problems, and the problems of hearing irregular sounds

Sindu Bhairavi – Removes sins and sorrows, and saves from unforeseen events

Sivaranjani – Powerful raga for meditation, bestows benevolence of God, removes sadness, diseases related to excess heat. Good for general health

Sandhya Kalyani – Cures ear, nose and eye diseases, relieves chronic colds, gives good sleep and freshness

Shankarabharanam – The power of this raga is incredible. It cures mental illness, soothes the turbulent mind and restores peace and harmony. If rendered with total devotion for a stipulated period, it can cure mental disorders said to be beyond the scope of medical treatment. It also is said to have the power to shower wealth.

Shanmugapriya – Sharpens the intellect, instills courage and replenishes the energy in the body

Subhapantuvarali – Alleviates mental dilemmas and indecisiveness

Suddha dhanyasi – Removes sorrow, creating a happy feeling, tonic for nerves, cures rhinitis and migraine.

Suruti – Mitigates stomach burn, insomnia, fear, disgust

Vakulab Soharanam – Alleviates asthma, bronchitis, heart disease, depression, skin disease and skin allergy

Varali Bhajan: Nakam Vinayakam – Good for heart, skin ailments and gastric problems

Vasanta / Vasanti – Controls high and low blood pressure, cures heart as well as nervous diseases, clears confusion when a series of medical tests has to be analyzed, and heals nervous breakdowns

Vasantham – Cures paralysis

Viswambari – General tonic, acts quickly

Jill Mattson
The Lost Waves of Time
www.Ancient–Music.com
www.JillsWingsOfLight.com
www.RedBubble.com/Jill Mattson

All of the artwork in this book - inside and out -
is based on original oil paintings by Jill Mattson.
Many of the paintings are available along with
prints. Visit JillaWingsOfLight.com for more
information.

Jill Mattson: Author, Composer, Musician and Artist

Jill Mattson is an author, artist, musician and widely recognized expert and composer in the emerging field of Sound Healing. She has written four books and produced seven CD's that combine intricate Sound Healing techniques with her original Award winning musical compositions *(Best CD of 2015 – People's Choice Award for **Contacting Angel & Masters**; 2012 Best New Age CD – Silver Award **Deep Wave Beauty CD**)*. The CD's consist of intriguing, magical tracks using ancient & modern techniques - with sound energy & special healing frequencies to achieve profound benefits.

Her cutting edge music includes: Sound Based Beauty Treatments, Frequencies of Flower Essences (emotional catharsis & virtue building), Celestial music with Tones from ancient Egypt and Celestial Bodies, Solfeggio/Reverse Solfeggio & Fibonacci tones, Binaural Beats & Meditative Music, Countering Negative Astrological Energies, Ascended Master & and Angelic Channeled Energies, Ancient Languages of Light, Tuning Notes for your body and more! These multilayered, multidimensional, deep layered, soulful works will uplift your heart - while offering a myriad of benefits.

Jill lectures throughout the United States on *"Ancient Sounds ~ Modern Healing"* taking followers on an exciting journey revealing the healing power of sound. She unveils secrets from ancient cultures as well as the latest findings of the modern scientific community showing the incredible potential and healing capabilities of sound, including how sound travels through your body. Jill draws on her extensive research of modern Sound Healing, and over 30 year study of ancient civilizations and secret societies in her music, lectures, workshops and writings.

Please visit her websites where you can learn more about her in-depth studies and work. Also available on the sites are additional free mp3's of her Sound Healing compositions, including Solfeggio Tones, Star Energy, Flower Frequencies, Fibonacci and nature tones. www.jillswingsoflight.com ~ www.musicforbeauty.com Experience some of the exercises described in this book in videos at www.Ancient-Music.com.

All of the artwork in this book - inside and out - is based on original oil paintings by Jill Mattson. Many of the paintings are available along with prints. Visit her website for more information

If you enjoyed this book, please consider leaving a review at amazon.com/Jill Mattson – to help spread these ideas! Thank you! Jill Mattson

Descriptions of Jill's other books and CDs follow.

Tomorrow's Total Wellness Today

Books

Mystical Accounts of Healing through Sound Energy

Secret Sounds ~ Ultimate Healing

Mysteries of the voice revealed; tuning the body with sounds; Sharry Edward's life story and BioAcoustics

Ancient Sounds ~ Modern Healing

Read how sound can alter a person's rain waves, increase relaxation, eliminate stress, aid the healing process, and help us become happier, healther, and more productive

CDs

Jill Mattson's CDs are multidimensional, deep-layered soulful works that offer a myriad of benefits.

Deep Wave Body Healing

Ancient wise Masters established conscious control of their physical bodies, specifically the organs. When they detected disharmony within an organ, they tuned it into harmony, which was associated with the health of the organ. In this meditation, connect with and tune your organs, with the help of frequencies associated with healthy body organs, other frequencies linked to health and ancient healing techniques.

Cutting Edge Vibratory CDs

Contacting Angels and Masters

INATS PEOPLE'S CHOICE AWARD FOR 2015 BEST CD OF THE YEAR
FINALIST FOR *INATS* BEST FREQUENCY HEALING CD OF 2015

An educational CD with guided meditations to bathe in the divine subtle energies, and meet your guides, angels and masters.

Become "enlightened" on how sounds and colors relate to angels, masters and yourself! Learn ways to communicate and recognize angels and masters!

Paint Your Soul

Etheric and angelic music: including the ancient spiritual musical codes of Solfeggio & Reverse Solfeggio frequencies. These complete 18 frequencies were employed in antiquity for elevating one's consciousness and soul. Also are the sounds found in nature - the Fibonacci and phi frequencies, singing gently the song of Mother Earth – getting you in tune and in harmony with nature. Lift and paint your consciousness with this deeply moving music.

Star Dust

The original music in **Star Dust** is derived from the motion and chemistry of the Heavenly Spheres. It transposes the motion and orbits of the planets into audible and hauntingly beautiful sounds – the "music of the Spheres". Also added are vibrational components based on the Celestial Elements – material literally made in the Stars. Cleverly combined with the heavenly music are intonations based on ancient methods to capture and realize the subtle energy blessings that comes from the Stars.

Cutting Edge Vibratory CDs

Healing Flower Symphonies
vols 1 & 2

The Healing Flower Symphonies are a remarkable 2 CD collection of original compositions containing the vibratory healing benefits of 12 Flower Essences. Each Healing Flower Symphony provides the healing potential of the associated flower. (Listening to the frequency of an item can subtly bestow the same benefits as ingesting the physical substance.) The music enables a cathartic release, then transitions into the successful triumph and mastery of the emotion (as in transforming fear into trust). The net effect is a wonderful blessing of the flower essences in a vibratory experience – resolving the emotional challenge involved and subtly strengthening the desirable emotional health of the listener.

Deep Wave Beauty

This amazing CD achieves the ultimate in combining a wonderful listening experience with numerous embedded vibrational frequencies - targeted to nourish, firm and renew your face's appearance. Enchanting New Age-Classical music provides the soothing structure for the overall adventure; spiritual peace, mental tranquility and Deep Wave body relaxation result. The vibratory essences associated with essential vitamins and nutrients along with the frequencies beneficial to collagen, muscles and skin tissues are injected. The CD was a silver prize winner at the **2012 INATS awards - Specialty Music** category.

Cutting Edge Vibratory CDs

Cosmic Streams
An Unrivaled Chakra Meditation Experience

» Tune Chakras with Special Frequencies, Rhythms, Colors, Elements, Vowel Sounds, Musical Instruments, Tibetan bowls, Emotional Subtle Energies and Affirmations
» Clear all Chakra layers and dimensions
» Harmonize and balance all major Chakra levels, including higher energy connections
» Clear all Chakra layers and dimensions
» Chakras are linked with specific glands, the control centers of your body. Activate and clear the Chakra/gland subtle energy connections.

Jill Mattson

"Jill Mattson is a researcher, writer, musical artist of great depth and sincerity. In a time when our adolescent modern society yearns for spiritual and academic truth, let her years of knowledge and enlightenment awaken you to your greatest inner potentials and our communities to their spiritual responsibilities."

Bessheen Baker, N.D., Director of Education and Founder of NITE

Websites & Social Media

Wings of Light
www.JillsWingsofLight.com

Ancient Music
www.Ancient-Music.com

Music For Beauty
www.MusicForBeauty.com

Twitter
https://twitter.com/wingsoflight

Facebook
https://www.facebook.com/pages/Jill-Mattson/286604571357944

YouTube
https://www.youtube.com/channel/UCAEuQdsjfce4m-ORTbxI6sA